13693

```
812                    13693
P545    PHILBRICK.

        Trumpets sounding.
```

DATE DUE

LIBRARY DISCARD

MEMPHIS UNIVERSITY SCHOOL
HYDE LIBRARY
6191 PARK ROAD
MEMPHIS, TENNESSEE 38138

Trumpets Sounding

Propaganda Plays of the American Revolution

ARNO PRESS
A New York Times Company
1976

TRUMPETS SOUNDING

EDITED BY NORMAN PHILBRICK

Reprint Edition 1976 by Arno Press Inc.

Copyright © 1972 by Benjamin Blom, Inc.

LC#   77-184007
ISBN   0-405-09803-0

Manufactured in the United States of America

For Kathie, Anne, Bob, and Virginia

Acknowledgments

Seven plays written during the period of the American Revolution (1775-81) are reproduced in this anthology to demonstrate how use was made of dialogues and presentations in dramatic and theatrical form to promote persuasion toward the American or the British cause.

The Introduction indicates not only why such forms were employed but also their limitations, which affected their proliferation. The editor is convinced that the pamphlet plays had an influence in the general war of words; although the production was slight, the pamphlets carried weight in all the colonies.

Trumpets Sounding, with its emphasis both on the dramatic composition and on the historical aspects of the material, should be of value to the student of the American theatre and of history. Our evolution from colony to new nation is revealed in a study of these plays.

The sources that were helpful are listed in the Bibliography, and the editor wishes to note his particular indebtedness to four works: *Pamphlets of the American Revolution,* edited by Bernard Bailyn, *Propaganda and the American Revolution* by Philip Davidson, *Origins of the American Revolution* by John C. Miller, and *Prelude to Independence* by Arthur M. Schlesinger.

A History of the American Drama from the Beginning to the Civil War by Arthur Hobson Quinn also has been a reliable compendium of the early development of the theatre in the United States.

Of the seven plays two, *A Dialogue Between a Southern Delegate and His Spouse* and *The Fall of British Tyranny,* are owned by the editor. The others, *The Blockheads, The Battle of Brooklyn, The Death of General Montgomery, The Patriots,* and *The Motley Assembly,* are reprinted by permission of the Henry E. Huntington Library, San Marino, California.

The editor should also like to acknowledge the initial encouragement given him by the late George Freedley, of the New York Public Library, and the constant care and attention of Benjamin Blom. The advising editors to whom the writer is indebted and without whose assistance the work would not have been accomplished are Professor Anthony Santaniello and Viola Roth, the former having guided with patience and wisdom the revisions over a period of time.

To my wife, Geraldine Philbrick, I should like to accord a paean of gratitude for her understanding and sympathy as well as her keen editorial judgment of the book as it was being brought to its completion.

Contents

Introduction   1

1
A Dialogue, Between a Southern Delegate, and His Spouse, on His Return from the Grand Continental Congress (1774)   27

2
The Fall of British Tyranny: or, American Liberty Triumphant (1776)   39

3
The Blockheads: or, The Affrighted Officers (1776)   135

4
The Battle of Brooklyn, A Farce of Two Acts (1776)   169

5
The Death of General Montgomery, In Storming the City of Quebec (1777)   211

6
The Patriots, A Comedy in Five Acts (1778)   265

7
The Motley Assembly, A Farce (1779)   347

Bibliography   359

Introduction

INTRODUCTION

ALARMS AND EXCURSIONS IN DRAMATIC FORM—war cries of the American Revolution penned by Tory-Loyalists and Whig-Patriots alike — are the substance of *Trumpets Sounding*. The emotional tone of these plays ranges from the deeply felt indignation of the Tory play *A Dialogue Between a Southern Delegate and His Spouse on His Return from the Grand Continental Congress* to the full fury of the Whig tirade in the scathing indictment of *The Blockheads*.

From pre-Revolutionary 1773 to the close of the conflict in 1783, at least thirteen propaganda plays and dialogues, exclusive of nontheatrical tracts, were printed in the colonies. Of these, seven have been selected for this anthology: *A Dialogue Between a Southern Delegate and His Spouse,* author unknown, New York, 1774; *The Fall of British Tyranny* attributed to John Leacock, Philadelphia, 1776; *The Blockheads; or, The Affrighted Officers* attributed to Mercy Otis Warren, Boston, 1776; *The Battle of Brooklyn,* author unknown, New York, 1776; *The Death of General Montgomery* by Hugh Henry Brackenridge, Norwich, 1777; *The Patriots* by Robert Munford, written between 1777 and 1779 but not printed until 1798 in Petersburg, Virginia; and *The Motley Assembly* attributed to Mercy Otis Warren, Boston, 1779.[1]

The First Continental Congress (the subject of the first play in this collection), convened in 1774, brought together a mélange of personalities and temperaments, conservative, moderate, and radical. Conciliation between the colonies and the mother country—urged by the old guard, encouraged by the temperate in the hope that strained relations would not reach a breaking point, and thwarted by the extreme Friends of Liberty, who were impatiently inclined toward independence—was the concern of the debates. The Congress of Arguments produced the first skirmishes of the Revolution, and although the confrontations were rhetorical, physical manifestations of anger were often apparent.

The jousting, feinting, parrying with words increased and intensified during and after the Congress, as the battle of words moved closer to actual war. In 1775 war came in the bloody action of Lexington and Concord, Breed's Hill, Long Island, and the Plains of Abraham. Shock, horrible realization, and uncontrollable anger were the responses of both sides to the chaos engulfing them, and their anguish found expression in abuse, satire, vilification, and caricature. On the battlefield of protest the pamphlet plays sounded their shrill notes, encouraging the combatants.

What is particularly striking about the plays when one reads them today is their immediacy—an instantaneous quality, as if one were participating with the playwright and the characters in the action of the moment. Yellowed and sometimes brittle as the pages are, with antique printing and the curious spelling, punctuation, and idiom of the eighteenth century, the event nevertheless springs clear from the confines of the pamphlet. One feels the kind of on-the-spot reaction that he might have to a relayed video-tape-recording of the turmoil. It is this involvement with the action, this direct contact with people caught in disaster, that gives these dramas a unique place in the propaganda war of the American Revolution. No other kind of persuasion written during that period has these qualities.

THE PLAYS ARE UNIQUE for another and more important reason: They explode with a short fuse of instant wrath, and the resulting pyrotechnic display is an original kind of propaganda. What semblance there is to formal dramatic structure is relatively unimportant in the total range and effect of the plays. The emotional drive sweeps the reader into the maelstrom of events. Searing and denunciatory or, by contrast, mocking and bitter, the dialogue and action ignore plot requirements, detailed characterization, and elaborate descriptions of setting and stage movement. Although the playwrights may have wished to take time to refine, edit, or reflect, it was impossible to do so.

They wished to report at once what they experienced, and they had no time to waste on artifice. When events of earth-shaking magnitude are happening just outside the study window, threatening to break glass and head, and the peaceful environment of an eighteenth century colonial parish is shattered by gunfire and bloody rout, the cries of the victims, whether Whig or Tory, must give rise to violent expression—those heard in the plays.

Throw out plot—no legend of the past is involved, no traditional pattern of writing need be followed. The riot of revolution is its own story, and the plays "tell it as it is," either in immediate reflections upon the occurrence or directly, begrimed and powder-burned from the battlefield. "Bleeding sergeants" with messages of dire consequence create the vivid passages of the plays; in the quieter moments patriotic emotions, often acerbic and disgusted, are never far from the surface. Contemporaneous with the moment itself, the happenings are the plot: a delegate's return from an unprecedented congress in *A Dialogue;* the insidious conferences of the ministers of King George, the battles and tortures, the infamous depredations on the Virginia coast in *The Fall of British Tyranny;* a famine and siege in *The Blockheads;* the shocking defeat of Americans in *The Death of General Montgomery;* the ill-usage of minorities in *The Patriots;* and a desiccated tea party in *The Motley Assembly.*

Throw out fine characterization—broad strokes of caricature suffice, and character is created from small seeds of fact, flowers in rumor, and over-the-teacups gossip about prominent figures, limned in patent exaggeration and prejudice. No holds are barred in attacking well-known persons, for laws of libel are hardly in question. Under fire are Lord Bute, Lord North, John Wilkes, General Gage, the brothers Sir William and Lord Richard Howe, Burgoyne, and the American heroes Washington, Putnam, Ethan Allen, Stirling, and Sullivan.

Shimmering through these works is the heat of personal passion. Such emotion gives to many scenes a nervous energy strong enough to overcome the convolutions of argument and the unwieldiness of structure. Often the pieces were written in great haste; Brackenridge in the preface to *The Death of General Montgomery* apologizes because he did not have time to correct the obvious deficiencies of his work. Some of the plays have all too obvious excesses. Some scenes are too long and others too short. And the plotting—what there is of it—frequently loses all causal logic, so that actions once started are not completed; for example, in the exchange between Lord Dapper and Tabitha in *The Blockheads,* plans for an elopement are set in motion and never reintroduced into the action.

The uneven writing and the lack of polish of the pamphlet plays preclude an evaluation of them as works of literature, but these very qualities, of rough-hewn style and personal commitment, raise them above the criticism that might dismiss them as eccentricities of dramatic literature. The grapeshot flew in many directions; not often the most effective satire, such ammunition has the advantage of hitting many targets at once. And we are not so far removed from the passions of that hour as to remain unaffected by the valor, the distress, and the fury of aroused and dissenting citizens.

Thus these pamphlet plays are first of all the raw stuff of propaganda, catching a moment in history, unrefined in presentation but shot through with sorely tried endurance. Suffering in silence has no place in the credo of these playwrights; they cry havoc and smite their enemies tooth and nail. As protest pieces, the Revolutionary dramas can stand alone, and they effectively served their purpose: to expose, decry, and mock; to hold the distorting mirror up to the knavery of the enemy, be he Whig or Tory, in order to reveal his perfidy, his immoral and unpatriotic ugliness.

BESIDES THEIR UNIQUENESS as a particular genre of persuasion, the plays have a supplementary and very important distinction: In depicting events on North American soil and the experiences of the principal characters of the plays in the history-making American rebellion and civil strife, the pamphlet plays are among the first dramas about native subjects to be written in the country, a portrait of the revolutionary activity of 1774 to 1779. Reflective of the pressing crises of the hour, the embattled condition of life, and the overwhelming conflict that beleaguered the writers, the plays are also colored by sectional individuality, parochial self-interest, and shrewd provincialism. The settings are local—besieged Boston, village greens, prison camps, the mudflats of Long Island, the Virginia tobacco lands, a drawing room in Boston. From the entire spectrum of the social scene, a potpourri of characters appears—shopkeepers, farmers, ministers, American and English generals, titled lords, tattered soldiers, seamstresses, ladies of quality, Yankees, Southerners, and New York merchants, many of them with dialects and idioms to match the regions from which they come. The immediacy of the plays and the underlying anger of the authors' purpose bring into sharp focus human beings whose individual and native features appear as on a stereoptican slide or as three-dimensional "living pictures."

The playwrights invite the reader to share their experiences, and because these chroniclers were directly involved in various aspects of the action or were close enough to be competent observers, their reports are charged with authentic recollections. Historical evidence supports a reported visit of Mercy Otis Warren to Charlestown immediately after the siege of Boston had been lifted; thus she would have seen at first hand the ruin left by the British. Description of similar destruction in Boston appears in *The Blockheads,* which she may have written. The writer of *The Battle of Brooklyn* suggests by his knowledge of Long Island and the details of the attack that drove the Americans to retreat to Manhattan that he was there during the engagement. Munford, the author of *The Patriots,* knew from his own experience how the minority Scots were treated in Virginia and how neutralists fared. By conviction he was a middle-of-the-road Whig but, being appointed a county lieutenant in charge of all military affairs in the Mecklenburg area of Virginia, he found it expedient to conceal any ambivalence he may have had toward the patriot cause.

The occasion and the playwrights' desire to report it as soon afterward as possible make the plays as timely as a daily newspaper report of a battle. (The one exception is *The Death of General Montgomery,* a delayed reaction because the news of Montgomery's defeat by Carleton at Quebec did not reach the colonies until almost two months had passed.) These revolutionary protests are, therefore, journalistic. But their novelty is not in the similarity to a newspaper account; it is in the recording of current history in dramatic dialogue with scene division and occasional stage directions. As such, the plays are linked to an earlier dramatic type.

The genre to which they are most closely allied is the English political drama of the last quarter of the seventeenth century and the first quarter of the eighteenth, of which *Venice Preserved* by Thomas Otway, *Lucius Junius Brutus* by Nathaniel Lee, *Tamerlane* by Nicholas Rowe, and *Cato* by Joseph Addison are outstanding examples. The English political play as a distinct theatrical expression was popular in the early eighteenth century when it was used to reflect party loyalties of Whig and Tory. The theatres were "to a degree, political institutions, and their managerial policies, including their choice of plays, were influenced by political considerations." Argument from the stage became so usual that audiences came expecting to hear a debate costumed as a play, and vociferously to take sides.[2]

The political plays in England held to a rigid and recognizable dramatic form, and they drew upon neoclassical sources, so that their lineaments were stamped with the features of seventeenth century drama. Furthermore, the audiences of London for whom political and party squabbles were meat and drink recognized contemporary controversies thinly disguised in archaic dress and language. Rhetorical donnybrooks over issues in the House of Lords and the House of Commons during the late Stuart and early Georgian eras not only were reflected by the playwrights and actors but also could be heard as rumbling thunder in the gallery, pit, and boxes, from which they were echoed the next day in pub, coffee house, and salon. Unraveling the parallels between ancient conflicts and current disputes was one of the amusements of the playhouse during the rage for party plays. An added fillip to pleasure was a kind of knowledgeable guessing-game played by the playwright with the spectators. Whom did Tamerlane represent in Rowe's tragedy? Obviously the defender of England, the frigid, unsmiling but extremely noble William III. And Bajazet, luxury mad and treacherous, whom Tamerlane destroyed in his iron cage? None other than Louis XIV, the fearful oppressor, determined to devastate England. *Cato,* dressed in its Roman robes, had an ambiguous reputation: the Whigs easily identified Cato as the Duke of Marlborough, for both were of heroic proportions and defenders of liberty; the Tories saw Marlborough as Caesar, the oppressor. The political plays had an impact on the times, the least of which were near riots in the theatres, but unlike the American Revolutionary pieces, they were about current affairs and not of them. The English audiences engaged in conjectures about the identity of heroes and events and publicly took sides, but the classical connotations and themes of many of the plays militated against the use of the propaganda dramas as a means of eyewitness reporting of actual conflict. Thus they lack the strong sense of urgency found in the works represented in this collection.

Both the English and the American political dramas had by their very nature another characteristic in common. Their purpose was the same: to persuade their readers to a particular point of view and often to a subsequent course of action. The English plays, however, were better dramas—that is, in the traditional pattern of neoclassical causal relationships, characterized by decorum, using subtle understatement rather than brash declaration to announce their prejudices. The American pieces proclaimed their defiance by verbal assaults or mockery and were more effective as instruments of propaganda than as formal plays. With no legendary pedigree, without pretense to literary values except in the scenes that were imitative of former models, the American plays represented unvarnished topicality in the familiar costumes of tragedy, comedy, farce, and melodrama, sometimes all combined in a single play, such as *The Fall of British Tyranny*.

Because the vigorous effect of the American works derives from the dramatization of a personally experienced conflict—which is, after all, the essence of drama—these pieces illuminate the broiling antagonisms surrounding and involving the authors and the first readers of the plays. The criticism that dismisses the plays as poor literature is beside the point: propaganda is their intention, simply that and nothing more. Dramatic form is used quite obviously only to heighten interest.

PROTEST LITERATURE today takes the form of letters to the editor, underground newspapers, books and articles, and lapel buttons; but in the eighteenth century much of it was published in pamphlet form in both England and the colonies. There was a brisk trans-Atlantic communication of ideas—British tracts were reprinted in the colonies and some colonial pamphlets appeared in England. Many arguments that were taken up in print were soon answered, and they in turn received a response. Thus, a continuing series became almost conventional, encouraged no doubt by printers who with Yankee ingenuity recognized the profit to be gained from controversy.

It is important to bear in mind that *pamphlet* is a generic term for a particular kind of printed work. Despite many definitions of the term, some tortuous in their ramifications, the essential characteristics of the pamphlet are clear. From the beginning of printing, the pamphlet has existed as a compact work, smaller than a book in both size and content, usually held together by stitching, and lacking a cover and sometimes even a title page. Some pamphlets were as short as a sudden and quickly resolved argument or as brief as a clever jingle printed on a single page. Others were considerably longer—disputations in a variety of forms, running from forty to one hundred pages.

Although some pamphlets were concerned with innocuous subjects, such as the arrangement of formal gardens or the latest medical treatment for consumption ("Do not allow the patient out-of-doors; it is better to have him breathe his own infected air to effect a cure"), the majority of the pamphlets were polemical in nature. The pamphlet as a printed form of communication meant to most people something doctrinaire.

In the fifteenth and sixteenth centuries the principal subject matter of propaganda pamphlets had been religious controversy; a century later the emphasis had become both religious and political, sometimes intermingled. By the eighteenth century the persuasive pamphlet had reached its apogee, and although it might appear in a variety of printed forms, such as an essay, an oration, a sermon, or addresses made to assemblies and other distinguished gatherings, it was primarily political in nature. The tone of the pamphlet could be dignified or scurrilous, arrogant or deceptively humble, sarcastic, ironic, scornful, ribald.

The literature of the American Revolution between 1764 and 1783[3] includes hundreds of such pamphlets—a violent, often chaotic battle of words, as the fortunes of war and the progress of rebellion led to the consumption of gallons of ink and tons of rag pulp. Amid all this ferment of protest, challenge, and vindication appeared the pamphlet play, an innovation in the propaganda war that presented the news of the Revolution in theatrical form. It sprang full-armed from the head of revolution and it joined in the battle for liberty, sharing in both the pamphlet and the dramatic tradition of the time.

The reason why some writers chose the pamphlet play as their means of expression can only be conjectured, but three assumptions can be made. Some of the authors had a very strong interest in drama to begin with. Three of the playwrights about whom we have some certain knowledge—Mercy Otis Warren, Hugh Henry Brackenridge, and Robert Munford—were all well read in classic and contemporary drama. Mrs. Warren highly approved of pieces written for the theatre and in one letter to Abigail Adams emphasized her admiration for satire, particularly that of Molière. As an undergraduate in the College of New Jersey, Brackenridge had considerable experience in writing dialogues, that is, disputations between two or more persons. Later, as a teacher, Brackenridge wrote plays for his pupils to perform. Munford was an enthusiastic playgoer when a student in England and became a patron of the drama in his native Virginia.

The second assumption as to the reason for the choice of the dramatic form is based upon the polemical nature of the subject matter. When the fate of a country and its very survival are being debated, abstract conjecture gives way to the cries of citizens, anguished and distracted by the fear that their blood may be spilled. Rounded periods, balanced argument, impersonal recitations of abuses, and conciliatory phrases have no place or time in actions of life and death. Drama itself, depending as it does on effective living speech, must use expletives, epithets, and crudities when its purpose is remonstrance. As the pamphlet plays demonstrate, the theatrical form is extremely effective for protest.

The third assumption concerning the writing of theatrical propaganda pieces is related to the very nature of drama: the articulation of emotions aroused by contention. Being in the midst of actual conflict, the writers of the pamphlet plays had ready grist for their mill; thus it was a simple matter to transfer the action of the day into theatrical form. The stirring event, the touching moment, could be more easily communicated by a medium that could accommodate the explosion of tensions.

It is significant that the pamphlet plays did not appear until both the propaganda and the military war had increased in intensity. Prior to 1774 the Tories had failed to realize how important a weapon the press could be. For the most part they produced controversial essays, soberly if not somberly argued, appealing to the literate and the intellectual. The Whigs also directed their written arguments to the intelligent reader, but early in the struggle they abandoned abstractions and moved to a more common style. They appealed to the heart and not so much to the head, calling on the baser instincts with language to match. The printed orations commemorating the Boston Massacre of March 5, 1770, and delivered on the anniversary of that event were popular reading, as were the printed sermons that supported the revolutionary cause. These sermons were characterized by the fire-and-brimstone techniques once used by ministers to describe the boiling pit of Hell gaping for a generation of sinners. The Tories woke up too late to the possibilities of propaganda, but as they became aware of the need for it and its effectiveness, they struck back, although without the vigor of their opponents. The frightful menace of "mobocracy," the world in chaos with unruly citizens running wild in the streets and usurping the seats of the mighty, inhibited the Tories, and they hesitated to arouse passions that might bring about reprisals. Their disdain of the ordinary citizen made them unwilling, if not unable, to sink to his level and appeal directly to him. Only occasionally did the Tories burst from their self-restriction and become even more violent than the most rabid Whigs (an example is *The Battle of Brooklyn*).

It was in the context of the heightening emotionalism of the rebellion that the pamphlet play was written. The battle of words begun with the passage of the Stamp Act in 1765 had a short-lived hiatus after the repeal of the act in March, 1766; but by 1774, when the First Continental Congress met, the tone of the propaganda changed from a mixture of passive but ever-threatening resistance to one of antagonism and hatred. The Whig-Patriots began to live with the fear that their liberties might be curtailed and their honor as free citizens destroyed. Their lives might be in jeopardy—those of Samuel Adams and John Hancock were. The Tory-Loyalists began to live in dread of being injured by their fellow citizens; such a possibility had been demonstrated by the physical attacks on the colonial representatives of the King during the Stamp Act crisis. The Tories felt a terror that their status would be violently changed and their properties destroyed—a disaster which had befallen Governor Hutchinson of Massachusetts when his home and library were sacked in 1765.

Shocking occurrences were to become commonplace—the bombarding of towns by the British, tar and feathers for the Tories, hangings of informers and spies, horrible conditions aboard British prison ships, destruction of property on both sides, hateful occupation of towns, and above all the tension of internecine strife. The pamphlet play reflected these events by direct, if exaggerated, reporting. It was printed, reprinted, advertised, and read, and its popularity added to the tinder of rebellion.

Exactly how influential was the pamphlet play in converting the colonists to either loyalist or patriotic cause? The answer can never be supplied adequately, any more than the precise effectiveness of other kinds of tracts can be ascertained. (The one obvious exception is *Common Sense*.) Both the dramatic and the nondramatic works exerted their particular power to persuade, and from the distance of today only indirect assumptions can be made about the measure of their dominance; yet conclusions concerning influence can be drawn from available and pertinent information relating to all pamphlets. Such knowledge is based on four factors: price, number of editions, distribution, and advertisements. Each is an indication of the great interest in pamphlets and in their intellectual and emotional impact.

Tracts came from the presses in great numbers in all the colonies, and one has the impression that almost everyone was writing them: the professional author, the literary hack, and the amateur correspondent who might hesitate to send a letter to the newspapers but was pleased to have his arguments printed in an independent pamphlet.

One obvious reason why the pamphlet was so popular was that it was inexpensive to produce; its cost to most readers was comparatively little. Some were sold for as little as a penny or two; those of greater length cost three shillings. *The Death of General Montgomery* sold in 1777 for "two-thirds of a dollar," or approximately four shillings or sixty-seven cents (at 1777 evaluation), making it fairly expensive for its time (the play was bound with several odes and elegiac pieces by diverse "hands"). As a single work, it would have cost much less.

An interested reader who could not afford the price probably took advantage of the opportunities for free reading supplied by the inns, barber shops, post offices, taverns, and coffee houses, where the latest public prints were available. These places of community service became very popular, particularly at times of crisis when people met to read, to discuss the latest news of the day, and to argue the merits and consequences of actions in London and in the colonies. Pamphlets and newspapers reflecting different persuasions were scattered about, and the plays were no doubt among them.

There were many illiterate men and women in the colonies, but if they could not read or write, they could be read to, as often occurred at public gatherings. And what is better designed for reading aloud than a play—an argument in dialogue? Free speech had never been an idle concept in the colonies; it was a birthright, practiced whenever two or three people were gathered together. Every man, woman, and child, it would appear from the records of town meetings, was moved to discuss what he heard.

In *The Americans Roused, in a Cure for the Spleen*, a pamphlet play attributed to Jonathan Sewall and published in 1775,[4] Trim, the barber, gives the following amusing account of political activity in a barber shop:

why, Sir, if I was denied the privelege of my shop to canvas politics, as a body may say, that is Lord North, East-India company, . . . duties and taxes, and the like of that, body o' me, Sir, strip me of this darling privelege, and you may e'en take my razors, soap, combs and all, and set fire to my shop. Why, Sir, I remember the time when every man minded his own business . . . and then my customers were in such a confounded hurry, that if they could not be shaved in a twinkling, without loss of time, they'd go to meeting with their beards hanging down to the waistbands of their breeches, and I must lose their custom; but now, Sir, if forty come in together, and all in the most freezing hurry, I have nothing to do but to souse plumb into a descant upon the times, and in the snap of a finger every man is as patient and still as any blockhead in my shop . . . they sit gaping, with solemn unmeaning phiz's, every one listens with silent attention to me, and forgets his beard, until I am pleased to dissolve the charm by closing my discourse; I tell them how I would trim Lord North, and have . . . Gov. Bernard, Gov. Hutchinson, &c. over head and ears in the suds . . . and then I rattle away upon grievances, opposition, rebellion and so on, only for the innocent purpose of supporting the credit of my shop.[5]

As the propaganda war gathered momentum the presses poured forth hundreds of political essays and their many mutations: sermons, orations, state papers, military pamphlets on the conduct of the war, poetry, and plays —all motivated by pro- and anti-American controversy.

"It is this form of writing," Moses Coit Tyler observes, "which is chiefly meant when historians now speak of what they are apt to call the political press, in America or in England. Thus, the power of the political essay in America during the Revolution is perfectly, even if unconsciously, described by Sir Erskine May when, of the political press in England during the same period, he says that, having first proved 'its influence as an auxiliary in party warfare' it began 'to rise above party, and to become a great popular power—the representative of public opinion.' "[6]

If a cheap price for a pamphlet is one gauge of its availability to citizens, and consequently of the possible influence it exerted, an analysis of the numbers and editions gives further evidence of the pervasiveness of pamphleteering. Statistics for the number of new pamphlets printed between 1763 and 1783 vary; 1200 to 1500 were published during that period, possibly more, in a country having a total population of only 2,780,369 in 1780 (an increase of 1,186,744 since 1760). These pamphlet figures do not include the various reprintings, and there is no precise figure for the number of copies in each edition. Figures indicating the size of any one edition of a pamphlet are scarce; Samuel Loudon, a New York printer, claimed that 1500 copies of an answer to *Common Sense* were destroyed.[7] Also, it is difficult to decide whether an edition was completely sold unless the printer made the statement that he was bringing out a later edition because the first was insufficient in number.[8]

The leading publication was *Common Sense* by Thomas Paine, which had a phenomenal record of twenty-five American and four foreign editions in 1776. More than 100,000 copies were sold in a very short time and eventually more than half a million. *Common Sense* outstripped all other pamphlets and was published in thirteen cities, but many other pamphlets also had a striking success.

One of these was the celebrated speech urging moderation in Britain's treatment of the colonies, written by Jonathan Shipley, Bishop of St. Asaph,[9] and published in London in 1774. There were twelve American editions, eight of which were reprinted in as many different towns. Other nondramatic pamphlets printed in the colonies created a demand for as many as seven editions; some reached five, and two or three were not uncommon. Of the pamphlet plays in this collection *The Fall of British Tyranny* was published in Philadelphia, Providence, and Boston in 1776, *The Battle of Brooklyn* in New York in 1776 and in Cork and Edinburgh in 1777, and *The Death of General Montgomery* in Norwich and Philadelphia in 1777.[10]

However low the cost of a pamphlet play or however many copies printed, the spread of propaganda would not have been ensured if there had not been numerous ways by which it could be disseminated and distributed. It could be read in public upon a patriotic occasion or passed from hand to hand; often provocative writings were sent by post or courier from one colony to another. The prolific letter writers—John and Mrs. Adams and Mercy Otis Warren, among others—often mention such enclosures. Pamphlets also gained wide circulation when they were printed in more than one city or town.

Enthusiasm for political treatises and the growing understanding of their value in strengthening morale created a public demand that was met in many instances by a double printing of a work; once in the columns of a newspaper and again as a separate tract. There were publishers whose business it was to specialize in tracts, state papers, public notices, and personal ephemera; there were others who printed only newspapers; and there were those who printed both, sometimes entirely separate from each other. If a printer published both a newspaper and individual pamphlets, he might test the effectiveness of a political essay by first printing it in his journal. If it proved popular, he would then issue it as a separate work, depending on the estimated market for a controversial article. He thus assured himself of wide dissemination of the article, because it benefited from the large distribution of the parent newspaper. Occasionally a reverse situation obtained: an independent work might be reprinted in a newspaper for the benefit of its readers.

James Rivington, the Tory printer-owner of the *New-York Gazetteer*, for example, not only controlled the most powerful press organ in the colonies between 1773 and 1775, but also printed separate pamphlets, among which was *A Dialogue Between a Southern Delegate and His Spouse*, the first play in this collection. *A Dialogue* aroused intense antagonism, as is indicated in a letter to James Madison from a friend in Philadelphia, who called it "grossly scurrilous."[11]

Rivington's Tory proclivities eventually destroyed his journalistic empire. On May 10, 1775, his presses were wrecked by an incensed mob, and he fled to a ship in New York harbor. In fact, so extreme did the Whig hatred of Rivington become that some of his tracts were burned, and some were literally tarred and feathered. Even more an expert at rabble-rousing was Isaiah Thomas, the printer-editor of *The Massachusetts Spy*. At the center of the rising storm, his notorious Whig news sheet was the talk of the citizenry. It was read avidly by the patriots and Tories alike and became in time a kind of revolutionists' handbook. As a result it attracted the contributions of the Friends of Liberty in Massachusetts Bay Colony. Thomas accepted *The Adulateur*, a pamphlet play by Mercy Otis Warren, and it appeared in *The Massachusetts Spy* in March, 1772. Mrs. Warren's attack on Governor Thomas Hutchinson in *The Adulateur* was so effective that it was reprinted as a separate pamphlet in 1773.

Although commercial notices are not necessarily as precise an indication of the popularity and value of propaganda pamphlets as are the factors of price, number of editions, and distribution, advertisements offer consequential evidence of the interest in rousing pamphlets which stimulated argument and made prejudice articulate. Exaggerated promotion of printed works, the not-so-gentle art of "puffing," became an increasingly popular adjunct to book and pamphlet publishing in the eighteenth century. Advertisements usually fell into two categories: the simple announcement of new titles and the more elaborate description of the contents of a work. Printers hawked mercantile wares as well as their own publications even though space was limited, and the pamphlets which they printed often were heralded with appropriate fanfare. The Whig press puffed Whig pamphlets, and the Tory press followed suit.

A number of pamphlet plays either received advance notices or were advertised on the day of publication. *The Blockheads* was noted on June 13, 1776, in *The New England Chronicle*, a Whig newspaper, with the following announcement: "Saturday next will be published, and to be sold by John Gill, in Queen-Street, The Blockheads; or the Affrighted Officers. A Farce." Four days later *The Constitutional Journal*, another Boston newspaper, ran a similar advertisement.

The Fall of British Tyranny was announced on July 24, 1776, in *The Pennsylvania Gazette*, the well-known and widely distributed journal that Franklin bought when it was failing in 1759 and made an outstanding success. In addition to the notice of publication of the play, the paper carried a full description of the scenes to entice the reader:

A pleasing scene between Roger and Dick, two shepherds near Lexington.

Clarissa, &c. A very moving scene on the death of Dr. Warren, &c., in a chamber near Boston the morning after the battle of Bunker's Hill. A humorous scene between the Boatswain and a Sailor on board a man-of-war, near Norfolk in Virginia. Two very laughable scenes between the Boatswain, two Sailors and the Cook, exhibiting specimens of seafaring oratory and peculiar eloquence of those sons of Neptune, touching Tories, Convicts and black regulars: and between Lord Kidnapper and Major Cudgeo. A droll scene, a council of war in Boston, Admiral Tombstone, Elbow Room, Mr. Caper, General Clinton and Earl Percy.

A shocking scene, a dungeon, between Colonel Allen and an officer of the guard.

Two affecting scenes in Boston after the flight of the Regulars from Lexington, between Lord Boston, messenger and officers of the guard. A patriotic scene in the camp at Cambridge, between the Generals Washington, Lee, Putnam, &c, &c.

The reputation of the play traveled north, and on August 22, 1776, *The New England Chronicle* announced:

Now in the Press, and speedily will be published and sold by Powars and Willis, and John Gill, in Queen Street,

> The Fall of British Tyranny
> or
> American Liberty Triumphant, the
> First Campaign
> A TRAGI-COMEDY, of Five Acts,
> Containing twenty-six scenes,
> Among which are the following, viz.

There follows the same description of scenes as printed in *The Pennsylvania Gazette,* to which is added:

With a dedication, preface, address to the Goddess of Liberty to the Congress, dramatis personae, prologue, epilogue, and a song in praise of King Tammany, the American Saint.

A truly dramatic performance, interspersed with wit, humour, burlesque, and serious matter, which cannot fail of affording abundant entertainment to readers of every disposition.

The Boston Gazette, one of the stanchest patriotic newspapers, printed a similar advertisement for the play on September 16, 1776. The announcement of the actual publication of the play in Massachusetts was made ten days later in *The New England Chronicle* with the added information that *The Fall of British Tyranny* would be sold in Watertown as well as in Boston, indicating the printer's anticipation of a large sale.

The great number of pamphlets published during this period, the low cost, the distribution of the pamphlets as separate works or through the medium of newspapers, and the many editions and advertisements indicate the value attached to the printed argument. The pamphlet plays were part of this ambitious propaganda campaign, but they were unique because of the direct and realistic communication by a reporter-playwright who recounted in theatrical terms what happened as recently as yesterday.

In addition to their satiric and persuasive qualities, the pamphlet plays bear a strong resemblance to two kinds of newspaper writing: the factual story and the feature article. The result is journalistic theatre, actual reporting heightened by dramatic form. Although they are not as sophisticated or as sociologically motivated as the "living newspaper" plays of the 1930s in America, they are similar: headlines transferred to the stage while the event is still alive in men's minds.

If these pamphlet plays were effective as propaganda, why were there not more of them? The answer hinges on several circumstances, moral, economic, and legal. Although, as we shall see, dramatic literature to be read in private was more or less acceptable, the theatre was stigmatized as a corrupter of morals. It was a place where evil persons congregated to prey upon the young; on stage, vice was often more attractive than virtue even though the latter was at the end triumphant. Theatre-going was a waste of time and money because the penny earned was not saved but spent on a frivolous and ephemeral commodity. In any case, participation in plays and attendance at them were illegal because of interdictions against both in many towns and colonies.

Staging plays before a public audience was condemned, but dramatic literature perused in the privacy of the study or occasionally presented as a "staged play reading" by one actor before an interested group of ladies and gentlemen escaped all but unenlightened censure. Such a reading occurred on February 8, 1770, and again in Boston on March 19, 1770, when one performer played all the roles in *The Provoked Husband*.[12] There were, of course, learned ministers and other respectable citizens, particularly in Boston and Philadelphia, who were pained if anyone chose to read a play as a pleasant occupation, but many persons were not so pained. They knew the latest works of the modern English playwrights; they had studied classical, Elizabethan, and Restoration dramas in college. There were even those who kept the Bible, Milton, and Shakespeare side by side on the bookshelf (de Tocqueville noted this when he visited a log cabin in western New York several decades later).[13]

In spite of the sometimes grudging approval of the drama, there was a pervasive vocal and written antagonism to the theatre, of which such terms of opprobrium as "sink of iniquity" and "devil's plaything" were understatements. The hatred of the theatre had been prevalent in varying degrees from the early days of colonial settlement. Most of the leaders in New England were adamant in their opposition and as late as 1750 Massachusetts reiterated its laws against the stage. The Middle States, however, became less censorious as the century advanced. In the South, where there had always been a more permissive attitude toward the theatre among the gentry if not among their more conservative associates and the representatives of the middle classes, traveling companies were welcome, especially during such occasions as Race Week in Charleston or when the Assembly met in Williamsburg. Moral censure, even in the South, was always a possible sword of Damocles, however, and theatre companies learned early to seek out the more obdurate officials in order to placate them with assurances that the production of plays need give no alarm.

Typical of the reaction against drama was the statement of Timothy Dwight, president of Yale, who declared that the pleasures of modern man should be simple—"riding, visiting, reading." All of these were much more acceptable than attendance at the theatre, where were produced works of Aeschylus, Sophocles, Euripides, Shakespeare, Corneille, Schiller, and Kotzebue, among which there is "scarcely one which an Apostle would read. . . . They are only a vast and fascinating system of profligacy."[14]

If Dwight considered the reading of drama not fit for an Apostle, and therefore too profane for ordinary mortals, he would have been outraged by the curriculum at Princeton, where Corneille and Racine were taught to students in "modern" French! Mercy Otis Warren of Plymouth, Massachusetts, a compatriot of Dwight's, would have found his attitude trying and his prejudices limiting. As she stated in her own somewhat prolix style: "Theatrical amusements may, sometimes, have been prostituted to the purposes of vice; yet, in an age of taste and refinement, lessons of morality, and the consequences of deviation, may, perhaps, be as successfully enforced from the stage, as by modes of instruction, less censured by the severe, while, at the same time, the exhibition of great historical events, opens a field of contemplation to the reflecting and philosophical mind."[15]

Another circumstance that militated against colonial dramatic writing, persuasive or otherwise, was the surfeit of theatrical fare that came directly from England or appeared at the booksellers under an American imprint. Published works were imported, but the reprinting of English drama in New York, Philadelphia, and Boston was an even brisker business, and plays were cheaper for that reason.

For those who did not consider the entering of a playhouse the first step to Hell, there were opportunities to see a variety of acted dramas. From 1752 to 1774 productions were given by the American Company under the aegis of Lewis Hallam and later of David Douglass. The acting and staging were professional, even if second rate, and Philadelphia, New York, Charleston, Williamsburg, and Annapolis became theatrical centers, although the season was sometimes short and there were months when no performances were presented. Financial security for the managers obviously meant the attraction of audiences, and the latter particularly desired the standard repertoire, which included the classics or the latest play from Drury Lane or Covent Garden. Native American drama in the pre-Revolutionary years rarely was given a hearing, no matter how expertly written, principally because it lacked the weight of public and critical acceptance enjoyed for the most part by the products of the English stage. It was not until after the Revolution that the clamor for American plays rose perceptibly.

The *coup de grâce* to the theatre profession in America took place on October 20, 1774, making its demise official and ostensibly final for the duration of the war. On that date the First Continental Congress, motivated more by political and economic than moral concerns, issued a resolution against performances. "We will in our several stations," the document read, "encourage frugality, economy, and industry, especially that of wool; and will discountenance and discourage every species of extravagance and dissipation, especially all horse-racing, and all kinds of gaming, cock-fighting, exhibition of shews, plays and other expensive diversions and entertainments."[16]

Although the proceedings of Congress had legal, if oftentimes unenforceable, status only if ratified by the separate colonies, this particular measure was approved rather quickly by all assemblies except those of New York and Georgia, indicating that a fair majority of citizens regarded the banning of theatrical entertainments (curiously equated with cock-fighting) as a political and moral expedient. The professional company led by Douglass admitted defeat and sailed for Jamaica on February 2, 1775, leaving a vacuum filled only by British officers who presented amateur theatricals under Burgoyne in Boston during the occupation (from April, 1775, to March, 1776), under the patronage of Sir William Howe in New York in 1777 and Philadelphia in

1778, and under Sir Henry Clinton in New York from 1778 to 1782.[17]

One exception to the British performances was the presentation by American soldiers of Addison's *Cato* at Valley Forge in May, 1778. The performance was attended, in spite of Congressional interdiction, by General and Mrs. Washington and Lord and Lady Stirling. "The Scenery was in Taste—and the performance admirable. . . . If the enemy does not retire from Philadelphia soon, our Theatrical amusement will continue—the Fair Penitent with the Padlock will soon be acted. The 'recruiting Officer' is also on foot."[18]

There may have been other performances by American soldiers in Philadelphia after the British had departed for New York. Whether plays were actually presented is not known, but in 1778 there were two other Congressional interdictions against the theatre, one of which forbade any member of the armed services to appear in or to attend plays, giving rise to the speculation that American officers were intending to emulate "Howe's Thespians," who had recently contributed to the amusements of Philadelphia before they departed ignominiously for the north.

The Revolution had forced professional players to leave the country and retire to Jamaica. The battle they had fought since 1752 to gain respectability, which was approaching at least an uneasy truce between them and the conservatives in the colonies, was suddenly turned by the action of Congress into a disastrous retreat. Had plays been allowed as a momentary surcease from the pressures of war or had drama been recognized as a source of stimulation to heroic actions, the theatre could have been used as a "happy and efficient instrument" instead of a dangerous one, as General "Mad Anthony" Wayne, who understood the value of propaganda under government control, argued in retrospect in 1785.[19]

To summarize the theatrical situation as it obtained during the Revolution: more pamphlet plays would have been written if the liberal exponents of the arts had been able to influence the majority to accept the playhouse as a medium in which events of importance to the colonial cause could be dramatized for patriotic motives. Such, however, was the unfavorable attitude toward the theatre that few writers dared attempt to write directly for it. When, after 1774, there were no opportunities for professional productions, the drama as a *pièce du théâtre* and as a public medium for propaganda was doomed. With the theatre closed to it, the only outlet for persuasive drama was the pamphlet play, distributed by the press, where the kind of censorship affecting the stage did not prevail.

There is evidence that three of the dramatic works which are included in this anthology — *The Death of General Montgomery*, *The Fall of British Tyranny*, and *The Patriots* — were given some kind of public presentation, probably only performances by nonprofessionals before invited friends in a college or in a private home. Hugh Henry Brackenridge wrote *The Battle of Bunker's-Hill* and *The Death of General Montgomery* for his students to perform. As he states in his preface to the latter play in 1777, he "would choose to have it considered only as a school piece. . . . It is intended for the private entertainment of Gentlemen of taste, and martial enterprize, but no means for the exhibition of the stage. The subject is not love but valor. I meddle not with any of the effeminating passions, but consecrate my muse to the great themes of patriotic virtue, bravery and heroism."[20] The emasculating complexities of love, as Brackenridge (perhaps slyly) affirms, have no place in a world where the drum beat rather than the heart beat rouses men to valiant action; romance is vitiating and not robust and must not interfere with more noble purposes. Brackenridge cannot resist his innate satirical temperament, but he must also give an earnest dedication, because, after all, *The Death of General Montgomery* is an object lesson in heroism, written for schoolboys—a "theatrical" oration rather than a play. By such rationalization the playwright rescues his dramatic poem from any taint of the stage and at the same time makes clear that he is conforming to the edict against stage performances.

We know also from the statement of Abbé Robin, a chaplain in the French Army in America in 1781, that *The Battle of Bunker's-Hill* and *The Death of General Montgomery*, as well as *The Fall of British Tyranny* attributed to John Leacock, were acted at Harvard.

> . . . their pupils often acted tragedies, the subject of which is generally taken from their national events, such as the battle of Bunker's Hill, the burning of Charlestown, the Death of General Montgomery, the capture of Burgoyne, the treason of Arnold, and the Fall of British tyranny. You must easily conclude, that in such a new nation as this, these pieces must fall infinitely short of that perfection to which our European literary productions of this kind are wrought up; but still, they have a greater effect upon the mind than the best of ours would have among them because these manners and customs are delineated, which are such as interest them above all others. The drama is here reduced to its true and ancient origin.[21]

Abbé Robin saw in these amateur attempts the seeds of a native and democratic drama, which included a strong strain of contemporary realism, arising from the immediate events of the day. The next thirty years would see a greater attempt to write and produce plays bearing an American hallmark, many of them concerning the political affairs of a new republic struggling for unity and combating the internal and external forces that would tear it asunder.

The third play that may have reached its audience in a semipublic presentation is *The Patriots*. One can make such an assumption because the author, Robert Munford, lived in a community in Virginia where the theatre and drama had a strong appeal and where there were many social gatherings at which plays were read aloud. The sophisticated William Byrd II describes how he was forced to stay several days at a plantation because of the rain, and there he discovered a copy of *The Beggar's Opera*, which he had seen in London in 1728. He assembled the household after dinner and read the opera to them, supplementing his account with observations on the production he had seen.[22] Munford could have likewise gathered his friends for such a reading, or it might even have been staged by amateurs in a private home.

Of the remaining four plays in the anthology, *A Dialogue, The Blockheads, The Battle of Brooklyn,* and *The Motley Assembly,* there is no evidence of production, although *The Battle of Brooklyn* could well have had a brief stage career in New York during the seven years the city was under British occupancy and the military "thespians" were performing for their fellow officers and the Loyalist elite.

THE SELECTION OF PLAYS in this collection was based on three criteria: their representation as examples of pro- or anti-American propaganda, their revelation of colonial reactions to actual events as they occurred, which give them historical authenticity, and finally their vividness in bringing to life a period of turmoil and anguish. These matters are more thoroughly treated in the introductions to each of the plays.

The plays are arranged in the chronological order of their date of composition, which is almost immediately upon the event itself. When the plays are read in sequence, one moves through a dramatized history of the American Revolution from the first agitation to a fully committed war. Taken as one aspect of social history these plays are an informal, vital, journalistic account of the movement of a revolution. It is possible to see in them the rising intensity of the conflict as it shifts from attempted conciliation to bloody strife, from delicately balanced adjustment between watchful compatriots to fractured loyalties among vengeful enemies.

The first play, *A Dialogue Between a Southern Delegate and His Spouse on His Return from the Grand Continental Congress,* was published in 1774, a year in which tensions were mounting and the atmosphere was filled with the recriminations of the Tories who honored the authority of the mother country and the Whigs who were disaffected by the lack of foresight and the stubbornness of the king's ministers. The anger of the Tories was heightened by the decision of the Whigs to send provincial delegates to an inter-colonial assembly in Philadelphia to discuss the wrongs perpetrated by Britain and to seek various avenues of conciliation in order to redress those wrongs. This meeting of continental representatives is the one that is under attack in the play.

Already England had taken punitive measures against Massachusetts, and it was feared that she might do likewise in the other colonies. There was a belief among the delegates to the Congress that with unity in America, arrangements could be made to strengthen the relationship of the child state to the parent. Home rule in the colonies was not actually anticipated; yet the stirrings of the idea of a commonwealth were present in the minds of many. As a matter of fact, had the conservative delegates, led by Galloway of Pennsylvania, carried the day, grievances might have been adjusted with England. That these delegates did not succeed was the result of the clever undercover work of the Massachusetts group, which included Sam and John Adams and John Hancock. These wily patriots knew how to play their cards, never openly accusing the king of tyranny, which would have antagonized the moderates at the convention, but emphasizing that the king's ministers were corrupt and were the real villains in the battle for colonial rights.

A Dialogue was much more effective as Tory propaganda than it may appear today. The Whigs thought it was scandalously defamatory because it ridiculed high-minded purpose and traduced the Friends of Liberty, who were both sincere in their concern for their freedom and angry at the treatment they were receiving from England.

No individual historical figures are selected for satire in the play; the whole assembly is derided. The propaganda is directed against the work of the Congress, ridiculed as the resolution of small minds. The cleverness of its attack lies in the manner of its presentation: the bickering of a man and his wife, which reduces the idealistic motivation of the patriots to a common domestic quibble. The wife scorns the presumptuous audacity of the Congress in defying Britain and asserts that if women had been the delegates they would have brought about a satisfactory *modus operandi* with Britain—women are adept at compromise and are less inclined than men to rash actions that threaten the security of home and family. From the point of view of its propaganda and what it reveals of the Anglo-American controversy in 1774, *A Dialogue* is a curtain raiser on the great conflict, the prologue to a bitter and lengthy war of words and men.

The Fall of British Tyranny, the second play, is a large historical panorama that continues the saga of the Revolution. This theatrical chronicle of English wickedness and American innocence begins in 1774, when the Intolerable or Coercive Acts were leveled against Massachusetts, and continues until early 1776, after the death of General Montgomery. The play is a patchwork quilt of incidents unified in design by a double Whig theme: the nefarious schemes of British ministers led by Lord Bute (Lord Paramount), the supposed manipulator of George III, and the dreadful effect of these ministerial machinations on the freedom-loving colonists.

The events—dramatized, reported, or briefly touched upon—are charged with life by a writer whose keen imagination, sensitivity to pathetic situations, and wry humor strip bare Tory and British pretensions. The first two acts take place in London where the Parliamentary enemies of the colonists set the wheels in motion while their own opponents, Englishmen who are sympathetic to America, voice a dismal chorus of despair at the evidence of Britain's tyranny—the effect of which is demonstrated as the scenes of the play move to the colonies and Canada in the last three acts, a panorama of the events of 1775 and early 1776.

The disarray of the Redcoats as they fly from Lexington and Concord, the horror of the battle of Bunker Hill, the recruiting of black slaves by Lord Dunmore in Virginia to murder their masters, and the sadistic imprisonment of Ethan Allen by Prescott at the beginning of the Canadian campaign are painted with brilliant strokes. In contrast are the somber emotions of fear of Britain's probable vengeance, of the anguish of women at the loss of husbands and sons, and of fear of the evil of English generals. Heroic hyperbole, pathos, sentimental pastoral, ribald verse and prose, colloquial speech, and satirical comment are combined in a vicious attack against the mother country.

The play is crowded with historical personages transmuted into theatrical characters, unsympathetically caricatured if they are enemies to liberty or enlarged to heroic proportions if defenders of the rights of man. The premise of the play is that all evils against America stem from one manipulator, Lord Bute, whose secret desire, according to rumor both in the colonies and in England, was to divide Britain and America, allowing each to destroy the other in the process so that Bute could reinstate on the throne his distant relatives, the Stuarts. The playwright uses this popularly accepted opinion of Bute to show how Bute's intrigues influence other officials of the crown. These ministers are thinly disguised: Lord Catspaw is Lord North; Lord Poltron, the Earl of Sandwich; Lord Hypocrite, the Earl of Dartmouth.

Opposing these creatures of Bute are the English ministers who, because of their defense of colonial freedom, were heroes to the Americans. Included among them are William Pitt the Elder, Earl of Chatham (Lord Wisdom), John Wilkes (Lord Patriot), and Edmund Burke (Bold Irishman).

The ineptitude of the British military men commanding the "occupational" forces on American soil receives the full measure of the playwright's scorn as he ridicules their stupidity, cowardice, arrogance, braggadocio, and sadism. These officers are aptly named: General Gage is Lord Boston, Admiral Graves is Lord Tombstone, General Burgoyne is Mr. Caper, General Sir William Howe is Elbow Room, and the Earl of Dunmore is Lord Kidnapper. The American generals Washington, Lee, and Putnam appear as themselves.

The large canvas upon which the author of *The Fall of British Tyranny* works reminds one of the immense paintings of Benjamin West or John Trumbull, in which the whole picture makes a statement about a critical event in history—"The Death of General Wolfe," "Penn's Treaty with the Indians," or "The Battle of Bunker's Hill"—but in which the details are as carefully depicted as in genre pieces.

Ridicule is the predominant device of the play, a combination of truth, half-truth, and rumor used to create hybrid caricatures. For example, Burgoyne is attacked for his dilettantism in the sophisticated social arts of music, dancing, and the theatre (for which he wrote plays); he is also mocked for his towering vanity and his reputed cowardice at Bunker Hill. A strong indictment of the British and a sentimental defense of the Americans in the early stages of the Revolution, the play is completed in historical time just before evacuation of the English from Boston, the subject of the next work in this collection.

The Blockheads, published later in 1776 than *The Fall of British Tyranny,* takes place in Boston between the time when Americans fortified Dorchester Heights on March 5, 1776 (thus restricting the British to the confines of the city with no escape except by sea), and the fateful day for the enemy, March 17, 1776, when General Howe decided to evacuate Boston and sail for Halifax. The predicament of the Loyalists caught between the retreating British and the advancing Americans was frightful; many were afraid to remain in Boston, but they had only one safe place to go—to Canada with the English. Many of them were huddled aboard ships, overcrowded as these already were, and began a long and perilous voyage to the northern sanctuary, from which a number fled to England.

The historical characters in *The Blockheads* are the complaining, starved British officers, once the pride of their country and now reduced to shuddering incompetence, and the fear-haunted Loyalists, regretting bitterly that they cast their lot with the perfidious English. Each of these two groups is satirized in portraits of actual officers and citizens. Among the former are Admiral Graves and General William Howe (who appeared in *The Fall of British Tyranny*), and among the latter, prominent local citizens who were known for their loyalty to the mother country. To these, the playwright adds three fictional Loyalist women.

The primary intention of the Whig propagandist is to curse Britain's military "blockheads" and their native-born adherents, but there is a secondary purpose, social in nature. The Loyalists are scorned for their sycophancy and their social pretensions, made evident by their groveling for awards and honors, the proper payment for allegiance to the king. They find, however, that they are reduced to the status of stable boys to the troops or, at best, to the position of social inferiors. The other object of attack by the playwright is the desire of certain rustic Loyalists to ape the customs and practices of London, turning their backs on the roughness and vulgarity of their "homespun" relatives, friends, and neighbors.

This second theme is the source for the only plot in *The Blockheads.* The Loyalist Simple family—Mr. Simple, his wife Jemima, and their daughter Tabitha—create a farcical domestic situation: Simple regrets leaving his farm to move to Boston to join the British, and his wife upbraids him for his lack of ambition to become one of the *beau monde.* The new social position would enable Tabitha to make a noble match, preferably with Lord Dapper, who would take them all to London where they could mingle with the aristocracy. The playwright shows that Dapper's intention is anything but honorable and makes the point that even the Loyalists cannot trust an Englishman, especially a lord, who "looks like a baboon on stilts" and is rumored to be impotent.

Retribution falls on the Simples and the other Loyalists as they flee the triumphant Americans. But the despair and the remorse of the Tories are presented without sympathy; suffering is their just reward for collaboration, and the playwright reveals their discomfort with gleeful pleasure.

Of the seven plays in this collection, the Tory *The Battle of Brooklyn* published in 1776 gives the strongest impression of being a direct report of the event itself. The action of *The Battle of Brooklyn* centers on the battle that took place on August 27, 1776, where Howe outmaneuvered Washington, causing him to abandon Long Island and retreat to Manhattan across the East River on August 30 to 31.

The defeat of the patriots on Long Island is a sorry chapter in the history of the Revolution, and the lack of foresight that caused it made it a ready subject for the Tory propagandist. The ineptitude of the American officers, their lack of knowledge of the terrain (which they should have known and had had the opportunity to learn), and the miscalculations on the part of the general staff all contributed to the inevitable disaster. Contrasted to the sorry display of rebel military logistics was the brilliance of Howe's strategy in using the undefended Jamaica Pass on the northeast of the Island, which resulted in the entrapment of the Americans. *The Battle of Brooklyn* is the Tory reverse of the coin of *The Blockheads,* even though the fiasco on Long Island was so complete and so obviously the result of misguided complacency that ridicule pales before the actual absurdity.

The Battle of Brooklyn presents a self-consciously smug attitude, not only about the immediate success of the British forces but about the eventual victory for England. The play is a vicious attack against the officers who led the patriot cause. They are not only made to look like fools but are pushed into the mire and tramped upon: Washington becomes a tawdry roué, buying a woman from his brother officer; Stirling a staggering alcoholic, frightened into a state of imbecility; Putnam a dishonest profiteer, reaping a financial windfall by selling horses stolen from the farmers of Connecticut and Long Island.

The Battle of Brooklyn is designed to belittle the rebels, to show them in the worst light and shatter any confidence the Americans may have in their leaders. The playwright-propagandist makes it apparent that Britain leads from strength; the triumph on Long Island presages a dramatic turn in the conflict, anticipating a quick end to the war and the subjugation of the colonies. Such optimism for the Loyalist and English success, based on the realities of colonial defeat by inexperienced bungling, written with unmitigated scorn of the principals, makes *The Battle of Brooklyn* effective propaganda; among the pamphlet plays, it is the best of the Tory attacks.

The Death of General Montgomery was published in 1777. The disastrous defeat for the Americans it reports took place in 1776, so that the play lacks the immediacy of the other works in this volume, but it does give a certain impression of verisimilitude, somewhat like a portrait taken from a photographic resemblance—in this instance the newspaper report of a battle. The action follows the neoclassical unities of place and time, the place being before the walls of Quebec on the Plains of Abraham, and the time being less than twenty-four hours between December 31, 1775, and January 1, 1776. Hugh Henry Brackenridge's concise chronicle presents one military event: the attack on Quebec in a raging snowstorm by the American commander Montgomery with his subordinate officer Benedict Arnold, their defeat by the British general Sir Guy Carleton, the death of Montgomery, and the withdrawal of the Americans.

The effectiveness of *The Death of General Montgomery* is weakened by the stilted unrhymed iambic pentameter in which it is written, but there are moving passages in it which reveal the playwright's dedication to liberty and his anger at those who would destroy it. The play is primarily, however, a eulogy for the brave men who perished in the wintry wilds of Quebec. Satire has no place in it; instead one finds bitter irony as well as a note of hope. The recompense for the soldiers who gave their lives willingly is that history will call them heroes and saviors of their country. It is on this note that the play is sustained. *The Death of General Montgomery* is also a heroic poem, flawed by writing that is sentimental and emotionally exaggerated. The Americans are painted in the splendid colors of adulation; the British in unrelieved black. There is also a hortatory element in this dramatic poem written to inspire young students, an admonition to follow the example of the heroes of Quebec, where the body of Montgomery was discovered frozen in the snow, his arm still upheld as he led the attack.

In pleasant contrast to the dirge-like *Death of General Montgomery*, *The Patriots* by Robert Munford is a cheerful domestic comedy with an underlying vein of serious intention. Written between 1777 and 1779, it is the only play in the collection that treats exclusively of the reaction of citizens not directly involved with the conflict but affected by it. The events take place in Virginia on the home front, in a section of the back country removed from the maelstrom of war, and the tone of the play contradicts a generalization that all colonists were irrevocably committed either to the red and gold of the English or the buff and blue of the Continentals. There was a middle ground in which a quieter kind of patriotism operated, one opposed to local chauvinism and the paranoiac suspicion that Tories were to be found under every bed or behind the wainscoting. It was a patriotism also antithetical to the hypocrisy of the turncoat who displayed one side or the other according to the political climate of the hour. Between the extremes lay neutralist opinion, which as the play demonstrates became more and more difficult to sustain as the fury of the Revolution increased.

The Patriots is named for the colonists whose judgment was balanced, who were the true believers in liberty, according to their own lights, and who had no self-esteem to mar their considered point of view. They are local heroes in the best sense, and they are introduced into an eighteenth century comedy in which the satire is confined to country matters and to political strife stemming from the larger issues of the Revolution.

The particular target of the propaganda of *The Patriots* is the Committees of Safety (or Observation or Inspection), which were established to seek out and prosecute those who did not adhere to the agreements of the First Continental Congress. These committees, although supposed to be fair and judicious, often were composed of bigoted men who saw traitors everywhere and stigmatized their fellow citizens as Tory at the merest hint of approval of British aims. Such prejudiced men literally prosecuted their personally chosen suspects upon gossip, rumor, and suspicion; they hated the minority groups, particularly the Scots, because the Scots were middlemen between the tobacco planters and the English commercial agents. Almost fanatically hated by the tobacco growers, the canny Scots were persecuted as enemies of the country, and the gentlemen farmers could pursue their attack on them with vigor unimpeded by any concern for justice.

The special quality of the propaganda in *The Patriots* lies in its defense of the right of the neutral to express opinions that run counter to the popular concepts embodied in the "watch dog" Committees of Safety. Meanwell and Trueman, the heroes of the play, declare they have every right to dissent even though such opposition to the patriot cause may mean a sacrifice of liberty or even of life. Using all the devices of eighteenth century sentimental and romantic comedy, *The Patriots* emphasizes that the home front had its particular perils, as did the battlegrounds.

The Motley Assembly, published in 1779, is a short trifle of manners. It is more than a simple social satire, however, because it attempts to accomplish two objectives. The first is an attack on the insipidity of those in the upper colonial classes who were still enchanted by British social graces. These Americans lived only for pleasure, were infected by *ennui,* and had forgotten the true meaning of the Revolution. The second objective is a reminder that the war was still in progress, that the collapse of the patriot cause was a very strong possibility and that men in battle need to have their morale strengthened by the active support and encouragement of the civilians.

The action of *The Motley Assembly* takes place in Boston several years after the British were driven from the city. It indirectly attacks those panjandrums among the elite who are busily hanging crepe for the demise of liberty, but its real target is the latent Loyalists in Boston, who pretend to be in favor of the American cause but are secretly drawn to the British. Those who deplore the loss of gaiety in the social round of the English and their American sycophants during the occupation of the city now give aid and comfort to the quasi-patriots who still infest the community. The present social leaders have forgotton the misery of the occupation, remembering only the gala parties and hating the present uncouth aspect of society. To these people, manners appear to be more important than convictions or defense of country. The lack of refinement, as noted by the majority of the characters, was nowhere more obvious than in the contrast between the Assemblies or balls formerly held by the British and continued with less éclat by the Americans. The playwright castigates the affected pseudopatriots who remember fondly the "brilliance" of the former social scene and deplore the lack of luster in the American imitation of "society." Such frivolities are more reprehensible because other more sober people are involved in a war of survival.

The Motley Assembly, a satirical vignette, opposing those who give lip service to the patriotic cause, indirectly attacks the malaise of indifference and apathy in the cities where the tide of war has retreated. Under fire also is the fruitless whining of those who live only in the past. The greatest scorn is for the demoralizers whose myopic point of view reduces the noble aims of the Revolution to petty bickering. These persons are not villains because they are not actually traitors, but their lack of enthusiasm for the American cause and their cold, "nasty-nice" reaction to those who defend them arouse in the playwright an intense scorn. For these reasons, *The Motley Assembly,* attacking an aspect of near-Loyalist folly not explored in the other pamphlet plays, has a particularly important place in the canons of Revolutionary propaganda.

THE AMERICAN REVOLUTION came to a triumphant conclusion in peace and independence after eight years of military and political defeats and victories. It was won in part because of the dogged determination of citizens turned soldier who became more and more proficient as they learned to take the full measure of their enemies and who were gradually unified in a dedication to freedom and liberty. *Freedom* and *Liberty* were catchwords, and the gradations of their meaning made them useful to Tory and Whig alike. Much depended on just how they were interpreted. Could one be independent if the physical ties were loosened and the spiritual ones retained? The Tories emphatically answered "Yes" and defended their point of view. Or should one reject the mother forthwith, sever relations and stop paying for dubious benefits? The reply of the majority of the Whigs was loudly affirmative. Obviously the contest was based on a vast complexity of considerations, many of them permutations of theories of government and the relationship of the rulers to their subjects, but the argument of independence or slavery became a major issue, and it turned into a propaganda war without which the force of the Revolution probably could not have been sustained until victory was achieved. Although the Tories were later than the Whigs in realizing the potentials of and the need for overt persuasion, after 1774 they maintained a healthy antagonism and many of their pamphlets were successful, if temporary, battles in the long controversy.

In the large corpus of writings occasioned by the Revolution plays were a small production, but they strike an original note. However biased the writers were, their presentation carried strong conviction, sincerity, and honesty according to their own lights. The writers of these pieces were violent in their attitudes because they were caught in an eruption of emotions stimulated by personal involvement and motivated by fear and distress. For the Tories—what they had known as a satisfactory way of life was being disrupted and would possibly suffer drastic change, and they were determined to oppose any threat to their security. In the Whig column of the balance sheet, however, from 1774 to 1776, there was more awareness of the uses of persuasion and more effective proselytes. The Whigs had begun their campaign of conversion as early as the Stamp Act crisis of 1765-66, and they had in their camp such powerful advocates as James Otis, Samuel Adams, Mercy Otis Warren, Patrick Henry, John Dickinson, Henry Laurens, and Thomas Jefferson—to name a few. They, each in his own way, added to the growing alarm. By 1775, and particularly after the military actions at Lexington and

Concord and the disaster at Bunker Hill occurred, the chimera of independence became a reality, and the agitation for complete severance from Great Britain became a consideration of the majority.

It was Thomas Paine and the declaration *for* independence, *Common Sense,* that brought into unmistakable focus the only possible goal of the American people. One can say incontrovertibly that after *Common Sense* was published propaganda soon avoided wariness or ambiguity when preaching independence, and the defense of it changed to outspoken and uncompromisingly forthright demands for its realization. The Whig pamphlet plays also came under Paine's influence. They display a rough and volatile force, a directness of attack and a timeliness that is also found in *Common Sense.* From Plymouth in Massachusetts to the plantations of the South civil war forced the colonists to voice their agony; this was a stage on which the dialogue of the actors was answered by no expected cues and no one knew on what tragic or comic conclusion the curtain would fall.

The plays in this anthology reflect that growing commitment, and when read in chronological sequence give insight into the rising emotional fever that affected all sorts and conditions of men. Extreme agitation in the major cities was matched by bloody combat on plains and fields. The battle of words became the battle of arms, increasing as the war became part of everyone's life.

In a remarkable way it is the rough and direct emotional quality in most of the plays that gives them their realistic pertinency and reconstructs for the reader a living experience of a time of great personal and national stress. Sermons and political orations were more plentiful than the pamphlet plays, but the plays hold their own with other forms of propaganda. Moreover, they have the added advantage of a theatrical appeal, which gives a "tuppence colored" tone to their divisive argument, as if make-up were applied to pen and ink cartoons. *A Dialogue* has a Punch and Judy quality, as do the domestic comic scenes in *The Blockheads.* The black and white and red of melodrama pervades many of the scenes of *The Fall of British Tyranny.* The language of the plays is often abrasive and contentious, full of scorn and satiric comment. The gallery of crudely drawn caricatures reminds one of Hogarth, Richardson, and Gillray; they are filled with raucous laughter rarely, if ever, tempered by good humor, for there was anger everywhere. Increasingly the times tried the most patient of souls, and mockery scarcely disguised its bitterness. The pamphlet plays, although small in number, were clearly heard in the battles of persuasion, and their trumpet notes sounded as loud and as clear as those of greater volume.

Notes

1. The six propaganda pieces not included are *The Adulateur,* Mercy Otis Warren, Boston, 1773; *The Americans Roused, in a Cure for the Spleen,* attributed to Jonathan Sewall, printed in New England and reprinted in New York, 1775; *The Group,* Mercy Otis Warren, Boston, 1775; *The Battle of Bunker's-Hill,* Hugh Henry Brackenridge, Philadelphia, 1776; *A Dialogue Between the Ghost of General Montgomery Just Arrived from the Elysian Fields; and an American Delegate in a Wood Near Philadelphia,* sometimes attributed to Thomas Paine, Philadelphia, 1776; *The Double Conspiracy,* attributed to John Trumbull, Hartford, 1783.

These plays are omitted for a variety of reasons: some have been reprinted a number of times; several are about local events, an area sufficiently covered by the included plays; some lack genuine dramatic or theatrical interest.

2. Allardyce Nicoll, *A History of the Restoration Drama,* 3rd ed. (Cambridge, England, 1940), pp. 10-11. See also Nicoll, *A History of the Early Eighteenth Century Drama,* 2nd. ed. (Cambridge, 1929), and John Loftis, *The Politics of Drama in Augustan England* (Oxford, 1963).

3. Thomas R. Adams, ed., "American Independence: The Growth of an Idea," *Publications of the Colonial Society of Massachusetts* (Boston, 1956), XLIII, p. 4. The entire bibliography, pp. 17-202, is an indispensable reference to numbers and editions of pamphlets of the period.

4. The play is not included in this collection because it is chiefly a prolix discussion in which the only action is the filling of tankards and the lighting of pipes. The work is a Tory document, and some of the arguments hit the mark, but it is principally a rhetorical exercise.

5. Pp. 4-5.

6. *The Literary History of the American Revolution* (New York, 1897), I, p. 21. The quotation from Sir Erskine May is in his *Constitutional History of England,* II, p. 247.

7. Peter Force, ed., *American Archives,* 4th Series (Washington, D. C.), V, pp. 438-40.

8. Homer L. Calkin, "Pamphlets and Public Opinion During the American Revolution," *Pennsylvania Magazine,* 64 (1940), pp. 23-27. Other authorities agree with his general estimate. Population statistics are from Mark M. Boatner III (ed.), *Encyclopedia of the American Revolution* (New York, 1966), p. 883.

9. For a good example of the American enthusiasm for the Bishop of St. Asaph, note how he is characterized in *The Fall of British Tyranny* as Lord Religion.

10. For bibliographical statistics of the pamphlets *see* Charles Evans, ed., *American Bibliography* (Chicago, 1903-05), V, p. 22.; Thomas R. Adams, ed., "American Independence, The Growth of an Idea," *Publication of the Colonial Society of Massachusetts* (December, 1956), XLIII, pp. 4-15.

11. *See* p. 32.

12. S. Foster Damon, "Varnum's 'Ministerial Oppression, a Revolutionary Drama'," *American Antiquarian Society* (October, 1945), p. 290; George O. Seilhamer, *History of the American Theatre* (Philadelphia, 1887), II, p. 16.

13. Phillips Bradley, ed., *Democracy in America,* 4th ed. (New York, 1948), II, p. 363.

14. *Travels in New England and New York* (New Haven, 1822), pp. 463-69.

15. *Preface to Poems, Dramatic and Miscellaneous* (Boston, 1790).

16. W. C. Ford, ed., *Journal of the Continental Congress, 1774-1779* (Washington, 1904), I, p. 78.

17. After the surrender of Cornwallis at Yorktown in 1781, the authority of Congress in respect to theatrical performances diminished and was not respected by all states. A theatre was built in Baltimore in 1781, and a regularly organized company of comedians performed in Baltimore, Annapolis, and New York for two years before the Peace Treaty of 1783. In the summer of 1783, from June 19 to August 16, Dennis Ryan gave thirty performances of familiar plays in New York. This theatrical activity preceded the official end of the Revolution when the last British forces departed from New York in November, 1783. *See* George O. Seilhamer, *History of the American Theatre*, chapters 2, 3, 4, 6, 7 of Vol. II for detailed explanation of these performances.

18. Letter from Colonel William Bradford to his sister Rachel, quoted by Paul Leicester Ford, *Washington and the Theatre* (New York, 1889), p. 26.

19. William Dunlap, *History of the American Theatre* (New York, 1832), pp. 56-58.

20. *The Death of General Montgomery*, preface.

21. Claude C. Robin, *New Travels through North America: In a Series of Letters* (Boston, 1784), p. 17. There is some doubt about whether Robin actually wrote the letters, which were translated by the Revolutionary poet Philip Freneau.

22. Louis B. Wright, ed., *The Prose Works of William Byrd of Westover* (Cambridge, Massachusetts, 1966), pp. 345-46.

✦✦✦✦✦✦✦✦✦✦✦✦✦✦✦✦✦✦✦✦✦✦✦✦✦✦✦✦✦✦✦
A DIALOGUE, BETWEEN
A SOUTHERN DELEGATE,
AND HIS SPOUSE,
ON HIS RETURN FROM
THE GRAND
CONTINENTAL CONGRESS
✦✦✦✦✦✦✦✦✦✦✦✦✦✦✦✦✦✦✦✦✦✦✦✦✦✦✦✦✦✦✦

Introduction to *A Dialogue*

WHEN pamphlets written for propaganda were cast in theatrical form, they followed one of two patterns. Either they were written with all the accessories of drama—plotting, characterization, act and scene division, and description of the scene—or they were presented as a simple dialogue, usually between two persons, a direct confrontation of playwright and reader or audience.

The dialogue was popular. People who lacked formal education responded to its conversational and argumentative presentation, for they were familiar with debates in town meetings where they listened to political oratory and participated in the harangues of the crowd. And the better educated merchants and members of the professions were acquainted with dialectical argumentation, since it was standard practice in collegiate training. Greek and Roman rhetoricians were used as models, and the British Parliament as well as the provincial legislatures furnished examples of style and brilliance in debate.

Other examples of rhetoric were available to the college man. Late seventeenth and early eighteenth century plays often contained passages of sharply developed argument, and students were encouraged to learn and recite these selections and engage in contests for prizes, thus returning the *agon* to its original intention. Such dialogues, often removed from the context of the play, were accepted not because they were in any way part of the theatre, but because they were excellent exercises in platform speaking. Original declamations given by students at term time were also part of the tradition of the colleges. The program at commencement usually included several newly prepared odes, well-organized debates, and lengthy, cleverly designed verbal exchanges, often heavily weighted with allegory and symbol but nonetheless sprightly and diverting.

A Dialogue Between a Southern Delegate and His Spouse on His Return from the Grand Continental Congress is in the tradition of the oral give-and-take of the town meeting as well as the carefully written and delivered disputation. It moves from its derivations into the current political contest of 1774 and in so doing uses as its method of attack a clearly individualized satire.

A Dialogue is engaging, with light touches of ridicule. The condemnation is neither severe nor violently angry for two particular reasons. In the first place, the event it mocks is not a battle or a physical conflict but the First Continental Congress, an assembly of sober-minded citizens alarmed by the course the parent government is taking and fearful for the liberties of the colonists. The play is, moreover, colored by a woman's laughter at the stupidity of men who gather solemnly in conclaves to protest against the inevitable —in this instance, the power and might of Great Britain. This aspect of woman's attacking the pretenses and political inclinations of a man's world introduces a typical situation of eighteenth century farces—the battle for superiority between the sexes.

The authorship of *A Dialogue* is unknown. The title page bears the name Mary V. V., but that is all the information we have about the playwright. A majority of the pamphlets of the period were anonymous. If men were fearful to admit to the writing of an attack against established government on the one hand or the patriotic cause on the other, women were even more likely to shy away from public protest. Furthermore, few women would admit they were so bold or unladylike as to invade the masculine arena of journalistic controversy.

It is, of course, possible that *A Dialogue* was written by a man, but its particular emphasis on the superiority of women to men in many matters suggests a woman's point of view: to shatter male vanity by reducing the male's vaunted "omniscience" to a showdown of its substance. Circumstantial evidence indicates that *A Dialogue* is woman's work.[1]

A Dialogue is an example of Tory propaganda, an attack on the radicals among the colonial lawyers, country gentlemen, and sophisticated urban merchants who met in Philadelphia in September and October, 1774. In general, these delegates represented the stable elements of property in the colonies but, as John Miller indicates, "The aristocratic complexion of Congress was no guarantee against its radicalism. Its delegates included both the well-heeled and the down-at-heel but the line which divided the extremists from the conservatives was not one of wealth or social position: some of the bluest-blooded members were among the most radical in combating British tyranny."[2]

Fear brought the delegates together, fear of the malign influence of Great Britain and its effect on their future. They were conscious of the emergency that drew them together and, in the First Continental Congress, patriotic enthusiasm affected them all so that they rose above sectionalism in an idealized common cause. No longer were they only Virginians or New Yorkers; they were Americans.

This meeting, then, is that which arouses the laughter of Mary V. V. To her it is absurd that little colonials, petty citizens, should meet with great solemnity and ostentation to defy the greatest power on earth, the might of England, of which they are an inextricable part. Obviously, they should know that their duty is to fear the King and Parliament and to keep the peace.

Underneath the chiding and the scorn explicit in the work, however, there is a serious warning: the colonists must stop the headlong race to disaster before it is too late. The delegates must rein in the radical elements in order to eliminate the danger of an actual break with England. The author views the mere calling of a congress as foolhardy, a step that could have fatal results. Fear of eventual independence and its dire consequences is implied. In effect the author asks: Why light a fire if it is going to consume you?

ALMOST as though making an inventory of stupid actions, if not actually traitorous felonies, the Wife in *The Dialogue* enumerates what she regards as the irresponsible decisions of the delegates. In particular, she opposes all radical moves of the Congress and approves any conciliatory efforts toward Britain. Her catalog of congressional sins includes one of its first acts—the approval of the Suffolk Resolves. These radical resolutions were an important milestone on the path to independence. They were the reaction to the coercive acts of Parliament that punished the Massachusetts Bay Colony. The Suffolk Resolves, adopted by Massachusetts patriots on September 9, 1774, under the leadership of Joseph Warren, defied Parliament, declaring that its acts in abrogating the liberties of Massachusetts "are gross infractions of those rights to which we are justly entitled by the laws of nature, the *British* Constitution and the charter of the Province."[3] The Resolves were so radical that they almost amounted to a declaration of war by the Bay Colony. When they were adopted by the Continental Congress on September 17, 1774, they became no longer the protest of one colony but of them all, a symbol of union that delighted the progressives and appalled the conservatives; Galloway of Philadelphia, Duane and Jay of New York were particularly incensed. These men were moderate conservatives, and the writer of *A Dialogue* allies herself with them.

The Wife of *A Dialogue* also directs her attack at the Association, which was the general agreement passed by the Continental Congress to stop imports from and exports to England and to forego the consumption of British goods. Attacked also are the proposed Courts of Inspection, which were to be established as a police organization in order to prevent any violation of the rules of the Association. In respect to this the Wife cries,

> "Could the Inquisition, Venice, Rome, or Japan,
> Have devised, so horrid, so wicked a Plan?"

The Wife's warning against the danger of misuse of such courts, which could result in invasion of privacy, was strongly within the realm of possibility, as events in the progress of the war were to prove. *The Patriots,* included in this volume, reveals a venal authoritarianism of the kind predicted by the Wife.

A Dialogue voices the indignation of the Tories because the Congress had betrayed the purpose for which it ostensibly met: To make apparent to the monarch that the restrictive acts of Parliament were causing a rift between England and America and that only by careful negotiation could the empire be preserved. Instead, the Congress turned away from conciliation and became, according to the Loyalist point of view, obdurate. The offensive radical elements from Massachusetts, Virginia, and South Carolina turned the tables on the conservatives. What was expected to be a dove-like assembly, hat in hand before the majesty of England, developed into an aggressive, rebellious force, designated by Samuel Johnson as "zealots of anarchy and dictators of sedition."

Aside from the political aspects of *A Dialogue,* the work has a theatrical quality in its scenes of bickering between husband and wife, a traditional comic device in eighteenth century plays. *A Dialogue* thus adds a comic note to the political battle. The Wife insists that men make foolish commitments in public life that women would not make: women are used to constant battle to preserve the security of the household and, in a larger sense, the community. Had they been allowed to participate in the Congress, the Wife declares, matters would have been different and the danger of a fateful break with England would have been avoided. Women, she says, are more practical and have an eye to the main chance.

A Dialogue follows the pattern of Hudibrastic meter—rhymed couplets in anapestic trimeter with irregularities—a popular structure for satiric verse of the period, especially in broadsides. The rhymes are obvious and rarely ingenious, but the galloping pace of the anapest is well suited to the duel between husband and wife, even though at times the underlying serious concern of the argument is belied by the rhythm.

A Dialogue was, perhaps, produced as a staged reading, although there is no evidence to support such an assumption. That it was disseminated and read widely is certain; the Tories must have been delighted with it. The influence of the work is indicated by a number of references that appeared in the press. William Bradford, a schoolmate of James Madison's, wrote to him from Philadelphia on January 4, 1775, commenting on the attitude of the colonies toward the increasing tension with Britain: "As to New-York, I think it has the least public virtue of any City on the Continent. I have heard several express their apprehensions of its Constancy. Rivington is encouraging the Cause of Administration there with all his might: he is daily publishing pamphlets against the proceedings of the Congress & the Cause they are engaged in. Some of them are grossly scurrilous, particularly 'A Dialogue between a Southern Delegate & his Spouse on his return from the Congress.' "[4]

Rivington, whose newspaper and pamphlets had the widest circulation in the colonies, published *A Dialogue,* thus assuring its dispersal through wide areas. It would seem very likely, therefore, that the anonymous pamphlet, which mocked the intentions of the First Continental Congress, was read by many who were not yet certain whether they wished to become involved in events that might sweep them to annihilation or at best to abject slavery. *A Dialogue* might well have made ardent Whigs apoplectic toward the Tories and at the same time also encouraged the Tories to fight against the radical cause.

Notes

1. Arthur Hobson Quinn states that "several authorities, who have evidently not read the dialogue, have attributed it to Thomas Jefferson" (*A History of the American Drama from the Beginning to the Civil War,* p. 57). Such identification of the author would seem to be patently absurd, particularly because the work is pro-Tory.

2. Miller, *Origins of the American Revolution,* p. 379.

3. Force, ed., *American Archives,* 4th Series (Washington, D. C., 1837), I, p. 777.

4. Hutchinson and Rachel, eds., *The Papers of James Madison* (Chicago, 1962), I, p. 132.

✦✦✦✦✦✦✦✦✦✦✦✦✦✦✦✦✦✦✦✦✦✦✦✦✦✦✦✦✦✦
A DIALOGUE, BETWEEN
A SOUTHERN DELEGATE,
AND HIS SPOUSE,
ON HIS RETURN FROM
THE GRAND
CONTINENTAL CONGRESS.
✦✦✦✦✦✦✦✦✦✦✦✦✦✦✦✦✦✦✦✦✦✦✦✦✦✦✦✦✦✦
A Fragment,
Inscribed
To the Married Ladies of America,
By their most sincere,
And affectionate Friend,
And Servant,
MARY V.V.
✦✦✦✦✦✦✦✦✦✦✦✦✦✦✦✦✦✦✦✦✦✦✦✦✦✦✦✦✦✦
Printed in the Year
M, DCC, LXXIV.
✦✦✦✦✦✦✦✦✦✦✦✦✦✦✦✦✦✦✦✦✦✦✦✦✦✦✦✦✦✦

Wife
In less than a Year,
Mark me Sir, you'll repent of't, as
sure as you're there.

Husband
Pray, for God's Sake, my Dear, be a little discreet;
As I hope to be sav'd, you'll alarm the whole Street;
Don't delight so in scolding yourself out of Breath;
To the Neighbours 'tis Sport, but to me it is Death.
I submit for Peace sake, to be led by the Nose;
Don't make the World think that we're come to Blows:
If once but a Crochet in your Head you have got,
For your Husband's Advice, Ma'm, you care not a Groat.
There are many wise People, I'd have you to know,
Who often have ask'd it, and have follow'd it too:
If I speak but a Word, you rave like a Fury,
The Patience of *Job*, Madam, wou'dn't, cou'dn't endure ye:
Had I a Million of Sons, Ah! by the Lord *Harry*,
I'd advise everyone of them never to marry.

Wife
Call the Doctor!—by this unusual Palaver,
I fear thou'st been bit, you so foam and so slaver:
Alas! never, — ah! — never, elect him again;
This pride of Delegation, turns many a Brain.

Husband
You mistook me, my Dear, I did not pretend,
Every Measure of Congress, right or wrong to defend;
Many Things they've left undone, they shou'd surely have done,
Many Things they have done, they shou'd have sure let alone:
a-The . . . Suffolk . . . Approbation
. . .
England . . . d-m-----n
. . . -a

b-Nice Discussions, a wise Man will ever decline,
When his Head and his Heart are oe'r heated with Wine;
Men, when drunk, are all Heroes, all prudent, all gallant;
Stark Fools, become Sages; rank Cowards, grow valiant:
High Matters of State should be plann'd before Dinner;-b
A Saint in the Morn, is at night oft a Sinner:
But grant their Resolves were more absurd than they are,
Could you really expect your meek Husband would dare
Oppose such a Torrent, when it's very well known,
He dares not say to your Face, his Soul is his own.

Wife
God bless us, and keep us! why, my Dearest, till now,
I ne'er heard you so wise, or so witty, I vow;

---

a–a
The . . . d-m-----n The omission of words here is a mystery. Perhaps the original printer could not read the text and therefore left it blank. One could make the romantic conjecture that the printer was a Whig who disagreed politically with the author, but if so he would have altered more of the text. Although the dashes in the original text indicate four lines are affected, probably only two are. Because of the rhyming of Approbation with d-m-----n, it seems logical to assume that these two lines are the couplet and that no complete lines are missing. It is difficult to deduce the meaning except insofar as the missing words relate to the Suffolk Resolves (*see* p. 30). In light of the Husband's second reference to the Resolves in the same speech, he may have thought them too radical, a sentiment indicating the Tory thinking of the writer, even though elsewhere the Husband favors the Whigs in Congress.

---

b–b
Nice . . . dinner These lines refer to the Tory calumny that members of Congress approved the Suffolk Resolves under the influence of Madeira, a canard which was blasted by the Whigs when they revealed that the approval of the resolutions took place in the morning and not late at night, when some of the members might have been under the influence of wine.

I protest this same Congress's a very fine School;
A man comes back a *Chatham*,^c who went there a Fool.

Husband
You're afraid to hear all, but for once I will speak,
Wherever I am known, I am called *Jerry Sneak*;^d
I bear, for all that, with your Caprice, and your Tricks,
But, prithee, Dear, dabble not in our Politics.

Wife
Prithee! ha, ha, ha, Prithee! my Senator grave!
Sir! I'll make you repent of that Speech, to your Grave;
Why had'st not said, KNOW THEN, like the mighty
     Congress,
I presume you'd a Hand in that ^{e-}civil Address^{-e}:
Indeed, my sweet Sir, when you treat with your Betters,
You should mind how you speak, and how you write Letters.

Husband
That Horse-laugh is all feign'd, with much better Grace,
You know, Ma'm, you cou'd hit me a Slap in the Face:
Consider, my Dear, you're a Woman of Fashion,
'Tis really indecent to be in such Passion;
Mind thy Household-Affairs, teach thy Children to read,
And never, Dear, with Politics, trouble thy Head.

Wife
Good Lord! how magnanimous! I fear Child thou'rt drunk,
Dost thou think thyself, Deary, a *Cromwel* or *Monck*?
Dost thou think that wise Nature meant thy shallow Pate,
To digest the important Affairs of a State?
Thou born! thou! the Machine of an Empire to wield?
Art thou wise in Debate? Shoud'st feel bold in the Field?
If thou'st Wisdom to manage Tobacco, and Slave,
It's as much as God ever design'd thee to have:
Because Men are Males, are they all Politicians?
Why then I presume they're Divines and Physicians,
And born all with Talents every Station to fill,
Noble Proofs you've given! no doubt, of your Skill:
Wou'd! instead of Delegates, they'd sent Delegates Wives;
Heavens! we cou'dn't have bungled it so for our Lives!
If you had ever consulted the Boys of a School,
Believe me, Love, you cou'd not have play'd so the Fool:
Wou'd it bluster, and frighten, its own poor dear Wife,
As the Congress does *England!* quite out of her Life?

Husband
This same Congress, my Dear, much disturbeth thy Rest,
God and Men ask no more, than that Men do their best;
'Tis their Fate, not their Crimes, if they've little Pretence,
To your most transcendent Penetration and Sense;
'Tis great Pity, I grant, they hadn't ask'd the Advice
Of a Judge of Affairs, so profound, and so nice;
You're so patient, so cool, so monstrous eloquent,
Next Congress, my Empress, sha't be made President.

---

^c
Chatham The Earl of Chatham, William Pitt, declared that the First Continental Congress was "the most honourable assembly of statesmen since those ancient Greeks and Romans in the most virtuous times," a statement which infuriated the Tories at home and in the colonies. Chatham thereby aroused a personal antagonism among the Loyalists in America, which is reflected in this *Dialogue*. The meaning of the line concerning Chatham could be that original fools become Chathams without ceasing to be foolish. Conversely, the line could also mean that fools assume the posture of Chatham once they have been to the school of Congress.

^d
Jerry Sneak The miserable henpecked Mayor of Garret, a farcical character in Samuel Foote's play *The Mayor of Garret*, produced in 1764.

^{e-e}
civil address The moderates in Congress wished to clarify their position. Not yet prepared for an abrupt break with England, they succeeded in having their colleagues approve a "loyal address" to the king, which, they hoped, would make it a matter of record that the quarrel of the colonies was not with the monarch but with his ministers and Parliament. Although she approves of the petition to the king, the Wife takes a critical view as to its content, making an assumption that it was not a sincere address, because she believes that all delegates were deluded or hypocritical.

Wife

I have said it, my Dear, and I'll say it again,
That your famous Congress were a strange set of men:
To you, my dear Love, I may be sometimes too pert,
But then, you know well, Dear, it is but for a Spirt:
Tho' I do now, and then, take the Freedom, to glance,
At your Dreams, and your Visions, I mind the main Chance;
Regard your true Interest, your Health, and your Ease,
And am ever dispos'd, to do just, as you please;
Sometimes, to be sure, it is not quite convenient,
But since I swore t'obey, I'm always obedient;
I defy you, to say now; you can't for your Life,
That I'm not, at the Bottom, a very good Wife:
Could I see you in Prison, or hang'd, without Pain?
Then, pray, have not I reason enough to complain?

Husband

Psha! for God's Sake, what Hazard of that do I run?

Wife

Psha, on, but beware, Dear, that you are not undone;
'Twou'd soon break my Heart, tho' we do now and then jar,
Were you ruin'd, or taken, or killed in War.
From the Love I bear you, and our dear Girls and Boys,
I have examin'd this Book, that makes so much Noise:
Without seeing thro' Mill-stones, its soon understood,
As sure as you are born, this will at last end in Blood:
A Cabal,[f] which the high sovereign Power defies,
No matter whether prompted, by Truth, or by Lies;
No Matter for us, whether without, or with Reason,
In Law, they say's deem'd, little short, of High Treason.
Three thousand Miles distant, we may crow and exult,
But can you hope, any State, will bear such Insult.
To your high mighty Congress, the Members were sent,
To lay all our Complaints, before Parliament;
Usurpation rear'd its head, from that fatal Hour,
You resolv'd, you enacted, like a sovereign Pow'r.
Acts, tho' not enjoin'd, on Pain of Gibbets, and Flames,
Disobey'd, at the Price, of our Fortunes, and Fames.
Your Non-Imports, and Exports, are full fraught with Ruin,
Of thousands, and thousands, the utter Undoing:
While, without daring to bite, you're shewing your Teeth,
You've contriv'd to starve, all the poor People to death.
Into all that's most sacred, you've made mad Inroad,
Morocco itself, wou'd be asham'd of your Code.
Pretty Sovereigns, in truth! God help us, what Things!
To make deep Politicians, or Statesmen, or Kings?
If *Philadelphia* or *York,* propos'd some wise Plan,
From that very Moment, you all branded the Man
[g]... of Sense and of Honour ... derive
  ... Carpenters-Hall ... alive
  ... murder or rob
  ... Pieces ... Mob.[g]

---

[f]
Cabal The belief was strong among provincial administrative officers that there existed "a secret, power-hungry cabal that professed loyalty to England while assiduously working to destroy the bonds of authority and force a rupture between England and her colonies." (Bernard Bailyn, ed., *Pamphlets of the American Revolution*, I, 88). Mary V. V. agrees with this currency of propaganda.

[g-g]
... of Sense ... Mob These omissions occur in the printed text. Since there is no extant manuscript, it is impossible to tell whether the tract was given to the typesetter in a corrupt state. Why it was not checked by the author is a mystery. Obviously, it is difficult to comprehend the meaning; however, the reference to Carpenters-Hall would indicate the writer's knowledge of the earliest conflict among the radicals and the conservatives at the convention. Galloway, the Philadelphia moderate, had offered the State House, a building associated with royal authority, for the meetings of the Congress. The artisans and lesser citizens wished to have the assembly gather in their hall, the Carpenters, arguing that it had ample space, was adjacent to the Philadelphia City Library, and had arcades for walking and conversing. Carpenters-Hall was chosen by vote, an action elating the radicals. Mary V. V. would have ridiculed the selection of the hall as a concession to an absurd democratic obsession among the delegates.

Instead of imploring, their Justice, or Pity,
You treat Parliament, like a Pack, of Banditti:
Instead of Addresses, framed on Truth, and on Reason,
They breathe nothing, but Insult, Rebellion, and Treason;
Instead of attempting, our Interests to further,
You bring down, on our Heads, Perdition, and Murder.
When I think how these Things must infallibly end,
I am distracted with Fear, and my Hair stands on end.

Husband
Youv'e been, heating your Brain, With Romances, and Plays,
Such Rant, and Bombast, I never heard in my Days.

Wife
Were your new-fangled Doctrines, as modest, and true,
'Twou'd be well for yourselves, and this poor Country too:
But supposing *Great-Britain,* quite out, of the Case,
And you all should be sav'd, by some high Act, of Grace;
Lets return to ourselves, if you've Eyes, you will see
Your Association, big with rank Tyranny.
Its hardly worth ones while, to show Indignation
At that foolish Bugbear, your Non-Importation;
For Men do so hunger, and so thirst, after Pelf,
That when thousands are starv'd, 'twill blow up, of itself.
You have read a great deal,—with patient Reflection,
Consider one Moment, your Courts of Inspection:
Could the Inquisition, *Venice, Rome,* or *Japan,*
Have devised, so horrid, so wicked a Plan?
In all the Records, of the most slavish Nation,
You'll not find an Instance, of such Usurpation.
If Spirits infernal, for dire Vengeance design'd,
Had been nam'd Delegates, to afflict Human kind,
And in Grand Continental Congress, had resolv'd,
"Let the Bonds of social Bliss, be from henceforth dissolved,"
They could not have plann'd, with more exquisite Skill,
Nor have found, a tame Race, more submiss to their Will.
Let Fools, Pedants, and Husbands, continue to hate
The Advice of us Women, and call it all Prate:
Whilst you are in Danger, by your good Leave, my Dear,
Both by Night and by Day, I will ring in your Ear——
Make your Peace:—Fear the King:—The Parliament fear.
Oh! my Country! remember, that a Woman unknown,
Cry'd aloud,—like *Cassandra,* in Oracular Tone,
Repent! or you are forever, forever undone.

****
THE FALL OF BRITISH TYRANNY
OR
AMERICAN LIBERTY TRIUMPHANT
****

Introduction to
*The Fall of
British Tyranny*

FILLED WITH dire prophecies about the future of the colonies unless action is taken against oppression, *The Fall of British Tyranny* is a tract, a pamphlet, a call to arms, a play. As Moses Coit Tyler observes, "It is simply a tremendous Whig satire, in dramatic form, first on the one deep treasonable motive attributed to the Tory conspirators who, in England and America, had forced the two countries into so monstrous a conflict; and, secondly, on the imbecility, the cowardice, and the grotesque failure thus far displayed by the military agents of these Tory conspirators in the execution of their horrid plot."[1] That *The Fall of British Tyranny* was popular enough to be printed in Philadelphia, Boston, and Providence in the same year, 1776, suggests the range of its influence.

The search for the true identity of the playwright has not yet been successful. There are tantalizing suggestions in various books and pamphlets, but the evidence is inconclusive and unsatisfactory. In *Annals of Philadelphia and Pennsylvania* John F. Watson, the editor, includes a note written by one J. H. J. of Cheviot, Ohio, who was a young man in Philadelphia at the time of the Revolution. J. H. J. reports, "Joseph Lacock, Coroner . . . wrote a play, with good humour, called 'British Tyranny.'"[2] Montrose J. Moses in his preface to his edition of *The Fall of British Tyranny* states that in his search through the colonial records of Pennsylvania he discovered "no less than three John Leacocks mentioned, all of whom were Coroners, as well as Joseph Leacock who occupied the same position."[3] George O. Seilhamer, in his *History of the American Theatre,* mentions a Joseph Leacock, jeweler and silversmith in Philadelphia, who wrote *The Disappointment,* a comic opera, which was intended for production in 1767 in Philadelphia but was abandoned because it characterized prominent citizens as credulous and foolish.

The confusion still remains. Was the author of *The Fall of British Tyranny* John Leacock, coroner, or Joseph Leacock, coroner or silversmith? Whoever wrote the drama was knowledgeable about American affairs, had read dispatches from England concerning parliamentary debates and was *au courant* regarding ministerial manipulations in London. News of the actions of the British government in the colonial press appeared with increasing regularity — too often in the opinion of the royal governors or councilors — and readily gave rise to rumors often regarded as fact. The author also could have and probably did read *The American Alarm, or The Bostonian Plea, for the Rights and Liberties, of the People,* a pamphlet by John Allen published in Boston in 1773, which imputed, as the principal cause of the Revolution, the Machiavellian contrivances of Lord Bute.[4]

THE PLAYWRIGHT'S major propaganda statement is that the American Revolution was indeed fomented by Lord Bute (Lord Paramount in the play). Paramount is characterized as an all-powerful and dangerous politician determined to triumph over both England and America in order to secure great privileges for himself and his distant relatives, the Stuarts. (Lord Bute did exert tremendous influence on George III before he was king and for several years after.)

The conventional belief in the power of Bute and the popular suspicion (assiduously reinforced ever since the Germanic royalty came to the throne in 1714) that disaffected Whigs when in opposition were tainted with Jacobitism or with Scots nationalism, created in the Scotsman Bute a ready-made villain acceptable to Americans, and thus he appears in the play.

Paramount is a double-dealing arch foe of American independence whose secret aim is to destroy America rather than to bring her in a healthy although repentant state back into the empire. In annihilating the colonies, he will drain England of men and materiel, leaving her so weak that she will be open to invasion by the Scots from the north and by France and Spain from the east and south. The Stuarts will then be restored and Lord Paramount will in truth become the power behind the throne, the dictator whose ambitions will at last be entirely satisfied.

In analyzing the play as an attack on Bute only, there is danger of minimizing the power of its propaganda. The cause of the Revolution lies in Bute, according to the playwright. It is he who rules Parliament by "shaking the treasury keys" in order to distribute largess in return for the support of his policies: this is seen at work in the first two acts of the play. Although there is little physical action, the dramatic interest is sustained by the maneuvering of Bute among his sycophants — Mansfield, Dartmouth, Sandwich, and others — and their conflict with the opposition in England — Chatham, the Bishop of St. Asaph, Camden, Wilkes, and Burke, the bitter enemies of Bute and his American policy.

When arguments substitute for action in the first part of the play, dramatic effectiveness arises more from the characterization of historic persons than from what they do. To understand the playwright's uses of persuasion, therefore, one must look first at the men who moved the events. Because of the bias of the play, it is necessary to accept the doubtful fact that Bute was the *eminence gris* in the king's government as late as 1776. (He had wielded his power between 1751 and 1763, but after that his decline began.) The truth is not that Bute was influential in 1776 but that the Americans and the English believed him to be so. George Trevelyan remarks, "As soon as Lord Bute was Prime Minister, he summoned southward, (beginning, but by no means ending, with his own kinsmen and retainers) a multitude of compatriots to partake of his good fortune. An assaulting force, which is active and enterprising, is always estimated above its real numerical strength by the party of the defence."⁵ Furthermore, as the result of the Scottish "invasion" by Bute and his supporters, a majority of Englishmen doubtless would have agreed with the author of *The Fall of British Tyranny* that the war in America was actually being conducted by Bute, and many called it a "Scotch War."⁶ Such an opinion had also swept across the Atlantic, and the Scottish minority in America suffered from its effects.

In the play Paramount sets his plan in motion to destroy the British empire. He is ably abetted by Mocklaw (William Murray, Lord Mansfield, a close friend of Bute's and another Scotsman). Mansfield is equally proscribed as an enemy of freedom and reviled as another Jeffries, opprobrium that still carried much weight after almost a hundred years.

Mansfield, similar to other ministers, was an opportunist but he was also a great justice (in the eighteenth century one could be both). He was determined to coerce America, and his remark that the killing of Americans was justified made him a fit subject for angry attacks in the colonies. In *The Fall of British Tyranny* he is a toady favoring expediency, but this caricature is the result of an American point of view based on hearsay and prejudice. Dora Mae Clark points out that "Lord Mansfield, legal authority for the imperialists, always wished to rule out the question of expediency and stick to the discussion of right."⁷ Mansfield, although a fair man, lacked strength of will, and this defect is also satirized in the play.

The next character in Paramount's establishment is Charley, actually Charles Jenkinson, secretary to Lord Bute. Charley serves chiefly as a servant who implements Paramount's schemes; he also acts as the commentator in Act I, Scene 4, where he and Paramount observe the procession going to an audience with the king with Wilkes at its head. Jenkinson was an important politician behind the scenes at Whitehall, said to have secret influence at court, "and, although he and Lord North always denied it, to have largely controlled Lord North's relations with the throne. This reputation secured him at once considerable authority and unrivalled odium."⁸ Jenkinson's role in the play is of minor importance, but that he is introduced at all suggests that he was thought to be prejudiced against America if only by his association with Bute.

The assemblage of characters in Act I, Scene 5, includes powerful opponents of the American cause whose evil intentions are made extremely explicit. The first of these is Poltron (the Earl of Sandwich), one of the most profligate men in the British government who served as First Lord of the Admiralty during the Revolution. Sandwich had a reputation, remarkable even in his time, for corruption and inefficiency. Although he was unable to create a strong navy because of Lord North's economies, he did little to improve the situation with what was available to him, and his administration of the Admiralty was a scandal. He was disdainful of the colonists, regarding them as boorish and stupid: one of his better known remarks, made in Parliament on March 16, 1775, was that the Americans were "raw, undisciplined, cowardly men. . . . Are these the men to fright us from the post of honour? Believe me, my Lords, the very sound of cannon would carry them off . . . as fast as their feet would carry them."⁹ This speech is echoed by the playwright in Act I, Scene 5.

Lord Hypocrite (the Earl of Dartmouth) would send a large force to crush the Americans, but he would color the action with an aura of "impartiality, forebearance and religion." He would also attempt to influence Methodist teachers, and particularly John Wesley with whom he was on friendly terms, in order to give coercion the sanction of religion. Dartmouth's cynical approach to the affairs in America is close to the general attitude of the British government.

As Secretary of State for the American Colonies and a friend of Lord North, Dartmouth held an important position in forming American policy. He appears to have been a weak minister, but there were forces preventing him from succeeding in efforts of conciliation that were uppermost in his mind. Benjamin Franklin, writing in 1773 to his son William, the royal governor of New Jersey, felt that Dartmouth was favorable to the colonies but was lacking in strength.[10] Dartmouth's latest biographer, B. D. Bargar, defends him against these charges, pointing out that he faced insuperable difficulties as a minister in a relatively new office. "If Dartmouth had accepted the American interpretation of the imperial relationship, he would have had to resign from the ministry. Conversely, his firm and consistent avowal of parliamentary supremacy made it impossible for him to accept the most moderate proposals from the colonies. The failure of conciliation was a great tragedy and no one man should bear the entire responsibility for it."[11]

Even though Dartmouth in the play is convinced that he can sway the Methodists to the cause of the government, he actually had no chance of success. In a letter written to him on June 14, 1775, Wesley points out, "All my prejudices are against the Americans. For I am an High Churchman, the son of an High Churchman, bred up from my childhood in the highest notions of passive obedience and non-resistance. And yet, in spite of all my rooted prejudice, I cannot avoid thinking (if I think at all) that an oppressed people asked for nothing more than their legal rights, and that in the most modest and inoffensive manner which the nature of the thing would allow." He ends by warning that the American affair may well be a disaster for the empire.[12]

Brazen (Mr. Wedderburn) is one of the most bloodthirsty and vociferous characters in the play. Although we see him only once, his famous speech in Parliament on October 26, 1775, is quoted in Act II, Scene 2. Wedderburn was another Scotsman closely allied to Bute and probably one of the most adventuresome of opportunists; he deserted the Whigs and became a devoted Tory, marking him a notorious turncoat, so flagrantly did he betray his original party.[13] He gained a reputation as a parliamentary debater by taking lessons in elocution from Thomas Sheridan, the father of Richard Brinsley Sheridan, and from Quin, the eminent actor.

Lord Catspaw (Lord North) is aptly named. He was the king's first minister from 1770 until 1782. Although Bute's influence was gone by then, the rumor persisted that North did in fact take orders from Bute; he was nicknamed Lord-Deputy North on the strength of this popular notion.[14] Dora Mae Clark also places North in a secondary position in the government but correctly names the king, not Bute, as his master. "After Townshend's death Lord North became Chancellor of the Exchequer, a man who from first to last seems to have been but the cat's-paw of the king. After 1770, in the position of prime minister, he uttered the views of the king, forced the royal policies through parliament, and for years repressed whatever private opinions he might have had in deference to those of his Majesty, George III. From the point of view of the king, Lord North was indeed a valuable addition to the cabinet."[15] This oftentimes indolent man, who fell asleep during parliamentary debate, so that Burke could say he hoped "the government was not dead, but only asleep,"[16] was good-humored and seemed able to disregard the attacks made on him by the great Whig orators of the day. North had a large following in Parliament, and for twelve years his power continued, a power that was often threatened but never reduced. "His tragedy was that the second half of his administration was burdened with a contentious and unsuccessful war for which his very qualities unfitted him; and he left a legend of ineptitude which is only half the story."[17]

Last in this intimate little conclave of anti-colonists is the man whom history will probably vindicate the more his motives and intentions are probed: Thomas Hutchinson (Judas), the last native royal governor of Massachusetts, serving from 1771 to 1774. An aristocrat in a colony of commoners (in part the cause of his downfall), he made personal profit from his position and obviously "sold" Massachusetts for many times thirty pieces of silver, as his enemies believed. Like Brutus, he was an honorable man according to his own lights, acting in the best interests of his province. Hutchinson was also a man of intense pride in his accomplishments and in the accumulation of public honors. Because he was native born he must have taken great personal satisfaction when he became royal governor. He knew his province well, but he misjudged the temper of the times and the growing desire for independence. He was, to give him credit, a man who hoped for eventual conciliation, but he wished to temper the wind of compromise so that any political changes would be within the limits of the law, backed if necessary by the force of military control. His downfall came through a set of circumstances that have never been satisfactorily explained. Hutchinson had written to his friend Thomas Whately, a member of Parliament, revealing private doubts about the growing radicalism in Massachusetts. He wished for a restoration of order so that the liberties of the colony under its royal charter would be safeguarded; otherwise, he felt that greater freedom would produce anarchy and that the British government, in order to preserve its empire, would have to level punitive measures. The irony, as history was to make clear, was that Hutchinson's apprehensions were well founded and what he feared might happen actually did occur.

Unfortunately for Hutchinson his letters were acquired by Benjamin Franklin, then acting as agent for Massachusetts in London and serving as deputy postmaster general in the colonies. In 1772 Franklin sent the letters to Thomas Cushing, Speaker of the Massachusetts House of Representatives, as well as to several other independence-minded colonists, with the "stipulation that no copies were to be made; they were to be shown only to confidential friends and then were to be returned to England."[18] In spite of these precautionary restrictions, no such secrecy was maintained. The letters were read by Samuel Adams before the House in June, 1773, and Adams had them printed. In justice to Franklin it may be said that he could have assumed that the letters would be kept private, but if this were the truth of the matter he displayed uncommon naïveté for so astute a politician. By sending such inflammatory matter to Massachusetts, knowing how quickly it would be used to discredit a man intensely hated by the radicals, Franklin was supplying tinder for a conflagration — and he may well have intended to do just that. Samuel Adams realized the explosive nature of the letters. He personally hated Hutchinson, but he was not alone in his anger against the native-born royal governor, for the latter had many bitter enemies in the colony, especially among the lower classes, who in 1765 had destroyed Hutchinson's mansion and all his papers, including a detailed history of the Massachusetts colony.

John Adams epitomizes the popular attitude toward Hutchinson in a letter to Abigail from Philadelphia on September 6, 1776, in which he writes of being chosen by the Congress to meet with Lord Howe to discuss conciliation: "An Idea has crept into many minds here, that his Lordship is such another as Mr. Hutchinson: and they may possibly think, that a Man who has been accustomed to Penetrate into the mazy Windings of Hutchinsons heart, and the serpentine Wiles of his head, may be tolerably qualified to converse with his Lordship."[19]

In Act I the playwright is concerned with the enemies of America in England, and he condemns them often with their own public utterances. Out of their own mouths he reveals their venality and corruption and the condescension of British officials toward the colonists. In Act II he presents the friends of America in England as they discuss the troubled political atmosphere. Their speeches, as well as those of Wilkes, Burke, and Barré, are often paraphrased public statements made in favor of America or against its political enemies, or a combination of both. The function of these pro-Americans in the play serves two purposes: to indicate that America is not without support among prominent persons in Britain and to present in dramatic form the bitterness and rage of those same people against the ministers in power and their shortsighted policy. The three friends of America who appear in Act II, Scene 1, are Lord Wisdom (The Earl of Chatham), Lord Religion (The Bishop of St. Asaph), and Lord Justice (The Earl of Camden).

William Pitt, the first Earl of Chatham, known as "the Great Commoner," had fallen out of royal favor by 1776, the date of the publication of the play. After the accession of George III in 1760, Pitt attacked Bute's plans for an immediate peace with Europe. He found himself in so much disfavor with the king that he resigned his offices in October, 1761, and went eventually into opposition, although he constantly maintained his attitude that he would not associate himself with any particular faction of the splintered Whigs. Upon the fall of the Rockingham ministry in 1776, Pitt was recalled to the government in spite of the king's personal opposition. Upon taking office Pitt accepted a peerage as Earl of Chatham, a move that shocked and antagonized the friends of liberty on both sides of the Atlantic. Once again, Bute was considered the evil genius behind the event, a manipulator who wished to bring Pitt under control of the king.

An American reaction (from the *Boston Evening-Post*) to Pitt's selection as a peer is amusing as well as bitter:

We hear that the new Chancellor [Lord Camden] will be applied to for a commission of Lunacy against the Earl of Chatham, and that the City of London are to sue it out.

The Pitt, a First Rate being much damaged in the Head in a late Cruise on the Coast of Scotland, is paid off and laid up at Chatham, where she is to serve as a Storeship. On examination, her timbers, which were supposed to have been true

English Heart of Oak, turn out to be nothing more than mere Scantlings of a rotten Scotch Fir, brought up by the Favourite from Mount Stuart in Buteshire and Hewn out by him into proper Form, at his Dock-yard, near the Pay-Office, Westminster.

It is much feared also, since this unhappy discovery, that the Timber of the Britannia, another First Rate, will be all found to be unsound, and that most of the ships in the Government's Service will turn out to be composed of the same rotten Materials.[20]

Although Chatham had lost the faith of Parliament, and his reputation was tarnished, he continued to defend America. Subsequent to his resignation from office in 1768 he became increasingly opposed to coercive measures abroad, denouncing American taxation, the Quebec Bill, and demanding that British troops be removed from Boston. In *The Fall of British Tyranny* Chatham is revealed as a man true to his principles, hating the excesses of English politicians and their corruptive influence, and as a defender of freedom. "Let us sound the trumpet of liberty and patriotism," he declares. He expresses his love for the Americans and his conviction that they will be triumphant and "become the glory of the earth." The implication is that the colonies will win their freedom; in reality, however, Chatham was violently opposed to independence. In his last speech in Parliament on April 7, 1778, he declared:

"I rejoice that the grave has not closed upon me; that I am still alive to lift up my voice against the dismemberment of this ancient and most noble monarchy. . . . Surely, my Lords, this nation is no longer what it was! Shall a people, that seventeen years ago was the terror of the world, now stoop so low as to tell its ancient inveterate enemy [France], take all we have, only give us peace? It is impossible!"[21]

Although a minor figure among the men who attempted to influence the affairs of America in England, Lord Religion (the Bishop of St. Asaph) nevertheless had a strong appeal for the colonists. In May, 1774, having been persuaded by Benjamin Franklin, the Bishop published a speech shortly after he had voted against the Massachusetts Charter Act. In his peroration he protested the enslaving of the colonies and warned that any such punitive measures as the Charter Act would ruin the peace of both countries. His attack against the government was published in five editions in London; there were two in Boston, Salem, and Philadelphia and one each in Newport, Hartford, New York, Lancaster, and Williamsburg.[22] His inclusion in the play adds a religious sanction to the American cause, one that contrasts strongly with the attitude of Dartmouth in the preceding scene.

Lord Justice is the Earl of Camden, and his favorable reputation in America arose from the fact that he had strongly supported Wilkes in the latter's opposition to the king and Parliament. Camden was also constantly in opposition to Mansfield (Mocklaw), denouncing almost all acts of Parliament that were inimical to the colonies. When the Stamp Act was repealed, for example, the Assembly of Maryland ordered a portrait of Camden to be hung in the state house. His often expressed warning that taxation without representation was wrong gave him heroic stature in the colonies. He held that taxation and representation are inseparable, "founded in a law of nature. It is more: it is itself an eternal law of nature."[23] In the play, as in his political utterances, Camden is fearful that the fabric of the British Constitution may be destroyed by unscrupulous men, and such a declaration would have evoked strong approval among the American readers of *The Fall of British Tyranny*.

The other three friends of America who appear in Act II, Scene 2, are even more vociferous than are those who discuss the situation in the previous scene. Lord Patriot (John Wilkes), the Bold Irishman (Edmund Burke), and the Colonel (Colonel Barré) are chiefly concerned with the speech made by Wedderburn (Brazen) on Thursday, October 26, 1775, a speech well known in America by the time *The Fall of British Tyranny* was written.

Wilkes's career in English politics was certainly one of the strangest in the annals of British party history. He seemed to have in him a passion for nonconformity and an inherent capacity for notoriety. He defied society by becoming a member of the infamous Medmenham Abbey, a scandalous "pleasure dome," sponsored by the Earl of Sandwich; even there Wilkes was notorious for loosing a baboon in the midst of the rites of the Black Mass. On April 23, 1763, he defied the king in Issue Number 45 of *The North Briton* — ironically named since its purpose was to attack the Scottish (Bute-ish) influence at court — intimating that the king was a liar in his recent message to Parliament. As a result Wilkes was accused of seditious libel and treason. Eventually, after vicissitudes that included exile from England and a financially difficult sojourn in France, he was elected to Parliament as a freeman of London. He finally surrendered to the authorities because of "his outlawry in the court of the king's bench, and after a formal arrest was committed by Lord Mansfield to . . . prison" on April 27, 1768.[24] He spent one year and eight months in prison, a privileged character who entertained lavishly and apparently thoroughly enjoyed his stay. He became idolized by the people, and friends on both sides of the Atlantic sent money to relieve him of his debts. By October, 1774, Wilkes was elected Lord Mayor of London. At one time Wilkes, who was loathed by George III, appeared before the king in a special audience to present a remonstrance against the coercion of America. The procession to the ceremony, which occurred on April 10, 1775, is reported by Charley in Act I, Scene 4, of the play.

"Wilkes and Liberty" became a slogan in England and America and was used throughout the Revolution; yet to this day there is question about the sincerity of Wilkes's interest in the colonies. "John Wilkes was so successful in turning the sympathy of Americans to his own personal advantage that his enthusiasm for the colonial cause appeared to be a pose."[25] Although he may not have been a poseur, he obviously was an opportunist. When money and flattery reached him, when his portrait appeared in the windows of the London streets, when Wilkes cockades and buttons were worn, at least publicly he changed some of his former declarations concerning independence. But there was never a change from his adherence to the supremacy of Great Britain. In the play, however, he is the epitome of patriotism, the defender of liberty and the opponent of those who would destroy freedom.

The Bold Irishman (Burke) was another hero to the Americans. He opposed the Townshend Act of 1767, that "nefarious" scheme that taxed glass, lead, painter's colors, tea, and paper imported into the colonies, from which revenue would come to pay officers of the crown, thus making them independent of the colonial assemblies and increasing the influence of the king. The act further infuriated the colonists because it reinvigorated the customs system, allowing royal customs commissioners to search and seize at will. Burke's disapproval and that of other powerful Whigs in Opposition brought about the repeal of the Townshend duties except that on tea, an omission that led to the Boston Tea Party. Burke also violently attacked the Boston Port Bill and the Massachusetts Charter decree, declaring, "What can the Americans believe but that England wishes to despoil them of all liberty, of all franchise, and, by the destruction of their characters, to reduce them to a state of the most abject slavery."[26]

In spite of his declaration for liberty in Act II, Scene 2, a reflection of his many utterances on the subject in Parliament, historians have established that he and Chatham as well "were by no means ready to embrace the American view of the empire, or even the rights of man."[27] As Commager and Morris also point out, Burke, Chatham, Camden, Wilkes, and others had some concept of the empire as becoming a commonwealth of nations, but their vision was limited, and they were principally concerned with protecting the Whig aristocracy from the encroachment of the king and his ministers on the one hand and the radical elements among the people on the other. There were, of course, more complications than these in the whole fragmented power structure of Parliament. Burke was inherently conditioned against any real threat to private property, and although he wanted reform in Parliament, it could only be to improve the situation for the ruling class. John Adams, in his usually astute manner, reflected long after the Revolution that Burke was really not a great friend to America and remarks that he himself saw in Parliament nothing in "all these attractions and repulsions, these dissolutions and coalitions, these conjunctions and oppositions in London, but national prejudices and family feuds between England, Scotland and Ireland."[28] And Adams was probably right.

Colonel (Colonel Barré), the third friend of America in Act II, Scene 2, was a soldier and a politician who had served under Wolfe at Quebec and had been a member of Parliament from 1761 to 1790. Although opposed to Chatham in the early days of his public career, he eventually became reconciled to him and incurred the hatred of George III. He was one of North's worst enemies, and it was said that "the terrors of his invective paralyzed Charles Townshend and dismayed Wedderburn."[29] He was probably best known in the colonies for his disgust at the Stamp Act and in a speech against it on February 7, 1765, coined a phrase that was to plague the British: "As soon as you began to care about them [the Americans], that care was exercised in sending persons to rule over them . . . to spy out their liberty, to misrepresent their actions, and to prey upon them; men, whose behaviour, on many occasions, has caused the blood of those SONS OF LIBERTY to recoil within them."[30] The name was adopted by secret societies in the colonies, and their radical members were responsible "for many acts of mob violence against loyalists."[31] In general, Barré was fearful of revolution and foresaw eventual independence. He did not support all the acts against the colonies, however, and was credited with strong prejudice toward the American cause. Wilkes-Barre, Pennsylvania, bears the names of two of the men in this scene and is testimony to the enthusiasm that rebels across the water held for them.

Thus Act II closes with six Englishmen of prominence, opposed to their own government's policies, bemoaning the fate of Britain and predicting the rising glories of America. Much of what they say is paraphrased from their public statements. What the colonists did not realize, however, is that these sympathizers would have fought violently against independence had they thought it an actual possibility or had they been in positions of power. John Miller acutely sums up their position when he notes, "the talents of the whigs were frittered away in oratory. . . . More and more they began to appear like professional crape hangers, and their speeches to sound like funeral orations over the British Empire,"[32] an empire they would have been the last to dissolve.

THE FIRST TWO ACTS of *The Fall of British Tyranny* consist chiefly of speeches; the rest of the work moves into action (with the exception of the shepherds' scene). There is an air of increasing tension as the evil manipulations of Paramount are felt in the colonies. The first two scenes of Act III show the effects of the new laws in America and the apprehensions felt by the Citizen, the Selectman, and the Minister — all common men. There will be great danger to the cause of freedom, for tyranny, popery, and dissension will be rife; the tree of liberty will be cut down and blood will be shed. The other note that is struck is one of proud assurance that America will rise above the conflict and will defend her rights or die.

Another part of the whole tapestry of cause and effect, of British pressure and American rigidity, is the meeting between Whig and Tory on their native soil in Act III, Scene 3. Patriot is pitted against Loyalist and the warning is explicit: the enemy may wear citizen's clothing as well as a red coat.

In Act III, Scenes 4 and 5, Lord Boston (General Gage), commander-in-chief of British forces and governor of Massachusetts, is supremely confident that the sortie to Lexington and Concord, which he had ordered, will be successful. He had sent Colonel Francis Smith to Concord to seize a store of arms there. That Gage also wanted to capture Samuel Adams and John Hancock, who were refugees from Boston in Lexington, in order to transport them to England to be hanged at Tyburn is still debatable, but rumors of such intention made for excellent propaganda. True or not there were some who wished to take no chances, among them the admirable Dr. Joseph Warren, president of the Massachusetts Provincial Congress. He sent Paul Revere to Lexington to warn the two, who made their escape.

In the play Gage's confidence rapidly abates when he learns the rebels have put the regular troops to flight and the Redcoats are retreating to Boston. It is small wonder that Gage was discomfited, and the playwright makes full use of his "bottling-up" and delights in making him ridiculous, for Gage was detested. When he first arrived at Boston in 1774, he came as a tyrant, making proclamations that antagonized not only Massachusetts but all the other colonies as well. Washington wrote to Bryan Fairfax on July 20, 1774, "And has not General Gage's conduct since his arrival, (in stopping the address of his council, and publishing a proclamation more becoming a Turkish bashaw, than an English governor, declaring it treason to associate in any manner by which the commerce of Great Britain is to be affected) exhibited an unexampled testimony of the most despotic system of tyranny, that ever was practised in a free government?"[33]

From the scene of action of the retreat from Lexington and Concord, the playwright suddenly shifts to a pastoral allegory in which two shepherds discuss both battles. (Their sheep are the colonists; the wolves are the redcoats.) The report, which Roger gives, contains many facts of the battles: the shouting and hurling of epithets by the British, a traditional custom as they moved into battle; the conduct of Smith and Pictairn; the eight Americans killed; the attack on Concord; and the retreat to Boston. There is also reference to an atrocity story: some Americans had sought sanctuary in the meetinghouse on the green and were slain there. The ferocity of the attack is not exaggerated, however, and the indirect presentation is more moving than a factual accounting.

In order to add still another persuasive element to the play, a song to Tammany is interjected. "Saint Tammany," the legendary Indian Sachem, was known throughout the colonies as a defender of liberty, and Tammany Societies had begun to spring up in many provinces during the last quarter of the eighteenth century, the first in Philadelphia. (Leacock would have known of the organization and might even have been a member of it.) That Tammany was a symbol of liberty would not have been lost on the readers, and the song, although somewhat inappropriate where it appears, adds zest to the propaganda.

The mood of the play changes in Act III, Scene 7. Once again a battle is reported, that of Bunker's Hill, June 17, 1775. The writing becomes highly emotional, displaying an intense anger toward the British and, in this particular context, fury against Gage. The battle and its horror is shown in the reactions of a woman who has lost her husband, son, and brother. Thus the scene presents vividly the anguish of the day for those who participated in the military action and those who watched it from Boston, for the families of both the British and the Americans were eyewitnesses to the carnage. The bombardment of Charlestown is described by Clarissa, and her concern for her loved ones is poignantly revealed. Clarissa's tragedy as a result of the loss of her men in the battle of Bunker's Hill is used by the playwright not only for pathetic response but also to praise Dr. Joseph Warren, a martyred hero of the military engagement.[34]

In the first six scenes of Act IV the action moves to Norfolk, Virginia. Lord Kidnapper (Lord Dunmore) brings Negroes on board his ship with the promise of freedom if they fight against their masters. That he probably never intended to keep his word but planned to use the slaves until they were no longer necessary and then sell them in the West Indies is still a moot point, but the possibility was strong. Thomas Jefferson, writing to John Page on August 20, 1776, says that Dunmore, having failed in his attacks along the coast and up the Potomac has sent his sick to Halifax, his good men to Staten Island, "and the blacks he shipped off to the West Indies."[35]

Volumes could be written on Dunmore, and almost none favorable; the playwright needed little exaggeration to add to the facts. Dunmore arrived in New York as royal governor in 1770 but two years later was sent to Virginia, where he failed to attract adherents to the British cause. By June, 1775, he was so unpopular that he had to shift the seat of government to a British man-of-war off Yorktown. The Virginia Assembly sent bills to him, but he refused to give his assent unless the assemblymen came on board. As a result the representatives took over the government, declaring that Dunmore had abdicated. The infuriated Dunmore raised a small attack fleet, set fire to Norfolk on January 1, 1776, and moved up and down the rivers of Virginia, making depredations where he wished. Washington, writing in December, 1775, said, "I do not think that forcing his Lordship on shipboard is sufficient. Nothing less than depriving him of life or liberty will secure peace to Virginia, as motives of resentment actuate his conduct to a degree equal to the total destruction of that colony."[36] Dunmore would have liked to have used the Indians as well as the Negroes against the provincials. One of his wildest schemes was to attempt to kidnap Mrs. Washington. George Washington, writing to his cousin Lund from Cambridge on August 20, 1775, remarked that "I can hardly think that Lord Dunmore can act so low, and unmanly a part, as to think of siezing [sic] Mrs. Washington by way of revenge upon me: howev'r, as I suppose she is, before this time gone over to Mr. Calvert's and will soon after retng., go down to New Kent, she will be out of his reach for 2 or 3 months to come."[37]

Having failed in all his attempts to block the colonists, Dunmore finally gave up the battle in 1776 and returned to England. Of all the royal governors he was probably the most inept, vociferous, and vulgar, and these qualities are aptly ridiculed by the playwright.

The last scene of Act IV is a wake held over the dreary remains of the Pyrrhic victory of Bunker's Hill. In the delineation of these ineffectual "champions" of British militarism, the officers — Lord Boston (Gage), Admiral Tombstone (Admiral Graves), Elbow Room (General William Howe), Mr. Caper (General Burgoyne), General Clinton, and Lord Percy — are met to render a post-mortem. The scene degenerates into backbiting and name-calling; accusations of cowardice, lack of leadership, and miscalculation of the strength and resolve of the rebels fly thick and fast. The officers apparently have no plan of action and resent the fact that they will be bottled up in Boston with food and drink running low. The most severe attack is against Gage and Burgoyne. While Howe led the troops on Bunker's Hill and was wounded in the engagement, Gage and Burgoyne watched the action from the safety of Copp's Hill in Boston.

The meeting of the generals has an interesting counterpart in a satire by Philip Freneau, *A Voyage to Boston, A Poem,* published in 1775 at New York and Philadelphia. It was republished in 1786, and subsequent editions appeared under the title *The Midnight Consultations; or, A Trip to Boston.* The poem has the same cast of characters as does Act IV, Scene 7, of the play. It tells the story of a traveler, made invisible, who arrives at General Gage's mansion in Boston. The stranger listens to the attacks made by each of the Englishmen on the others and paints them all in a disdainful light.

Freneau's poem calls to mind the curious, although minor, confusion surrounding the derivation of the sobriquet Elbow Room. Trevelyan points out that the Americans used it for Burgoyne even before his arrival in Boston on May 25, 1775. Burgoyne was presumed to have remarked when he heard that "British Regulars were shut up by only twice their number of Provincials: 'What! . . . Well, let us get in, and we'll soon find elbow room!'" In the poem, however, the sobriquet is linked to another in the lines:

> "Howe, vexed to see his starving army's doom,
> In prayer, besought the skies for elbow room—."

The author of *The Fall* attributes the name to Howe, which suggests he had seen Freneau's poem.[38]

A new shift of mood now occurs as the first two scenes of Act V move to Canada for a violent conflict between General Prescott and Ethan Allen, Prescott's prisoner. On September 25, 1775, Ethan Allen, who had been sent by Montgomery to recruit Canadians for the American army, had made an abortive and foolish attempt to take Montreal. Governor Guy Carleton of Canada captured Allen and turned him over to Brigadier General Prescott. Prescott had always had a bad image among Americans, and there is no doubt that he was cruel and arrogant. That he himself was twice a prisoner of the rebels made him the butt of cartoons and jokes in England and a ready object of contempt in the colonies. On December 30, 1775, Richard Smith, a member of the Continental Congress from New Jersey, noted in his diary that "Gen'l Washington has sent to Gen. Howe a spirited Letter informing Him that whatever Severities are inflicted on Col. Allen shall be retaliated on Brig. Gen. Prescott."[39] Smith also recorded in 1776 that Prescott claimed that he was only acting under Carleton's orders.

News that Allen was harshly treated must have spread through the colonies after his capture, because the meeting between Prescott and Allen and the subsequent punishment inflicted on Allen as presented in *The Fall of British Tyranny* bears some relation, however remote, to the facts. When Allen published a narrative of his experiences in 1779, the legends about him grew. His account is forceful, at times violent, and full of native Connecticut humor. In spite of the exaggeration it was true that he was shackled in irons, that he suffered long imprisonment on shipboard, and that he constantly berated the British in the violent language for which he was famous.

The last three scenes of Act V take place in the headquarters of Washington in Cambridge. Washington, meeting there with Generals Lee and Putnam, castigates the British and mourns the death of Montgomery;[40] because of Montgomery's sacrifice they determine never to sheathe their swords until independence has been won and tyranny defeated.

Putnam, represented as the epitome of patriotism, was after all a human being with incredible weaknesses. He was unpredictable because his egomania made him foolhardy and unreliable.[41] Charles Lee, even in the early days of the Revolution, was beginning to show signs of an instability that still, in retrospect, makes him enigmatic. He may have been either a traitor or a patriot. Washington called him "fickle." He had peculiarities of temperament that affected his loyalty but, unlike Benedict Arnold, the variations in his character represented momentary shifts of personality. Douglas Southall Freeman notes Lee's dirty habits and his obscenity, which antagonized gentlemen of New England in 1775, but such characteristics are not mentioned by the author of *The Fall of British Tyranny*.[42]

THE PLAY thus ends on a note of high resolve. Its purpose was to attract allegiance to the American idea of liberty. Whatever literary quality exists in the play is subordinated to its intention. Leacock was obviously making no pretensions to prominence as an artist. He was simply recording in theatrical form the events leading up to and including the early phases of the Revolution. What he does succeed in accomplishing, if only by inadvertence, is a kind of structural control over his material. The first two acts set the motivation for the action through discussion. They can be labeled the *cause*, for in them we see Paramount as Lord High Manipulator, arranging the strings and proceeding to set his marionettes in action. The counterforces, opposed to him but incapable of making decisive moves, combine to form a chorus of dissent, throwing into high relief the dastardly plans to enslave the colonies, defeat the Hanoverians, and restore the Stuarts. The *cause* is effective propaganda, having an authenticity based on actual speeches or letters. The motivation for the destruction of America is thus clearly exposed.

The final three acts of the play represent in a diversity of action the *result*. The machinery has been successfully activated, and in America events occur which had their secret springs in the villainous decisions made at St. James's. Throughout the remainder of the play, reference is constantly made to Paramount and his cohorts, either indirectly or directly, as forces that brought about a sanguinary civil war. Thus the purposes of propaganda are well served in the constant reminder to the reader that England intended always to punish the colonies and bring them to heel no matter who their master — a George III or a Lord Bute whose presumably sinister intentions toward dictatorship obsessed him and made him seek increasing power.

Slight though it may be, some aspect of artistic organization is present in *The Fall*. It has several scenes that particularly arouse the reader because they transcend the prosaic style of journalistic reporting. The shepherds' scene, for example, is well handled; it has a naïveté that effectively contrasts with the horrible action it symbolizes. The allegory of wolves and lambs gives it a rough charm and would have found ready response from readers accustomed to depredations upon grazing flocks. Furthermore, clever satiric barbs are hidden in the pastoral allusions, and the pathetic elements in the writing rely more on sentiment than sentimentality.

The first six scenes of Act IV — the Lord Dunmore sequence — are earthy and violent. Echoes of Fielding and some Swiftian comment can be found in the portrayal of the debauched Dunmore, and the total effect reminds one of Rowlandson caricatures. The minor characters, such as the boatswain, the cook, and the chaplain, are memorable vignettes, and the Negro leader, Cudjo, is well drawn in his ignorance and his eagerness to serve Lord Kidnapper by destroying his white colonial masters.

What emerges from *The Fall of British Tyranny* is an inspired proclamation against the immorality and wickedness of a British plot against America, symbolized in the arch-villain Bute. In a sense this pamphlet play is an engrossing editorial condemning the men who are manipulating the machinery of destruction both in England and in America and supporting those who are defending the rights of man. Another skein in the tapestry of the play is the attention paid to common men and the sufferings they endure because of the disruption caused by a civil war. It is through these innocent persons, the selectman, the citizen, the minister, Clarissa, the shepherds, the Negroes under the domination of Dunmore, and the prisoners in Canada that one is made conscious of the inclusive nature of *The Fall of British Tyranny* as it reveals the indignation of an embryonic nation against those who would prevent it from realizing its destiny.

Notes

1. Tyler, *The Literary History of the American Revolution* (New York, 1897), II, p. 200.

2. Watson, ed., *Annals of Philadelphia and Pennsylvania*, rev. ed. (Philadelphia, 1855), I, p. 104.

3. Moses, *Representative Plays by American Dramatists* (New York, 1918), I, p. 279.

4. So many crimes were placed at Bute's door that the literature concerning them would fill a volume in itself. (*See* the discussion in the introduction to this volume.)

5. Trevelyan, *The American Revolution* (London, 1905), III, p. 182.

6. *Ibid.*, p. 184.

7. Clark, *British Opinion and the American Revolution* (New Haven, 1930), p. 242.

8. Archbold, "Jenkinson, Charles," *DNB*, X, p. 747.

9. Force, ed., *American Archives*, 4th Series (Washington, D. C., 1848-53), I, pp. 1682-83.

10. Barker, "Legge, William," *DNB*, XI, p. 859.

11. Bargar, *Lord Dartmouth and the American Revolution* (Columbia, 1965), p. 159.

12. Telford, ed., *The Letters of John Wesley* (London, 1931), VI, pp. 155-60.

13. Millar, "Wedderburn, Alexander," *DNB*, XX, p. 1044.

14. Barker, "North, Frederick," *DNB*, XIV, pp. 604-09.

15. Clark, *op. cit.*, p. 200.

16. Quoted by Miller in *The Triumph of Freedom*, third printing (Boston, 1948), p. 25.

17. Mackesy, *The War for America* (Cambridge, Mass., 1964), p. 521.

18. Miller, *Origins of the American Revolution*, rev. ed. (Stanford, 1959), p. 331.

19. Butterfield, ed., *Diary and Autobiography of John Adams* (Cambridge, Mass., 1961), III, p. 430.

20. *Boston Evening Post*, September 29, 1766 (Number 1620).

21. Thackeray, *A History of the Right Honorable William Pitt, Earl of Chatham* (London, 1827), II, p. 378.

22. Butterfield, ed., *Adams Family Correspondence* (Cambridge, Mass., 1963), I, p. 154n.

23. Lossing, *The Pictorial Field-Book of the Revolution* (New York, 1890), II, p. 194; I, p. 472.

24. Rigg, "Wilkes, John," *DNB*, (London, 1921-22), XXI, pp. 242-50.

25. Clark, *op. cit.*, p. 153.

26. Lossing, *op. cit.*, I, p. 505.

27. Commager and Morris, eds., *The Spirit of 'Seventy-Six* (Indianapolis, 1958), I, p. 227.

28. Butterfield, ed., *Diary*, III, p. 135n.

29. Courtney, "Barré, Isaac," *DNB*, I, p. 1196.

30. *The Parliamentary History of England, from the earliest period to the year 1803* (London, 1813), XVI, p. 39.

31. Miller, *Sam Adams, Pioneer in Propaganda*, 2nd ed. rev. (Stanford, 1960), p. 51.

32. Miller, *Triumph of Freedom* (Boston, 1948), p. 34.

33. Fitzpatrick, ed., *The Writings of George Washington* (Washington, D. C., 1931-1944), III, p. 232.

34. For a further evaluation of Warren, see Frothingham, *The Life and Times of Joseph Warren* (Boston, 1865). *The Diary and Autobiography of John Adams,* edited by L. H. Butterfield, contains many references to Warren, who was a close friend to John and Abigail Adams.

35. Boyd, ed., *The Papers of Thomas Jefferson* (Princeton, 1950), I, pp. 497-98.

36. Sabine, *Biographical Sketches of Loyalists of the American Revolution* (Boston, 1864), I, p. 399.

37. Fitzpatrick, *op. cit.*, pp. 432-33.

38. *See* Trevelyan, *op. cit.*, I, p. 299; Pattee, ed., *The Poems of Philip Freneau* (Princeton, 1902), I, pp. 158-82.

39. Burnett, ed., *Letters of Members of the Continental Congress* (Washington, D. C., 1921), I, p. 291.

40. *See* introduction to *The Death of General Montgomery.*

41. *See* introduction to *The Battle of Brooklyn.*

42. Freeman, *George Washington* (New York, 1951), III, p. 373.

****
THE FALL OF BRITISH TYRANNY
OR
AMERICAN LIBERTY TRIUMPHANT

The FIRST CAMPAIGN

A TRAGI-COMEDY of FIVE ACTS,
AS LATELY PLANNED
At the Royal Theatrum Pandemonium,
At St. James's
****
THE PRINCIPAL PLACE OF
ACTION IN AMERICA

Publish'd According to Act of Parliament

Quis furor ô cives! quae
tanta licentia ferri?
Lucan, lib. I. ver. 8

What blind, detested madness could afford
Such horrid licence to the murd'ring sword?
Rowe

****
PHILADELPHIA:
Printed by STYNER and CIST, in Second-street,
near Arch-street. M DCC LXXVI

The Dedication

To

LORD BOSTON,¹ and the REMNANT of the ACTORS,ᵃ
MERRY ANDREWS, and strolling PLAYERS,
in BOSTON, LORD KIDNAPPER,ᵇ and the rest of the PIRATES
and BUCCANEERS, and the innumerable and never-ending ᶜ-CLAN of MACS and DONALDS upon DONALDS,-ᶜ
in AMERICA.²

My Lords and Gentlemen,
Understanding you are vastly fond of plays and farces, and frequently exhibit them for your own amusement, and the laudable purpose of ridiculing your masters (the *Yankees*, as you call 'em) it was expected you would have been polite enough to have favoured the world, or America at least, (at whose expense you act them) with some of your playbills, or with a sample of your composition.

I shall however not copy your churlishness, but dedicate the following Tragi-Comedy to your patronage, and for your future entertainment; and as the most of you have already acted your particular parts of it, both comic and tragic, in reality at Lexington, Bunker's-hill, the Great-Bridge,ᵈ etc. etc. etc. to the very great applause of yourselves, tho' not of the whole house, no doubt you will preserve the marks, or memory of it, as long as you live, as it is wrote in capital American characters and letters of blood on your posteriors: And however some Whigs may censure you for your affected mirth (as they term it, in the deplorable situation you are now in, like hogs in a pen, and in want of elbow room) yet I can by no means agree with them, but think it a proof of true heroism and philosophy, to endeavour to make the best of a bad bargain, and laugh at yourselves, to prevent others from laughing at you; and tho' you are deprived of the use of your teeth, it is no reason you should be bereaved of the use of your tongues, your eyes, your ears, and your risible faculties and powers. That would be cruel indeed! after the glorious and fatiguing campaign you have made, and the many signal victories obtained over whole herds of cattle and swine, routing flocks of sheep,ᵉ lambs and geese, storming hen-roosts, and taking

---

ᵃ
Remnant . . . Actors An implication that the siege of Boston has left a remnant of actors or clowns rather than British officers. The allusion is apt and satirical because the British performed in plays under Burgoyne's direction, one of which may have been written by him. (See *The Blockheads*.)

ᵇ
Lord Kidnapper The Earl of Dunmore, a Scottish villain. (*See* the introduction to *The Fall*, dramatis personae, and Act IV, Scenes 1-6.)

ᶜ-ᶜ
Clan . . . Donalds The Scots were severely criticized, strongly suspected, and often reviled and harmed. (*See* the introduction to *The Patriots*.)

ᵈ
Great-Bridge This skirmish, which might have resulted in a battle, took place at Norfolk on December 9, 1775. When the American militia leader William Woodford moved toward Norfolk, Governor Dunmore took the initiative. His redcoats, however, were turned back to their ships in the harbor. The defeat of the British at Lexington and Great-Bridge and the disastrous results of Bunker's Hill supplied grist to the mill of the American propagandist.

ᵉ
routing flocks of sheep There are numerous references in the plays and other satirical works to the British having to resort to sheep and cattle stealing to keep alive. They made forays against the islands in Boston Harbor and secured provender for themselves. Moses Coit Tyler indicates that there is something grotesque about the invincible troops of Britain forced by a provincial militia into a victory of sheep-stealing. (*The Literary History of the American Revolution,* I, p. 422.)

them prisoners, and thereby raising the glory of Old England to a pitch she never knew before. And ye Macs, and ye Donalds upon Donalds, go on, and may our gallows-hills and liberty poles be honour'd and adorn'd with some of your heads: Why should Tyburn and Temple-bar make a monopoly of so valuable a commodity?

Wishing you abundance of entertainment in the re-acting this Tragi-Comedy, and of which I should be so proud to take a part with you, tho' I have reason to think you would not of choice let me come within three hundred yards of your stage, lest I should rob you of your laurels, receive the clap of the whole house, and pass for a second Garrick among you, as you know I always act with applause, speak bold—point blank[f]—off hand—and without a prompter.

I am, My Lords and Gentlemen Buffoons,
  Your always ready and humble servant,

DICK RIFLE[g]

---

[f]
point blank The British are reminded by the playwright that although unprompted and seemingly casual in their military discipline, the colonial militiamen were effective as sharp-shooters, firing directly and with precision.

---

[g]
Dick Rifle The individualistic riflemen caused Washington more pain than promise when he realized they defied discipline and even could become mutinous if they thought their rights as men were threatened. The weapon used by many was the Dickert, a long rifle made by Jacob Dickert of Lancaster, Pennsylvania. Rifles had been manufactured in that area since 1720 for use principally on the frontier, and a Dickert rifle would have been known for its deadly potential. If the playwright was a native Pennsylvanian, presumably he was acquainted with the particular firearm. Dick Rifle, therefore, was an extra gibe at the English, and the reference would have aroused a smug satisfaction in the Americans. (*See* Boatner, *Encyclopedia of the American Revolution* [New York, 1966] p. 329.)

The Preface

SOLOMON SAID,[3] "Oppression makes a wise man mad,"[4] but what would he have said, had he lived in these days, and seen the oppression of the people of Boston, and the distressed situation of the inhabitants of [h-]Charlestown, Falmouth, Stonnington, Bristol, Norfolk,[-h] etc. Would he not have said, "The tongue of the sucking child cleaveth to the roof of his mouth for thirst; the young children ask for bread, but no man breaketh it unto them?"[5] "They that did feed delicately, perish in the streets; they that were brought up in scarlet, embrace the dung."[6] What would he have said of rejected petitions, disregarded supplications, and contemned remonstrances? Would he not have said, "From hardness of heart, good Lord, deliver us?"[7] What would he have said of a freeborn people butchered—their towns desolated, and become an heap of ashes—their inhabitants become beggars, wanderers and vagabonds—by the cruel orders of an unrelenting tyrant, wallowing in luxury, and wantonly wasting the people's wealth, to oppress them the more? Would he not have said, it was oppression and ingratitude in the highest degree, exceeding the oppression of the children of Israel? and, like Moses, have cried out, let the people go? Would he not have wondered at our patience and long-suffering, and have said, 'Tis time to change our master!—'Tis time to part!—And had he been an American born, would he not have showed his wisdom by adopting the language of independency? Happy then for America in these fluctuating times, she is not without her Solomons, who see the necessity of heark'ning to reason, and listening to the voice of COMMON SENSE.[8]

h-h
Charlestown . . . Norfolk All these towns were threatened by the British at one time or another and several were bombarded and burned, causing the Americans to rise in indignation against the oppressors.

The GODDESS of LIBERTY

Hail! *Patriots, hail! by me inspired be!
Speak boldly, think and act for Liberty,
United sons, America's choice band,
Ye patriots firm, ye Sav'ours of the land.
Hail! Patriots, hail! rise with the rising sun,
Nor quit your labour, till the work be done.
Ye early risers in your country's cause,
Shine forth at noon, for Liberty and Laws.
Build a strong tow'r, whose fabric may endure
Firm as a rock, from tyranny secure.
Yet would you build my fabric to endure,
Be your hearts warm—but let your hands be pure.
Never to shine, yourselves, your country sell;
But think you nobly, while in place act well.
Let no self-server general trust betray,
No picque, no party, bar the public way.
Front an arm'd world, with union on your side:
No foe shall shake you—if no friends divide.
At night repose, and sweetly take your rest;
None sleeps so sound as those by conscience blest:
May martyr'd patriots whisper in your ear,
To tread the paths of virtue without fear;
May pleasing visions charm your patriot eyes;
While Freedom's sons shall hail you blest and wise.
Hail! my last hope, the cries, inspired by me,
Wish, write, talk, fight, and die—for LIBERTY.

---

*The Congress

The Prologue

Spoken by Mr. Peter Buckstail[9]

Since 'tis the fashion, preface, prologue next,
Else what's a play?—like sermon without text!
Since 'tis the fashion then, I'll not oppose;
For what's a man if he's without a nose?
The curtain's up—the music's now begun,
What is't?—Why murder, fire, and sword, and gun.
What scene?—Why blood!—What act?—Fight and be free!
Or be ye slaves—and give up liberty!
Blest Continent, while groaning nations round
Bend to the servile yoke, ignobly bound,
May ye be free—nor ever be opprest
By murd'ring tyrants, but a land of rest!
What say ye to't? what says the audience?
Methinks I hear some whisper COMMON SENSE.
Hark! what say them Tories?—Silence—let 'em speak,
Poor souls! dumb—they hav'n't spoke a word this week,
Dumb let 'em be, at full end of their tethers,
'Twill save the expense of tar and of feathers:
Since old [i·]Pluto's lurch'd 'em, and swears he does not know
If more these Tory puppy curs will bark or no.[·i]
Now ring the bell[j]—Come forth, ye actors, come,
The Tragedy's begun, beat, beat the drum,
Let's all advance, equipt like volunteers,[k]
Oppose the foe, and banish all our fears.
We will be free—or bravely we will die,
And leave to Tories tyrants legacy,
And all our share of its dependency.

---

i-i

Pluto's . . . no Lurch'd is the archaic sense, meaning deceived. The playwright suggests that the devil, or Hades, has deceived the Tories but whether they will respond to British Satan and support him in his endeavors is still an unanswered question; in other words, how can he be sure that the Loyalists will rise in defense of the mother country?

---

j

bell A bell or three knocks on the floor from backstage announced that the play was to begin and the actors were to appear.

---

k

volunteers The rebels are voluntary soldiers, not professionals, and the prologue returns to the satirical leit-motif anticipated in the title page and the dedication. The play is not an illusion, for it is enacted upon the actual stage of Britain and America where murder, fire, and the sword create the action of freedom. *Common Sense* is reiterated as a call for independence, and Americans are urged to die for freedom.

Dramatis Personae

LORD PARAMOUNT   *Chief Officer of the Government Party in power, the Tories*
LORD MOCKLAW   *Tory Lord Chief Justice*
LORD HYPOCRITE   *Secretary of State for the American Colonies*
LORD POLTRON   *First Lord of the Admiralty*
LORD CATSPAW   *Parliamentary leader under Paramount*
LORD WISDOM   *Leader of the Whig Party, now out of office. Opposed to Paramount*
LORD RELIGION   *Whig religious leader*
LORD JUSTICE   *Whig justice in opposition to Mocklaw*
LORD PATRIOT   *Radical politician, opposed to Paramount*
BOLD IRISHMAN   *Distinguished Whig orator*
JUDAS   *Former Royal Governor of Massachusetts*
CHARLEY   *Secretary to Paramount*
BRAZEN   *Whig turncoat and Tory advocate*
COLONEL   *Whig politician, master of invective*
LORD BOSTON   *Commander-in-Chief, British forces in America*
ADMIRAL TOMBSTONE   *British Naval Commander*
ELBOW ROOM   *British General, tactician for the Battle of Bunker Hill*
MR. CAPER   *British General*
LORD KIDNAPPER   *Royal Governor of Virginia*
GENERAL WASHINGTON   *Commander-in-Chief, American forces*
GENERAL LEE   *American General*
GENERAL PUTNAM   *American General*
ROGER and DICK   *Two shepherds*
CLARISSA   *Boston matron*
GENERAL PRESCOT   *British Officer*
ETHAN ALLEN   *Colonel in the American army*
Officers
  Soldiers
    Sailors
      Citizens
        Slaves

ACT I

Scene 1

At St. James's.

[*Lord Paramount solus, strutting about.*]

Lord Paramount
Many long years have rolled delightfully on, whilst I have been basking in the sun-shine of grandeur and power, whilst I have imperceptibly (tho' not unsuspected) guided the chariot of state, and greased with the nation's gold the imperial wheels.

'Tis I that move the mighty engine of royalty, and with the tincture of my somniferous[10] opiate (or, in the language of a courtier) by the virtue of my secret influence, I have lulled the ª⁻axletree to sleep,⁻ª and brought on a pleasing insensibility.

Let their champion, ᵇ⁻Lord Wisdom, groan, he is now become feeble and impotent, a mere cripple in politics;⁻ᵇ their Lord Patriot's squint has lost its basilisk effect:ᶜ and the bold Irishman may bellow the *Keenew*ᵈ till he's hoarse, he's no more when compar'd to me than an Irish salmon to a Scotch herring: I care not a bawbeeᵉ for them all. I'll reign in Britain, I'll be king of their counsels, and chief among the princes.

Oh! ambition, thou darling of my soul! stop not 'till I rise superior to all superlative, 'till I mount triumphantly the pinnacle of glory, or at least open the way for one of my own familyᶠ and name to enter without opposition.

The work is now cut out, and must be finish'd, I have ventur'd too far to recede, my honour's at stake my importance, nay my life depends upon it!

Last night's three hours closeting has effectually done the business; then I spoke my mind in such terms as to make a lasting impression, never to be eradicated—all—all was given up to me, and now since I hold the reins of government, since I am possessed of supreme power, every thing shall be subservient to my royal will and pleasure.

Scene 2

[*Enter Mocklaw.*ᵍ]

Mocklaw
I am your Lordship's most obedient humble servant.

Paramount
Be seated.—I sent for you to have a small conference with you—and to let you know, your advice respecting certain

---

a-a
axletree . . . sleep Having "greased" the wheels of the chariot of state with gold, Paramount also contrived to stop the axletree upon which the wheels revolve, causing an apathy that will allow him to work his nefarious schemes.

b-b
Lord Wisdom . . . politics Reference to the incapacity of the Earl of Chatham. (See p. 46.)

c
basilisk effect John Wilkes (Lord Patriot) was one of the ugliest of men. His most famous "portrait" is the caricature by Hogarth, which, Peter Quennell states, "was savage; but Hogarth was too genuine an artist to be able to handle so striking a personage without some touches of involuntary appreciation. The expression is cunning and the leer malevolent; nevertheless there is a look of resolute, almost diabolical, energy about that tall forehead . . . the crooked prognathous grin, and sharply squinting eyes." (*The Profane Virtues*, p. 190.) Paramount notes that Wilkes's eyes have lost the effect of the basilisk, the legendary reptile with a hypnotic, fatal glance.

d
Keenew A lamentation or dirge for the dead, oftentimes a wordless cry or wail, sometimes recounting the glories of the past and calling for vengeance. Bold Irishman (Burke) was well known for his angry attacks against the government in defense of America, and his lamentations could be well likened to keening.

e
bawbee A Scottish coin of small value issued under Charles II and William III; a trifle.

f
my own family Paramount is referring to the Stuarts, part of his own family. (See p. 42.)

g
Mocklaw Lord Mansfield. (See the introduction to *The Fall*.)

h
Mr. Brazen Wedderburn. (See the introduction to *The Fall*.)

i
Attorney General Edward Thurlow, attacked by the playwright because he stanchly defended the rights of Britain against the colonies and insisted that England was clearly pursuing her destiny in prosecuting the subjugation of America.

j-j
Lord Justice . . . Glynn Lord Justice (Camden) is a friend of America. (See the introduction to *The Fall*.) Dunning was solicitor-general in the Duke of Grafton's administration in 1768 but, disaffected with the government, resigned in 1770. He continued as a member of Parliament where he was a strong antagonist of ministerial measures opposed to America. He vehemently argued against the act to change the Massachusetts Charter and said, "We are now come to that fatal dilemma, 'Resist, and we will cut your throats; submit, and we will tax you'; such is the reward of obedience." (*DNB*, VI, p. 214.) John Glynn was a supporter of Wilkes and a convinced defender of American rights. Glynn was known for his vast legal knowledge and liberal interests. "It was of him that Wilkes remarked to George III, 'Sir, he was a Wilkite, which I never was.'" (*DNB*, VIII, p. 13.)

k
statute Although the law had been disregarded for many years, someone, presumably Mansfield, discovered it was applicable. Thus the House of Lords in January, 1769, recommended the "transmission of instructions to the Governor of Massachusetts (Bernard) to obtain full information of all treasons, and to transmit the offenders to England, to be tried there under a statute of the 35th of Henry VIII, which provided for the punishment of treason committed out of the kingdom." Burke and

points of law, I have found, succeeded to admiration, even beyond my most sanguine expectations.

Mocklaw
I am heartily glad of it, altho' the advice I gave your Lordship, I cannot say, was law; yet, your Lordship can easily pass it as such by a royal proclamation: and should it ever be disputed, I have quirks and quibbles enough at your service, with Mr. Brazen[h] and Mr. Attorney General's[i] assistance, to render it so doubtful, obscure and ambiguous, as to puzzle [j]Lord Justice, perplex Dunning, and confound Glynn.[j]

Paramount
Can you show me an instance of a royal proclamation passing for law? or advise me how to make it such, if you can, I shall make it well worth your study.

Mocklaw
My Lord as you have now got a parliament exactly to your mind, ev'ry thing you propose will be granted: but in order that you may see precedents are not wanting—there is a statute[k] in the reign of Henry 8th that expressly shows the then parliament passed a law that the king's proclamation should be the law of the land—

Paramount
Are you sure of that?

Mocklaw
My Lord, here it is—this is the real law: *Luce meridiana clariora*.[l] When we find anything of this kind, ready made to our hands, it's a treasure we should never part with. *(Paramount reads.)*

Paramount
I see it plain! this, this alone is worth a ton of gold—Now, by St. Andrew! I'll strike a stroke that shall surprise all Europe, and make the boldest of the adverse party turn pale and tremble—Scotch politics, Scotch intrigues, Scotch influence, and Scotch impudence (as they have termed it) they shall see ere long shine with unheard of splendour, and the name of Lord Paramount the mighty, shall blaze in the annals of the world with far greater lustre (as a consummate politician) than the name of Alexander the Great, as an hero!

Mocklaw
That day I much wish for,—but, with your Lordship's permission, I would just mention, that secrecy and dissimulation are the soul of enterprise; your Lordship hath many enemies, who watch ev'ry movement of state with a jealous and wary eye.

Paramount
I know it, but the futile attempts of my timid adversaries have hitherto proved abortive—so far I have borne down

all opposition, and those (even some of the greatest of them) who not long since were my most open, as well as secret enemies, I now behold with the most princely pleasure, the earliest to attend, to congratulate me on my birth day, tho' uninvited, bow down and make the most obsequious[11] congees.[m] Have you not seen this, Mocklaw? and how I keep them in expectation of something, by now and then bestowing part of a gracious smile amongst a dozen of 'em?

Mocklaw
I have, my Lord, and no doubt they interpret that as a favourable omen;—however, policy, my Lord, would dictate that to you, if there were no other consideration.

Paramount
True, and yet they are cursedly mistaken—and now, Mocklaw, as I have ever found you to be well dispos'd towards me, and the cause I espouse, and as I trust you continue satisfy'd with my former bounty, and my promise now of granting you a pension for life, with liberty to retire, I shall make you my confidant and disclose to you a secret no man except myself yet knows, which I expect you have so much honour to let it remain a secret to all the world (I mean as to the main point I have in view).

Mocklaw
Depend upon it, my Lord, I am sincerely devoted to your Lordship, command me, I care not what it is, I'll screw, twist and strain the law as tight as a drumhead to serve you.

Paramount
I shall at this time but just give you a hint of the plan I have drawn up in my own mind. You must have perceived in me a secret hankering for majesty for some time past, notwithstanding my age;—but as I have considered the great dislike the nation in general have, as to my person, I'll wave my own pretensions, and bend my power and assiduity to it in favour of one, the nearest a kin to me, you know who I mean, and a particular friend of yours, provided I continue to be dictator, as at present; and further, I intend America shall submit.—What think you of it so far?

Mocklaw
A day I've long wish'd to see! but you stagger me, my Lord, not as to my honour, secrecy, or resolution to serve you, but as to the accomplishment of such grand designs.

Paramount
'Tis true, I have undertaken a mighty task, a task that would have perplexed the Council of Nice, and stagger'd even Julius Caesar—but—

Mocklaw
You have need, my Lord, of all your wisdom, fortitude and

other friends of America denounced the measure, the former declaring, " 'At the request of an exasperated governor, we are called upon to agree to an address advising the king to put in force against the Americans the Act of Henry VIII. And why? Because you cannot trust the juries of that country! Sir, that word must convey horror to every feeling mind.' " (Lossing, I, p. 482.) To remove treasonable offenders to England for a trial by British judges was anathema to the colonists who recognized that there would be no justice when 3,000 miles of ocean lay between the guilty party and his accusers. In spite of strong remonstrances, however, the address and resolutions were passed. The Americans' fury against this infringement of their rights as well as other coercive acts was constantly fed by the propagandists as is indicated in this scene and others which take place in England.

1-1
Luce . . . clariora At noontime the light is brighter.

---

m
congees A ceremonial departure; in the eighteenth century an elaborate manner of bowing oneself out of the presence of a distinguished person.

power, when you consider with whom you have to contend. —Let me see—Lord Wisdom—Lord Religion—Lord Justice —Lord Patriot—the bold Irishman, etc. etc. etc. and the wisdom of the United Colonies of America, in Congress to cope with; as individuals they are trifling, but in league combined may become potent enemies.

Paramount
Granted—But are you so little of a lawyer as not to know the virtue of a certain specific I'm possess'd of, that will accomplish any thing, even to performing miracles? Don't you know there's such sweet music in the shaking of the treasury keys, that they will instantly lock the most babbling patriot's tongue! transform a Tory into a Whig, and a Whig into a Tory? make a superannuated old miser dance, and an old Cynic philosopher smile? How many thousand times has your tongue danc'd at Westminster Hall to the sound of such music?

Mocklaw
Enchanting sounds, powerful magic, there's no withstanding the charms of such music, their potency and influence are irresistible—that is a point of law I can by no means give up, of more force than all the acts of parliament since the days of king Alfred.

Paramount
I am glad you acknowledge that—Now then for a line of politics—I propose to begin first by taxing America, as a blind—that will create an eternal animosity between us, and by sending over continually ships and troops, this will of course produce a civil war—weaken Britain by leaving her coasts defenceless, and impoverish America; so that we need not fear any thing from that quarter. Then the united fleets of France and Spain with troops to appear in the channel, and make a descent, while my kinsman with thirty thousand men lands in Scotland, marches to London, and joins the others: What then can prevent the scheme from having the wish'd for effect? This is the main point, which keep to yourself.

Mocklaw
If it has failed heretofore, 'tis impossible it should fail now; nothing within the reach of human wisdom was ever planned so judiciously; had Solomon been alive, and a politician, I would have sworn your Lordship had consulted him.—But I would beg leave to hint to your Lordship the opposition to be apprehended from the militia of England; and the German forces that may be sent for according to treaty.

Paramount
As to the militia, they are half of them my friends, witness Lancaster, Manchester, Liverpool, etc. etc. etc. the other half scarce ever fired a gun in their lives, especially those

of London, and I shall take care by shaking the keys a
little to have such officers appointed over them, who are
well known to be in my interest. As to the German forces,
I have nothing to apprehend from them; the parliament
can soon pass an act against the introduction of foreign
troops,[n] except the French or Spaniards, who can't be called
foreign, they are our friends and nearest neighbors. Have
you any thing further to object against the probability of
this plan?

Mocklaw
Nothing my Lord, but the [o-]people of Ireland, who must
be cajoled or humbugg'd.

Paramount
As to that, let me alone, I shall grant the Roman Catholics,
who are by far the most numerous, the free exercise of their
religion,[-o] with the liberty of bearing arms, so long unjustly
deprived of, and disarm in due time all the Protestants in
their turn.

Mocklaw
That will be a noble stroke; the more I consider it, the
more I'm surpris'd at your Lordship's profound wisdom and
foresight: I think success is certain.

Paramount
Then this is the favourable crisis to attempt it; 'tis not the
thought of a day, a month, or a year. Have you any more
objections?

Mocklaw
I have one more, my Lord—

Paramount
Well, pray let's hear it; these lawyers will be heard.

Mocklaw
The Bishops and Clergy are a powerful, numerous body; it
would be necessary, my Lord, to gain them over, or keep
them silent—A religious war is the worst of wars.

Paramount
You are very right, I have 'em fast enough—Mammon will
work powerfully on them—The keys—the keys—His Grace
my [p-]Lord of Suffolk, and Dean Tucker,[-p] are managing this
business for me, and feeding them with the hopes of being
all created Arch-bishops here, and each to have a diocese,
and Bishops of their own appointment in America; not a
city or town there but must be provided with a Bishop:
There let religion erect her holy altars, by which means
their revenues will be augmented beyond that of a Cardinal.
All this we must make 'em believe.

Mocklaw
True, my Lord, what is a Bishop without faith? This is the

THE FALL | 69

n
foreign troops The use of foreign
mercenaries was abhorrent both to
English lovers of liberty and to
their American counterparts, and
the playwright seizes on this
point to arouse his readers'
anger by reminding them of the
British policy. When the question
was first raised the Whigs in
Opposition inveighed against the
proposal but to no avail. The
princes of small German princi-
palities were willing to supply
men for money, snuffing, as
Burke said, "the cadaverous
taint of lucrative war," and
Britain secured 30,000 German
mercenaries at a total cost of
4,700,000 pounds.

o-o
people . . . religion The Irish
question had long plagued
Britain. Paramount's simple
solution is obviously impractical
as a political measure. This
passage served as excellent
propaganda, however, because in
May, 1774, Parliament had passed
the Quebec Act by which the
French Canadians were permitted
to worship openly as Roman
Catholics. The analogy to Ireland
in this instance would not have
passed unnoticed. Furthermore,
Paramount (Bute) supposedly
aligned himself to the Stuarts,
of whom James II privately
endorsed the Roman Church.

p-p
*Lord of Suffolk . . . Dean
Tucker* This is a strange
combination. The Earl of Suffolk
was Secretary of State for the
Northern Department from 1771
to 1779, and he approved the
king's policy of military coercion
against the colonies, but Dean
Josiah Tucker of Gloucester was
notorious for his insistence that
separation from the colonies
was inevitable and would, in the
long run, prove beneficial for
England and America. Dean
Tucker is omitted from the New
England and Providence printings,
which leads to interesting
conjecture. Perhaps the publishers
in New England also saw the
incongruity of linking the two
men as opponents to America.

grandest stroke of religious circumvention that ever was struck.—I've done, my Lord.

Paramount
Very well; you'll not fail to meet the privy council here this evening; in the mean time you'll go and search the statutes for other precedents to strengthen the cause; and remember I have enjoin'd you to secrecy.

Mocklaw
Depend upon it, my Lord, I cannot prove ungrateful to your Lordship, nor such an enemy to myself.

[*Exit Mocklaw.*]

Scene 3

[*Lord Paramount solus.*]

Paramount
This Mocklaw is a cursed knowing dog, and I believe the father of Brazen; how readily he found an old act of parliament to my purpose, as soon as I told him I would make it worth his study; and the thoughts of a pension will make him search his old worm-eaten statute books from the reign of king Arthur down to this present time; how he raises objections too to make me think his mind is ever bent on study to serve me. The shaking of the treasury keys is a fine bait. *(Rings the bell.)* Charters, magna Chartas, bill of rights, acts of assembly, resolves of congresses, trials by juries (and acts of parliament too) when they make against us, must all be annihilated; a suspending power I approve of, and of royal proclamations.—

[*Enter Charley.*[q]]

Charley
I wait your Lordship's orders.

Paramount
Write a number of cards, and see that the Lords of the privy council, and Mr. Judas,[r] be summoned to give their attendance this evening at six o'clock, at my Pandemonium.[s]

Charley
I'm gone, my Lord. *(Exit Charley.)*

[*Paramount solus.*]

Paramount
How do we show our authority? how do we maintain the royal prerogative? keep in awe the knowing ones of the opposite party, and blind the eyes of the ignorant multitude in Britain? Why, by spirited measures, by an accumulation of power, of deception, and the shaking of the keys, we

---

[q] *Charley* Charles Jenkinson, secretary to Lord Bute. (*See* the Introduction to *The Fall.*)

[r] *Mr. Judas* An apt sobriquet for Thomas Hutchinson, former governor of Massachusetts, whom many colonists considered a betrayer of his native country. (*See* the introduction to *The Fall.*)

[s] *Pandemonium* The abode of all the demons; in Milton the capital of Hell or the palace of Satan.

may hope to succeed; should that fail, I'll enforce them with the pointed bayonet; the Americans from one end to the other shall submit, in spite of all opposition; I'll listen to no overtures of reconciliation from any petty self-constituted congress, they shall submit implicitly to such terms as I of my royal indulgence please to grant. I'll show them the impudence and weakness of their resolves, and the strength of mine; I will never soften; my inflexibility shall stand firm, and convince them the second Pharaoh is at least equal to the first. I am unalterably determined at every hazard and at the risk of every consequence to compel the colonies to *absolute* submission, I'll draw in treasure from every quarter, and, Solomon-like, wallow in riches; and Scotland, my dear Scotland, shall be the paradise of the world. Rejoice in the name of Paramount, and the sound of a bawbee shall be no more heard in the land of my nativity.—

Scene 4

[*Enter Charley in haste.*]

Charley
My Lord, the notices are all served.

Paramount
It's very well, Charley.

Charley
My Lord, be pleased to turn your eyes, and look out of the window, and see the ᵗ⁻Lord Mayor, Aldermen, Common council and Liverymen going to St. James's with the address.⁻ᵗ

Paramount
Where? Sure enough—Curse their impudence; how that squinting scoundrel swells with importance—Mind, Charley, how fond he is a bowing to the gaping multitude, and ev'ry upstart he sees at a window—I hope he'll not turn his blare[12] eyes t'wards me—I want none of his bows, not I—Stand before me, Charley—

Charley
I will, my Lord, and if he looks this way, I'll give him such a devilish grin as best suits such fellows as him, and make him remember it as long as he lives.

Paramount
Do so, Charley; I hate the dog mortally, I religiously hate him, and hope ere long to have satisfaction for his insolence, and the freedoms he has taken with me and my connexions; I shall never forget the many scandalous verses, lampoons and pasquinadesᵘ he made upon us.

t-t
Lord Mayor . . . address On April 10, 1775, Wilkes, as Lord Mayor of London, with the Aldermen and Livery of the City of London presented an Address and Remonstrance to George III in which coercion against America was strongly deplored. The petition was printed in the Philadelphia papers in June of 1775 so that the author of *The Fall of British Tyranny* could have known of it and used it in this descriptive scene, thereby enhancing Wilkes's reputation in America.

u
scandalous . . . pasquinades Wilkes in his pamphlet-periodical, *The North Briton*, constantly attacked Bute in verse and in political satire; the pasquinade was oftentimes an anonymous libel printed for distribution in public places. The reference to the effective kind of propaganda in which Wilkes indulged, and which was successfully imitated in America, would have had a response among colonial readers, arousing them to similar oral or written reactions.

Charley
Indeed he has used your Lordship too ill ever to be forgotten or forgiven.

Paramount
Damn him, I never intend to do either—See again how he bows—there again—how ᵛ˙the mob throw up their hats, split their throats, how they huzza too; they make a mere god of the fellow; how they idolize him—Ignorant brutes!˙ᵛ

Charley
A scoundrel; he has climb'd up the stilts of preferment strangely, my Lord.

Paramount
Strangely, indeed; but it's our own faults.

Charley
He has had better luck than honester folks; I'am surpris'd to think he has ever rose to the honour of presenting a remonstrance, or rather, that he could ever have the impudence to think of remonstrating.

Paramount
Aye, Charley, you see how unaccountably things turn out; his audacity is unparalleled—a Newgate dog.ʷ

Charley
My Lord, I believe the fellow was never known to blush; and indeed 'tis an observation I made some time since, and I believe a just one, without an exception, that those who squint never blush.

Paramount
You must be mistaken, Charley.

Charley
No, my Lord, it's a fact, I had an uncle squinted exactly like him, who was guilty of many scandalous things, and yet all the parish, with the parson at their head, could not make him blush, so that at last he became a bye-word— Here comes old shame-the-devil; this dog is the very spawn of him.

Paramount
Hoot, mon! ye give your uncle a shokingˣ character.

Charley
I only mention it, my Lord, for the similarity's sake.

Paramount
For the spawn of him, and the similarity's sake, I'm apt to think you've been abusing your own cousin all this while.

Charley
God forbid, my Lord, I should be anyhow allied to him.

ᵛ⁻ᵛ
the mob ... brutes This passage is reminiscent of the description of the idolators of Caesar in *Julius Caesar,* Act I, Scene 2. Paramount (Bute) would be envious of Wilkes's popularity with the masses.

ʷ
Newgate dog Wilkes's incredible career included actual outlawry as well as election to the office of Lord Mayor of London. (*See* the introduction to *The Fall.*)

ˣ
shoking The word in the New England and the Providence editions is correctly spelled: shocking.

THE FALL | 73

Paramount
I fancy, Charley, if the truth was known, your uncle did not mention you in his will, and forgot to leave you the mansion house and farm at Gallows-hill. Am I right, Charley?

Charley
You're right, my Lord, upon my honour—but—

Paramount
I thought so—Well, never mind—Ha, ha, ha, who are those two fat fellows there that go in such state?

Charley
I suppose them to be a couple of Livery Tallow-chandlers,^y my Lord, by their big bellies.

Paramount
Ha, ha,—what work the guards would make amongst them—but they must not be called yet.—And who are those other two behind 'em?

Charley
This is Mr. Hone, and the other Mr. Strap, a couple of the Corporation barbers,^z forsooth.

Paramount
Ha, ha, ha, I thought they had been a couple of Dukes;—and that one—who is he with the Beehive^{aa} wig?¹³

Charley
That is Mr. Alderman Pipeshank, in Newgate-street.

Paramount
A parcel of Newgate dogs altogether—Well, it is a good deal of satisfaction to me to think how this fellow will be received at St. James's; he'll not return back so pleas'd as he seems to be now, I warrant you—I have taken care he shall meet with a d----d cold reception there; he will have to make his appearance before ^{bb-}Lord Frostyface, Lord Scarecrow, Lord Sneerwell, Lord Firebrand, Lord Mawmouth, Lord Waggonjaws, Lord Gripe, Lord Brass, Lord Surly and Lord Tribulation,^{-bb} as hard-fac'd fellows as himself; and the beauty of it is, not one of them loves him a whit more than I do.

Charley
That will be rare diversion for them that are present; he'll look then, my Lord, like Sampson making sport for the Philistines.

Paramount
Aye, but I wish he was as blind too, as Sampson was.—Well, Charley, we have been dispos'd to be a little merry with this ridiculous parade, this high life below stairs. I wish you had begun your description a little sooner, before

y
Livery Tallow-chandlers On the occasion of an Address to the King made by the City of London it was the custom for the mayor, the aldermen, who were magistrates ranking next to the mayor, and members of various livery companies, which were trade associations descended from medieval guilds, to march in procession to the king's palace to present the address to the king. The two men described would be members of the livery company of candlemakers and sellers.

z
Corporation barbers The body of municipal officers of a town or city was the Corporation. Thus Hone and Strap, aptly named, were barbers by profession but members of the Corporation of the City of London.

aa
Beehive By the 1770s wigs of men and women were reaching alarming proportions similar to those of the late seventeenth century. They represented different shapes or actually had on top of them miniature ships, fruits, or whatever the current fad might suggest. This particular character wore a very high wig, shaped like a beehive.

bb-bb
Lord Frostyface . . . Lord Tribulation It would not be practical to attempt to identify these characters, and since they do not appear in the play it is irrelevant to do so. They could be any of a number of peers who might confront Wilkes at the King's levee. The humor lies in the obvious caricatures conjured up by the names—a Hogarthian gallery.

they were all gone; the looks of these wiseacres affords us some mirth, tho' we despise them and their politics, and it's not unlikely it may end in blood—Be it so, I'm prepared for the worst.

Charley
Rather so, my Lord, than to submit to such rascals.

Paramount
I'll give up my life first for a sacrifice.

[*Exit Charley.*]

Scene 5

[*Enter Mocklaw, Poltron, Hypocrite, Catspaw,*[cc] *Brazen, Judas. (All seated.)*]

Paramount
My Lords, and Gentlemen, it seems opposition to our measures are making hasty strides; the discontented faction, the supporters and encouragers of rebellion, and whose hearts are tainted therewith, seem bent, if possible, on the destruction of Britain, and their own aggrandisement. Are not the daily papers filled with treasonable resolves of American congresses and committees, extracts of letters, and other infamous pieces and scurrilous pamphlets, circulating with unusual industry throughout the kingdom, by the enemies of Britain, thereby poisoning the minds of our liege subjects with their detestable tenets?—And did you not this day see the procession, and that vile miscreant Lord Patriot at their head, going to St. James's with their remonstrance, in such state and parade as manifestly tended to provoke, challenge and defy majesty itself, and the powers of government? and yet nothing done to stop their pernicious effects.—Surely, my Lords and Gentlemen, you must agree with me, that it is now become highly expedient that an immediate stop should be put to such unwarrantable and dangerous proceedings, by the most vigorous and coercive measures.

Mocklaw
I entirely agree with your Lordship, and was ever firmly of opinion, that licentiousness of every kind, (particularly that of the Press) is dangerous to the state; the rabble should be kept in awe by examples of severity, and a proper respect should be enforced to superiors. I have sufficiently shown my dislike to the freedom of the press,[dd] by the examples I have frequently made (tho' too favourable) of several printers, and others, who had greatly trespassed, and if they still persist, other measures should be taken with them, which the laws will point out; and as to Lord Patriot, he's a fellow that has been outlaw'd, scandal proof, little to be

---

[cc] *Poltron, Hypocrite, Catspaw* The Earl of Sandwich, the Earl of Dartmouth, and Lord North. (*See* the introduction to *The Fall.*)

[dd] *freedom of the press* Mocklaw (Mansfield) could speak with feeling on this matter. It was the result of too much freedom of the press from the conservative point of view that allowed Wilkes to print *The North Briton*, the issue of April 23, 1763 (No. 45) being considered particularly seditious. The publication had a strong effect on the political theories of the American Revolution. The playwright thus includes another indictment against Britain, the repression of the press. Mansfield was involved because as judge he heard the various trials against Wilkes and sentenced him to prison. (For further details, see the introduction to *The Fall.*)

got by meddling with him; I would advise to let him alone for the present, and humble America first.

Mr. Brazen
I am very clear in it, please your Lordship; there are numbers of men in this country who are ever studying how to perplex and entangle the state, constantly thwarting government, in ev'ry laudable undertaking; this clamourous faction must be curbed, must be subdued and crush'd—our thunder must go forth, America must be conquered. I am for blood and fire to crush the rising glories of America—They boast of her strength; she must be conquered, if half Germany is called to our assistance.

Lord Poltron
I entirely agree with you, Mr. Brazen; my advice is, that Lord Boston and Admiral Tombstone[ee] be immediately dispatch'd to Boston, with two or three regiments (tho' one would be more than sufficient) and a few ships to shut up their ports, disannul their character, stop their trade, and the pusillanimous beggars, those scoundrel rascals, whose predominant passions are impudence and fear,[14] would immediately give up, on the first landing of the regulars, and fly before 'em like a hare before the hounds; that this would be the case, I pawn my honour to your Lordships, nay I'll sacrifice my life: My Lords, I have moreover the testimony of General Amherst and Colonel Grant to back my assertion; besides here's Mr. Judas, let him speak.

Lord Hypocrite
If this is the same Colonel Grant[ff] that was at Fort Duqesne, the same that ran away from the French and Indians, the same that was rescued by Colonel Washington, I have no idea of his honour or testimony.

Lord Poltron
He's a Gentleman, my Lord Hypocrite, of undoubted veracity.

Lord Hypocrite
You might as well have said courage too; I have exceptions against both; and as to General Amherst's assertion that he could drive all America with five thousand men, he must have been joking, as he is quite of a diff'rent opinion now.

Lord Catspaw
What is your opinion of your countrymen, Mr. Judas, with respect to their courage?

Judas
The same that I ever told you, my Lord; as to true courage they have none, I know 'em well—they have a plenty of a kind of enthusiastic zeal, which they substitute in the room of it; I am very certain they would never face the regulars, tho' with the advantage of ten to one.

ee
Lord Boston and Admiral Tombstone General Gage and Admiral Graves. (*See* the introduction to *The Fall*.)

ff
Colonel Grant The implication made by Lord Hypocrite that Grant ran away during the battle for Fort Duquesne (Pittsburgh) in 1758 and was rescued by Washington is erroneous. It would have made excellent propaganda, however, because Grant was genuinely disliked in the colonies for his strongly anti-American sentiments.

gg

the olive-branch By 1776, when *The Fall* was published, both the English and the Americans had sought means of conciliation. The Earl of Chatham (Lord Wisdom) made his proposal on February 1, 1775; it was rejected by the ministers and Parliament and was attacked viciously by Lord Sandwich (Lord Poltron) and others in the ministry. After its rejection, Lord North (Mr. Catspaw) on February 20, 1775, presented his conciliatory plan. In it, North proposed "that when any of the colonies should offer adequate provisions for the common defence, as well as for the support of its civil government—including the administration of justice—it would be proper, if approved by the King and Parliament, to forbear from levying any duty or tax upon this colony, except duties designed for the regulation of commerce, the net revenue of which would be credited to the complying colony." (Gipson, XII, p. 295). The opposition, which included Colonel Barré (Colonel) and Edmund Burke (Bold Irishman), attacked the plan, saying that it was an "act of insidious cunning by which he [North] was practising the art of divide and rule." Burke, in his great speech on reconciliation on March 22, noted that the plan was " 'one of a ransom by auction,' " a playing off of one or several colonies by others. (Gipson, XII, pp. 296 and 304.) The various olive branches had been held out and had been rejected for good, if prejudiced, reasons by the colonists because, as B. D. Bargar has aptly expressed it, "the rod of chastisement was never far from the olive branch," and to shift the metaphor, only the naive among the Americans would have failed to recognize the fist of iron in the velvet glove. (*Lord Dartmouth and the American Revolution*, p. 141.)

---

hh-hh

Methodist . . . Bishop Dartmouth

Lord Hypocrite

All this, and a great deal more, would never convince me of the general cowardice of the Americans—but of the cowardice of Grant I've been long convinced, by numbers of letters formerly from America—I'am for doing the business effectually; don't let us be too sanguine, trust to stories told by every sycophant, and hurry heels over head to be laugh'd at; the Americans are bold, stubborn and sour; it will require foreign assistance to subdue 'em.

Lord Catspaw

These sour Americans, ignorant brutes, unbroke and wild, must be tamed; they'll soon be humble if punish'd; but if disregarded, grow fierce.—Barbarous nations must be held by fear, rein'd and spurr'd hard, chain'd to the oar, and bow'd to due controul, 'till they look grim with blood; let's first humble America, and bring them under our feet; the olive-branch[gg] has been held out, and they have rejected it; it now becomes us to use the iron rod to break their disobedience; and should we lack it, foreign assistance is at hand.

Lord Hypocrite

All this I grant, but I'm for sending a force sufficient to crush 'em at once, and not with too much precipitation; I am first for giving it a colour of impartiality, forbearance and religion.—Lay it before parliament; we have then law on our side, and endeavour to gain over some or all of the [hh]Methodist Teachers, and in particular my very good friend Mr. Wesley, their Bishop,[hh] and the worthy Mr. Clapum, which task I would undertake; it will then have the sanction of religion, make it less suspected, and give it better grace.

Lord Catspaw

I should choose it to be done by consent of parliament; we stand then on firmer ground; there's no doubt they'll grant ev'rything your Lordship proposes upon my motion: but to tell the truth, I'd rather be in purgatory so long, than to run the gantlet of the Bold Irishman's tongue.

Mocklaw

Aye, aye, don't part with the law while it's in our favour, or we can have it by asking for—and as to the Bold Irishman, don't be brow-beaten, you must summon all your brass, and put on a rugged highwayman's face like his; I expect some work of that kind too, but the devil himself shan't brow-beat me.

Paramount

I am glad to find, my Lords and Gentlemen, you all see the necessity of sending over troops and ships; [11]I intend my Lord Catspaw shall lay it before parliament, and am very certain they'll pass any acts I can desire. I thank you, Lord Hypocrite, for your kind offer, and accept of it; his Grace my Lord of Suffolk and Dean Tucker are negotiating the same business with the rest of my Lords the Bishops, and will succeed; so that it will carry the appearance of law and of religion, and will be sufficiently grac'd; I'll warrant you no one shall have cause to complain of its wanting grace."[ii] And now, my Lords and Gentlemen, as it's so late, and we have gone through all the business at this time proposed, you are at your liberty to withdraw.

[*Exeunt.*]

[*Paramount solus.*]

"-----*The great, th' important day,*
"*Big with the fate of Britain and of America,*"[15]

is now fixed, irrevocably fixed; the storm is ready to burst; the low'ring clouds portend their fate my glory, their fall my triumph—But I must haste to be gone, the ceremonies await my presence; deeds of darkness must be done by night, and, like the silent mole, work under ground:[16]

Now rushing forth in sober twilight gray,
Like prowling wolf, who ranges for his prey,
With eager grasp I'll seize th' imperial crown.
But if I fail, thou world, turn upside down;
Nor mortal leave alive, my fall to mourn.[17] (*Exit.*)

(Lord Hypocrite) was a close friend of the Methodists', being acquainted with John Wesley, Augustus Toplady, and others. Dartmouth's confidence in the support of the Methodists does not follow truth of the matter. (*See* reference to Wesley's letter in the introduction to *The Fall*.)

ii-ii

I intend . . . wanting grace Paramount summarizes the meeting, as an astute chairman should, saying that the matter of force will be laid before the Parliament and both law and religion will give sanction to it (as acts of Parliament and religious affirmation can be twisted into a semblance of reasonable conduct); the whole business will be given for the sake of public appearance and private ambition the sanctity of grace—the indefinable charismatic quality that impresses everyone.

ACT II

Scene 1

[*Lord Wisdom, Lord Religion, Lord Justice.*ª]

Lord Wisdom
I much lament, my Lords, the present unhappy situation of my country; where'er I turn my eyes, to Europe, Asia, Africa, or America, the prospect appears the same.—Look up to the throne, and behold your king, if I may now call him by that soft title—Where is the wisdom, the justice, the religion, that once adorn'd that throne, and shed the benign influence of their bright rays through the four quarters of the globe? Alas! they're flown!

Mark his forlorn looks—his countenance dejected, a sullen greatness fixed on his brow, as if it veil'd in blood some awful purpose, his eyes flaming and sanguinary; how I bewail him for[18] his predecessor's sake!—Long—long have I been an old, and I trust a ᵇ-faithful servant in the family—Can I then restrain one tear? No, 'tis impossible! —View that arch-dragon, that old fiend, Paramount, that rebel in grain, whispering in his ear. View his wretched ministers hovering round him, to accomplish their accursed purpose, and accelerate his destruction—View the whole herd of administration (I know 'em well) and tell me if the world can furnish a viler set of miscreants? View both houses of parliament, and count the number of Tyrants, Jacobites, Tories, Placemen, Pensioners, Sycophants and Panders.ᐧᵇ View the constitution, is she not disrob'd and dismantled? Is she not become like a virgin deflower'd? View our fleets and armies commanded by bloody murdering butchers! View Britain herself as a sheep without a shepherd! And lastly view America, for her virtue bleeding and for her liberty weltering in her blood!

Lord Religion
Such hath, and ever will be the fate of kings, who only listen to the voice of pleasure, thrown in their way by the sirens of administration, which never fail to swallow them up like a quicksand—like a serpent, who charms and fascinates, bewitches and enchants with his eye the unwary bird; witness the fatal catastrophe of ᶜ-Rehoboam, who rejected the counsel of the wise and experienced, and gave up all to the advice and guidance of young, unskilful and wicked councillors.ᐧᶜ Had he listen'd to you, my Lord, had he followed your advice, all, all would have gone well—Under your auspicious administration Britain flourished, but ever since has been on the decline, and patriotism, like religion, scarcely now more than a sounding brass or a tinkling cymbal.

ª
Lord Wisdom, Lord Religion, Lord Justice The Earl of Chatham, the Bishop of St. Asaph, the Earl of Camden. (*See* the introduction to *The Fall*.)

---

b-b
faithful servant . . . Panders Chatham had served the king and Britain brilliantly until turned out of office upon the accession of George III. (*See* the introduction to *The Fall*.) The administration of which he speaks, which began in 1770 under Lord North, was notorious for chicanery and cynicism. Horace Walpole, whose memoirs of the reigns of George II and George III have an acid quality, nevertheless spoke clearly to the point when he commented on certain persons in the ministry of Lord North. He is devastating but he hits the mark. "Lord North was a pliant tool, without system or principle; Lord George Germaine of desperate ambition and character; Wedderburn (Brazen) a thorough knave; Lord Sandwich (Poltron) a more profligate knave, Lord Gower a villain capable of any crime, Elliott, Jenkinson (Charley), Cornwall mutes that would have fixed the bowstring round the throat of the constitution." (*Last Journals*, II, p. 5.)

---

c-c
Rehoboam . . . councillors. I Kings 12.

Lord Wisdom
My counsel has been rejected—my conciliatory plan thrown under the table, and treated with contempt; the experience of gray hairs called the superannuated notions of old age—my bodily infirmities—my tottering frame—my crazy carcase, worn out in the service of my country, and even my very crutches, have been made the subject of their ridicule.

Lord Justice
Gratitude, like religion and patriotism, are about taking their flight, and the law of the land stands on tiptoe; the constitution, that admirable fabric, that work of ages, the envy of the world, is deflower'd indeed, and made to commit a rape upon her own body, by the avaricious frowns of her own father, who is bound to protect her, not to destroy —her pillars are thrown down, her capitals broke, her pedestals demolish'd and her foundation nearly destroy'd.— Lord Paramount and his wretched adviser Mocklaw baffles all our efforts.—The statutes of the land superseded by royal proclamations and dispensing powers, etc. etc. the bloody knife to be held to the throats of the Americans, and force them to submit to slav'ry.—Administration have commenced bloody tyrants, and those that should protect the subject, are become their executioners; yet will I dispute with them inch by inch, while there's a statute book left in the land. Come forth, thou grand deceiver! I challenge thee to come forth!

Lord Wisdom
Our friends must bestir themselves once more, perhaps we may yet turn the scale.—If the voice of religion, wisdom, and justice should fail, let us sound the trumpet of liberty and patriotism, that will conquer them in America, I know; let us try to storm them here with the united whole, and if by a base majority they still carry their point, we can nevertheless wash our hands and be clean.

Lord Religion
From the pulpit, in the house of God, have I spoken aloud, I have lifted up my voice like a trumpet, Oh! Britain, how art thou fallen! Hear now, O house of Britain, is it a small thing for you to weary man, but will you weary your God also? In the house of Lords have I borne my testimony:[d] Hear now, O ye Princes, and I will yet declare in Britain, and show forth in America, I will not cease 'till I bring about (if possible) unity, peace and concord.

Lord Wisdom
Much to be wished for; but alas! I fear it's now too late; I foresee the tendency and consequence of those diabolical measures that have been pursued with unrelenting fury. Britain will ruin her trade, waste her wealth, her strength, her credit and her importance in the scale of Europe. When a British king proves ungrateful and haughty, and strives to be independent of his people, (who are his sole support) the people will in their turn likewise strive to be independent of him and his myrmidons,[e] and will be free; they will

[d] *testimony* The Bishop's most celebrated speech for America was one that opposed the Massachusetts Charter Act and warmly defended the colonies. (*See* the introduction to *The Fall*.)

[e] *myrmidons* The devoted Thessalians who accompanied Achilles to Troy; henchmen or hirelings who obey their leader without question.

erect the anfractuous[f] standard of independency, and thousands and tens of thousands will flock to it, and solace themselves under its shade.—They have often been told of this, but effected to dispise it; they know not America's strength, they are ignorant of it; fed by the flatt'ry of every sycophant tale, imagine themselves almighty, and able to subdue the whole world. America will be lost to Britain forever, and will prove her downfall. America is wise, and will shake off the galling yoke before it be riveted on them; they will be drove to it, and who can blame them? Who can blame a gally slave for making his escape?—Britain will miscarry in her vile projects, her knight errant, her Don Quixotte schemes[19] in America: America will resist; they are not easily to be subdued; (nay 'tis impossible) Britain will find it a harder task than to conquer France and Spain united, and will cost 'em more blood and treasure than a twice seven years war with those European powers; they will stand out 'til Britons are tired. Britain will invite her with kind promises and open arms; America will reject them; America will triumph, rejoice and flourish, and become the glory of the earth; Britain will languidly hold down her head, and become first a prey to a vile Pretender, and then be subject to the ravagers of Europe. I love the Americans, because they love liberty. Liberty flourishes in the wilds of America. I honour the plant, I revere the tree, and would cherish its branches. Let us, my friends, join hands with them, follow their example, and endeavour to support expiring liberty in Britain; whilst I have a tongue to speak, I will support her wherever found; whilst I have crutches to crawl with, I will try to find her out, and with the voice of an arch-angel will demand for a sacrifice to the nation those miscreants who have wickedly and wantonly been the ruin of their country. Oh, Liberty! Oh, my country!

Lord Religion
Oh, Religion! Oh, Virtue! whither art thou fleeing? Oh, thou Defender of the Faith! Oh, ye mighty Lords and Commons! Oh, ye deluded Bishops! ye learned props of our unerring church, [g-]who preach up vengeance, force and fire,[-g] instead of peace! be wise in time, lest the Americans be driven to work out their own salvation without fear or trembling.
[*Exeunt.*]

Scene 2

[*Lord Patriot. Bold Irishman, Colonel.*[h]]

Bold Irishman
That Brazen Lawyer,[20] that Lord Chancellor, that wou'd be, held forth surprisingly last night, he beat the drum in your ears, brother soldier.

---

[f] *anfractuous* Torturous.

[g-g] *who preach ... fire* There is from the point of view of the playwright unintentional irony in this speech or a case of the pot calling the kettle black. The clergy in England with a few exceptions, among them the Bishop of St. Asaph, defended the government. But the fulminations of the American preachers became strong media for propaganda; these men of the cloth preached resistance to Britain. As war became inevitable, the pulpit orators promised God's support and rose to powerful heights of rhetoric in describing the wickedness and cruelty of the enemy and justified the taking up of arms. As Philip Davidson notes, a favorite text was "Cursed be he that keepeth back his sword from blood." (*Propaganda and the American Revolution*, p. 206n).

[h] *Lord Patriot, Bold Irishman, Colonel* John Wilkes, Edmund Burke, Colonel Barré (*See* the introduction to *The Fall.*)

Colonel
I think he did; he beat a Tatoo for us all.

Lord Patriot
No politicians but lawyer politicians, it seems, will go down; if we believe him, we must all turn lawyers now, and prate away the liberties of the nation.

Colonel
Aye, first we must learn to rail at the clamorous faction, disappointed politicians — ever restless — ever plotting — constantly thwarting government, in laudable and blameable purposes.—Inconsiderable party—inconsistent in their own politics—hostile to all government, soured by disappointment, and urged by want—proceeding to unjustifiable lengths—and then found the magnanimity of a British senate, animated by the sacred fire caught from a high-spirited people—

Bold Irishman
And the devil knows what beside—Magnanimity and sacred fire, indeed!—Very magnanimous sounds, but pompous nothings! Why did he not tell us where was the magnanimity of the British senate at the time of the dispute about Falkland's Island?[1] What sort of fire animated them then? —Where was the high spirit of the people? Strange sort of fire, and strange sort of spirit, to give up to our inveterate enemies, the Spaniards, our property unasked for, and cut our best friends and brethren the American throats, for defending theirs against lawless tyranny; their sacred fire became then all fumo,[21] and the strength of their boasted spirits evaporated into invisible effluvium; the giant then sunk sure enough spontaneously into a dwarf; and now, it seems the dwarf having been feeding upon smoky fire and evaporated spirits, is endeavouring to swell himself into a giant again, like the frog in the fable, 'till he bursts himself in silent thunder—But let the mighty Philistine, the Goliath Paramount, and his oracle Mocklaw, with their thunder bellowed from the brazen mortar-piece of a turn-coat lawyer, have a care of the little American David!

Lord Patriot
Aye, indeed! America will prove a second Sampson to 'em; they may put out his eyes for a while, but he'll pull their house down about their ears for all that. Mr. Brazen seem'd surpris'd at the thought of relinquishing America, and bawl'd out with the vociferation of an old miser that had been robb'd—Relinquish America! relinquish America! forbid it heavens! But let him and his masters take great care, or America will save 'em the trouble, and relinquish Britain.

Colonel
Or I'm much mistaken, Brazen says, establish first your superiority, and then talk of negotiating.

[1]
Falkland's Island A group of islands in the South Atlantic ocean, settled by the French in 1764. In 1765 the islands were claimed for Great Britain by Captain John Byron. A small group of English settlers was left at Port Egmont. In 1766, the French settlement was withdrawn at the insistence of Spain, and in 1770 the Spanish evicted the English colonists. There was great agitation in Britain against this action, and in 1771 Port Egmont was restored to the British. In 1774 England, fearful of antagonizing Spain, voluntarily gave up the islands to Spain, which brought about violent attacks against Lord North's government by the opposition.

Lord Patriot
That doctrine suits 'em best; just like a cowardly pickpocket, or a bloody highwayman, knock a man down first, and then tell him stand and deliver.

Colonel
A just comparison, and excellent simile, by my soul! But I'm surpris'd he did not include the Clergy among the number of professions unfit (as he said) to be politicians.

Bold Irishman
Did you ever know a lawyer to meddle with religion, unless he got a see by it?[j] he'll take care and steer clear of that; if it don't come in his way, he'll never break his neck over a church bible, I warrant you—Mammon is his god—Judge Jeffereys is his priest—Star-chamber doctrine is his creed—fire, flames and faggot, blood, murder, halters and thund'ring cannon are the ceremonies of his church—and lies, misrepresentations, deceit, hypocrisy and dissimulation are the articles of his religion.

Lord Patriot
You make him a monster, indeed.

Bold Irishman
Not half so bad as he is, my Lord; he's following close to the heels of that profound sage, that oracle, Mocklaw, his tutor: I can compare the whole herd of them to nothing else but to the swine[k] we read of running headlong down the hill, Paramount their devil, Mocklaw the evil spirit, and Brazen their driver, as unfit to guide the chariot of state as Phaeton[l] was to guide the chariot of the sun.[22]

Colonel
And thus they'll drive liberty from out the land, yet I hope they'll meet the ambitious Phaeton's fate; but when a brave people, like the Americans, from their infancy us'd to liberty (not as a gift, but who inherit it as a birth-right, but not as a mess of pottage, to be bought by, or sold to, ev'ry hungry glutton of a minister) find attempts made to reduce them to slavery, they generally take some desperate successful measure for their deliverance. I should not be at all surpris'd to hear of independency proclaim'd throughout their land, of Britain's armies beat, their fleets burnt, sunk, or otherwise destroy'd. The same principle which Mr. Brazen speaks of, that inspires British soldiers to fight, namely the ferment of youthful blood, the high spirit of the people, a love of glory, and a sense of national honour, will inspire the Americans to withstand them; to which I may add, liberty and property.—But what is national honour? Why, national pride.—What is national glory? Why national nonsense, when put in competition with liberty and property.

---

[j] *got a see by it* Bold Irishman's (Burke) speech is a clever assessment of Wedderburne as an infamous politician-lawyer. The combined metaphor of religion and politics is well handled, and the speech is colored with the caustic comment on human affairs for which Burke was well known by his orations. Burke notes that politicians steer away from religious matters unless there is gain for them, such as the control of a see to which a grateful bishop might be appointed. He shifts ground to the particular condemnation of Wedderburne as tyranny personified and a danger to both England and America.

[k] *swine* An allusion to the three passages in the Bible wherein Jesus drove the devils out of men and allowed them to enter a herd of swine that "ran violently down a steep place into the sea and perished in the waters." Mat. 8: 28-32; Mark 5: 11-14; Luke 8: 31-33.

[l] *Phaeton* Phaeton, son of Apollo, asked the favor of driving his father's chariot. Reluctantly Apollo granted the request, and Phaeton, unequal to the task, all but destroyed the world until he in turn was annihilated by Jove's thunderbolt.

Lord Patriot
Of Britain I fear liberty has taken its farewell, the aspiring wings of tyranny hath long hovered over, and the overshadowing influence of bribery hath ecclips'd its rays and dark'ned its lustre; the huge Paramount, that temporal deity, that golden calf, finds servile wretches enough so base as to bow down, worship and adore his guilded horns;—let 'em e'en if they will:—But as for me, tho' I should stand alone, I would spurn the brute, were he forty-five[23] times greater than he is; I'll administer, ere long, such an emetic to him, as shall make the monster disgorge the millions[m] yet unaccounted for, and never shall it be said, that Patriot ever feared or truckled to him, or kept a silent tongue when it should speak.

Bold Irishman
There I'll shake hands with you, and my tongue shall echo in their ears, make their arched ceiling shake,[24] the treasury bench crack,[n] and the great chair of their great speaker tremble, and never will I cease lashing them, while lashing is good, or hope remains; and when the voice of poor liberty can no longer be heard in Britain or Hibernia, let's give Caledonia a kick with our heels, and away with the goddess to the American shore, crown her, and defy the grim king of tyranny, at his peril, to set his foot there.—Here let him stay, and wallow in sackcloth and ashes, like a beast as he is, and, Nebucadnezzar-like, eat grass and thistles.
(*Exeunt.*)

> *See Paramount, upon his awful throne,*
> *Striving to make each freeman's purse his own!*
> *While Lords and Commons most as one agree,*
> *To grace his head with crown of tyranny,*
> *They spurn the laws, force °-constitution locks,*
> *To seize each subject's coffer, chest and box;*
> *Send justice packing, as tho' too poor unmix'd,-°*
> *And hug the tyrant, as by law he's fix'd.*

---

[m] *the millions* The attack on Bute continues with this reference to an alleged private income from bribery and, specifically, from a supposed payment to Bute from abroad as the result of his effecting the peace treaty ending the Seven Years' War. The rumor of an enormous bribe given Bute by European governments persisted throughout his life. (The New England and Providence editions specify forty millions.)

[n] *treasury bench crack* The first minister of the king was the First Lord of the Treasury who occupied the principal seat in the House of Commons on the treasury bench. This leader of the party in power later became known as Prime Minister, although in the eighteenth century it was not as common a designation as it is today. In fact, Lord North refused to use the title.

[o-o] *constitution locks . . . unmix'd* These lines refer to writs of assistance by which officials could search private dwellings and storehouses for smuggled goods. "Search and seizure" became anathema to the colonists, partly because many were guilty of smuggling. The playwright attacks the invasion of privacy, which would have been regarded as unconstitutional and illegal.

ACT III

Scene 1

In Boston.

[*Selectman, Citizen.*]

Selectman
At length, it seems the bloody flag is hung out, the ministry and parliament, ever studious in mischief, and bent on our destruction, have ordered troops and ships of war to shut our ports,[a] and starve us into submission.

Citizen
And compel us to be slaves; I have heard so. It is a fashionable way to requite us for our loyalty, for the present we made them of [b]Louisburg, for our protection of Duquesne, for the assistance we gave them at Quebec, Martinico, Guadaloupe, the Havannah,[b] etc. etc. Blast their councils, spurn their ingratitude! Soul of Pepperel![c] whither art thou fled?

Selectman
They seem to be guided by some secret demon; this stopping our ports and depriving us of all trade is cruel, calculated to starve and beggar thousands of families, more spiteful than politic, more to their own disadvantage than ours: But we can resolve to do without trade; it will be the means of banishing luxury, which has ting'd the simplicity and spotless innocence of our once happy asylum.

Citizen
We thank heaven, we have the necessaries of life in abundance, even to an exuberant plenty; and how oft' has our hospitable tables fed numbers of those ungrateful monsters, who would now, if they could, famish us?

Selectman
No doubt, as we abound in those temporal blessings, it has tempted them to pick our pockets by violence, in hopes of treasures more to their minds.

Citizen
In that these thirsters after gold and human blood will be disappointed.—No Perus or Mexicos here they'll find—but the demon you speak of, tho' he acts in secret is notoriously known. Lord Paramount is that demon, that bird of prey,

---

[a] *shut our ports* The scene now shifts to America. The news of the Boston Port Act of March, 1774, has reached the colonists and the two citizens are discussing its frightening implications.

[b-b] *Louisburg . . . Havannah* The British claim—that England had been the protector of the colonies during the French and Indian War and was therefore owed allegiance if not gratitude—was answered by the patriots who argued that they had participated as much as had the British in their own defense, even though they were led by British officers and for the most part followed strategy designed in London. The six locations named by the Citizen refer to the places in which the British defeated the French.

[c] *Soul of Pepperel* The reference to Pepperal (or Pepperrell) would have added force to the argument concerning the ability of the colonists to be aggressive in their own interests. In 1745 Pepperel, a native of Maine, led the American forces against Louisburg, an undertaking considered foolhardy by many. Fort Louisburg was impregnable, it was thought, and to have the proud fortress humbled by colonial militia with a few British ships was unthinkable, to both the French and the English. The attack and siege was effective and the fortress capitulated June 16, 1745.

that ministerial cormorant, that waits to devour, and who first thought to disturb the repose of America; a wretch no friend to mankind, who acts thro' envy and avarice, like satan, who escap'd from hell to disturb the regions of paradise; after ransacking Britain and Hibernia for gold, the growth of hell, to feed his luxury, now waits to rifle the bowels of America.

Selectman
May he prove more unsuccessful than satan; blind politics, rank infatuation, madness detestable, the concomitants of arbitrary power! They can never think to succeed; but should they conquer, they'll find that he who overcometh by force and blood, hath overcome but half his foe—Captain Preston's massacre[d] is too recent in our memories; and if a few troops dar'd to commit such hellish unprovok'd barbarities, what may we not expect from legions arm'd with vengeance, whose leaders harbour principles repugnant to freedom, and possess'd with more than diabolical notions? Surely, our friends will oppose them with all the power heaven has given them.

Citizen
Nothing more certain; each citizen and each individual inhabitant of America are bound by the ties of nature; the laws of God and man justify such a procedure; passive obedience for passive slaves, and non-resistance for servile wretches who know not, neither deserve, the sweets of liberty. As for me and my house, thank God, such detestable doctrine never did, nor shall ever, enter over my threshold.

Selectman
Would all America were so zealous as you.—The appointment of a general Continental Congress was a judicious measure, and will prove the salvation of this new world, where counsel mature, wisdom and strength united, will prove a barrier, a bulwark, against the encroachments of arbitrary power.

Citizen
I much approve of a choice of a congress; America is young, she will be to it like a tender nursing mother, she will give it the paps of virtue to suck, cherish it with the milk of liberty, and fatten it on the cream of patriotism; she will train it up in its youth, and teach it to shun the poison of British voluptuousness, and instruct it to keep better company. Let us, my friend, support her all in our power, and set on foot an immediate association; they will form an intrenchment, too strong for ministerial tyranny to o'erleap.

Selectman
I am determined so to do, it may prevent the farther effusion of blood—and—

d
Captain Preston's massacre The reference is to the so-called Boston Massacre of March 5, 1770, considered by many of the patriots to have been the first overt act in the Revolution. The city had been in a state of high tension as the result of non-importation disagreements and the murder on February 22 of a young boy by the merchant Richardson, who had been selling proscribed articles and who had shot the youth under provocation. Although Richardson was condemned for murder, Lieutenant-Governor Hutchinson refused to sign a death warrant. By March 5 the mood of the citizens was dangerous, and eventually the riot occurred in which the British fired into a crowd, killing three and mortally wounding two others. Captain Preston, who was officer of the day and present at the event, was arrested as were six other soldiers. Much to the surprise of their friends, John Adams and Josiah Quincy agreed to defend the soldiers. Preston and four soldiers were acquitted, the others were discharged from military service. There have been rumors ever since that Sam Adams may have initiated the event. Whatever the truth of the matter, there is little doubt that the "massacre" proved to be useful for the propagandists of the American cause. The fifth of March became a day of martyrs and from 1770 forward, that day was an occasion for violent orations depicting the cruelty and heartlessness of the British.

Scene 2

[*Enter a minister.*]

Minister
My friends, I yet will hail you good morrow, tho' I know not how long we may be indulged that liberty to each other; doleful tidings I have to tell.

Selectman
With sorrow we have heard it—good morrow, Sir.

Minister
Wou'd to God it may prove false, and that it may vanish like the dew of the morning.

Citizen
Beyond a doubt, Sir, it's too true.

Minister
Perhaps, my friends, you have not heard all.

Selectman
We have heard too much, of the troops and ships coming over, we suppose you mean; we have not heard more, if more there be.

Minister
Then worse I have to tell, tidings which will raise the blood of the patriot, and put your virtue to the proof, will kindle such an ardent love of liberty in your breasts, as time will not be able to exterminate—

Citizen
Pray let us hear it, I'm all on fire.

Selectman
I'm impatient to know it, welcome or unwelcome.

Minister
Such as it is, take it; your character is annihilated; you are all, all declared rebels; your estates are to be confiscated; your patrimony to be given to those who ever[25] labor'd for it; popery to be established in the room of the true catholic faith; the Old South,[e] and other houses of our God, converted perhaps into nunneries, inquisitions, barracks and common jails, where you will perish with want and famine, or suffer an ignominious death; your wives, children, dearest relatives and friends, forever separated from you in this world, without the prospect of receiving any comfort or consolation from them, or the least hope of affording any to them.

Selectman
Perish the thought!

Citizen
I've heard enough;—To arms! my dear friends, to arms! and death or freedom be our motto!

---

[e] *the Old South* On October 19, 1775, General William Howe ordered one of his worst acts of depredation, the conversion of the Old South meeting-house, scene of religious worship and political gatherings, into a riding school for the cavalry. The pews were stripped from the church, and one of the most beautiful pews was used for a hog pen. The effect of the act increased the fury against the British and was a fit subject for propaganda. (Lossing, I, p. 574.) Another string to the bow of the propagandist was the recurrent rumor that the British were going to turn America into a Roman Catholic nation. The Quebec act of 1774, which in part granted religious freedom to Roman Catholics in Canada, added strength to the suppositions concerning British intentions.

Minister
A noble resolution; Posterity will crown the urn of the patriot who consecrates his talents to virtue and freedom; his name shall not be forgot; his reputation shall bloom with unfading verdure, while the name of the tyrant, like his vile body, shall moulder into dust. Put your trust in the Lord of hosts, he is your strong tower, he is your helper and defence, he will guide and strengthen the arm of flesh, and scatter your enemies like chaff.

Selectman
Let us not hesitate.

Citizen
Not a single moment;—'tis like to prove a mortal strife, a never-ending contest, tyranny or death.[26]

Minister
Delays may be dangerous.—Go and awake your brethren that sleepeth;—rouse them up from their lethargy and supineness, and join with confidence temporal with spiritual weapons.—Perhaps they be now landing, at this moment, this very moment, may be the last of your liberty.—Prepare yourselves—be ready—stand fast—ye know not the day nor the hour.—May the Ruler of all send us liberty and life.—Adieu! my friends.

Scene 3

In a Street in Boston.

[*Frequent town-meetings and consultations amongst the inhabitants;*—f·*Lord Boston arrives with the forces and ships;—lands and fortifies Boston, etc.*·f]

[*Whig, Tory.*]

Whig
I have said and done all that man could say or do.—'Tis wrong, I insist upon it, and time will show it, to suffer them to take possession of g·Castle William and fortify Boston Neck.·g

Tory
I cannot see, good Sir, of what advantage it will be to them; —they've only a mind, I suppose, to keep their soldiers from being inactive, which may prejudice their health.

Whig
I wish it may prove so, I would very gladly confess your superior knowledge in military manoevres; but till then, suffer me to tell you, it's a stroke the most fatal to us,—no less, Sir, but to cut off the communication between the town and country, making prisoners of us all by degrees,

---

f-f
Lord Boston . . . fortifies Boston
In May, 1774, General Gage (Lord Boston) became governor-in-chief and captain-general of the province of Massachusetts Bay, succeeding Thomas Hutchinson (Mr. Judas), who sailed for England never to return to his homeland. (See the introduction to *The Fall*.)

---

g-g
Castle William . . . Boston Neck
Castle William was a fortress on Castle Island in Boston Harbor. When Howe evacuated Boston, he destroyed the fortress. Peter Oliver, the Loyalist, reported that the "conflagration was the most pleasingly dreadful that I have ever beheld: sometimes it appeared like the eruption of Mount Etna." (Adair and Schutz, eds., *Origin and Progress of the American Revolution*, p. 143n.)

and give 'em an opportunity of making excursions, and in a short time subdue us without resistance.

Tory
I think your fears are groundless.

Whig
Sir, my reason is not to be trifled with. Do you not see or hear ev'ryday of insults and provocations to the peaceable inhabitants? This is only a prelude. Can men of spirit bear forever with such usage? I know not what business they have here at all.

Tory
I suppose they're come to protect us.

Whig
Damn such protectors, such cut-throat villains; protect us? from what? from whom?—

Tory
Nay, Sir, I know not their business;—let us yet bear with them 'till we know the success of the petition from the Congress;—if unfavourable, then it will be our time.

Whig
Then, I fear, it will be too late; all that time we lose, and they gain ground; I have no notion of trusting to the success of petitions, waiting twelve months for no answer at all. Our assemblies have petitioned often, and as often in vain; 'twould be a miracle in these days to hear of an American petition being granted; their omnipotencies, their demi-godships (as they think themselves) no doubt think it too great a favour done us to throw our petitions under their table, much less vouchsafe to read them.

Tory
You go too far;—the power of King, Lords and Commons is uncontroulable.

Whig
With respect to tyrannizing they would make it so, if they could, I know, but there's a good deal to be said and done first; we must have more than half the bargain to make.

Tory
Sure you would not go to dispute by arms with Great-Britain.

Whig
Sure I would not suffer you to pick my pocket, Sir.

Tory
If I did, the law is open for you—

Whig
I have but a poor opinion of the law, when the devil sits judge.

Tory
What would you do then, Sir, if I was to pick your pocket?

Whig
Break your head, Sir—

Tory
Sure you don't mean as you say, Sir—

Whig
I surely do—try me, Sir—

Tory
Excuse me, Sir, I am not of your mind, I would avoid every thing that has the appearance of rashness.—Great-Britain's power, Sir—

Whig
Great-Britain's power, Sir, is too much magnified, 'twill soon grow weak, by endeavouring to make slaves of American freemen; we are not Africans yet, neither bond-slaves. —You would avoid and discourage every thing that has the appearance of patriotism, you mean.—

Tory
Who? me, Sir?

Whig
Yes, you, Sir;—you go slily pimping, spying and sneaking about, cajoling the ignorant, and insinuating bugbear notions of Great-Britain's mighty power into weak people's ears, that we may tamely give all up, and you be rewarded, perhaps, with the office of judge of the admiralty, or continental hangman, for ought I know.

Tory
Who? me, Sir?

Whig
Aye, you, Sir;—and let me tell you, Sir, you've been long suspected—

Tory
Of what, Sir?

Whig
For a rank Tory, Sir.

Tory
What mean you, Sir?

Whig
I repeat it again—suspected to be an enemy to your country.

Tory
By whom, Sir? Can you show me an instance?

Whig
From your present discourse I suspect you—and from your connexions and artful behavior all suspect you.

Tory
Can you give me a proof?

Whig
Not a point blank proof, as to my own knowledge; you're so much of a Jesuit, you have put it out of my power;—but strong circumstances by information, such as amount to a proof in the present case, Sir, I can furnish you with.

Tory
Sir, you may be mistaken.

Whig
'Tis not possible, my informant knows you too well.

Tory
Who is your informant, Sir?

Whig
A gentleman, Sir; and if you'll give yourself the trouble to walk with me, I'll soon produce him.

Tory
Another time; I cannot stay now;—'tis dinnertime.

Whig
That's the time to find him.

Tory
I cannot stay now.

Whig
We'll call at your house then.

Tory
I dine abroad, Sir.

Whig
Begone, you scoundrel! I'll watch your waters;[h] 'tis time to clear the land of such infernal vermin.

[*Exeunt both different ways.*]

Scene 4

In Boston, while the Regulars were flying from Lexington.

[*Lord Boston, surrounded by his guards and a few officers.*]

Lord Boston
If Colonel Smith[i] succeeds in his embassy, and I think there's no doubt of it, I shall have the pleasure this ev'ning,

---

[h] *I'll watch your waters* To keep a strict watch on anyone's actions.

[i] *Colonel Smith* Brevet Lieutenant Colonel Francis Smith (1723-1791), an inept soldier but professionally acceptable because of his age and experience in the British army, was selected to command the move on Lexington and Concord, April 19, 1775.

I expect, of having my friends Hancock and Adams's good company; I'll make each of them a present of a pair of handsome iron ruffles, and Major Provost shall provide a suitable entertainment for them in his apartment.

Officer
Sure they'll not be so unpolite as to refuse your Excellency's kind invitation.

Lord Boston
Shou'd they, Colonel Smith and Major Pitcairn[j] have my orders to make use of all their rhetoric and the persuasive eloquence of British thunder.

   [*Enters a messenger in haste.*]

Messenger
I bring your Excellency unwelcome tidings—

Lord Boston
For Heaven's sake! from what quarter?

Messenger
From Lexington plains.

Lord Boston
'Tis impossible!

Messenger
Too true, Sir.

Lord Boston
Say—what is it? Speak what you know.

Messenger
Colonel Smith is defeated, and fast retreating.

Lord Boston
Good God! What does he say? Mercy on me!

Messenger
They're flying before the enemy.

Lord Boston
Britons turn their backs before the Rebels!—The Rebels put Britons to flight? Said you not so?

Messenger
They are routed, Sir;—they are flying this instant;—the Provincials are numerous, and hourly gaining strength;—they have nearly surrounded our troops. A reinforcement, Sir—a timely succour may save the shatter'd remnant. Speedily, speedily, Sir! or they're irretrievably lost!

Lord Boston
Good God! What does he say? Can it be possible?

---

[j] *Major Pitcairn* Pitcairn (1722-1775) was second in command under Smith at Lexington.

Messenger
Lose no time, Sir.

Lord Boston
What can I do?—O dear!

Officer
Draw off a detachment—form a brigade; prepare part of the train; send for Lord Percy; let the drums beat to arms.

Lord Boston
Aye do, Captain; you know how, better than I. *(Exit Officer.)* Did the Rebels dare to fire on the king's troops? Had they courage? Guards, keep round me.

Messenger
They're like lions; they have killed many of our bravest officers and men; and if not checked instantly, will totally surround them, and make the whole prisoners. This is no time to parley, Sir.

Lord Boston
No, indeed; what will become of me?

[*Enter Earl Percy.*]

Earl Percy
Your orders, Sir.

Lord Boston
Haste, my good Percy,[k] immediately take command of the brigade of reinforcement, and fly to the assistance of poor Smith!—Lose no time, lest they be all cut off, and the rebels improve their advantage, and be upon us; and God knows what quarter they'll give.—Haste, my noble Earl!—Speedily!—Speedily! Where's my guard?

Earl Percy
I'am gone, Sir.

[*Exeunt Percy and officers—drums beating to arms.*]

Lord Boston
What means this flutt'ring round my heart? this unusual chillness? Is it fear? No, it cannot be, it must proceed from my great anxiety, my perturbation of mind for the fate of my countrymen. A drowsiness hangs o'er my eyelids;—fain would I repose myself a short time;—but I must not;—I must wait;—I'll to the top of yon eminence,—there I shall be safer. Here I cannot stay;—there I may behold something favourable to calm this tumult in my breast,—But, alas, I fear—Guards, attend me.

[*Exeunt Lord Boston and guards.*]

---

k

my good Percy Hugh, Baron Percy, was opposed to the government's attitude toward the colonies. Nevertheless, he sailed for America early in 1774 and was placed by Gage in command of the camp in Boston. On April 19, 1775, he moved swiftly from Boston and rescued Smith and his troops.

Scene 5

THE FALL | 93

[Lord Boston and guards on a hill in Boston, that overlooks Charlestown.]

Lord Boston
Clouds of dust and smoke intercept my sight; I cannot see; I hear the noise of cannon—Percy's cannon—Grant him success!

One of the Guard
Methinks, Sir, I see British colours waving.

Lord Boston
Some ray of hope.—Have they got so near?—Captain, keep a good look out; tell me every thing you see. My eyes are wondrous dim.

Officer
The two brigades have join'd—Now Admiral [1]·Tombstone bellows his lower tier on the Provincials.·[1] How does your Excellency?

Lord Boston
Right;—more hope still.—I'm bravely to what I was. Which way do our forces tend?

Officer
I can distinguish nothing for a certainty now; such smoke and dust.

Lord Boston
God grant Percy courage!

Officer
His ancestors were brave, Sir.

Lord Boston
Aye, that's no rule—no rule, Captain; so were mine.—A heavy firing now.—The Rebels must be very numerous—

Officer
They're like caterpillars; as numerous as the locusts of Egypt.

Lord Boston
Look out, Captain, God help you, look out.

Officer
I do, Sir.

Lord Boston
What do you see now? Hark! what dreadful noise!

One of the Guard
(Aside.) How damn'd afraid he is.[m]

[1-1]
Tombstone—Provincials Percy finally succeeded in saving what British he could by reaching Charlestown Neck where he was under protection of naval guns. Tombstone (Graves) had his ships in position so that they could protect the retreating regulars, and the lower tier on his gunships thundered against the advancing Americans.

---

[m]
How damn'd afraid he is. This sentence and other lines suggesting that Gage was a coward are presented for the purpose of propaganda. Inept as Gage may have been or guilty of errors of judgment, he was not a coward. That he failed politically to understand the American situation was not entirely his fault but it reflected the British ministers' almost complete lack of comprehension of the colonists and their temper.

Another of the Guard
(*Aside.*) He's one of your chimney corner Generals—an old granny.

Officer
If I mistake not, our troops are fast retreating; their fire slackens; the noise increases.

Lord Boston
Oh, Captain, don't say so!

Officer
'Tis true, Sir, they're running—the enemy shout victory.

Lord Boston
Upon your honour?—say—

Officer
Upon my honour, Sir, they're flying t'wards Charlestown. Percy's beat; I'm afraid he's lost his artillery.

Lord Boston
Then 'tis all over—the day is lost—what more can we do?

Officer
We may, with the few troops left in Boston, yet afford them some succour, and cover their retreat across the water; 'tis impossible to do more.

Lord Boston
Go instantly; I'll wait your return. Try your utmost to prevent the Rebels from crossing. Success attend you, my dear Captain, God prosper you! (*Exit Officer.*) Alas, alas! my glory's gone; my honour's stain'd. My dear guards, don't leave me, and you shall have plenty of porter and sour-crout.[n]

Scene 6

[*Roger and Dick, two shepherds near Lexington, after the defeat and the flight of the Regulars.*]

Roger
Whilst early looking, Dick, ere the sun was seen to tinge the brow of the mountain, for my flock of sheep, nor dreaming of approaching evil, suddenly mine eyes beheld from yon hill a cloud of dust arise at a small distance; the intermediate space were thick set with laurels, willows, evergreens, and bushes of various kinds, the growth of wild nature, and which hid the danger from my eyes, thinking perchance my flock had hither stray'd; I descended, and straight onward went; but, Dick, judge you my thoughts at such a disappointment: Instead of my innocent flock of

---

[n] *porter and sour-crout* Staples in the diet of the soldiers. The latter almost became a cause célèbre in one of Burke's orations after the disclosure that Howe had evacuated Boston in March, 1776. He declared that "every measure which had been adopted or pursued was directed to impoverish England and to emancipate America; and though in twelve months nearly one thousand dollars a man had been spent for salt beef and sour-krout." (Lossing, I, pp. 590-91.)

sheep, I found myself almost encircled by a herd of ravenous British wolves.

Dick
Dangerous must have been your situation, Roger, whatever were your thoughts.

Roger
I soon discovered my mistake; finding a hostile appearance, I instantly turn'd myself about, and fled to alarm the shepherds.

Dick
Did they pursue you?

Roger
They did; but having the start, and being acquainted with the bye-ways, I presently got clear of their voracious jaws.

Dick
A lucky escape, indeed, Roger; and what rout did they take after that?

Roger
Onwards, t'wards Lexington, devouring geese, cattle and swine, with fury and rage, which, no doubt, was increased by their disappointment; and what may appear strange to you, Dick, (tho' no more strange than true) is, they seem'd to be possessed of a kind of brutish music, growling something like our favourite tune Yankee Doodle,º (perhaps in ridicule) 'till it were almost thread bare, seeming vastly pleased (monkey-like) with their mimickry, as tho' it provoked us much.

Dick
Nature, Roger, has furnish'd some brute animals with voices, or, more properly speaking, with organs of sound that nearly resemble the human. I have heard of crocodiles weepingᵖ like a child, to decoy the unwary traveler, who is no sooner within their reach, but they seize and devour instantly.

Roger
Very true, Dick, I have read of the same; and these wolves, being of the canine breed, and having the properties of blood-hounds, no doubt are possess'd of a more acute sense of smelling, more reason, instinct, sagacity, or what shall I call it? than all other brutes. It might have been a piece of cunning of theirs, peculiar to them, to make themselves pass for shepherds, and decoy our flocks; for, as you know, Dick, all our shepherds both play and sing Yankee Doodle, our sheep and lambs are as well acquainted with that tune as ourselves, and always make up to us whene'er they hear the sound.

Dick
Yes, Roger; and now you put me in mind of it I'll tell you of something surprising in my turn: I have an old ram

THE FALL | 95

º
Yankee Doodle "Yankee Doodle" almost became the American national anthem. It was sung and played by the British on numerous occasions as a derisive air and was answered constantly as a song of defiance by the Americans. There are many explanations for its origin, and the accretion of its verses continued far into the nineteenth century.

ᵖ
crocodiles weeping The analogy of the ancient belief that crocodiles weep over their victims and attract them by cries similar to those of children as here applied to the British would have appeared very apt to the reader.

and an old ewe, that, whenever they sing Yankee Doodle together, a skilful musician can scarcely distinguish it from the bass and tenor of an organ.

Roger
Surprising indeed, Dick, nor do I in the least doubt it; and why not, as well as Balaam's ass,[q] speak? and I might add, many other asses, now-a-days; and yet, how might that music be improved by a judicious disposition of its various parts, by the addition of a proper number of sheep and young lambs; 'twould then likewise resemble the counter, counter tenor, treble,[r] and finest pipes of an organ, and might be truly called nature's organ; methinks, Dick, I could forever sit and hear such music,

> *Where all the parts in complication roll,*
> *And with its charming music feast the soul!*

Dick
Delightful, indeed; I'll attempt it with what little skill I have in music; we may then defy these wolves to imitate it, and thereby save our flocks: I am well convinced, Roger, these wolves intended it rather as a decoy than by way of ridicule, because they live by cunning and deception; besides, they could never mean to ridicule a piece of music, a tune, of which such brutes cannot be supposed to be judges, and, which is allowed by the best masters of music to be a composition of the most sublime kind, and would have done honor to a Handel or a Correllius.[s] Well, go on, Roger, I long to hear the whole.

Roger
When they came to Lexington, where a flock of our innocent sheep and young lambs, as usual, were feeding and sporting on the plain, these dogs of violence and rapine with haughty stride advanc'd, and berated them in a new and unheard of language to us.

Dick
I suppose learn'd at their own fam'd universities—

Roger
No doubt; they had teachers among them—Two old wolves their leaders, not unlike in features to Smith and Pictairn, as striving to outvie each other in the very dregs of brutal eloquence, and more than Billingsgate jargon, howl'd in their ears such a peal of new-fangled execrations, and hell-invented oratory, 'till that day unheard in New-England, as struck the whole flock with horror, and made them for a while stand aghast, as tho' all the wolves in the forest had broke loose upon them.

Dick
Oh shocking!—Roger, go on.

---

[q] *Balaam's ass* Numbers 22: 21-31. The angel of the Lord appeared to Balaam's ass in order that Balaam might not proceed to Moab. Balaam struck the beast of burden who spoke and reprimanded Balaam.

[r] *counter, counter tenor, treble* Counter, counter tenor is the alto male singing voice of high value; the treble is the highest boy's voice, approaching the soprano.

[s] *Correllius.* Corelli (1653-1713), one of the first great violin teachers and composers.

Roger
Not content with this, their murdering leaders, with premeditated malice, keen appetite, and without provocation, gave the howl for the onset, when instantly the whole herd, as if the devil had entered into them, ran violently down the hill, and fixed their talons and jaws upon them, and as quick as lightening eight young innocent lambs[t] fell a sacrifice to their fury, and victims to their rapacity; the very houses of our God were no longer a sanctuary; many they tore to pieces, and some at the very foot of the altar; others were dragged out as in a wanton gamesome mood.

Dick
Barbarity inexpressible! more than savage cruelty! I hope you'll make your master pay for 'em; there is a law of this province, Roger, which obliges the owner of such dogs to pay for the mischief they do.

Roger
I know it, Dick; he shall pay, never fear, and that handsomely too; he has paid part of it already.

Dick
Who is their master, Roger?

Roger
One Lord Paramount; they call him a free-booter; a fellow who pretends to be proprietor of all America, and says he has a deed for it, and chief ranger of all the flocks, and pretends to have a patent for it; has been a long time in the practice of killing and stealing sheep in England and Ireland, and had like to have been hang'd for it there, but was repriev'd by the means of his friend GEORGE—I forgot his other name—not Grenville[u]—not GEORGE the Second—but another GEORGE—

Dick
It's no matter, he'll be hang'd yet; he has sent his dogs to a wrong place, and lugg'd the wrong sow by the ear; he should have sent them to Newfoundland, or Kamptschatka,[v] there's no sheep there—But never mind, go on, Roger.

Roger
Nor was their voracious appetites satiated there; they rush'd into the town of Concord, and proceeded to devour everything that lay in their way; and those brute devils, like Sampson's foxes,[w] (and as tho' they were men) thrice attempted with firebrands to destroy our corn, our townhouse and habitations.

Dick
Heavens! Could not all this provoke you?

Roger
It did; rage prompted us at length, and found us arms 'gainst such hellish mischief to oppose.

---

t
eight young innocent lambs The number of Americans killed at Lexington.

---

u
Grenville George Grenville succeeded Bute as First Lord of the Treasury, or Prime Minister, in 1763. It was he who promulgated the Stamp Act with its disastrous results. He resigned from office in 1765. Roger's forgetfulness as to the name of George III is, of course, an intended insult.

---

v
Kamptschatka The Kamptschatka Peninsula is located in northeastern Russia.

---

w
Sampson's foxes Judges 15: 4-5. Samson caught 300 foxes, attached firebrands to their tails and set them among the cornfields and vineyards of the Philistines, thus destroying the harvests.

Dick
Oh, would I have been there!

Roger
Our numbers increasing, and arm'd with revenge, we in our turn play'd the man; they, unus'd to wounds, with hideous yelling soon betook themselves to a precipitate and confused flight, nor did we give o'er the chase, 'till Phoebus grew drowsy, bad us desist, and wished us a good night.

Dick
Of some part of their hasty retreat I was a joyful spectator, I saw their tongues lolling out of their mouths, and heard them pant like hunted wolves indeed.

Roger
Did you not hear how their mirth was turn'd into mourning? their fury into astonishment? How soon they quitted their howling Yankee Doodle, and chang'd their notes to bellowing? how nimbly (yet against their will) they betook themselves to dancing? And he was then the bravest dog that beat time the swiftest, and footed Yankee Doodle the nimblest.

Dick
Well pleased, Roger, was I with the chase, and glorious sport it was: I oft perceiv'd them tumbling o'er each other heels over head; nor did one dare stay to help his brother—but, with bloody breech, made the best of his way—nor ever stopped 'till they were got safe within their lurking-holes—

Roger
From whence they have not the courage to peep out, unless four to one, except (like a skunk) forc'd by famine.

Dick
May this be the fate of all those prowling sheep-stealers; it behooves the shepherds to double the watch, to take uncommon precaution and care of their tender flocks, more especially as this is like to be an uncommon severe winter, by the appearance of wolves so early in the season—but, hark!—Roger, methinks I hear the sound of melody warbling thro' the grove—Let's sit a while, and partake of it unseen.

Roger
With all my heart.—Most delightful harmony! This is the First of May; our shepherds and nymphs are celebrating our glorious St. Tammany's day; we'll hear the song out, and then join in the frolick, and chorus it o'er and o'er again—This day shall be devoted to joy and festivity.

SONG

[Tune. The hounds are all out, etc.]

Of St. George, or St. Bute,^x let the poet laureate sing,
Of Pharaoh or Pluto of old,
While he rhymes forth their praise, in false, flattering lays,
I'll sing of St. Tamm'ny the bold, my brave boys.

Let Hibernia's sons boast, make Patrick their toast;
And Scots Andrew's fame spread abroad.
Potatoes and oats, and Welch leeks for Welch goats,
Was never St. Tammany's food, my brave boys.

In freedom's bright cause, Tamm'ny pled with applause,
And reason'd most justly from nature;
For this, this was his song, all, all the day long:
Liberty's the right of each creature, brave boys.

Whilst under an oak his great parliament sat,
His throne was the crotch of the tree;^y
With Solomon's look, without statutes or book,
He wisely sent forth his decree, my brave boys.

His subjects stood round, not the least noise or sound,
Whilst freedom blaz'd full in each face:
So plain were the laws, and each pleaded his cause;
That might BUTE, NORTH, and MANSFIELD disgrace,
  my brave boys.

No duties, nor stamps, their blest liberty cramps,
A king, tho' no tyrant, was he;
He did oft 'times declare, nay sometimes wou'd swear,
The least of his subjects were free, my brave boys.

He, as king of the woods, of the rivers and floods,
Had a right all beasts to controul;
Yet, content with a few, to give nature her due:
So gen'rous was Tammany's soul, my brave boys.

In the morn he arose, and a-hunting he goes,
Bold Nimrod^z his second was he.
For his breakfast he'd take a large venison stake,
And despis'd your flip-flops^{aa} and tea, my brave boys.

While all in a row, with squaw, dog and bow,
Vermilion adorning his face,
With feathery head he rang'd the woods wide:
St. George sure had never such grace, my brave boys.

His jetty black hair, such as Buckskin saints wear,
Perfumed with bear's grease well smear'd,
Which illum'd the saints face, and ran down apace.
Like the oil from Aaron's old beard,^{bb} my brave boys.

---

^x
St. George or St. Bute The reference is to the loyalist Society of St. George; Bute is an example of the use of topical satire.

^y
Whilst . . . tree Tammany supposedly was present at the great meeting of conciliation between Penn and the Indian tribes that took place "under the elm tree at Sachamaxou" in 1682. (See *DAB*, VII, pt. 2, p. 435.)

^z
Nimrod Nimrod, son of Cush, a mighty hunter. (Genesis 10: 8-9.)

^{aa}
flip-flops Probably misspelling of "flip-flaps," a kind of tea cake.

^{bb}
Aaron's old beard Reference is to the precious oil of priesthood that was poured upon Aaron's head and ran down upon his beard and garments. (Psalm 133:2.)

The strong nervous deer, with amazing career,
In swiftness he'd fairly run down:
And, like Sampson, wou'd tear wolf, lion or bear.
Ne're was such a saint as our own, my brave boys.

When he'd run down a stag, he behind him wou'd lag;
For, so noble a soul had he!
He'd stop, tho' he lost it, tradition reports it,
To give him fresh chance to get free, my brave boys.

With a mighty strong arm, and a masculine bow,
His arrow he drew to the head,
And as sure as he shot, it was ever his lot,
His prey it fell instantly dead, my brave boys.

His table he spread where the venison bled,
Be thankful, he used to say;
He'd laugh and he'd sing, tho' a saint and a king,
And sumptuously dine on his prey, my brave boys.

Then over the hills, o'er the mountains and rills
He'd caper, such was his delight;
And ne'er in his days, Indian history says,
Did lack a good supper at night, my brave boys.

On an old stump he sat, without cap or hat,
When supper was ready to eat,
Snap, his dog, he stood by, and cast a sheep's eye;
For ven'son, the king of all meat, my brave boys.

Like Isaac of old, and both cast in one mould,
Tho' a wigwam was Tamm'ny's cottage,
He lov'd sav'ry meat, such that patriarch eat,
Of ven'son and squirrel made pottage, brave boys.

When fourscore years old, as I've oft'times been told,
To doubt it, sure, would not be right,
With a pipe in his jaw, he'd buss his old squaw,
And get a young saint ev'ry night, my brave boys.

As old age came on, he grew blind, deaf and dumb.
Tho' his sport, 'twere hard to keep from it,
Quite tired of life, bid adieu to his wife,
And blaz'd like the tail of a comet, brave boys.

What country on earth, then, did ever give birth
To such a magnanimous saint?
His acts far excel all that history tell,
And language to feeble to paint, my brave boys.

Now, to finish my song, a full flowing bowl
I'll quaff, and sing all the long day,
And with punch and wine paint my cheeks for my saint,
And hail ev'ry First of sweet May, my brave boys.

Dick
What a seraphic voice! how it enlivens my soul! Come away —away Roger! the moments are precious.

[*Exeunt Dick and Roger.*]

Scene 7

In a chamber, near Boston, the morning after the battle of Bunker's Hill.

Clarissa
How lovely is this new-born day!—The sun rises with uncommon radiance after the most gloomy night my wearied eyes ever knew.—The voice of slumber was not heard—the angel of sleep was fled—and the awful whispers of solemnity and silence prevented my eye-lids from closing. —No wonder—the terrors and ideas of yesterday—such a scene of war—of tumult—hurry and hubbub—of horror and destruction—the direful noise of conflict—the dismal hissing of iron shot in vollies flying—such bellowing of mortars—such thund'ring of cannon—such roaring of musquetry—and such clashing of swords and bayonets—such cries of the wounded—and such streams of blood—such a noise and crush of houses, steeples, and whole streets of desolate Charlestown falling—pillars of fire, and the convulsed vortex of fiery flakes, rolling in flaming wreaths in the air, in dreadful combustion, seemed as tho' the elements and the whole earth were envelop'd in one general, eternal conflagration and total ruin, and intermingled with black smoke, ascending, on the wings of mourning, up to heaven, seemed piteously to implore the almighty interposition to put a stop to such devastation, lest the whole earth should be unpeopled in the unnatural conflict—Too, too much for female heroism to dwell upon—But what are all those to the terrors that filled my affrighted imagination the last night? — Dreams—fancies—evil bodings—shadows, phantoms, and ghastly visions continually hovering around my pillow, goading and harrowing my soul with the most terrific appearances, not imaginary, but real—Am I awake—Where are the British murderers?—where's my husband?—my son?—my brother?—Something more than human tells me all is not well: If they are among the slain, 'tis impossible.—I—Oh! *(She cries.)*

[*Enter a neighbour, a spectator of the battle.*]

Neighbour
Madam, grieve not so much.

Clarissa
And I wont to grieve without a cause? Wou'd to God I did; —mock me not—What voice is that? Me thinks I know it—

some angel sent to comfort me?—welcome then. (*She turns about*) O, my neighbour, is it you? My friend, I have need of comfort. Hast thou any for me?—say—will you not speak? Where's my husband?—my son?—my brother? Hast thou seen them since the battle? Oh! bring me not unwelcome tidings. *(Cries.)*

Neighbour
(*Aside:* What shall I say?) Madam, I beheld them yesterday from an eminence.

Clarissa
Upon that very eminence was I. What then?—

Neighbour
I saw the brave man Warren, your son and brother.

Clarissa
What? O ye gods!—Speak on friend—stop—what saw ye?

Neighbour
In the midst of the tempest of war—

Clarissa
Where are they now?—That I saw too—What is all this?

Neighbour
Madam, hear me—

Clarissa
Then say on—yet—O, his looks!—I fear!

Neighbour
When General Putnam bid the vanguard open their front to the—

Clarissa
Oh, trifle not with me—dear Neighbour!—where shall I find them?—say—

Neighbour
(*Aside:* Heavens! must I tell her!) Madam, be patient—right and left, that all may see who hate us, we are prepar'd for them—

Clarissa
What then?—Can you find 'em?—

Neighbour
I saw Warren and the other two heroes firm as Roxbury stand the shock of the enemy's fiercest attacks, and twice put to flight their boasted phalanx.—

Clarissa
All that I saw, and more; say—wou'd they not come to me, were they well?—

Neighbour
Madam, hear me—

Clarissa
O! He will not speak.

Neighbour
The enemy return'd to the charge, and stumbling o'er the dead and wounded bodies of their friends, Warren received them with indissoluble firmness, and notwithstanding their battalious aspect, in the midst of the battle, tho' surrounded with foes on ev'ry side—

Clarissa
O, my neighbour!—

Neighbour
Madam—his nervous arm, like a giant refresh'd with wine, hurl'd destruction where'er he came, breathing heroic ardour to advent'rous deeds, and long time in even scale the battle hung, 'till at last death turn'd pale and affrighted at the carnage—they ran—

Clarissa
Who ran?

Neighbour
The enemy, Madam, gave way—

Clarissa
Warren never ran—yet—oh! I wou'd he had—I fear— (*Cries.*)

Neighbour
I say not so, Madam.

Clarissa
What say ye then? he was no coward, neighbour—

Neighbour
Brave to the last. (*Aside:* I forgot myself.)

Clarissa
What said you? O heavens! brave to the last! those words— why do you keep me thus?—cruel—

Neighbour
(*Aside:* She will know it.) I say, Madam, by some mistaken orders on our side, the enemy rallied and return'd to the charge with fresh numbers, and your husband, son and brother—Madam—

Clarissa
Stop!—O ye powers!—What?—say no more—yet let me hear—keep me not thus—tell me, I charge thee—

Neighbour
(*Aside:* I can hold no longer, she must know it.) Forgive me, Madam—I saw them fall—and Michael, the arch-angel, who vanquish'd satan, is not more immortal than they.—(*Aside:* Who can relate such woes without a tear?)

Clarissa
Oh! I've heard enough—too too much (*cries*) yet—if thou hast worse to tell—say on—nought worse can be—O ye gods!—cruel—cruel—thrice cruel—cou'd ye not leave me one—(*She faints, and is caught by her friend, and placed in a chair, he rings the bell, the family come in, and endeavour to bring her to.*)

Neighbour
With surprising fortitude she heard the melancholy relation, until I came to the last close—she then gave me a mournful look, lifted up her eyes, and immediately sunk motionless into my arms.

Woman
Poor soul!—no wonder—how I sympathize with her in her distress—my tender bosom can scarcely bear the sight! A dreadful loss! a most shocking scene it was, that brothers should with brothers war, and in intestine fierce opposition meet, to seek the blood of each other, like dogs for a bare bone, who so oft in generous friendship and commerce join'd, in festivals of love and joy unanimous as the sons of one kind and indulgent father, and separately would freely in a good cause spend their blood and sacrifice their lives for him.

Neighbour
A terrible black day it was, and ever will be remembered by New-England, when that vile Briton, (unworthy the name of Briton) Lord Boston, (curse the name!) whose horrid murders stain American soil with blood; perish his name! a fratricide! 'twas he who fir'd Charlestown, and spread desolation, fire, flames and smoke in ev'ry corner—he was the wretch, that waster of the world, that licens'd robber, that blood-stain'd insulter of a free people, who bears the name of Lord Boston, but from henceforth shall be called Cain, that pillag'd the ruins, and dragg'd and murder'd the infant, the aged and infirm—(But look, she recovers.)

Clarissa
O ye angels! ye cherubims and seraphims! waft their souls to bliss, bathe their wounds with angelic balsam, and crown them with immortality. A faithful, loving and beloved husband, a promising and filial son, a tender and affectionate brother: Alas! what a loss!—Whom have I now to comfort me—What have I left, but the voice of lamentation: (*She weeps.*) Ill fated bullets—these tears shall sustain me—yes, ye dear friends! how gladly wou'd I follow you—but alas! I must still endure tribulation and inquietudes, from which you are now exempt; I cannot cease to weep, yet brave men, I will mourn your fall—weep on—flow, mine eyes, and wash away their blood, 'till the fountain of sorrow is dried up—but, oh! it never—never will—my sympathetic soul shall dwell on your bosoms, and floods of tears shall water

your graves; and since all other comfort is deny'd me, deprive me not of the only consolation left me of meditating on your virtues and dear memories, who fell in defence of liberty and your country—ye brave men—ye more than friends—ye martyrs to liberty!—This, this is all I ask, 'till sorrow overwhelms me—I breathe my last; and ye yourselves, your own bright spirits, come and waft me to your peaceful abode, where the voice of lamentation is not heard, neither shall we know any more what it is to separate.

Eager the patriot meets his desperate foe
With full intent to give the fatal blow;
The cause he fights for animates him high,
His wife, his children and his liberty:
For these he conquers, or more bravely dies,
And yields himself a willing sacrifice.

[*Exeunt.*]

ACT IV

Scene 1

Near Norfolk, in Virginia, on board a man of war, Lord Kidnapper in the state-room, a boat appears rowing towards the ship.

[*Sailor, Boatswain.*]

Sailor
BOATSWAIN!

Boatswain
Holla.

Sailor
Damn my eyes, Mr. Boatswain, but here's a black flag of truce coming on board.

Boatswain
Sure enough—where are they from?

Sailor
From hell, I suppose—for they're as black as so many devils.

Boatswain
Very well—no matter—they're recruits for the Kidnapper.[a]

Sailor
We shall be all of a colour by and by—damn me—

Boatswain
I'll go and inform his Lordship and his pair of doxies[b] of it. I suppose by this time they have trim'd their sails, and he's done heaving the log. [*Exit Boatswain.*]

Scene 2

Near the state-room.

Boatswain
Where's his Lordship?

Servant
He's in the state-room.

Boatswain
It's time for him to turn out, tell him I want to speak to him.

Servant
I dare not do it, Boatswain; it's more than my life is worth.

---

[a] *the Kidnapper* Lord Dunmore. (*See* the introduction to *The Fall.*)

[b] *pair of doxies* Davidson states that Dunmore was accused of "impressing a hundred and sixty people into his service; he finally returned all of them . . . except two maidens 'detained as bedmakers to his lordship.'" (*Propaganda and the American Revolution*, p. 149.) The immorality of noble lords who were chosen as royal governors was a constant irritation to puritanical common folk in the colonies. With few exceptions provincial rulers appointed in London were tarred by the brush of innuendo in the press and the pamphlets, leading the ordinary reader to assume that a man's private immorality would make him a venal public official.

Boatswain
Damn your squeamish stomach, go directly, or I'll go myself.

Servant
For God's sake! Boatswain—

Boatswain
Damn your eyes, you pimping son of a bitch, go this instant, or I'll stick my knife in your gammons.^c

Servant
O Lord! Boatswain. (*Servant goes.*)

Boatswain
(*Solus.*) What the devil—keep a pimp guard here, better station the son of a bitch at the mast head, to keep a look out there, lest Admiral Hopkins^d be upon us.

[*Enter Kidnapper.*]

Kidnapper
What's your will, Boatswain.

Boatswain
I beg your Lordship's pardon, (*Aside:* But you can soon fetch up ^{e-}Leeway, and spread the water sail^{-e} again) please your honour, here's a boat full of fine recruits along side for you.

Kidnapper
Recruits, Boatswain? you mean soldiers from Augustine,^f I imagine; what reg'mentals have they on?

Boatswain
Mourning, please your honour, and as black as our tarpawling.

Kidnapper
Ha, ha, well, well, take 'em on board, Boatswain, I'll be on deck presently.

Boatswain
With submission to your honour, d'ye see (*scratching his head*) I think we have gallows-looking dogs enough on board already—the scrapings of Newgate, and the refuse of Tyburn, and when the wind blows aft, damn 'em they stink like polecats—but d'ye see, as your honour pleases, with submission, if it's Lord Paramount's orders, why it must be so, I suppose—but I've done my duty, d'ye see—

Kidnapper
Ha, ha, the work must be done, Boatswain, no matter by whom.

Boatswain
Why, aye, that's true, please your honour, any port in a storm—if a man is to be hand'd, or have his throat cut, d'ye see—who are so fit to do it as his own slaves especially

THE FALL | 107

c
gammons Legs

d
Admiral Hopkins. The Continental Congress, having decided to establish a fleet for defensive purposes against the British Navy, on December 22, 1775, appointed Esek Hopkins of Rhode Island commander-in-chief. In January, 1775, he took charge of "his little fleet of eight small ships, hastily altered to meet their new requirements." Hopkins was directed by Congress to move southward and attack the ships of the enemy along the Virginia and Carolina coasts. Among the British ships was the Fowey man-of-war, which Dunmore had made the seat of the Virginia government after a riot against him on June 5, 1775. (See *DAB*, V, pt. 1, p. 209.)

e-e
Leeway . . . sail Obviously a reference to Dunmore's revels with the doxies on board; the implication of the nautical metaphor is witty, the water sail being a small sail set under a lower studding sail or under a spanker boom extending nearly to the water.

f
Augustine Kidnapper is expecting British reinforcements from Florida, under English control after the Seven Years War.

as they're to have their freedoms for it; nobody can blame 'em, nor your honour neither, for you get them for half price, or nothing at all, d'ye see me, and that will help to lessen poor Owld England's taxes, and when you have done with 'em here, and they get their brains knock'd out, d'ye see, your honour can sell them in the West Indies, and that will be something in your honour's pocket, d'ye see—well, ev'ry man to his trade—but, damn my impudence for all, I see your honour knows all about it—d'ye see.

[*Exit Boatswain.*]

Scene 3

[*Lord Kidnapper returns to his state-room, the Boatswain comes on deck and pipes.*]

Boatswain
All hands ahoi—hand a rope, some of you Tories, forward there, for his worship's reg'ment of black guards to come aboard.

[*Enter Negroes.*]

Boatswain
Your humble servant, Gentlemen, I suppose you want to see Lord Kidnapper?—Clear the gangway there of them Tyburn tulips. Please to walk aft, brother soldiers, that's the fittest birth for you, the Kidnapper's in the state-room, he'll hoist his sheet-anchor presently, he'll be up in a jiffin —as soon as he has made fast the end of his small rope athwart Jenny Bluegarter and Kate Common's stern posts.

First Sailor
Damn my eyes, but I suppose, messmate, we must bundle out of our hammocks this cold weather, to make room for these black regulars to stow in, tumble upon deck, and choose a soft birth among the snow?

Second Sailor
Blast 'em, if they come within a cable's length of my hammock, I'll kick 'em to hell through one of the gun ports.

Boatswain
Come, come, brothers, don't be angry, I suppose we shall soon be in warmer latitude—the Kidnapper seems as fond of these black regulars (as you call 'em Jack) as he is of the brace of whores below; but as they come in so damn'd slow, I'll put him in the humour of sending a part of the fleet this winter to the coast of Guinea, and beat up for volunteers, there he'll get recruits enough for a hogshead or two of New-England rum, and a few old pipe-shanks, and save poor Owld-England the trouble and the expence of clothing them in the bargain.

First Sailor
Aye, Boatswain, any voyage, so it's a warm one—if it's to hell itself—for I'm sure the devil must be better off than we, if we are to stay here this winter.

Second Sailor
Any voyage, so it's to the southward, rather than stay here at lazy anchor—no fire, nothing to eat or drink, but suck our frosty fists like bears, unless we turn sheep-stealers again, and get our brains knock'd out. Eigh, master cook, you're a gentleman now—nothing to do—grown so proud, you wont speak to poor folks, I suppose?

Cook
The devil may cook for 'em for me—If I had any thing to cook—a parcel of frozen half-starved dogs. I should never be able to keep 'em out of the cook-room, or their noses out of the slush tub.

Boatswain
Damn your old smoky jaws, you're better off than any man aboard, your trouble will be nothing,—for I suppose they'll be disbursted in different messes among the Tories, and it's only putting on the big pot, cockey. Ha, ha, ha.

Cook
What signifies, Mr. Boatswain, the big pot or the little pot, if there's nothing to cook? no fire, coal or wood to cook with? Blast my eyes, Mr. Boatswain, if I disgrace myself so much, I have had the honour, damn me (tho' I say if that shou'dn't say it) to be chief-cook of a seventy four gunship, on board of which was Lord Abel-Marl and Admiral Poke-Cock.

Boatswain
Damn the liars—old singe-the-devil—you chief cook of a seventy-four gun ship, eigh? you the devil, you're as proud as hell, for all you look as old as Matheg'lum,g hand a pair of silk stockings for our cook here, d'ye see—lash a handspike athwart his arse, get a ladle full of slush and a handful of brimstone for his hair, and step one of you Tories there for the devil's barber, to come and shave and dress him. Ha, ha, ha.

Cook
No, Mr. Boatswain, it's not pride—but look'e (as I said before) I'll not disgrace my station, I'll throw up my commission, before I'll stand cook for a parcel of scape gallows, convict Tory dogs and run-away Negroes.

Boatswain
What's that you say? Take care, old frosty face—What? do you accuse his worship of turning kidnapper, and harbouring run away Negroes?—Softly, or you'll be taken up for a Whig, and get a handsome coat of slush and hogs

g
Matheg'lum Methuselah

feathers for a christmas-box, cockey: Throw up your commission, eigh? throw up the pot-halliards,[h] you mean, old piss-to-windward? Ha, ha, ha.

Cook
I tell you, Mr. Boatswain—I—

Boatswain
Come, come, give us a chaw of tobacco, Cook—blast your eyes, don't take any pride in what I say—I'm only joking, d'ye see—

Cook
Well, but Mr. Boatswain—

Boatswain
Come, [i]avast, belay the lanyards of your jaws,[i] and let's have no more of it, d'ye see. (*Boatswain pipes.*) Make fast that boat along side there.

[*Exeunt ev'ry man to his station.*]

Scene 4

[*Lord Kidnapper comes up on the quarter deck.*]

Lord Kidnapper
Well, my brave blacks, are you come to list?

Cudjo
Eas, massa Lord, you preazee.[j]

Kidnapper
How many are there of you?

Cudjo
Twenty-two, massa.

Kidnapper
Very well, did you all run away from your masters?

Cudjo
Eas, massa Lord, eb'ry one, me too.

Kidnapper
That's clever; they have no right to make you slaves, I wish all the Negroes wou'd do the same, I'll make 'em free—what part did you come from?

Cudjo
Disse brack man, disse one, disse one, disse one, disse one, come from Hamton, disse one, disse one, disse one, come from Nawfok, me come from Nawfok too.

---

[h] *pot-halliards* Ropes in the galley by which pots were hung.

[i-i] *avast . . . jaws* Be quiet, fasten the ropes of your jaws.

[j] *Eas, massa Lord, you preazee.* Cudjo and his compatriots represent probably the second time that the Negro appeared in native American drama. The first such character was Ralpho in *The Candidates* by Robert Munford, a play written in 1770. It was published in 1798, but there is no record of a performance. (*See* Richard Moody, ed., *Dramas from the American Theatre 1762-1909* for the latest reprint of the Munford play.)

Kidnapper
Very well, what was your master's name?

Cudjo
Me massa name Cunney Tomsee.

Kidnapper
Colonel Thompson—eigh?

Cudjo
Eas, massa, Cunney Tomsee.

Kidnapper
Well then I'll make you a major—and what's your name?

Cudjo
Me massa cawra me Cudjo.

Kidnapper
Cudjo?—very good—was you ever christened, Cudjo?

Cudjo
No, massa, me no crissen.

Kidnapper
Well then I'll christen you—you shall be called major Cudjo Thompson, and if you behave well,—I'll soon make you a greater man than your master, and if I find the rest of you behave well, I'll make you all officers, and after you have serv'd Lord Paramount a while, you shall have money in your pockets, good clothes on your backs, and be as free as them white men there. (*Pointing forward to a parcel of Tories.*)

Cudjo
Tankee, massa, gaw bresse, massa Kidnap.

Sailor
(*Aside.*) What a damn'd big mouth that Cudjo has—as large as our main hatch-way—

Cook
(*Aside.*) Aye, he's come to a wrong place to make a good use of it—it might stand some little chance at a Lord Mayor's feast.—

Kidnapper
Now go forward, give 'em something to eat and drink there. (*Aside:* Poor devils, they look half starved and naked like ourselves.)

Cook
(*Aside.*) I don't know where the devil they'll get it; the sight of that fellow's mouth is enough to breed a famine on board, if there was not one already.

Sailor
Aye, he'd tumble plenty down his damn'd guts and swallow it, like Jones[27] swallow'd the whale.

Kidnapper
To morrow you shall have guns like them white men—Can you shoot some of them rebels ashore, Major Cudjo?

Cudjo
Eas, massa, me try.

Kidnapper
Wou'd you shoot your old master, the Colonel, if you could see him?

Cudjo
Eas, massa, you terra me, me shoot him down dead.

Kidnapper
That's a brave fellow—damn 'em—down with them all—shoot all the damn'd rebels.

Sergeant
(*Aside.*) Brave fellows indeed!

Kidnapper
Sergeant!

Sergeant
I wait your Lordship's commands.

Kidnapper
Sergeant, to-morrow begin to teach those black recruits the exercise, and when they have learn'd sufficiently well to load and fire, then incorporate them among the regulars and the other Whites on board; we shall in a few days have some work for 'em, I expect—be as expeditious as possible. (*Aside to him.*) Set a guard over them every night, and take their arms from them, for who knows but they may cut our throats.

Sergeant
Very true, My Lord, I shall take particular care.

[*Exit Kidnapper, Sergeant and Negroes walk forward.*]

Scene 5

Sergeant
Damn 'em, I'd rather see half their weight in beef.

Boatswain
Aye, curse their stomachs, or mutton either; then our Cook wou'dn't be so damn'd lazy as he is, strutting about the

deck like a nobleman, receiving Paramount's pay for nothing.

Sergeant
Walk faster, damn your black heads. I suppose, Boatswain, when this hell-cat reg'ment's complete, they'll be reviewed in Hyde Park?—

Boatswain
Aye, blast my eyes, and our Chaplain with his dirty black gown, or our Cook, shall be their general, and review 'em, for he talks of throwing up his pot-halliards commission, in hopes of it.

Sergeant
Ha, ha, ha.—

Cook
I'd see the devil have 'em first.—

[*Exeunt Sergeant, etc.*]

Scene 6

In the cabin.

[*Lord Kidnapper, Captain Squires, Chaplain.*]

Kidnapper
These blacks are no small acquisition, them and the Tories we have on board, will strengthen us vastly; the thoughts of emancipation will make 'em brave, and the encouragement given them by my proclamation, will greatly intimidate the rebels—internal enemies are worse than open foes.—

Chaplain
Very true, My Lord; David prayed that he might be preserved from secret enemies.

Kidnapper
Aye, so I've heard, but I look upon this to be a grand manoeuvre in politics; this is making dog eat dog—thief catch thief—the servant against his master—rebel against rebel—what think you of that parson?

Chaplain
A house divided thus against itself cannot stand, according to scripture—My Lord, your observation is truly scriptural.

Kidnapper
Scripture? Poh, poh—I've nothing to do with scripture—I mean politically, parson.

Chaplain
I know it very well; sure, My Lord, I understand you perfectly.

Kidnapper
Faith, that's all I care for; if we can stand our ground this winter, and burn all their towns that are accessible to our ships, and Colonel Connolly[k] succeeds in his plan, there's not the least doubt but that we shall have supplies from England very early in the spring, which I have wrote for; then, in conjunction with Connolly, we shall be able to make a descent where we please, and drive the rebels like hogs into a pen.

Chaplain
And then gather them (as the scriptures say) as a hen gathereth her chickens.

Kidnapper
True, Mr. Scripture.

Captain Squires
Very good, but you must take care of the hawks.

Kidnapper
What do you mean by the hawks, Captain?

Captain Squires
I mean the shirt-men, the rifle-men, My Lord.

Kidnapper
Aye, damn 'em, hawks indeed; they are cursed dogs; a man is never safe where they are, but I'll take care to be out of their reach, let others take their chance, for I see they have respect to persons—I suppose they wou'd shoot at me, if I were within their reach.

Chaplain
Undoubtedly, they would be more fond of you than of a wild turkey; a parcel of ignorant unmannerly rascals, they pay no more respect to a Lord than they wou'd to a devil.

Kidnapper
The scoundrels are grown so damn' impudent too, that one can scarcely get a roasting pig, now-a-days, but I'll be even with some of 'em by and by.

Chaplain
I hope we shall get something good for our Christmas dinner—so much abstinence and involuntary mortification, cannot be good for the soul—a war in the body corporal is of more dangerous consequence than a civil war to the state, or heresy or schism to the church.

Kidnapper
Very true, parson—very true—now I like your doctrine—a full belly is better than an empty sermon; preach that

---

[k] *Colonel Connolly* Connolly was a Loyalist doctor from Pennsylvania who, having been granted land in Virginia, eventually became an unscrupulous land speculator as well as an agent of Lord Dunmore. In August, 1775, Connolly joined Dunmore aboard his warship off Portsmouth, Virginia, where the two concocted a plan to raise a regiment on the western frontier and "launch an offensive that would capture Pittsburgh and Alexandria" and take Virginia. The plan was discovered in good time. Connolly was imprisoned in Philadelphia until the end of 1776, removed to Baltimore until 1780, exchanged, continued his conspiracies, was retaken, and released in 1782 on condition that he go to England. He appeared again with a plan to seize New Orleans and gain control of the Mississippi but was frustrated in his scheme by Washington. (For further details *see* Boatner, pp. 261-62; Carl Van Doren, *Secret History of the American Revolution*, pp. 23-26; Sabine, I, pp. 331-32.)

doctrine;—stick to that text, and you'll not fail of making converts.

Chaplain
The wisest of men said, there is nothing better, than that a man should enjoy that which he hath, namely, eat, drink, and be merry, if he can.

Kidnapper
You're very right—Solomon was no fool, they say—(*he sings*)
    Give me a charming lass, Twangdillo cries,
    I know no pleasure, but love's sweet joys.

Chaplain
(*Sings.*) *Give me the bottle, says the red face sot,*
    For a whore I'd not give six-pence, not a groat.

Yet two is better than one, my Lord, for the scriptures further say, if one be alone, how can there be heat? you seem to be converted to that belief, for you have a brace of them, as the Boatswain says.

Kidnapper
Ha, ha. It's a pity but you were a bishop, you have the scriptures so pat—now I'll go take a short nap, meanwhile; Captain, if any thing new happens, pray order my servant to wake me.

Captain Squires
I will, My Lord.

    [*Exit Kidnapper.*]

Chaplain
And you and I'll crack a bottle, Captain: (bring a bottle, boy!) 'tis bad enough to perish by famine, but ten thousand times worse to be chok'd for want of moisture. His Lordship and two more makes three; and you and I and the bottle make three more, and a three-fold cord is not easily broken; so we're even with him.

Captain Squires
With all my heart.—Boy, bear a hand!

Tom
Coming, Sir.

Chaplain
Tom, Tom! make haste, you scoundrel!— fetch two bottles; I think we can manage it.

    [*Enter Tom with the bottles.*]

Chaplain
That's right, Tom.—Now bring the glasses, and shut the door after you.

    [*Exit Tom.*]

Scene 7

In Boston. A council of war after the battle of Bunker's Hill.

[*Lord Boston, Admiral Tombstone, Elbow Room, Mr. Caper,*[1] *General Clinton, Earl Percy.*]

Lord Boston
I fully expected, with the help of the last reinforcement you brought me over, and the advice and assistance of three accomplish'd and experienc'd Generals, I should have been able to have subdued the rebels, and gain'd immortal laurels to myself—have return'd to Old England like a Roman Consul, with a score or two of the rebel Generals, Colonels and Majors, to have grac'd my triumph.

Elbow Room
You have been vastly disappointed, Sir—you must not look for laurels (unless wild ones) nor expect triumphs (unless sham ones) from your own victories or conquests in America.

Lord Boston
And yet not more disappointed than you, Sir—witness your thrasonical speeches on your first landing, provided you had but elbow room—and Mr. Caper too to bring over Monsieur Rigadoon, the dancing-master, and Signior Rosin, the fiddler forsooth; he thought, no doubt, to have country danc'd the rebels out of their liberty with some of his new cuts—with his soft music to have fascinated their wives and daughters, and with some of 'em, no doubt, to have taken the tour of America, with his reg'ment of fine sleek prancing horses, that have been feeding this six months on codfish tails; he thought to have grown fat with feasting, dancing, and drinking tea with the Ladies, instead of being the skeleton he now appears to be—not to mention any thing of his letter, wherein he laments Tom's absence; for "had Tom been with him (he says) he wou'd have been ᵐ·out of danger,·ᵐ and quite secure from the enemy's shot."[28]

Percy
I think, Gentlemen, we're even with you now; you have had your mirth and frolick with us, for dancing Yankee Doodle, as you called it, from Lexington.—I find you have had a severer dance, a brave sweat at Bunker's Hill, and have been obliged to pay the fiddler in the bargain.

Clinton
However, Gentlemen, I approve (at proper seasons) of a little joking, yet I can by no means think (as we have had such bad success with our ⁿ·crackers) that this is a proper time to throw your squibs.·ⁿ

1
Lord Boston, Admiral Tombstone, Elbow Room, Mr. Caper General Gage, Admiral Graves, General William Howe, Burgoyne. (*See* the introduction to *The Fall.*)

mm
out of danger On June 25, 1775, Burgoyne wrote a letter to his close friend Lord Stanley in which he reports that the Battle of Bunker's Hill was a great achievement for the British, a masterly action and a great victory. He vividly describes the battle that he witnessed with Clinton in the comparative safety of a battery directly opposite to Charlestown. He remarks, "I much lament Tom's absence; . . . and had he been with me he would likewise have been out of danger; for, except for two cannon balls that went a hundred yards over our heads, we were not in any part of the direction of the enemy's shot." (Force, *American Archives,* 4th Series, II, pp. 1094-95.) The obvious implication that English generals remain safely out of danger during battle would not have been lost on colonial readers.

n-n
crackers . . . squibs The *double-entendre* simply means that the effect of the firecrackers or large field pieces gained the British nothing; because of the near disaster to the English this is not the time to quibble or to throw little firecrackers, which do not explode but burn with a fizz.

Lord Boston
I grant you, Sir, this is a very improper time for joking; for my part, I was only speaking as to my own thoughts, when Mr. Elbow Room made remarks, which he might as well have spared.

Elbow Room
I took you, Sir, as meaning a reflection upon us for our late great loss, and particularly to myself, for expressing some surprise on our first landing, that you should suffer a parcel of ignorant peasants to drive you before 'em like sheep from Lexington; and I must own I was a little chagrin'd at your seeming so unconcern'd at such an affair as this, (which had nearly prov'd our ruin) by your innuendoes and ironical talk of accomplish'd Generals, Roman Consuls and triumphs.

Lord Boston
My mentioning accomplish'd Generals, surely, Sir, was rather a compliment to you.

Elbow Room
When irony pass current for compliments, and we take it so, I shall have no objection to it.

Mr. Caper
The affair of Lexington, My Lord Boston, at which you were so much affrighted (if I am rightly inform'd) was because you then stood on your own bottom, this of Bunker's Hill you seem secretely to rejoice at, only because you have three accomplish'd and experienc'd Generals to share the disgrace with you, besides the brave Admiral Tombstone —you talk of dancing and fiddling, and yet you do neither, as I see.

Lord Boston
And pray, Sir, what did you do with the commission, the post, the Duke of Grafton gave you, in lieu of your losses at Preston election, and the expences of your trial at the king's bench for a riot, which had emptied your pockets?— Why you sold it—you sold it, Sir—to raise cash to gamble with.—

Admiral Tombstone
Damn it, don't let us kick up a dust among ourselves, to be laugh'd at fore and aft—this is a hell of a council of war—though I believe it will turn out one before we've done—a scolding and quarrelling like a parcel of damn'd butter whores—I never heard two whores yet scold and quarrel, but they got to fighting at last.

Clinton
Pray, Gentlemen, drop this discourse, consider the honour of England is at stake, and our own safety depends upon this day's consultation.

Lord Boston
'Tis not for argument sake—but the dignity of my station requires others should give up first.

Elbow Room
Sir, I have done, lest you should also accuse me of obstructing the proceedings of the council of war.

Mr. Caper
For the same reason I drop it now.

Lord Boston
Well, Gentlemen, what are we met here for?

Admiral Tombstone
Who the devil shou'd know, if you don't?—damn it, didn't you send for us?

Lord Boston
Our late great loss of men has tore up the foundation of our plan, and render'd all further attempts impracticable—'twill be a long time ere we can expect any more reinforcements—and if they should arrive, I'm doubtful of their success.

Clinton
The provincials are vastly strong, and seem no novices in the art of war; 'tis true we gain'd the hill at last, but of what advantage is it to us—none—the loss of 1400 as brave men as Britain can boast of, is a melancholy consideration, and must make our most sanguinary friends in England abate of their vigour.

Elbow Room
I never saw or read of any battle equal to it—never was more martial courage display'd, and the provincials, to do the dogs justice, fought like heroes, fought indeed more like devils than men; such carnage and destruction not exceeded by °-Blenheim, Minden, Fontenoy, Ramillies, Dettingen, the battle of the Boyne, and the late affair of the Spaniards and Algerines-°—a mere cock-fight to it—no laurels there.

Mr. Caper
No, nor triumphs neither—I regret in particular the number of brave Officers that fell that day, many of whom were of the first families in England.

Admiral Tombstone
Aye, a damn'd affair indeed—many powder'd beaus—ᵖ-petit maitres—fops—fribbles—skip jacks—macaronies—jack puddings-ᵖ—noblemen's bastards and whores sons fell that day—and my poor marines stood no more chance with 'em than a cat in hell without claws.

---

o-o
Blenheim . . . Algerines These are all English battles, from the Battle of the Boyne in 1690 (the defeat of James II by William III) to the attack of Charles III of Spain against Algiers in 1775. As the playwright notes, these engagements were violent affairs, which anticipated a change from "gentlemanly" warfare to that in which no holds were barred.

p-p
petit maitres . . . jack puddings These are all denigrative terms for insignificant and affected persons: fribbles are triflers, skip jacks are conceited fops, macaronies were effete young gentlemen who wore elaborate hair dress in the Venetian style, jack puddings were scorned as mountebanks or clowns. The passage is obviously a castigation of the minor officers in the British army. It generally bore some truth, however, because many of the subalterns were unseasoned in warfare, particularly the rugged and ungentlemanly kind they encountered in America.

Lord Boston
It can't be help'd, Admiral; what is to be done next?

Admiral Tombstone
Done?—why, what the devil have you done?—nothing yet, but eat Paramount's beef, and steal a few Yankee sheep—and that, it seems, is now become a damn'd lousy, beggarly trade too, for you haven't left yourselves a mouthful to eat.
(Aside:) "Bold at the council board, But cautious in the field, he shunn'd the sword."

Lord Boston
But what can we do, Admiral?

Admiral Tombstone
Do? why suck your paws—that's all you're like to get. *(Aside:)* But avast, I must ᑫ·bowse taught there,ᑫ or we shall get to logger heads soon, we're such damn'd fighting fellows.

Lord Boston
We must act on the defensive this winter, 'till reinforcements arrive.

Admiral Tombstone
Defensive? aye, aye—if we can defend our bellies from hunger, and prevent a mutiny and civil war among the small guts there this winter, we shall make a glorious campaign of it indeed—it will read well in the American Chronicles.

Lord Boston
I expect to be recalled this winter, when I shall lay the case before Lord Paramount, and let him know your deplorable situation.

Admiral Tombstone
Aye, do—and lay it behind him too; you've got the weather-gage of us this tack,ʳ mess-mate; but I wish you a good voyage for all—and don't forget to tell him, the poor worms are starving too, having nothing to eat, but half starv'd dead soldiers and the ships bottoms. *(Aside.)* A cunning old fox, he's gnaw'd his way handsomely out of Boston cage—but he'll never be a WOLF,ˢ for all that.

Mr. Caper
I shall desire to be recalled too—I've not been us'd to such fare—and not the least diversion of entertainment of any sort going forward here—I neither can nor will put up with it.

Admiral Tombstone
I think we're all a parcel of damn'd boobies for coming three thousand miles upon a wild goose chase—to perish

---

ᑫ⁻ᑫ *bowse taught there* Nautical term meaning to haul hard; he must restrain himself from speaking too candidly or the argument will become more heated.

ʳ *weather-gage of us this tack* "A ship was said to have the weather-gage, or 'the advantage of the wind,' when she could steer straight for an opponent while the latter would have to tack against the wind." (Boatner, p. 1177.)

ˢ *WOLF* General James Wolfe, the hero of the capture of Quebec from the French, September 13, 1759, who died at the moment of his victory on the Plains of Abraham.

with cold—starve with hunger—get our brains knock'd out, or be hang'd for sheep-stealing and robbing hen-roosts.

Lord Boston
I think, Admiral, you're always grumbling—never satisfied.

Admiral Tombstone
Satisfied? I see no appearance of it—we have been here these twelve hours, scolding upon empty stomachs—you may call it a council of war, (and so it is indeed,—a war with the guts) or what you will—but I call it council of famine.

Lord Boston
As it's so late, Gentlemen, we'll adjourn the council of war 'till to-morrow at nine o'clock—I hope you'll all attend, and come to a conclusion.

Admiral Tombstone
And I hope you'll then conclude to favour us with one of them fine turkeys you're keeping for your sea store, *(Aside: or that fine, fat, black pig you or some of your guards stole out of the poor Negro's pen)* as it's near Christmas, and you're going to make your exit—you know the old custom among the sailors—pave your way first—let us have one good dinner before we part, and leave us half a dozen pipes of Mr. Hancock's wine[t] to drink your health, and a good voyage, and don't let us part with dry lips.

Such foolish councils, with no wisdom fraught,
Must end in wordy words, and come to nought;
Just like St. James's, where they bluster, scold,
They nothing know—yet they despise being told.

[*Exeunt.*]

---

[t] *pipes . . . wine* John Hancock's house was one of the most impressive in Boston and his wine cellar was of the best. His mansion was countermanded by the chief British officers. After the evacuation of Boston it was discovered that Hancock's residence suffered little damage, the elaborate furnishings and most of the wine remained secure. Abigail Adams writing to John Adams, March 31, 1776, referring to Hancock by his title of President of the Continental Congress, says, "The Mansion House of your President is safe and the furniture unhurt whilst both the House and Furniture of the Solisiter [sic] General [Samuel Quincy] have fallen a prey to their own merciless party." (*Adams Family Correspondence*, I, p. 369.) The British disregard of American private property and the misuse of it during the occupation of Boston added still another indictment.

ACT V

Scene 1

At Montreal

[*General Prescot, Officer.*]

General Prescot
So it seems indeed, one misfortune seldom comes alone—The rebels, after the taking of Ticonderoga and Chamblee, as I just now learn by a Savage, marched immediately to besiege St. John's, and are now before that place, closely investing it, and no doubt intend paying us a visit soon.

Officer
Say you so? then 'tis time to look about us.

General Prescot
They'll find us prepar'd, I'll warrant 'em, to give 'em such a reception as they little dream of—a parcel of Yankee dogs.

Officer
Their success, no doubt, has elated them, and given 'em hopes of conquering all Canada soon, if that's their intent.

General Prescot
No doubt it is—but I'll check their career a little.—

[*Enter Scouting Officer, with Colonel Allen, and other Prisoners.*]

Scouting Officer
Sir, I make bold to present you with a few prisoners—they are a scouting detachment from the army besieging St. John's.

General Prescot
Prisoners? Rebels, I suppose, and scarcely worth hanging.

Colonel Allen
Sir, you suppose wrong—you mean scarcely worth your while to attempt.

General Prescot
Pray who are you, Sir?

Colonel Allen
A man, Sir, and who had the honour, 'till now, to command those brave men, whom you call rebels.

General Prescot
What is your name? if I may be so bold?

Colonel Allen
Allen.

General Prescot
Allen?

Colonel Allen
Yes, Allen.

General Prescot
Are you that Allen, that Colonel Allen (as they call him) that dar'd to take Ticonderoga?

Colonel Allen
The same—the very man.

General Prescot
Then rebels you are, and as such I shall treat you, for daring to oppose Lord Paramount's troops, and the laws of the land.

Colonel Allen
Prisoners we are, 'tis true—but we despise the name of a rebel—With more propriety that name is applicable to your master—'tis he who attempts to destroy the laws of the land, not us—we mean to support them, and defend our property against Paramount's and parliamentary tyranny.

General Prescot
To answer you, were a poorness of spirit I despise; when Rebels dare accuse, power that replies, forgets to punish; I am not to argue that point with you: And let me tell you, Sir, whoever you are, it now ill becomes you thus to talk—You're my prisoner—your life is in my hands, and you shall suffer immediately—Guards! take them away.

Colonel Allen
Cruel insult!—pardon these brave men!—what they have done has been by my orders—I am the only guilty person (if guilt there be) let me alone suffer for them all (opening his breast) Here! take your revenge—Why do you hesitate?—Will you not strike a breast that ne'er will flinch from your pointed bayonet?

General Prescot
Provoke me not—Remember you're my prisoners.

Colonel Allen
Our souls are free!—Strike, cowards, strike!—I scorn to beg my life.

General Prescot
Guards! away with them—I'll reserve you for a more ignominious death—your fate is fix'd—away with them.

Colonel Allen
(*Going off.*) Be glutted, ye thirsters after human blood—Come, see me suffer—mark my eye, and scorn me, if my expiring soul confesses fear—Come, see and be taught virtue, and to die as a patriot for the wrongs of my country.

[*Exeunt prisoners and guards.*]

Scene 2

A dungeon.

Colonel Allen
What! ye infernal monsters! murder us in the dark?—What place is this?—Who reigns king of these gloomy mansions?—You might favour us at least with one spark of light—Ye cannot see to do your business here.

Officer
'Tis our orders.

Colonel Allen
Ye dear, ye brave wretched friends!—now wou'd I die for ye all—ye share a death I wou'd gladly excuse you from—'Tis not death I fear—this is only bodily death—but to die noteless in the silent dark, is to die scorn'd, and shame our suff'ring country—we fall undignify'd by villains hands—a sacrifice to Britain's outcast blood-hounds—This, this shakes the soul! Come then, ye murderers, since it must be so—do your business speedily—Farewell, my friends! to die with you is now my noblest claim, since to die for you was a choice deny'd—What are ye about?—Stand off, ye wretches!

Officer
I am order'd to lay you in irons (*they seize him*) you must submit.

Colonel Allen
What, do you mean to torture us to death with chains, racks and gibbets? rather despatch us immediately—Ye executioners, ye inquisitors, does this cruelty proceed from the lenity I shewed to the prisoners I took?—Did it offend you that I treated them with friendship, generosity, honour and humanity?—If it did, our suff'rings will redound more to our honour, and our fall be the more glorious—But remember, this fall will prove your own one day.—Wretches! I fear you not, do your worst; and while I here lay suff'ring and chain'd on my back to the damp floor, I'll yet pray for your conversion.

Officer
Excuse us, we have only obey'd orders.

Colonel Allen
Then I forgive you; but pray execute them.

> *Oh! my lost friends! 'tis liberty, not breath,*
> *Gives the brave life. Shun slav'ry more than death.*
> *He who spurns fear, and dares disdain to be,*
> *Mocks chains and wrongs—and is forever free;*
> *While the base coward, never safe, tho' low,*
> *Creeps but to suff'rings, and lives on for woe!*

[*Exeunt guards.*]

Scene 3

In the camp of Cambridge.

[*George Washington, General Lee, General Putnam.*]

General Washington
Our accounts from the Northward, so far, are very favourable; Ticonderoga, Chamblee, St. John's and Montreal our troops are already in possession of—Colonel Arnold,[a] having penetrated Canada, after suff'ring much thro' cold, fatigue and want of provisions, is now before Quebec, and General Montgomery, I understand, is in full march to join him; see these letters (*they read*).

General Lee
The brave, the intrepid Arnold, with his handful of fearless troops, have dar'd beyond the strength of mortals—Their courage smil'd at doubts, and resolutely march'd on, clamb'ring (to all but themselves) insurmountable precipices, whose tops, covered with ice and snow, lay hid in the clouds, and dragging baggage, provisions, ammunition and artillery along with them, by main strength, in the dead of winter, over such stupendous and amazing heights, seems almost incredible, unparallelled in history!—'Tis true, Hannibal's march over the Alps comes the nearest to it; it was a surprising undertaking, but when compar'd to this, appears but as a party of pleasure, an agreeable walk, a sabbath day's journey.

General Putnam
Posterity will stand amazed, and be astonish'd at the heroes of this new world, that the spirit of patriotism should blaze to such a height, and eclipse all others, should outbrave fatigue, danger, pain, peril, famine, and even death itself, to serve their country: that they should march, at this inclement season, thro' long and dreary deserts, thro' the remotest wilds, covered with swamps and standing lakes, beset with trees, bushes and briars, impervious to the cheering rays of the sun, where are no traces or vestiges of human footsteps, wild, untrodden paths, that strike terror into the fiercest of the brute creation.
   No bird of song to cheer the gloomy desert!
   No animals of gentle love's enliven!

General Lee
Let Britons do the like—no—they dare not attempt it—let 'em forth the Hanoverian, the Hessian, the hardy Russian, or, if they will, the wild Cossacks and Kalmucks of Tartary, and they would tremble at the thought! And who but Americans dare undertake it? The wond'ring moon and stars stood aloof, and turn'd pale at the sight!

General Washington
I rejoice to hear the Canadians received them kindly, after

---

[a] *Colonel Arnold* The respect for Arnold in the early days of the war seems ironic when one recalls his subsequent betrayal of the American cause. He was intrepid and he was brave; he became disaffected later when his ambitions were frustrated, and he felt that he was not respected by the Congress and by Washington. Furthermore, he was abetted by his wife, the former Peggy Shippen, who fancied power and glory as the wife of a British officer.

their fatigue furnish'd them with the necessaries of life, and otherwise treated them very humanely—And the savages, whose hair stood on end, and look'd and listen'd with horror and astonishment at the relation of the fatigues and perils they underwent, commiserated with them, and afforded all the succour in their power.

General Lee
The friendship of the Canadians and savages, or even their neutrality alone, are favourable circumstances that cannot fail to hearten our men; and the junction of General Montgomery will inspire 'em with fresh ardour.

General Putnam
Heavens prosper 'em!

[*Enter Officer and Express.*]

Officer
Sir, here's an express.

Express
I have letters to your Excellency.

General Washington
From whence?

Express
From Canada, Sir.

General Washington
From the army?

Express
From the head-quarters, Sir.

General Washington
I hope matters go well there.—Had General Montgomery join'd Colonel Arnold when you left it?

Express
He had, Sir—these letters are from both those gentlemen. (*gives him the letters.*)

General Washington
Very well. You may now withdraw and refresh yourself, unless you've further to say—I'll dispatch you shortly.

Express
Nothing further, Sir.

[*Exeunt Officer and Express.*]

Scene 4

General Washington
(*Opens and reads the letters to General Lee and Putnam.*)
I am well pleased with their contents—all but the behavior of the haughty Carleton[b]—to fire upon a flag of truce, hitherto unprecedented, even amongst Savages or Algerines—his cruelty to the prisoners is cowardly, and personal ill treatment of General Montgomery is unbecoming a General—a soldier—and beneath a Gentleman—and leaves an indelible mark of brutality—I hope General Montgomery, however, will not follow his example.

General Lee
I hope so too, Sir—if it can be avoided; it's a disgrace to the soldier, and a scandal to the Gentleman—so long as I've been a soldier, my experience has not furnish'd me with a like instance.

General Putnam
I see no reason why he shouldn't be paid in his own coin.—If a man bruises my heel, I'll break his head—I cannot see the reason or propriety of bearing with their insults—does he not know it's in our power to retaliate fourfold?

General Lee
Let's be good natur'd, General—let us see a little more of it first—

General Putnam
I think we have seen enough of it already for this twelve-months past. Methinks the behaviour of Lord Boston, the ill treatment of poor Allen, to be thrown into a loathsome dungeon like a murderer, be loaded with irons, and transported like a convict, would sufficiently rouse us to a just retaliation—that imperious red coat, Carleton, should be taught good manners—I hope to see him ere long in our College at Cambridge—

General Lee
I doubt; he'll be too cunning, and play truant—he had no notion of learning American manners; ev'ry dog must have his day (as the saying is); it may be our time by and by—the event of war is uncertain—

General Putnam
Very true, Sir; but don't let us be laugh'd at forever.

[*Enters an Officer in haste.*]

Officer
Sir, a messenger this moment from Quebec, waits to be admitted.

General Washington
Let him enter. (*Exit Officer.*)

[*Enters Messenger.*]

---

[b] *Carleton* Montgomery and Arnold were the American commanders who attempted an assault against Quebec and its British defender, Carleton. The disastrous attack in which Montgomery was killed occurred on December 31, 1775, and January 1, 1776. Prior to the engagement Montgomery endeavored to send Carleton an order to surrender. The bearer of the flag of truce was fired upon. Subsequently a letter from Montgomery did reach Carleton, but the demand for capitulation was ignored. (For discussion of Carleton's ambivalent character and the use made of it by American propagandists, *see* the introduction to *The Death of General Montgomery*.)

General Washington
What news bring you?

Messenger
I am sorry, Sir, to be the bearer of an unpleasing tale—

General Washington
Bad news have you?—have you letters?

Messenger
None, Sir—I came off at a moment's warning—my message is verbal.

General Washington
Then relate what you know.

Messenger
After the arrival and junction of General Montgomery's troops with Colonel Arnold's, Carleton was summoned to surrender; he disdaining any answer, fir'd on the flag of truce—

General Washington
That we have heard—go on.

Messenger
The General finding no breach could be effected in any reasonable time, their walls being vastly strong, and his cannon rather light, determined to attempt it by storm—The enemy were apprized of it—however he passed the first barrier, and was attempting the second, where he was unfortunately killed, with several other brave Officers—

General Washington
Is General Montgomery killed?

Messenger
He is certainly, Sir.

General Washington
I am sorry for it—a brave man—I could wish him a better fate!—

General Lee
I lament the loss of him—a resolute soldier—

General Putnam
Pity such bravery should prove unsuccessful, such merit unrewarded;—but the irreversible decree of Providence!—who can gainsay?—we may lament the loss of a friend, but 'tis irreligious to murmur at pre-ordination. What happ'ned afterwards?

Messenger
The Officer next in command, finding their attacks at that time unsuccessful, retired in good order.

General Washington
What became of Colonel Arnold?

Messenger
Colonel Arnold, at the head of about three hundred and fifty brave troops, and Captain Lamb's company of artillery, having in the mean time passed through St. Roques, attacked a battery, and carried it, tho' well defended, with the loss of some men—

General Putnam
I hope they proved more successful.

General Lee
Aye, let us hear.

Messenger
The Colonel about this time received a wound in his leg, and was obliged to crawl as well as he cou'd to the hospital, thro' the fire of the enemy, and within fifty yards of the walls, but, thro' Providence, escap'd any further damage.—

General Putnam
Aye, providential indeed!

General Washington
Is he dangerously wounded?

Messenger
I am told not, Sir.

General Washington
I am glad of it.—What follow'd?

Messenger
His brave troops pushed on to the second barrier, and took possession of it.

General Washington
Very good—proceed.

Messenger
A party of the enemy then sallying out from the palace-gate, attacked them in the rear, whom they fought with incredible bravery for three hours, and deeds of eternal fame were done; but being surrounded on all sides, and overpowered by numbers, were at last obliged to submit themselves as prisoners of war.

General Putnam
Heav'ns! could any thing prove more unlucky? such brave fellows deserve better treatment than they'll get (I'm afraid) from the inhuman Carleton.

General Lee
Such is the fortune of war, and the vicissitudes attending a military life; to-day conquerors, to-morrow prisoners.

General Washington
He dares not treat them ill—only as prisoners. Did you learn how those brave fellows were treated?

Messenger
It was currently reported in the camp they were treated very humanely.[29]

General Washington
A change for the better.

General Putnam
Produc'd by fear, no doubt from General Montgomery's letter—but no matter from what cause.

General Lee
How far did the remainder of the army retire?

Messenger
About two miles from the city, where they are posted very advantageously, continuing the blockade, and waiting for reinforcements.

General Lee
Did the enemy show any peculiar marks of distinction to the corpse of General Montgomery?

Messenger
He was interred in Quebec, with ev'ry possible mark of distinction.

General Washington
What day did the affair happen on?

Messenger
On the last day of the year.

General Washington
A remarkable day! When was the General interred?

Messenger
The second of January.

General Lee
What number of men in the whole attack was killed? did you learn?

Messenger
About sixty killed and wounded.

General Washington
Have you any thing further to communicate?

Messenger
Nothing, Sir, but to inform you they are all in good spirits, and desire reinforcements and heavy artillery may be sent them as soon as possible.

General Washington
That be our business—with all dispatch. You may for the present withdraw. Sargeant!

   [*Enter Sargeant.*]

Sargeant
I wait your orders, Sir.

General Washington
See that the Messenger and his horse want for nothing.

Sargeant
I shall, Sir. (*Exeunt Sargeant and Messenger.*)

Scene 5

General Washington
I'll dispatch an express to the Congress. This repulse, if I mistake not, (or victory, as Carleton may call it) will stand 'em but in little stead—'twill be only a temporary reprieve—we'll reinforce our friends, let the consequences be what it may—Quebec must fall, and the lofty strong walls and brazen gates (the shield of cowards) must tumble by an artificial earthquake; should they continue in their obstinacy, we'll arm our friends with missive thunders in their hands, and stream death on them swifter than the winds.

General Lee
I lament the loss of the valiant Montgomery and his brave officers and soldiers (at this time more especially) 'tis the fortune of war, 'tis unavoidable; yet, I doubt not, out of their ashes will arise new heroes.

General Putnam
Who can die a more glorious, a more honourable death than in their country's cause?—let it redouble our ardour, and kindle a noble emulation in our breasts—let each American be determined to conquer or die in a righteous cause.

General Washington
I have drawn my sword, and never will I sheathe it, 'till America is free, or I'm no more.

General Lee
Peace is despaired of, and who can think of submission? The last petition from the Congress, like the former, has been disregarded; they prayed but for liberty, peace and safety, and their omnipotent authoritative supremeships will grant them neither: War, then, war open and understood, must be resolved on; this, this will humble their pride, will bring their tyrant noses to the ground, teach 'em humility, and force them to hearken to reason when 'tis too late. My noble General, I join you (*drawing his sword*) I'll away with the scabbard, and sheathe my sword in the bosom of tyranny.

General Putnam
Have you not read the speech, where frowning revenge and sounds of awful dread for disgrace at Lexington and loss

at Bunker's-hill echo forth? Not smiling peace, or pity, tame his sullen soul; but, Pharaoh-like, on the wings of tyranny he rides and forfeits happiness to feast revenge, 'till the waters of the red sea of blood deluge the tyrant, with his mixed host of vile cut-throats, murderers, and bloody butchers.

General Washington
Yet, finding they cannot conquer us, gladly would they make it up by a voluntary free will offering of a million of money in bribes, rather than be obliged to relish the thoughts of sacrificing their cursed, pride and false honour, they're sending over to amuse us (to put us off our guard) a score or two of commissioners, with sham negotiations in great state, to endeavour to effect, by bribery, deception, and chicanery, what they cannot accomplish by force. Perish such wretches!—detested be their schemes!—Perish such monsters!—a reproach to human understanding—their vaunted boasts and threats will vanish like smoke, and be no more than like snow falling on the moist ground, melt in silence, and waste away—Blasted, forever blasted be the hand of the villainous traitor that receives their gold upon such terms—may he become leprous, like ᶜ·Naaman, the Syrian, yea, rather like Gehazi, the servant of Elisha,·ᶜ that it may stick to him forever.

General Putnam
I join you both, and swear by all the heroes of New-England, that this arm, tho' fourscore and four *(drawing his sword)* still nervous and strong, shall wield this sword to the last in the support of liberty and my country, revenge the insult offer'd to the immortal Montgomery, and brutal treatment of the brave Allen.
   Oh, liberty! thou sun-shine of the heart!
   Thou smile of nature, and thou soul of art!
   Without thy aid no human hope cou'd grow,
   And all we cou'd enjoy were turn'd to woe.

[*Exeunt.*]

ᶜ·ᶜ *Naaman . . . Elisha* Naaman, the Syrian, was cured of his leprosy by Elisha. Elisha's servant, Gehazi, by trickery, received money and clothes from Naaman, whereupon Elisha, in great anger, declared, "The leprosy therefore of Naaman shall cleave unto thee, and unto thy seed forever." II Kings 5.

The Epilogue

Spoken by Mr. Freeman.

Since tyrants reign, and lust and lux'ry rule;
Since kings turn Nero's—statesmen play the fool;
Since parli'ment in cursed league combine,
To sport with rights that's sacred and divine;
Destroying towns with direful conflagration,
And murder subjects without provocation!
These are but part of evils we could name,
Not to their glory, but eternal shame.
Petitions—waste paper—great Pharoah cries,
Nor care a rush for your remonstrances.
Each Jacobite, and ev'ry pimping Tory,
Waits for your wealth, to raise his future glory:
Or pensions sure, must ev'ry rascal have,
Who strove his might, to make FREEMAN a slave,
Since this the case, to whom for succour cry?
To God, our swords, and sons of liberty!
Cast off the idol god!—kings are but vain!
Let justice rule, and independence reign.
Are ye not men? Pray who made men, but God?
Yet men make kings—to tremble at their nod!
What nonsense this—let's wrong with right oppose,
Since nought will do, but sound, impartial blows.
Let's act in earnest, not with vain pretense,
Adopt the language of sound COMMON SENSE,
and with one voice proclaim INDEPENDENCE.
Convince your foes you will defend your right,
That blows and knocks is all they will get by't.
Let tyrants see that you are well prepar'd,
By proclamations, sword, nor speeches scar'd;
That liberty freeborn breathe in each soul!
One god-like union animate the whole!

END of the FIRST CAMPAIGN.

****
THE BLOCKHEADS:
OR
THE AFFRIGHTED OFFICERS
****

Introduction to *The Blockheads*

WRITTEN after the evacuation of the city by English forces under General William Howe, *The Blockheads; or, The Affrighted Officers* is an indictment of the British and the Loyalists in Boston. The play celebrates an American triumph in logistics on March 2, 1776: the fortification in record time of Dorchester Heights overlooking Boston, thus weakening Boston's defenses for the besieging colonial forces. As a result the only recourse left to Howe was to remove his troops, as well as frantic Loyalists, from the city. On March 17, 1776, Howe boarded ship and sailed to the haven of Halifax. The apparently sudden decision and its effect upon the citizens who were loyal to the English cause are vividly presented by a playwright who also attacks the overweening British and the deluded colonists who still believed in the ultimate success of the forces of the empire. There is in *The Blockheads* a strong desire on the part of the playwright to persuade the citizens of Boston who still had doubts about an American victory that the English would abandon whenever expedient any who were faithful to them. In the point and counterpoint of the British and Loyalist scenes in *The Blockheads* it is made evident that the former were exploiting the latter and the "King's friends" in America were becoming disenchanted with their loyalty. In this respect *The Blockheads* is a clever example of one phase of propaganda: to influence wavering colonists to recognize the perfidy of Albion and join the patriot cause.

The Blockheads; or, The Affrighted Officers[1] was printed as a pamphlet play in 1776. Although no author is indicated, for reasons not entirely clear Paul Leicester Ford ascribes the play to Mercy Otis Warren.[2] It is difficult without definite evidence to assert that Mrs. Warren wrote *The Blockheads*, but there are substantive and circumstantial considerations that lead to that possibility.

The Blockheads was a riposte to *The Blockade of Boston*, a satire against the Americans generally believed to have been written by General John Burgoyne, although no copy of this effort has survived. Mrs. Warren's anger at the desecration of Boston during the siege and her well-known hatred of Burgoyne might very well have motivated her to write *The Blockheads*. The historical facts give some credence to this postulate.

Clinton, Howe, and Burgoyne had arrived at Boston on May 25, 1775, assured before they left England that their duties would be superficial, mostly military "show." Within three weeks' time they encountered the Battle of Bunker's Hill and the siege of Boston. After the Battle of Bunker's Hill on June 17, 1775, Boston was blockaded by the Americans; Washington and the Continental Army and various militias lay at Cambridge. British egress from the city was cut off except by sea. Through the latter part of 1775 and the early part of 1776 the situation worsened in the town; food and fuel were in short supply, the weather was severe, and the lack of activity, except for occasional skirmishes with the colonials, made the English hungry, restless, uneasy, and very short of temper,[3] a situation reflected in *The Blockheads*.

In spite of all the difficulties, however, the colorful Burgoyne made the best of a bad case. He had a love for all pleasures and particularly enjoyed writing for the theatre, and he was no novice, having established a reputation for witty comedies in London where his play *The Maid of the Oaks* had been produced by Garrick at Drury Lane in 1774. While in Boston, Burgoyne continued his dramatic activity, writing a new prologue to *Zara* by Aaron Hill. The prologue was proclaimed when the play was produced late in 1775; Burgoyne's verse made a direct appeal to the Loyalists, who were obviously being encouraged, if not actually commanded, to support a cause that would eventually triumph.

Burgoyne returned to England in November, 1775. Before quitting America he may have written *The Blockade of Boston* or, at least, left behind the general idea of the satirical skit (it was probably a short afterpiece) with the officer-actors remaining in Boston. They continued their theatrical entertainments — part of the social round that also included elaborate balls and card parties given while the common soldiers and many Loyalists as well as colonists suffered.[4]

A notice in the *New England Chronicle* of December 21, 1775, almost a month after Burgoyne's departure, states:

We are informed that there is now getting up at the theatre, and will be performed in the course of a fortnight a new farce called The Blockade of Boston. [*It is more probable before that time the poor wretches will be presented with a tragedy called the Bombardment of Boston.*][5]

Whether it actually was Burgoyne who wrote the piece, he was generally supposed to be the author, and the prologue to *The Blockheads* contains the line "Their gen'ral turn'd the blockade to a play" — an assumption based on his association with the officer-actors and the fact that he was a well-known playwright.

PREPARATIONS for the farce were completed, and the play was ready on the night of January 8, 1776. Various accounts of what happened, some of the details plainly apocryphal, have appeared. *The Busybody* by Susannah Centlivre had been given, and *The Blockade* was about to be performed as an afterpiece. According to one report, a character "designed to burlesque Washington" entered in "an uncouth gait, with a large wig, a long rusty sword, attended by a country servant with a rusty gun. At that moment a sergeant suddenly appeared and exclaimed, 'The Yankees are attacking our works on Bunker's Hill!' "⁶ The audience at first assumed that the alarm was part of the play but soon realized it was authentic. Great confusion resulted: "The officers jumping over the orchestra, breaking the fiddles on the way; the actors rushing about to get rid of their paint and disguises, the ladies alternately fainting and screaming; and the play brought to great grief and summary conclusion."⁷ A Rowlandson cartoon indeed! What had actually occurred was that the patriots under Major Knowlton had attacked the few remaining houses in Charlestown, occupied by the British after Bunker's Hill, and the resultant alarm led to the panic both inside and outside the theatre.

The Blockade may have been presented again several times, for it was announced in the *Boston News-Letter* that as soon as the officers who had been called to Charlestown were replaced, the piece would be given as a double bill with *Tamerlane*.⁸ *The Blockade of Boston* and Burgoyne thus became the laughingstock of the patriots, fitting objects for the mockery of respectable citizens, among them Mercy Otis Warren. She also was aroused to a fever pitch of indignation by the intolerable punitive occupation of Boston. The scorn she used in her known pamphlet plays and in her letters is comparable to similar emotions in *The Blockheads*. Furthermore, her violent antagonism toward Burgoyne, to her the symbol of the arrogance and cruelty of the British officers, could have led her to condemn the English military hierarchy in America.

Mrs. Warren's opinion of Burgoyne was expressed in a letter written on July 17, 1775, to her friend Abigail Adams, who a week later wrote to her husband paraphrasing Mrs. Warren's remarks on the English general.

As to Burgoyne I am not Master of Language sufficient to give you a true Idea of the Horrible wickedness of the Man. His designs are dark, his Dissimulation of the deepest die, for not content with deceiving Mankind he practices deceit on God himself, by Assuming the Appearance (like Hutchinson) of great attention to Religious Worship when every action of his life is totally abhorant to all Ideas of true Religion, Virtue or common Honesty. An Abandoned Infamous Gambler of Broken fortune and the worst Most detestable of the Bedford Gang who are wholly bent on Blood, tyrany and Spoil, and therefore the darling Favorite of our unrivalled Ruler Lord Bute.⁹

Another piece of evidence relating to the authorship of the play lies in the political involvement of Mrs. Warren in the Revolution. She was the wife of James Warren of Plymouth, Massachusetts, an avid patriot, and the sister of James Otis, one of the most perceptive, even though considered to be somewhat erratic, of the early protesters against the English. With Samuel Adams, he became a resolute defier of the ministerial party at home and abroad as well as a violent agitator against the king. Both he and Samuel Adams were able propagandists. The Warrens' home in Plymouth became a center for the planning of strategy against the royal government, and it was there that Mercy Warren not only listened to conversations and knew of the secret plans for a change in the relation of the colonies to the mother country but also contributed her share to the councils of war. Mercy Warren engaged in voluminous correspondence with leading patriots of her day, particularly Abigail and John Adams. She also wrote many poetical satires in the tradition of Dryden and Pope.

On September 5, 1769, however, a personal tragedy occurred which probably affected her subsequent writing. On the evening of that day, as a result of a quarrel of long bitterness James Otis was brutally assaulted in a coffee house by John Robinson, a commissioner of customs, and his friends. Otis, a man of promise and brilliance, was so severely beaten that he was forced to retire from active life, except for rare public appearances, and he never completely recovered his reason. Because of the injury to her brother, Mercy Warren apparently moved from a general condemnation of the British to a more personal one against those she could no longer recognize as partners in a ministerial-colonial contract but as enemies of a nation.

One of the results of such a change was *The Adulateur,* a play in which she attacked the villain of the colony of Massachusetts Bay, Thomas Hutchinson, the native-born royal governor. The first half of *The Adulateur* appeared in *The Massachusetts Spy* in March, 1772, and the second part a month later. It was published anonymously, but in achieving popular success it acquired not only imitators but also an immediate collaborator. "A memorandum in Mercy's handwriting in the Massachusetts Historical Society reads: 'Before the author thought proper to present another scene to the public, it was taken up and interlaced with productions of an unknown hand. The plagiary swells *The Adulateur* to a considerable pamphlet.'" [10] The initial theme of Mrs. Warren's play was an unmasking of Hutchinson; the additional material turned her work into a protest against the Boston Massacre of 1770.

On May 24 and on July 19, 1773, a year after *The Adulateur* was published, a play entitled *The Defeat* appeared in *The Boston Gazette.* Once again Rapatio, the sobriquet given to Hutchinson in *The Adulateur,* appears as the chief villain. The style of *The Defeat* is much the same as that of the earlier play, and the theme is concerned with rapacious tryanny as opposed to struggling patriotism, ready for martyrdom, if necessary, to ensure freedom. Rapatio-Hutchinson became so well known as the corrupter of Massachusetts that Abigail Adams, in a letter to Mercy Warren on December 5, 1773, could refer to the "Dark designs of a Rapatio Soul." [11]

A second villain was Hazelrod (Peter Oliver), Lord Chief Justice of Massachusetts Bay Colony. He appears as an aide and supporter of Rapatio in *The Adulateur,* and both men are encouraged by Limpit (Andrew Oliver, brother to Peter and married to Hutchinson's sister-in-law), who is a character in both *The Adulateur* and *The Defeat.* The name Hazelrod also became well known and was used as another term of opprobrium in correspondence among the patriots. John Adams, for example, mentions "the strains of Hazelrod" in a letter to James Warren in April, 1774.[12]

Mercy Warren's most-well-known play, one that she eventually acknowledged as her own, was *The Group,* published in Jamaica, Philadelphia, and Boston in 1775. There is again stylistic similarity to *The Adulateur* and *The Defeat,* and some of the same names are used for the leading characters. In fact one might consider that the three pamphlet plays constitute a trilogy. The "group" includes the leading Tories in Boston, among them Hazelrod (Peter Oliver), Judge Meagre (Foster Hutchinson, brother of Thomas Hutchinson), Brigadier Hateall (Timothy Ruggles, who appears in *The Blockheads* as Surly), Hector Mushroom (Colonel Murray, who is Bonny in *The Blockheads*), Scriblerious Fribble (Harrison Grey, who is Meagre in

The Blockheads), and Dupe (Thomas Flucker). Incidentally, both in *The Defeat* and in *The Group* the character who can be hired to write for any cause ("Crito, a Scribbler" in the former and "Scriblerius" in the latter), is satirized as a hack who can veer with the political wind.

The nature of her recrimination in *The Group* is similar to that in *The Blockheads,* but the tone of the latter is more derisive and has a note of triumph because the wicked receive their punishment. *The Group* was a success in Philadelphia and Boston, and despite Mercy Warren's wish to have the name of the author unknown, certainly the intimate circle at Plymouth, Braintree, and Boston suspected or knew who the writer was. John Adams publicized the work (although without revealing the name of the playwright) and encouraged Mrs. Warren to continue her satirical writing.

Thus encouraged by Adams and further applauded by his Abigail,[13] Mrs. Warren certainly did not lay down her pen. She continued to write, but her modesty, reinforced by a fear of endangering her position as a "proper" female in society, made her overly cautious in declaring her authorship of subsequent satires. If she did not admit to the writing of *The Adulateur, The Defeat,* and *The Group* at the time they were written, it is not likely that she would have acknowledged any connection with *The Blockheads,* a more severe castigation than the other three pamphlet plays.

At this distance it is difficult to determine exactly what was written by Mrs. Warren and what are imitations by others — plagiarism and outright piracy were common enough in eighteenth-century literary circles. Eventually Mercy Warren would acknowledge *The Group* publicly, however, as well as publish a small volume of poems containing two romantic plays, *The Sack of Rome* and *The Ladies of Castile,* and write a three-volume history of the Revolution (which cast aspersions on John Adams and brought about a rift in their friendship).

Still another circumstantial link of evidence connecting Mrs. Warren with *The Blockheads* is possibly of importance. Benjamine Edes and John Gill were publishers of *The Boston Gazette,* which had "for a long time been the main organ of the popular party; and it was through its columns that Otis, the Adamses, Quincy, and Warren addressed the public."[14] The printing house of Edes and Gill was in Queen Street, Boston, and the imprint of *The Blockheads* indicates that the place of publication was Queen Street. Obviously the printers were interested in publishing in addition to a newspaper a variety of anti-British pamphlets by various writers, and one can assume that a new work by Mrs. Warren would have been immediately set in type and distributed, particularly because her former writings had seized the public imagination.

A stronger point of internal proof, indicating that Mrs. Warren wrote *The Blockheads,* lies in the fact that three persons scourged in *The Group* — Timothy Ruggles, Harrison Gray, and John Murray — are indicted afresh in *The Blockheads,* although under different character names.

The principal argument brought by scholars against Mrs. Warren's having written *The Blockheads* is that certain scenes are too vulgar for a woman of her sensibilities. Mrs. Warren had been reared among farming people; she knew the language of those who were beneath her in the social strata and, protected by her anonymity, perhaps she felt free to lapse into vulgarisms occasionally. Simple and his wife, for example, indulge in coarse allusions to natural functions, an attempt on the part of the playwright to give them a lower-class reality.

The identity of the author of *The Blockheads* will probably always remain a matter of conjecture. What is certain is that the play made a forceful case against the British and was printed and distributed by publishers known for their anti-British bias.

THE FIRST SCENE of *The Blockheads* opens with a picture of the British officers in Boston who through their own stupid blunders have been made victims of the siege of Boston. Although the characters are easily identifiable as enemy officers,[15] there is nothing to distinguish them one from another, particularly in this first scene. Emphasis underlines two points: a reiterative lament about lack of supplies, which means imminent starvation for both officers and the common soldier; and the need to prevent the Yankees from occupying Dorchester Heights, from which they could command the city and make its defense impossible.

The playwright reduces the proud British soldier from "the terror of the world" to a craven self-pitying wretch who shakes in his boots every time he goes outside the walls. His great fear lies in the power of American arms, particularly the rifles, and his early claims to superiority are mocked by jeering comments. The scene ends with the acknowledgment that the English are in dire straits for lack of food and the only thing they can do is attack the Heights, not only to dislodge the rebels and to protect themselves in Boston but, more importantly, to save their honor, such as it is. The next scene of the play reveals the playwright's scorn for another group, the Loyalists, immured with the English in Boston. As these miserable people bewail the fate that has reduced them to lackeys to the British, the playwright obviously takes pleasure in emphasizing their disillusionment and despair.

The greater part of Act II moves away from politics to social satire as criticism is leveled against the ordinary American who would ape the aristocratic class. Mrs. Simple, having arrived in the city after escaping with her husband and daughter from the country wishes at once to affect a new style but is opposed by her husband, who regrets his decision to seek protection in Boston, where he feels ill at ease among the grand folk.

By Act III, Scene 1, the worst has happened — Dorchester Heights has been fortified and Boston is an easy prey to the Americans. The consternation of the British when they discover the success of the rebels on the Heights is effectively dramatized, as is the bravery of the colonists.

Act III, Scene 2, returns to the subplot; the Loyalists have heard of the imminent retreat of the English and are near panic, realizing that they may have to leave their homes and escape with the government forces by sea. They must make haste to flee or they will be destroyed. The last scenes of the play depict a nightmare of a city gone mad with fear. The British are in retreat and even the regulars are bitterly mocking the authority that sent them on a fool's errand. Everything has become chaotic; the generals have been confined within the city, "writing and acting comedies," and the whole business is "INCOMPREHENSIBLE," says the soldier in the final scene of the play.

The Loyalists are in worse panic than the soldiers, and the description of the confusion in the city is filled with a kind of black humor. Whether the playwright was actually present at the scene or not, reports of the evacuation must have made gleeful stories throughout the colony. Mrs. Warren may have come to Boston soon after the British left; we know she was there one month after the city had been returned to the Americans. On April 17 she wrote to Abigail Adams stating she and Mrs. Washington had seen "the deserted Lines of the Enemy and the Ruins of Charleston, a Melancholy Sight, the last which Evinces the Barbarity of the Foe and leaves a deep impression of the Sufferings of that unhappy Town."[16] The epilogue reiterates the plight of the Loyalists in a scene in their miserable quarters in Halifax. Although the ex-patriots are full of regret for their adherence to Britain and are treated somewhat sympathetically, the underlying hostility of the playwright is obvious.

THE PARTICULAR historical interest of *The Blockheads* is obviously in its treatment of the Loyalists. Mercy Warren, as well as many of her compatriots, looked with undisguised contempt upon those who would not support the patriot cause. They were all about — the Tory ladies who drank the controversial tea, the Tory men who secretly applauded the success of British arms, the Anglican churchmen who saw God on the side of the anointed monarch, and even those common folk who had never questioned the validity or the benevolence of a patriarchal government three thousand miles away.

The Loyalists in the play are Gray, Ruggles, Brattle, and Edson. According to avowed patriots they had much to answer for, but they themselves feel no guilt in defending the rule of their fathers. In *The Blockheads*, however, their only motive for clinging to the past is of a materialistic nature, not idealistic. They are, nevertheless, completely disillusioned by the treatment they have received from the British; most of them had anticipated being welcomed as supporters of the government, rewarded by place and position because they had been faithful to the king, but the opposite occurred. They were treated as subordinates, almost as inferiors, not accepted by either the civil or the military authorities. There were exceptions, of course, but in general the plight of the Loyalist was a desperate one, and this condition, which might have been remedied by Britain early in the conflict, was in the long run one of the causes for the loss of the colonies.

There was always the hope in London that once the army moved into any area, the local Loyalists would inevitably rise in support of the military. Such a hope was gratified on several occasions, but for the most part the "inevitable" did not happen, largely because of the stupid treatment by the British of those who might have aided them. For example, men who volunteered to serve in the English army were formed into regiments of "provincials," regarded with condescension and generally treated with contempt.

The author of *The Blockheads* delineates the Loyalists with careful attention. The character Meagre is Harrison Gray, Receiver-General of Massachusetts and father of Elizabeth Gray Otis, who had married Samuel Allyne Otis, Mrs. Warren's brother. Gray maintained his Tory principles and attempted to dissuade others from becoming involved in the patriot cause; he was, in addition, a Mandamus Councillor.[17] In his work on the Loyalists, Lorenzo Sabine notes that "Mr. Gray was a timid man; and was accused of being on both sides in politics, according as he met Whig and Tory. In private life he was remarkably exemplary."[18] In 1776 Gray left Boston for Halifax in the general evacuation, and in June of that year he arrived in England and never returned to his native land. As he states in *The Blockheads*, he left behind him an estate and possessions (among which incidentally were a horse and chaise, indications of affluence).[19]

Timothy Ruggles (Surly) had opposed James Otis since the agitation over the Stamp Act in 1765. They became implacable enemies — a fact Mercy Warren would have known. Eventually Ruggles became a violent Tory, and in *The Blockheads* he is in despair because Hutchinson, on whom he depended, has fled to England, and the honors and profit which he had expected to gain have vanished with the royal governor. He has lent money to the government on British security, as did Gray, only to discover that such security was nonexistent. Ruggles, too, was a Mandamus Councillor, which as Sabine indicates, "increased his unpopularity to so great a degree that his house was attacked at night, and his cattle were maimed or poisoned."[20] So bitter did Ruggles become that he accepted an appointment by General Howe "to command three companies of volunteers, to be called the Loyal American Associators, but it is doubtful if Ruggles ever fought in the field against the American army."[21] Surly is used to voice the bitterness of the Loyalists against the British upon whom they depended for succor. In Act III, Scene 2, with the evacuation from Boston a reality, he is forced to accept the fact that the British troops are in disgrace and that retreat is the only possible course. Howe has announced that he will not attack Dorchester Heights because of the wild weather, but Surly believes, as did other Loyalists, that Howe used the storm as an excuse, being afraid to attack any high-ground fortifications, remembering the Pyrrhic victory at Bunker's Hill.

William Brattle (Brigadier Paunch), another Loyalist, was Brigadier General of the Massachusetts Militia. Sabine points out that he was a man of great talent, excelling as physician and lawyer and serving as clergyman as well as military man. He was known for his high living and his physical weight — hence his sobriquet in the play. He seems to have been adept at pleasing all sides in the mounting crisis, and his downfall and censure came about by accident. On August 24, 1774, he wrote to General Gage stating that the militia in towns of the province were in readiness "to meet at one Minute's Warning, equipt with Arms and Ammunition" and that powder was being withdrawn from the arsenal at Quarry Hill. As the editors of *The Adams Family Correspondence* point out, "Gage at once ordered a detachment of regulars to remove the powder to Castle Island, but with extraordinary carelessness he dropped the letter on a street in Boston." It was soon published in the *Boston Gazette* by Edes and Gill, and Brattle fled to Boston.[22] That Brattle was also a close friend of Hutchinson's added to his unpopularity. Brattle himself, as indicated in the play, left with the British troops in 1776. He arrived in Halifax and died there a few months later.

John Murray (Bonny) makes a very brief appearance in the play. He was another Mandamus Councillor. According to Sabine, "A party of about five hundred, with the Worcester Committee of Correspondence, repaired to

Rutland (where Murray lived) to ask Colonel Murray to resign his seat in the Council. On the way, they were joined by nearly one thousand persons from other sections. A delegation went to the house, and reported that he was absent. A letter was accordingly addressed to him, to the effect that, unless his resignation appeared in the Boston papers, he would be waited upon again. He abandoned his house on the night of the 25th of August of that year (1774), and fled to Boston."[23] In 1776 he sailed for Halifax with the British. His estates in Massachusetts were confiscated and, as he states in the play, he ruined his fortune "tagging after these poltroons." He died in exile in 1794.

The last of the Mandamus Councillors to be presented is Josiah Edson (Simple). There is a slight confusion about his identity: in the Clothier Collection at the University of Pennsylvania, the name given for Simple is Eaton, but so far as can be judged, there was no Loyalist of prominence of that name. Josiah Edson, however, was a Mandamus Councillor from Bridgewater, Massachusetts, and a colonel in the militia. Simple in the play says that all of his fellow Loyalists were "fond of the titles of Col. Esq. etc. — a gewgow of a commission was sufficient to render us enemies to our country . . . . Sometimes I am ready to heave myself upon the mercy of my injur'd country, but the awful ideas of committees, courts of enquiry, etc. terrify me from this expedient: — Besides, shall we stoop to submission to these miscreants; — we, Col's Esq'rs Judges."

There is additional evidence indicating that Simple is meant to represent Edson. In one of the most important pieces of the literature of propaganda, the Hudibrastic epic *M'Fingal* attributed to John Trumbull,[24] published in January, 1776, Edson is referred to as that "old simplicity of Edson." One might assume that the author of *The Blockheads* knew *M'Fingal* and made an easy transference from Edson to Simple. Edson was obliged to flee to Boston because of the attack by the mob on his house, and he left for Halifax in March, 1776. Eventually he returned to New York and died there or on Long Island. Sabine remarks that Edson was "a deacon of the church, and a respectable, virtuous man."[25]

All this may have been true of the actual man, but in the play Simple reveals characteristics that are earthy and somewhat gross. That he came from Bridgewater in the farming community would give credence to his farm interests and to his repenting his action in moving from the country to Boston; yet in the play it is not indicated that he was driven from Bridgewater. The playwright wants to make the point that Loyalists were disillusioned not so much by the cause they espoused but by the treatment they received from those who should have welcomed them and made use of their services. Hutchinson spoke of Edson in 1771, making the significant point that the latter was one of several persons of prominence who would have carried great weight in normal times but were overwhelmed by great opposition against them and thus remained silent or inactive.

The theatrical qualities of *The Blockheads* that are especially effective are seen in the realistic bickering between Simple and his wife, which add a low comedy energy to the play, making a clear contrast between the genteel world of fashion to which Mrs. Simple aspires and the rustic life they knew before removing to Boston. The literary merit of *The Blockheads* lies in its depiction of the increasing dismay and anger directed against the interloping British by the weak-willed American Tories who would support them. There is impatience with former friends who cannot or will not comprehend the disunity that their adherence to the Crown creates.

Probably no production of *The Blockheads* was presented; certainly not in Boston, for no colonial acting company was established to replace the British actors after the evacuation of the city. The Americans were too occupied with the war for such frivolity, and the Congressional ban against plays simply reinforced what had been a historical precedent in New England. Because the limited number of performers during the Revolution were British, they obviously would not have presented *The Blockheads*. As an advertised pamphlet, however, the play no doubt had a good audience. In the military, political, social, and religious arenas men were beginning to lose what reasonable perspective they might have had. In such a climate the violent diatribe of *The Blockheads* would have flourished, and it would have been greeted with enthusiasm by the patriots.

Notes

1. A comic opera printed in 1782 at New York entitled *The Blockheads; or, Fortunate Contractor*, has sometimes been confused with the earlier work.

2. Ford, *Some Notes towards an Essay on the Beginnings of American Dramatic Literature, 1606-1789* (New York, 1893), p. 15.

3. Deacon Timothy Newell of the Brattle Street Church reports in his *Journal*, August 1, 1775: "This day was invited by two gentlemen to dine, upon *rats*." Quoted by Henry Steele Commager and Richard B. Morris, *The Spirit of 'Seventy-Six* (Indianapolis, 1958), I, p. 148.

4. Faneuil Hall, that "sacred political arena, where cries for freedom had often been heard," was turned into a theatre, an act of profanation that increased the bitterness toward Howe.

5. Seilhamer, *History of the American Theatre* (Philadelphia, 1889), II, p. 20.

6. *Ibid*.

7. Winsor, ed., *The Memorial History of Boston* (Boston, 1882), III, p. 162.

8. Seilhamer, *op. cit.*, p. 21.

9. Butterfield, ed., *Adams Family Correspondence*, I, p. 262. This comment is in a letter from Abigail Adams to John Adams, July 25, 1775. The editor notes that Abigail Adams is quoting from a letter she received from Mercy Otis Warren written July 17, 1775 (p. 264n).

10. Anthony, *First Lady of the Revolution: The Life of Mercy Otis Warren* (New York, 1958), p. 82.

11. Ford, ed., *Warren-Adams Letters* (Boston, 1917), I, p. 18.

12. *Works* (Boston, 1856), IX, p. 336.

13. *Adams Family Correspondence*, I, p. 185. Letter from Abigail Adams to Mercy Warren, February, 1775.

14. *The Memorial History of Boston*, p. 137.

15. All the characters, except Grant, are discussed in the introduction and the edited text of *The Fall of British Tyranny* in this volume. Grant had been defeated in the French and Indian War in September, 1758, when he attempted to take Fort Duquesne. He was Governor of the Floridas from 1764 until 1771 and after sick leave abroad, returned to America with Howe, arriving in Boston in May, 1775. Grant was violently anti-American, declaring in the House of Commons on February 2, 1775, "that the Americans could not fight, and that he would undertake to march from one end of the continent to the other with 5000 men." Freeman, *George Washington*, New York, 1951, IV, p. 377. (*See also* Boatner, *Encyclopedia of the American Revolution*, New York, 1966, p. 443.) Grant's boast was never forgotten or forgiven. In *The Fall of British Tyranny*, the remark concerning 5000 men is attributed to Lord Amherst.

16. Ford, ed., *Warren-Adams Letters*, I, pp. 228-29.

17. In order to punish the Massachusetts Bay Colony for its transgressions against the Crown, the British government enacted a series of laws against the inhabitants of Boston and its environs on May 20, 1774. These regulations came to be known as the Intolerable Acts, among which was one decreeing that the Massachusetts Council would no longer be an elective body but would be appointed by the Governor on a "'royal writ of Mandamus.' The 36 appointed by Gage became marked men." (Boatner, *op cit.*, pp. 671-72.)

18. Sabine, *Biographical Sketches of the Loyalists of the American Revolution* (Boston, 1864), I, p. 488.

19. *Ibid.*

20. Sabine, *op. cit.*, II, p. 243.

21. Fairman, "Ruggles, Timothy," *DAB*, VIII, p. 221.

22. Sabine, *op. cit.*, II, p. 114.

23. *Ibid.*

24. John Trumbull, *M'Fingal* (Boston, 1826), p. 31. In the same part of Canto I, Trumbull also ridicules Murray and Ruggles.

25. Sabine, *op. cit.*, I, p. 403.

****
THE BLOCKHEADS:
OR
THE AFFRIGHTED OFFICERS
****

A Farce

****

BOSTON:
Printed in Queen-Street
M,DCC,LXXVI

****

Prologue*

> Your pardon first I crave, for this intrusion,
> The topic's such it looks like a delusion;
> And next your candor, for I sware and vow,
> Such an attempt I never made 'till now.
> But constant laughing at the desp'rate fate,
> The bastard sons of Mars endur'd of late,
> Induc'd me thus to minute down the notion,
> Which put my risibles in such commotion.
> By yankees frighted too! oh dire to say!
> Why yankees sure at red-coats faint away!
> Oh yes—they thought so too—for lack-a-day,
> Their gen'ral turn'd the blockade to a play:
> Poor vain poltroons—with justice we'll retort,
> And call them blockheads for their idle sport.

*In the published text, the prologue is printed at the end of the pamphlet; it is restored to its proper place here.

Dramatis Personae

CAPTAIN BASHAW	Ad----l [*Admiral Graves*]	⎫
PUFF	G-----l [*General William Howe*]	⎬ Officers
LORD DAPPER	L--d P---y [*Lord Percy*]	⎬
SHALLOW	G---t [*Grant*]	⎬
DUPE	Who you please	⎭
MEAGRE	G--y [*Harrison Gray*]	⎫ Refugees
SURLY	R-----s [*Timothy Ruggles*]	⎬ and
BRIGADIER PAUNCH	B-----e [*William Brattle*]	⎬ Friends
BONNY	M----y [*John Murray*]	⎬ to
SIMPLE	E---n [*Josiah Edson*]	⎭ Government
JEMIMA	Wife to Simple	
TABITHA	Her daughter	
DORSA	Her maid	

Soldiers, Women, etc.

The Dramatis Personae appears as above in the printed play (1776), including the elliptical identifications. For anyone with a knowledge of the prominent British officers and the well-known Loyalists in Boston during the period, the ellipses in the actual titles, or names of real people, would have been easily supplied by the readers. Arthur Hobson Quinn in *A History of the American Drama from the Beginning to the Civil War* notes that a "key" to the characters is written in a copy of the play in the Clothier Collection of the University of Pennsylvania. The key is correct except for one omission and one error. Internal evidence in his speech in the play suggests that "Dupe —Who you please" is Clinton, who arrived with Burgoyne and Howe to bring about a quick victory in the colonies and who with the others suffered disillusionment in regard to a speedy end of the war. The character is treated lightly; his only complaint is a real one, that he and the others were brought 3,000 miles under a false impression. The fact that Dupe is not severely castigated could add another slight piece of evidence that Mercy Warren wrote *The Blockheads*. In her evaluation of British officers written to her friends she has less contempt for Clinton than for the others. The key also indicates that "E---n" is Eaton instead of Edson, but the internal evidence of the play and the facts suggest that this character was a likeness of Josiah Edson, still another violent Loyalist. The error could lie in faulty transcription or ignorance concerning the leading Loyalists in Boston and its environs.

SCENE, Boston

ACT I

Scene 1

A Room with the Officers, etc.

Puff
Well, gentlemen, a pretty state for British generals and British troops — the terror of the world become mere scare-crows to themselves. — We came to America, flush'd with high expectations of conquest, and curbing these sons of riot.—We tour'd away[a] in the senate as if our success was certain; as if we had only to curb a few licentious villains, or hang them as spectacles for their brethren.—But how are we deceiv'd?—Instead of this agreeable employ, we are shamefully confin'd within the bounds of three miles, wrangling and starving among ourselves.

Shallow
Curs'd alternative, either to be murder'd without, or starv'd within.—These yankey dogs treat us like a parcel of poltroons; they divert themselves by firing at us, as at a flock of partridges.—A man can scarcely put his nose over the intrenchments without losing it;—another loses his eyes, only looking thro' the ambuseirs.[b]—They have a set of fellows called rifflers; they would shoot the very devil if he was to come within a league of them.

Captain Bashaw
Gentlemen, it will not do to set groaning here; let us determine upon some plan quickly to be done, otherwise I shall bid you farewell, and you may follow after as well as you are able.—You find every night brings them nearer and nearer; they raise a hill and fortify it in 6 hours—I expect soon to see a fortification grow out of the channel, and our ships of war to be blown up by some damn'd machine.— Such devils are capable of any thing; the power of miracles is put into their hands, and they improve the patent to admiration.—You must do something to dispossess them of those fortifications, otherwise we shall not only be starv'd, but absolutely murder'd.

Lord Dapper
Starv'd or murder'd are trifles, compar'd to being taken prisoners, to be drag'd before their congresses, committees, etc.—A pack of mutton-headed fellows, with their rusty musqets, are more dread visitors, than a tribe of furies, just arriv'd from h--l; therefore let us do something in earnest, or perhaps we shall be too late for relief.

---

[a] *tour'd away* Using an adroit turn or twist of phrase.

[b] *ambuseirs* Openings in fortifications through which one could fire on the enemy.

Puff
The eminence on Dorchester-hill,[c] which they began last night, they must at all hazards be dispossess'd of; we must rally our weak numbers, and drive them if possible; but such is our situation, our men are become meer skeletons; their present diet renders them more capable of terrifying their enemies, than fighting of them:—They will think the ghosts of their forefathers are coming to battle against them.—Poor devils! I pity their miserable state, but so the fates have order'd it, we can only laugh or pity each other.

Lord Dapper
Curss'd cruel fate! that we should thus be pen'd up.—Churchill's description of *Scotland* is but a shadow to it;—if that great genius was now alive, we should soon have a new edition with amendments.—He represents their flies and spiders, etc. as starving, but here they are absolutely starv'd—poor innocent insects, I forgive ye your tormenting of my legs; ye suck'd 'till you could find no nourishment, and then fell at my feet and died—Thousands have lain gasping within the small circle of my chair; their case was truly deplorable—I felt their state by experience.—My case is somewhat parallel to the prodigal son.—I may well adopt his words, "how many hired servants of my father's, have bread enough and to spare, while I perish with hunger."

Shallow
We shall all be oblig'd to follow his example; I never thought to make an improvement of a parable, but our case is now so truly deplorable that necessity prompts me to it.—Hard crusts and rusty bones have never till now become my diet; they do not suit my digestion.—My teeth are worn to stumps, and my lips are swell'd like a blubber-mouth negro's, by thumping hard bones against them; my jaw bone has been set a dozen times, dislocated by chewing hard pork, as tough as an old swine's ass.

Puff
Well, gentlemen, we are all acquainted with each other's circumstances, but however, we cannot mend them by recounting them—Let us rally our men and drive those rebels from their fortifications, or else we may soon expect to be introduc'd to their honor's Adams and Hancock, with sundry other gentlemen of distinction.—My L--d Dapper must have the command, and I doubt not we shall be able to dispossess them. Let us keep up our spirits, for we have nothing else to feed on, tho' it is a poor dish for a greedy appetite.

Lord Dapper
Some pretense must be made, as our honor is at stake.

[*Exeunt omnes.*]

---

c
Dorchester-hill See the introduction to *The Blockheads.*

Scene 2

A room with refugees, and friends to government

Surly

Nothing can be more wretched than our state,—vagabonds and outcasts[d] in the world!—here we are,—friends we have none,—we fled here for protection, but how are we disappointed!—Those on whom we depended, are as miserable as ourselves!—we have been cajol'd into all this by that curs'd H--------n,[e]—and he pleas'd us with pensions, posts of honor, and profit, but the villain has fled, and left us to shirk for ourselves.—My dwellings I have forsaken, my family are left to feed on the charity of friends, if they can find any; while I, poor wretch, have thrown myself upon the mercy of those who are unable to help me.—My money I have let out on government security—and poor security too, I am afraid;—from affluence and splendor, I am reduc'd to wretchedness and misery and skulk about the streets like a dog that has lost one ear.—Oh curss'd ambition! much better had it been if I had stay'd among my countrymen, and partook quietly of the produce of my farm.—Why need I have medled in politicks, or burnt my fingers dabbling in this sea of fire—My tenants and my oxen would have been much more agreeable companions than these herd of stalking poltroons, swaggering with their swords at their a— and afraid to draw them from the scabbard.

Simple

We have reason to blame ourselves—we have brought affairs to the present state—we were fond of the titles of Col. Esq. etc.—a gewgow[f] of a commission was sufficient to render us enemies to our country—We contriv'd a thousand tricks to make ourselves obnoxious to our countrymen, that we might be noticed as friends to government; we thought this would recommend us to some lucrative post:—We embrac'd the shadow of grandeur, but the substance has fled—A bow from a general or a fifer is all the satisfaction we have for our loyalty.—I am become almost asham'd of my company; a pack of [g]strutting pedanticks,[g] looking like elopers from the grave, "grinning horribly their ghastly smiles"; [h]gallanting their drosly nymphs, hag'd with constant use[h]—Sometimes I am ready to heave myself upon the mercy of my injur'd country, but the awful ideas of [i]committees, courts of enquiry,[i] etc. terrify me from this expedient:—Besides, shall we stoop to submission to these miscreants:—we, Col's Esq'rs. Judges, etc. bow to the lordly sway of these vile villains? I will rather perish than do it.

Surly

Our pride is our only cordial[j]—we have nothing else to feed on;—d-m'd poor nourishment!—we have been long

[d] *vagabonds and outcasts* The Loyalists have been promised much by Hutchinson, but he had given them little. Before the opening of the play Hutchinson has fled to England, leaving those who depended on him with absolutely nothing. The British were of no assistance, regarding the Loyalists as unwanted appendages except when they could be used for official advantage.

[e] *H--------n* Hutchinson.

[f] *gewgow* Probably should be "gewgaw," meaning a trifle, lacking in substantial value.

[g-g] *strutting pedanticks* Used in the sense that the British with whom they must consort are ostentatious and demonstrate a condescension toward those who presumably have less knowledge of the world.

[h-h] *gallanting—use* Escorting or paying court to their common women, older than their years by the wearing nature of their profession.

[i-i] *committees, courts of enquiry* Committees of Safety and Courts of Enquiry were established by the colonists during the Stamp Act crisis. They became more powerful as the Revolution grew; many Loyalists were exposed by these groups and forced to recant or were imprisoned or exiled when they refused to do so. The committees and courts were officially supported by the Second Continental Congress on July 18, 1775. The playwright warns his Loyalist readers of the power of the committees and the fear of excessive punishment that they engender.

[j] *cordial* A cordial in this sense means any medicine, food, or drink by which one is invigorated.

fed on the sumptuous dish of expectation of relief, but alas! we have so keen an appetite for that, we quickly devour'd it;—the general has no further supply left him, and we are now left to famish till a fresh supply comes.—We have fled here as friends to government, but how are we treated?—We are despised, our wives ravag'd, and our daughters debauch'd;—honor or profit we have none—abuse and ruin we have our ample shares of.—Much happier had we been, if instead of bowing and cringing to the great, we had minded the concerns of our farms; and instead of calculating the revenue of the nation, we had considered the income of our own stocks.

Paunch
Alas! we have all been deceived;—we have been pleased with the expectation of large reinforcements;—that conquest was certain;—and that the rebels would be speedily crushed.—Flush'd with these sanguine hopes, we have buoyed ourselves amidst these seas of tumult and outrage, but now we find ourselves woefully deceived, without any remedy.—Victory seems to declare in favor of the country; she has fled from these brave sons of mars, and takes refuge within the cells and cottages of America.

Surly
Well, gentlemen, you may all whine and cry, for my part I am determined to keep up my spirits, and hope for better times—why should we be so discomforted, because we have met with a little rugged treatment?—we must expect to encounter with many such trifles, but shall they discourage us? can we expect to gain honor in a silver slipper? no, we must engage with all H--l rather than give up our point.—Its true, friend Paunch cannot meet with his Dainty Soups, nor feast on his favorite Fish and Oil, but shall this render him peevish and fretful? I hope not—we are now to try our Loyalty, by the grand touchstone of Affliction; let us act like men, and I doubt not we shall be well rewarded.—HIS MAJESTY will regard us as the faithful of the land, and will recompence our fidelity with ample tokens of his affection—Your poor dejected Countenances are a disgrace to the cause we are engag'd in; reconcile yourselves to your present state, and I doubt not a happy deliverance will speedily arrive.

Meagre
Deliverance is a poor worn out, unmeaning word—I am tir'd with the sound—a word with so little meaning you cannot produce in a groce (sic) of dictionaries—Loyalty and Deliverance are pleasing words when us'd with propriety, but they are now maim'd with often handling.

Simple
Loyalty, d--m the word and its meaning—It is only a ᵏ-Court Watch Word,-ᵏ to entrap men, and then fleece them of their property.

In this instance, only pride is left upon which to feed, and such a circumstance is small comfort when one considers what might have been expected as reward.

---

k-k
Court Watch Word The reference is to words made general by the English ministerial politicians for purposes of propaganda in order to attract the imagination of the people and bind them to the British cause, thus exploiting the citizens in the name of a high-sounding principle.

ACT II

Scene 1

A room.

[*Tabitha and Dorsa*]

Tabitha
When did you receive this letter?

Dorsa
His servant left it with me last night.

Tabitha
He acquaints me that he intends to attend at the back gate this evening, and that he shall expect me there. I shall put great confidence in your friendship; if you deceive me I am undone.

Dorsa
If I deceive you, may your ruin fall on me.

Tabitha
Lord Dapper has address'd me in very honorable terms; he proposes to carry me to England, after the present campaign, but my father (an old prig) is greatly against it, and seems tired with the company of these red coats, (as he calls them)—but this person I am determined to have at all hazards.—Why should I deny myself the pleasures and honors of this life, to please an old fool that is just leaving of them.—The title of lady is very agreeable; it is what many would jump at;—such matches do not offer every day, and I shall improve the time as dextrous as I can.

Dorsa
Make hay while the sun shines, is a very good maxim.—Indeed, madam, I approve your determination; I should think you quite mad to determine otherways—who would not have a young spark if they could meet with one?—For my part I would not lodge another night without one, if I could meet with a good offer.

Tabitha
All our correspondence must go thro' your hands, you must be cautious, and watchful, for the least mishap will disconcert the whole plan.

Dorsa
I am us'd to these tricks of gallantry; I have introduc'd many a young sweet-heart—you may safely trust your security in my hands.—But one thing I wou'd mention (excuse my boldness) this Lord Dapper labours under the disgrace of Inability.

Tabitha
Inability, what do you mean? I hope he is not wanting in any thing to render the marriage agreeable.—If he is, I shall quickly throw him out of window, and appoint a better person in his room—its true, since you hint this, it makes me somewhat suspicious, he looks like a baboon upon stilts, and I begin to be fearful of his abilities—however, he will serve for a cully[a] to fleece for my indulgencies in dress and fashion.

Dorsa
That he may do, but for anything else (if reports are true) I had rather marry my old grandfather.

[*Exeunt.*]

Scene 2

[*Simple and his Wife*]

Simple
The worst job that ever I did, to move to this accurss'd place.—A friend to government! d--m connection!—my family ruin'd—myself a despis'd old fool.

Wife
My dear, do not be so childish—I am sure we are agreeably situated, excepting our scantiness of provisions; but great folks do not mind such trifles—roast beef, etc. only becomes hard-skin'd ploughjoggers[b]—eating and drinking became us while we were rough farmers, but now I should be asham'd to be seen setting round a smoking table of provisions, cramming and stuffing like a yoke of oxen. These delicate gentlemen and ladies would despise us as yankees, to see us maunching bread and cheese, etc.—they would have very nasty ideas about us, for what goes in must come out;—Oh it makes me sick to think of it!

Simple
You will be more sick before it is over—I wish I had now a good belly-full of what you mention; I would willingly bear the ridicule, as to the manner of it's coming out.—I believe the most delicate lady among them, would be glad of such stable contents, and risque the hazard of it's appearing again to the world—however, my dear, I have no notion of being merry—I have more serious affairs to think of.—I must acquaint you, that I am absolutely ruin'd—my whole fortune is fell either into the hands of the rebels without, or lent upon the security of chance, to those within —my resources are entirely exhausted—I have pleas'd myself with some appointment in office, but I find that will fail—we have so many needy fellows among us, that one must make interest to be even groom to the light horse.[c] What to do I know not.

---

[a] *cully* A dupe or a fool who can be used for gain, especially by a woman.

[b] *ploughjoggers* A ploughman.

[c] *groom to the light horse* The corruption in the British army and in colonial civil life is emphasized. To achieve even a very low rank—groom to the light horse cavalry—bribery is necessary.

Wife
Now forsooth you are going upon your old whining scheme —because you see I am acquainted with the gentry, you begin on these canting topics—you are afraid I shall ask you for a silk gown, or a new cap; that I shall want to see the plays, etc. and that you must have to bring forth some of those rusty joannes,[d] which you have pilfer'd from your neighbours, when you was a justice.—You may depend upon it, I shall begin to want these things, and shall expect no hesitation or denial.—Do not think I am to lead my life like a mope,[e] as when we were rusty farmers—we are now gentle-folks, and shall expect to do like gentle folks.—Our daughter Tabitha, she must also be introduc'd into the fashionable company, not always be a drudge about the house—she has now no filthy butter to churn; she is no longer a dairy-maid, but a lady, and a GOVERNMENT LADY[f] too, and as such she shall be supported.—Who knows but some rich gentleman may fancy her, and carry her to London, and perhaps take us with her—then for it, we shall see life, and perhaps then you may get a little beef, or something else to fatten your paunch.—In short, you look so much like a skeleton, I am afraid to go to bed to you—almost begin to wish for another husband.—Come, my dear, rouse yourself, don't think about your fat farm, let it go, it is all dirty stuff, only fit for yankees.

Simple
Poor foolish woman! how you feast on pride! is it possible you are in earnest? Can so much folly dwell in women?—I always thought women to be but one degree above a she ass, but you seem many degrees below.—You pretend to vaunt in all these prudish airs, but depend on it, you shall get no support from me.—As to your daughter, she may expect to incur my displeasure, if she goes romping among these ladies of quality.—As to rich upstarts, I had rather marry her to a good monkey, than to any figure of a man in the garrison.—What signifies putting a young girl to bed with a poor famish'd image!

Wife
You old fool, do you think I am to be frightened out of my designs?—No, I will learn you to treat your wife with a little more good manners—I wish you would become a little more polish'd, and go into the company of gentlemen and ladies—You would there hear nothing of she asses and such filthy farm terms.—My dear, and my honey, are the terms there made use of—thousand pretty things which I never before heard of, are whisper'd round—they can talk to one another with their eyes, and you can almost guess what they mean—none of your coarse language defiles their conversation—nothing but pure refinement.—I would not for the world go back to my former habitation, to hear the grunting of hogs—I should die with the spleen. As to your not supplying me, I am no way concern'd about

---

[d] *rusty joannes* Gold coin that Simple has hoarded. The joannes were of Portuguese origin, worth about $8.81 in their day, and were issued from 1722 to 1835; the name is derived from John V of Portugal.

---

[e] *mope* A dullard.

---

[f] *Government Lady*. Daughter Tabitha has risen in the world; she no longer can be treated as a servant. She has become a Tory lady and in time may marry English wealth and fortune.

it; if you won't another will, and you may expect a pair of horns grow out of your head as large as your old bulls.

Simple
Do, and welcome, but stand clear if you come within reach of them.

[*Exeunt.*]

Scene 3

A Garden.

[*Enter Lord Dapper and Tabitha.*]

Lord Dapper
Well, my dear, we have met, agreeable to appointment—I hope your old dad of a father has become more reconcil'd—the old prig[g] is as obstinate as a mule; neither offers of profit or friendship have any avail with him—however, let us not disappoint ourselves of the pleasure of matrimony, for to gratify the whim of a grey-headed old fool. All things are ready; fly from this place of confinement, and let us celebrate our long expected nuptials.

Tabitha
My papa, Sir, remains as determined as ever—he seems tir'd with being confin'd within the garrison—he had rather be among his farm neighbours, which makes him so fretful with all of your party—I do not think it possible ever to get his consent, but such a trifle shall never baulk my inclination—I shall throw off all reserve, and put myself entirely under your protection—shall quit the family, and depend on your honor.

Lord Dapper
Poor girl, you will find but little of that. (*Aside.*)—Come let us hasten as fast as possible, as delays of this kind may prove fatal.

[*As they are going off, her father appears.*]

Simple
Villain, what business have you with my daughter?

[*Lord Dapper draws his sword, and Simple runs away.*]

---

[g] *old prig* "Prig" is a general cant term, meaning petty thief or of a thievish disposition.

Scene 4

Here is exhibited a prospect of the light horse, being so weak, are supported by ropes to keep them on their legs; the groom busy in giving them glisters — also, a review of their troops — the whole looking like French cooks, in a hot day's entertainment; each company favor'd with a close stool pan.[h]

Officers
Gentlemen soldiers, we are now agoing to fight against these rebel dogs; be not discouraged, but let us play the man.

Soldiers
We had much rather fight for a good pudding.

[h] *close stool pan* Chamber pot.

ACT III

Scene 1

[Enter officers, etc.]

Puff

Heaven and earth are against us, the party are entirely defeated from heaven, the wind has been so boisterous as to drive them back. You see, gentlemen, our situation, our enemies are gaining upon us hourly, one night more perhaps will make us their prisoners—for heaven's sake let us determine upon something speedily, whether to quit the town, or try once more to rout these rebels.

Shallow

Why will you desire us to go to battle?—are you for seeing another Bunker-Hill frolic?—those devils would glory to have us come out to them, it would be sport to the dogs, to see us breaking our shins, tumbling over each other. —I esteem my life beyond my honor, and am not for throwing it away for the diversion of a parcel of yankees—If we cannot hold the garrison by keeping in, for God's sake, let us beat a retreat; but the LORD knows where; however, I had rather heave myself upon the mercy of the sea, than to be taken their prisoner.—Who but a mad man would trust himself out of these entrenchments? it is certain death.—I am for fighting, where there is some prospect of coming off clear; but here venture yourself out, and I would not insure you for 100 per cent.—d--n the devils, they excel their very father Belzebub for fighting.—I had rather engage with a squadron just arrived from the lower-regions, than with those curst fellows on yonder hill.

Lord Dapper

You are quite right—such herds of men are enough to scare Hannibal, and all the heroes that ever lived,—look! what millions there are!—the inhabitants of the four quarters of the globe (excepting ourselves) are now on those hills!—for heaven's sake, let us improve the time, and retreat as fast as possible.—I shall expect all the fishes of the sea to turn men, and become our enemies, let us improve our passport while the inhabitants of the sea are at peace.

Dupe

Now B------e,[a] here is more matter for humor, you may give us a second edition of your farce.—This is beyond all expectation!—a fine story to tell my L--d N--h! but he is at helm, he may risk his own head if he will, I am determined not to hazard mine for his whims—he may go fight them one after another, if he pleases, he shall not catch me to

---

[a] B------e In all probability this is simply an apostrophe to the absent Burgoyne, because there is no explanation possible from the context of the play as published. Of the officers who are gathered together in the scene there is none whose name begins with B and ends in e, yet the line is addressed to B------e.

run his tom-fool errands—the ministry and the parliament may come over, and hold their courts in Boston, and may send forth, and execute their acts if they think fit, they shall not find me fool enough to run my head against a cannon ball, to execute their d--m silly acts. I never would have come on this expedition, if I had had the least intimation of the bravery of this people.—I thought a bright sword, a smart cock'd hat, would effectually have terrified these fellows into submission, but I find the contrary, and have no inclination to try their skill at man killing.

Shallow
If I had a scolding wife, perhaps I would venture myself within a hundred yards of those hills; but while I have not, you shall find me far enough from them; and I don't care how much farther.—Our ministry think soldiers were made to be fir'd at as sport, but I hope on this occasion they will find themselves deceived,—for my part, I am determined to secure a place of safety;—if any have a mind to go out, let them; they have my good wishes for their return; but if they regard their lives, I advise all, and every one to keep within the entrenchments—I would rather sh-t my breeches than go without these forts to ease myself.

Puff
D--m them, I know the fellows by experience,—I remember Bunker-Hill—I shall never forget them, for their civility to me—their cock'd eye taking fight, makes my very blood run cold—how I came off alive is a miracle; whiz, whiz, whiz, good Lord, how it makes me shudder to think of it!—no, no, my lads, you shan't catch me among you, while I am out of your reach, I will keep out—In short, gentlemen, it will not do to be looking at them; they seem preparing to come nearer us, let us give out the alarm for a retreat immediately; we must determine where to go, after we are without the reach of these disagreeable visitors.

All
As speedy as possible.

Scene 2

A Room with Refugees and Friends to Government.

Surly
A retreat, is it possible!—shall the British troops ever suffer such disgrace, as to flee from a parcel of yankees?—we have been fed up with high notions of the power and resolution of these troops—but I find, when the matter becomes serious, they are as terrify'd as old women—the General has made a sham attempt[b] to dispossess them of their fortifications, but has withdrawn them with the pretense of the wind being too boisterous—what a pretty

[b] *sham attempt* The playwright adds to the general derision of Howe as the result of his rescinding his orders for an attack on Dorchester Heights on the night of March 5, 1776. A violent storm had arisen, and this circumstance was used as the official excuse for abandoning the sortie.

hobble[c] are we in, to be drove away from our only place of security—but I find our strong holds are become meer shadows of safety.—A very agreeable employ, for gentlemen to be running after a pack of cowards, and what is more miserable to depend on them for protection.—If I could once get clear of my present state, you should never find me again to depend upon a broken reed.

Bonny
It signifies nothing to fret, and find fault among ourselves, but let us be for securing a retreat as fast as possible—let us be packing up our alls,[d] and making our best way off.—I have ruin'd my fortune, tagging after these poltroons—I will now trouble them with my company—if they cannot protect me, they shall maintain me; while they have anything to eat themselves, I am determined to partake.—Poor encouragement for friends to government; if they don't find better reception than we have met with, they will have but few volunteers.

Simple
As for depending on their generosity for maintenance, I have no notion of. I have a more effectual way to support myself—I shall look out for snacks among the booty, left in the town, by their runaway owners—I shall improve the opportunity while pilfering is in the fashion; the [e]General has set us a very pretty example.[e]

Meagre
Is this the sad alternative, either to heave ourselves upon the mercy of our countrymen, or run away with a parcel of cowards?—but however, as matters are so circumstanced, we must make the best of it.—I have a considerable quantity of the province money, which will serve to procure me a scanty maintenance in our retreat—sad state! half famish'd on land, and pent within the garrison for 10 months, am now oblig'd to put to sea, to vomit up what little guts I have remaining! crust cruel fate! are our high expectations come to this? reinforcements, and the Lord knows what all become meer bug-bears?[f] farewel Boston, the once happy seat of my residence—farewel friends, and countrymen, I leave ye all, to go I know not where.

Brigadier Paunch
Gentlemen, we have just received orders from the General to prepare speedily for a retreat, the garrison is all in alarm, every one is driving helter skelter—you must be careful how you walk the streets, otherwise you will break your shins, or perhaps your necks, in the general confusion—if I was not so intimately convinc'd, the fight would be the most diverting that ever I beheld—but our circumstances will not admit of speculation, let us be gone, for the rebels are just upon us.

[*Exeunt.*]

---

[c] *hobble* As a hobbled horse; hampered and troubled.

[d] *alls* A workman's term for his tools.

[e-e] *General . . . example.* Rumors were rife that the British officers upon evacuating Boston took with them valuable property, and the testimony of returning householders verified the facts, which added to the general indignation against the British.

[f] *bug-bears* Hobgoblins to frighten children; an imaginary terror or object of dread.

Scene 3

A Room with Simple and Wife.

Simple
Well, my dear, what think you now of your agreeable situation; your filthy farm, and coarse roast beef, etc. nasty stuff!—what is the matter with your refined company that they fly away so abruptly, methinks they might have been polite enough to give us some little notice of their retreat; not run away like a parcel of mice, when the cat comes among them. I have for a long while been fearful of this, but found my mistake too late—I have outstay'd my day of grace, and find I must follow these ranters a wild goose chase over land and sea—I am tir'd of the chase! my family is ruin'd, and my daughter I am afraid, is debauch'd by a painted monkey, who I saw with her at the gate—the villain drew his sword upon me, but like a true British general, I thought fit to run away.

Wife
I wonder, my dear, you should complain at going abroad—I am fond of seeing the world—what signifies always to be pen't up within the smoke of our own chimnies? why should we not travel like other gentlefolks, to learn the manners and customs of other nations? must we always remain as ignorant as our brown bread[g] neighbors, and know nothing more of the world than what is transacted within our own parish?—for my part I am determined to extend my knowledge, and follow the fleet from one end of the world to the other, rather than remain as ignorant as our parson's wife. The rumour is, that we are going to Halifax; a rich, flourishing populous city, where nature wantons in all her luxury; here we may enjoy and divert ourselves without being teaz'd with the constant alarms of the devilish yankees — curse them, I wish they were all under your cyder press, and I had the screwing of it.—Rouse up you old Lazarus, and betake yourself, with your wife and family, aboard the ships; don't you hear the drums beat the alarm?

Simple
Worse and worse! greater fool than ever; it seems to grow upon you—I presume you have made geography your study, you are so well acquainted with the clime and soil of Halifax—rich and luxurious to admiration!—experience is the best school master—you are for seeing the world, and here perhaps you may be satisfy'd by seeing the a-s of it.—I find you are a fresh water sailor, and will make but a miserable figure aboard the ship, along side of your polite company.—I shall pity your modesty, when what is in will come out, and perhaps at both ends.—Pray, my dear, was you ever sea sick?—I presume not—oh! I shudder at the thought!

---

[g] *brown bread* A staple of the diet in New England was for generations the common brown bread, eaten usually with pork and beans on a Saturday night.

Wife
Don't tantalize me longer—I will not bear any more of your freedom—pray what do you mean by coming out at both ends?—I like no such coarse phrazes; if I had fifty ends, my modesty should forbid any thing from coming out of either—I know how to behave myself, and keep all ends safe.—Let us be going quickly.

Simple
Gang along, with the devil to you.—Curse my fate, to be yok'd to an old fool of a wife, and scampering after a herd of runaway cowards.

A Barrack--------with Soldiers and Women.

Soldier
Ha, ha, ha,—yankee doodle forever—I wish Lord North was here, to see his brave troops in their present plight, running away with their breeches down—who can help laughing at what a tom fool's errand we have been sent upon—we were sent here to ransack the country, and hang up a parcel of leading fellows for the crows to pick, and awe all others into peace and submission—instead of this, in our first attempt we were drove thro' the country, like a pack of jack asses, nor stop'd running 'till we had got within Boston, where we had been fortify'd for six months —here we were confin'd, reduc'd to skeletons, our bones standing sentry thro' our skins—we ventur'd out once more to dispossess them of Bunker-hill, we gain'd the ground, but if we are to purchase the whole land of America at so dear a rate, the Lord have mercy upon us.—We have receiv'd reinforcements, but they only serv'd to fill up the vacancies made at Bunker-hill frolic—large force of artillery, light horse, and the devil knows what, have come to our assistance, but what has been our luck? loss of men, of honor, of flesh, and to crown the whole, are now running away, as fast as we can scamper.

Soldier
A pretty story this in the British annals—an ever-lasting disgrace will attend the transactions in America.—Our best generals, with a force of artillery, sufficient one would think, to storm the regions of Belzebub—the most experience'd troops his Majesty has; a capital navy; yet, with all this force, our generals dare not peep over the entrenchments—are confin'd within three miles of garrison, writing and acting comedies[h]—dismantling meeting houses to exercise their horses, to prevent their having the scurvy—our troops hag'd[i] and famished, for want of refreshments—our navy lying at anchor, while the [j]privateers are depriving us of our supplies.[j]—"MYSTERIOUS! UNEXAMPLED! INCOMPREHENSIBLE!"—Disgrace too great for the spirit of Britons!—Not an action have we done, that has been any way to our honor or profit—it is true, we have set a few towns on fire, but like champions, took care to go where there was not even a pistol for defence.

---

[h] *writing and acting comedies* (See the introduction to *The Blockheads*.)

[i] *hag'd* Gaunt, lean, and wild looking.

[j-j] *privateers . . . supplies* The inaction of the British navy for long periods of time was a subject of continued ridicule in the colonies, while the success of the privateers was applauded. The latter made handsome profit by attacking and securing supply ships from Britain, which they towed to free American ports in order to sell the contraband.

Soldier

Nothing can be more diverting, than to see the town in its present situation—all is uproar and confusion—carts, trucks, wheel barrows, hand barrows, coaches, chaise, are driving as if the very devil was after them. Our generals look as wild as stags, when pursu'd by the hounds; they are startled at every noise; they think the rebels are just upon them.—Orders are given for blocking up the streets, that the rebels may break their shins, if they pursue us—we have also a [k]parcel of stuff'd images, looking like devils behind the pope, to be fix'd up as sentries; a fit emblem of ourselves—Burgoyne could not have contriv'd a prettier satyr—our ambuseirs are fill'd with wooden guns; d--m such wooden-headed commanders—to crown the whole, they should have had an effigy with a barber's block-head, as engineer.[k]—Oh Briton! your disgrace makes my very blood dance the hornpipe.—The poor yankee refugees, run backwards and forwards, like a parcel of cats let out of a bag—I would give half my pay, that some droll blade was here to describe the ludicrous scenery.

Soldier

The beauty of the whole is aboard the ships—the yankee refugees with their wives, cut a most ridiculous figure—vomiting, crying, cooking, eating, all in a heap.—I was ready to burst my sides in laughing, to see the ladies scampering into the vessels, tumbling one over another, showing their legs, etc.—One fellow in his hurry, pitch'd over board, and was kind enough to remain there—the whole scene was sufficient to raise the risibles of the crying philosopher—in short, words cannot describe it; they stow like a litter of pigs, or like a young brood of spaniels; they even spew in one another's mouths.

Women

Good enough for them, they have brought it upon themselves; they had better have minded their farms, not have run here to be a ridicule to both parties,—If I had a good farm, I would see government to the devil, before they should catch me here, to be froz'd, famish'd, ridicul'd—curse them and their spiritless protectors, and let's conclude with huzzas for America.

FINIS.

---

k-k
parcel—engineer The old ruse of using stuffed figures with wooden guns hidden behind windows or other openings in buildings to give the impression of a larger number of defendants than actually existed has a long history. The Soldier indicates that the whole effect is farcical. To make it more so, he sarcastically suggests that the wooden block upon which a barber displays a wig should have been used, mounted upon an effigy of an engineer identified by his uniform. Such a symbol would have been indeed appropriate for the blockheads, which the British officers appeared to be to the colonists.

Soliloquy, by way of epilogue

Spoken by Mrs. Simple, after her arrival at Halifax.

Modest! polite! genteel! Heavens what deceit,
Dwells in the breasts of those I termed great!
But now too late, my shame and grief appear;
I'm lost! undone! stop'd short in my career.
A barn my dwelling—paltry fish my food,—
With insults, scorn, and execrations lude.
Oh sad disgrace!—but this is not the worst,—
I'm by my husband and my daughter curs'd;
Our Bashaw[a] too, forever in a teaze,
Vents his dire spleen on us, poor refugees.
Accursed state—from tow'ring hopes I've fell,
To herd with transports, and such devils dwell.—
One tear my injur'd country weep for me,
And for that tear, may you be ever free.

[a] *Our Bashaw* Admiral Graves (see dramatis personae); bashaw, a variant of pasha—a man of high rank or office—is used here in a pejorative sense.

****

THE
BATTLE OF BROOKLYN
A
FARCE
OF
TWO ACTS

****

Introduction to *The Battle of Brooklyn*

A FRONTAL ASSAULT on the patriot cause, *The Battle of Brooklyn*, written in the autumn of 1776, succeeds mainly because of its invective and is one of the most important examples of Tory pamphleteering in theatrical form. The playwright makes fools of the rebels and ridicules their aspirations by caricaturing prominent persons and attacking the weakness of the patriot amateurs who opposed the British professionals.

The play was first published in New York in 1776 and was published in Edinburgh and Cork in 1777. The New York edition with some variations was reprinted in Brooklyn in 1873. The question of authorship, however, remains baffling. The little information we have about the playwright appears in an advertisement in the Cork edition, which states that the "following little Piece was written by an Officer in New-York." The "Officer" could have been an Englishman in the expeditionary forces or he could have been a native of Long Island who had been given a commission by the English. Whoever he was, his knowledge of the geography of Long Island, his acquaintance with citizens of the area, and his use of native peculiarities of language and custom—all concluded from internal evidence in the play—suggest that he was born on Long Island or was a resident for a period of years. (There is, of course, the possibility that the advertisement in the Cork edition was a form of puffing to give authenticity to the play for Irish readers.)

The Battle of Brooklyn has a striking immediacy. The battle itself has just been fought, and although news of it and the details could have been pieced together shortly thereafter, clearly the playwright had direct knowledge of the events of the British triumph of August 27, 1776, on Long Island. He could have been there and then moved to New York with the victorious English and written his play within the next two weeks.

The exact date of the writing cannot be ascertained, but internal evidence indicates that it was sometime in late August, between the day of the battle (August 27) and the early part of September. Although the writer is aware of many details of the engagement, he is not certain of the fate of Stirling and Sullivan, leading characters in the play. They are, as Noah says in the last scene, "Killed or taken prisoners." Apparently the author did not know that both Stirling and Sullivan had surrendered and were aboard the flagship of Admiral Lord Richard Howe.

On September 2 Sullivan appeared before Congress with a message from Lord Howe proposing a conference with the Americans, but Congress refused to negotiate privately with the admiral and decided to "send a committee to see whether Howe had any authority to treat with persons authorized by Congress."[1] They did send such a committee, composed of Benjamin Franklin of Pennsylvania, John Adams of Massachusetts, and Edward Rutledge of Virginia, but the possible reconciliation with Britain came to nothing, partly because Howe insisted that the Declaration of Independence be rescinded before peace talks could take place.

On September 4, however, the Congress agreed to exchange Sullivan and Stirling for British officers. The Americans subsequently returned to their own lines in early September, but not to New York City, which had been evacuated on September 14, 1776.

The playwright might not have known about their circumstances until after New York was in the hands of the British on September 14. The assumption then is that *The Battle of Brooklyn* was written shortly after the American defeat on August 27, 1776, and before the British controlled New York on September 14. It must remain an assumption only, given the proposition that, once the British had invested New York, the playwright would have heard of Sullivan's appearance before the Congress.

The value of the play as propaganda for the British cause lies not so much in its treatment of the battle of Long Island as in the delineation of the characters involved: the colonists, their leaders, and the ancillary characters whose function is not to advance the "plot," such as it is, but to cast aspersions on the major actors. There was no need for the playwright to exaggerate the stupidity of American strategy and the alarms and excursions of the day of battle; the event itself was an incredible disaster. However, before examining the treatment of characters, a brief explanation of the battle itself is needed. When the British evacuated Boston on March 17, 1776, as dramatized in *The Blockheads,* the rebel leaders were uncertain about the enemy's movements. The assumption was that the English would attempt to occupy New York. Instead, they went to Nova Scotia, and it was not until July that the royal fleet appeared in the Narrows off Long Island. During the interval, between March and July, the Americans fortified New York and built heavy entrenchments on Brooklyn Heights. The rebels felt doubly assured of their position because the Heights were protected on the southwest by Gowanus Creek and by millponds and treacherous marshlands that figure dramatically in the play when the Americans flee from the British; on the northeast, Wallabout (Wallabrocht) Bay gave additional natural defense. As William Dunlap notes, "The Americans lines and encampment extended from Gowanus Creek to the Wallabout, from water to water, on the high grounds commanding each."[2] It seemed an impregnable position, for in order to take New York, the Americans argued, the British would have to sail between the city and Long Island and thus be caught in a trap.

Under Admiral Lord Richard Howe and General William Howe the English did nothing of the kind. Instead they took Staten Island, off the New Jersey coast, and then waited until August 22, 1776, before they landed on Long Island, debarking at Gravesend Bay in the southeast with 24,000 men, including Loyalists from Staten Island and New York, and Hessian mercenaries under De Heister, to oppose 19,000 or 20,000 Americans.[3]

Washington and his general staff did not intend to let the enemy reach the Heights and were determined to hold them off by a protective action on the plains below the fortifications, where there were connecting roads from the villages of Gravesend, New Utrecht, Flatbush, and Bedford. These roads, fortified by small redoubts and breastworks similar to those Putnam boasts about in the play, were considered to be an effective defense.

The Americans had anticipated attacks from the southeast and southwest. If they could not make a stand on the plains, the Heights were their refuge. They failed to consider the open end far to the northeast where a road led from Jamaica through Jamaica Pass to Bedford. The enemy could move along that road, thus bypassing the Heights, and come onto the plains behind the American defenders who were expecting assaults from the south.

So matters stood on the night of August 26 and the morning of August 27. Sullivan was in the southeast to oppose De Heister at Flatbush Pass. Stirling was near the village of Gowanus to defend the American lines against Major General Grant, who was on the southwest Narrows Road near the Red Lion tavern. Putnam had ordered Stirling there early that morning when he heard that Grant was attacking at the Red Lion. (Later evidence raises question, however, as to whether Putnam actually knew what was transpiring.)

De Heister and Grant were part of a diversionary strategy to catch the Americans off guard while Howe and his officers—Percy, Cornwallis, and Clinton—moved with a formidable array from the northeast down the Jamaica Pass to the plains and caught the rebels in a trap. As Grant, De Heister, and Howe were encircling them, the only escape for the Americans was across the creeks and marshlands. Chaos resulted. The rebels ran for their lives into the marshes and up the wooded terrain, leaving behind a thousand dead or prisoners; only remnants reached the Heights.[4]

With the retreat of the American soldiers who were to protect him on his left, Stirling had to draw back, only to find part of Howe's army under Cornwallis at his rear. Showing none of the cowardice attributed to him in *The Battle of Brooklyn,* Stirling attacked the superior British forces. From 11:30 A.M. until noon he put up a violent fight that belies the fearful hysteria of the character in the play who pleads with Sullivan to save him. As a matter of fact, at this juncture of the battle the two men were not even together. Sullivan, surrounded by De Heister's men at Flatbush Pass, fought valiantly from 9:30 until noon, at which time he surrendered.[5]

The disaster was complete. The Americans were in retreat; Sullivan and Stirling were captured. Washington, on the Heights when the panic occurred, was left with a disintegrated force, many of his supplies gone, morale at low ebb, and the future doubtful. All that remained was for Howe to advance on the Heights and in a few hours destroy what was left of the American army. The East River was at Washington's back, and ships of the line were there—the British navy in full force. The panic on Long Island increased; soldiers and sympathetic civilians were desperate to escape. (In the play the sentry gives a graphic report of the situation.) It seemed obvious that Howe would storm the American position; the British and the Hessians had come into the area just below the Heights, and if they had attacked the whole affair would have been over. But Howe delayed, not knowing exactly how many men were opposing him at Brooklyn, and probably thinking of a similar situation when the British were faced with insurgents on the commanding position of Breed's Hill and Bunker's Hill. Besides, there was no reason to make unnecessary sacrifice; the royal navy was patrolling the East River and the escape of the Americans to New York City would be almost impossible.

In *The Battle of Brooklyn* Washington appears to be obtuse about the situation after the retreat of the Americans from the plain of Long Island and the capture of Sullivan and Stirling. He wishes to defend the line as well as the Heights, although Putnam argues for the removal of the army to New York. Washington allows Putnam to make the decision, afraid to do so himself, and thus the commander-in-chief is revealed as a weak military leader who must rely on others for his choices.

It is, of course, known that Washington actually took sole responsibility for the retreat, and on the night of August 29 and the following morning he effected the crossing of the East River with the entire army. Even nature seemed to assist as a heavy fog moved over the river at Brooklyn Ferry and prevented the British from knowing what was happening. Howe did not appear on Brooklyn Heights until after the American army had vanished. His dismay must have been great, for once again, as at Dorchester Heights, God and nature appeared to be on the side of the Americans.

Because the pamphleteer in *The Battle of Brooklyn* is primarily interested in disillusioning the Americans by showing their leaders to be poltroons or worse, the actual defeat takes a secondary place. The military situation did not need to be ridiculed; the facts spoke eloquently enough, and the Americans condemned themselves by their own incompetence.

WILLIAM ALEXANDER, Lord Stirling, is the most obvious of the caricatures, and he is constantly indicted as a drunken fool. When we first see him he has just risen at noon after a night of debauch and he has a splitting headache. He immediately calls for something to drink, and his drunkenness continues as a theme throughout the play. In the council scene with Washington he is rhetorically as well as literally inebriated. Sullivan in an aside says of him: "Pompous, flimsey, drunken fool." In the first scene of Act II at the critical moment when the battle is beginning, Stirling appears in disarray, terribly frightened when he hears about the shooting near the Red Lion. He fortifies himself by taking a "whistle" from his canteens.

Another element in the portrait of Stirling is his cowardice. A knocking on the door in the first scene frightens him out of his wits because he thinks that the Redcoats have arrived to seize him. In the scenes of battle he displays abject fear and lacks the wit of a Falstaff that might make the cowardice acceptable. He calls for Sullivan because he wants protection. Sullivan arrives but is unable to prevent the retreat. Stirling cries in despair, "Dear General, what shall we do?" At the end of the battle scene when he is about to be left alone, he begs Colonel Clark not to leave him, and they run off together.

The playwright underlines Stirling's incompetence as a general as well.

The general has one solution to all problems of strategy: he is "for surrounding—surround! is the word with me; if they were twenty times the number, I say surround them all!" Later on, during the battle, Sullivan maliciously asks Stirling if he now wishes to surround the British, although it is obvious that the tables have been turned. Stirling replies, "For God's sake, dear General, don't mention it. I did not expect them this way: our whole dependence is upon you, my dear General; but do not let them cut off our retreat." Thus Stirling is seen as an incompetent ass who should never have been placed in command.

The playwright's invective is not limited to charges of drunkenness, cowardice, and incompetence, for he also impugns the general's honesty. In the first scene of *The Battle of Brooklyn* Stirling's servant, King, alludes to "paper manufactory." Shortly after King leaves, Stirling expresses the wish that his servant will be shot because, Stirling declares, "he has been my evil genius, ever since I was concerned with him in counterfeiting paper currency." (The truth of the matter, discussed later, is that Stirling was involved in the case of counterfeiting not as a criminal but as a judge.)

To separate fact from fiction is always a difficult task, but there is little doubt that Lord Stirling was colorful, extravagant, and vain and a heavy imbiber. Jonathan Odell, the Tory satirist, a good friend and literary protégé of the Tory governor of New Jersey, William Franklin, the illegitimate son of Ben Franklin, paused in his scourging of the members of the Congress in 1779 to ask:

> "What matters what of Stirling may become?
> The quintessence of whiskey, soul of rum;
> Fractious at nine, quite gay at twelve o'clock;
> From thence till bed-time stupid as a block."[6]

If only the Tories commented on Stirling's habits there might be some room to doubt his interest in rum, peach brandy (which he craves in the play), and other liquors, but Dr. Benjamin Rush makes the same criticism. Rush was opinionated, as John C. Miller observes, a "somewhat waspish Philadelphia physician and member of Congress . . . inclined to hold generals solely responsible for victory or defeat; he could not see the army for the generals."[7] He was a civilian first and, like many another member of the Congress, was not willing to surrender his rights as a representative of the people to the military. Although tactless, he expressed a point of view held by many in regard to even the highest officers of the Continental Army, including Washington. In October, 1777, Rush visited Washington's camp and took notes, describing Stirling as "a proud, vain, lazy, ignorant drunkard."[8]

Twenty-three years later Rush wrote his autobiography; having mellowed considerably in the interval, he concludes that Stirling was "A learned sensible man, but somewhat vain, and like Charles II apt to tire his company by a repetition of the same stories. He was prudent and wise in council, and brave in the field. His manners were gentle and agreeable. His misfortunes before the war had led him to seek relief in toddy, with which he sometimes impaired his judgment. Congress honored him with a vote of approbation and praise after his death."[9]

Stirling's addiction to "toddy" seems incontestable, but that he was an inebriated rascal with no value to the American cause is most certainly not true. The allegations of his extreme intemperance can be laid to rest—allowing for some degree of familial prejudice—by the portrait of Stirling drawn by his grandson William Alexander Duer: "Remarkable for the cheerfulness and hilarity of his disposition . . . and confirmed in those convivial habits that increased upon him in after life, though never to such a degree as to interfere with the performance of his public duties, or deprive him of the esteem and confidence of his official superiors, or private friends."[10]

From all evidence the Tory condemnation of Lord Stirling as a coward is also false. His action on Long Island, and a number of other exploits, prove his bravery. For example, he defied Governor Franklin of New Jersey in 1776, when it was traitorous to oppose a royal governor, by seizing the transport *Blue-Mountain-Valley* off Sandy Hook as she anchored under the guns of the man-of-war *H. M. S. Asia*, and brought her to Perth Amboy.[11]

Although the bravado in Stirling's character made him exaggerate his own importance, he was not incompetent. His early education included mathematics and astronomy, subjects in which he particularly excelled. He became known for careful organization, and his appointment as surveyor-general of New Jersey attests to the high regard accorded him for his professional capacity.[12] Much could be written of his engineering capabilities; Fort Washington and Fort Lee on the Hudson were built by him, and he also fortified Harlem Heights and established Fort Stirling on Brooklyn Heights.

Stirling served under Putnam on Long Island and under Sullivan at Brandywine and in other engagements, but he never commanded an offensive on his own. Washington seemed to have some doubts about his ability in battle, yet the commander-in-chief was impressed by him and evidently considered him an able administrative officer. Under Washington's orders, Stirling participated in several courts of inquiry, including those involved with the Conway Cabal against Washington, the fate of Andre, and the court-martial of Major General Charles Lee.[13] These were all matters of great moment to the American cause, and one must assume that Washington would have been careful to select intelligent and trusted officers to serve as judges.

Stirling's link with counterfeiting (referred to by Joe King in Scene 1) is based on a celebrated case in New Jersey in 1773. Among the suspects was John King, and the chief culprit was Samuel Ford, who was arrested on the charge. William Duer reports that Ford "with the assistance of one John King, a subordinate confederate . . . effected his escape, and in company with King and Richardson [another confederate] fled to the western wilderness."[14] Lord Stirling was not one of the criminals; rather he acted as a judge on the Council of Governor Franklin. The author of *The Battle of Brooklyn* must have known of the circumstances, which were common knowledge by 1776, and he twists the facts to blacken Stirling's character, suggesting a connivance between Stirling and King and using the name of the latter for Stirling's servant.

In spite of a weakness for alcohol and vanity (his impressive wardrobe consisted of 412 garments, including 119 pairs of hose, 31 coats, 58 vests, 43 pairs of breeches, 2 pairs of trousers, and 6 powdering gowns, worn when hair was being powdered),[15] Stirling was nonetheless devoted to the patriot cause. He believed in constitutional liberty, and although a friend of Chatham and Bute he protested against the tyranny inflicted upon America and suffered loss of property because of the Revolution. He enjoyed the admiration of such men as John Adams, who wrote to Abigail that he was "vastly pleased" with Stirling's character.[16] Washington's letter of condolence to the Countess of Stirling (as she was styled) expressed a generally held opinion: ". . . how deeply I share the common affliction, on being deprived of the public and professional assistance, as well as the private friendship, of an officer of so high a rank, with whom I have lived in the strictest habits of amity, and how much those military merits of his Lordship, which rendered him respected in his lifetime, are now regretted by the whole army."[17]

THE FIRST APPEARANCE of Israel Putnam in *The Battle of Brooklyn* occurs at the council with Washington. Putnam was fifty-eight at the time, a legendary warrior, often impulsive and theatrical in his actions but so renowned for his exploits that no one could deny his superiority. He was praised and likened to Cincinnatus for having left his workshop, possibly even his plough, to ride to Lexington upon news of the conflict there. He was often flamboyant, but in spite of his mismanagement of affairs and his lack of generalship he was essentially an honest fighter and courageous. In the play he is concerned only with minor defenses, totally lacking in comprehension of the important tactics that could result in victory, and made to look a fool. Even though Putnam was no fool, by 1775 age was beginning to lessen his effectiveness, and the playwright touched closer to the truth than the Americans cared to admit. Putnam's appointment as major general had been opposed by many congressmen because of his age and impulsiveness but, as a member of the Continental Congress, Eliphalet Dyer, wrote to Joseph Trumbull on June 20, 1775, "his fame as a warrior has been so far extended thro the Continent that it would be in Vain to urge any of our Gen'll officers in Competition with him and he Carried by Universal Voice."[18]

The distrust of Putnam's ability and judgment increased, however, and in February, 1777, John Adams wrote Abigail that "Many persons are dissatisfied with Numbers of the General Officers of the highest Rank. I don't mean the Commander in Chief, his character is justly very high, but Schuyler, Putnam, Spencer, Heath are thought by very few to be capable of the great commands they hold. We hear of none of their heroic Deeds of Arms. I wish they would all resign."[19]

Later in the year when Putnam was in command in the Hudson Highlands, he proved so incapable that Alexander Hamilton (at the time aide-de-camp to Washington), who had been sent to investigate the situation, wrote to his chief, "I find everything de[ranged] by General Putnam." He suggested that Putnam be relieved of his command, a decision that had already been made by Congress.[20]

The principal accusation against Putnam in the play, however, is that of dishonesty. He is in league with criminals through the thief Skinner to steal horses and goods from the inhabitants of Long Island and to sell them in other colonies. Of all the charges that might have been leveled—incompetence, foolhardiness, impulsiveness—dishonesty was probably furthest from the truth. If Dr. Timothy Dwight, President of Yale College and Putnam's intimate friend, is to be believed, Putnam was a man "whose generosity was singular, whose honesty was proverbial."[21] On the other hand, Captain John Montressor, a British chief engineer who was with Putnam under Colonel Bradstreet in 1764, states in his journal that "Even Israel Putnam, of Connecticut, might have been bought, to my certain knowledge, for *one dollar per day.*"[22]

The truth about Putnam may, of course, lie somewhere between the two points of view, but because his integrity was rarely questioned even by those who severely criticized him for other frailties, one is inclined to the opinion that he was always honest within the limits of his colossal egotism and lack of imagination. The playwright could have emphasized the obvious weaknesses, making his condemnation of Putnam ring more true for those who knew the man, but he used the character for other purposes. In the next to the last scene of the play Putnam urges Washington to give up Long Island and retreat to New York. In this encounter Putnam embodies common sense, and the scene is devised to cast aspersions on Washington's lack of command and his stubbornness, thereby effectively demonstrating the incompetence of the Americans. Putnam is the wiser man, and Washington submits to him.

THE PLAYWRIGHT'S TREATMENT of John Sullivan is less condemnatory than are those of the other "Rebel Chiefs." In the only two scenes in which he appears, he is levelheaded and displays good judgment within the limitations of too great a confidence in his own ability. In the council scene he encourages Washington by saying that he is acquainted with all the "woods and defiles" of the island, a knowledge that was not as extensive as he implies, but the playwright makes little of this point. Sullivan demonstrates his generalship when he maintains a cool and detached attitude even at the moment of retreat. His speeches are ironic (they remind one of Burgoyne in Shaw's *The Devil's Disciple*). "This I now know, my Lord, that we heaven-sent Generals are exceedingly apt to lead our troops to the devil." In reply to Stirling's plaintive "What shall we do?" Sullivan answers, "Just as you please: every man is now his own general."

The attack on Sullivan is presented through the speeches of his servant Noah, who appears only in the last scene, rather than through caricature. Noah remarks that Sullivan was a lawyer who "maintained a suit for me against my mother" and won it—which appalls Joe King, to whom Noah tells the story. Noah says that Sullivan exploited the common people of Berwick in order to benefit himself, and that he gained his wealth by imposing on the weak and ignorant. On the whole, however, the portrait of Sullivan is of a fairly able general, condemned mainly because in the past he was a sly New England lawyer.

In truth Sullivan was a man of great ambition and very eager to obtain property. In June, 1776, for example, a petition with 133 signatures was presented to the General Court of New Hampshire protesting against Sullivan's holding of notes and suing for the money lent, presumably exactly when due, without giving the debtors an extension of time. He "constantly pressed for debts owed him"[23] and was convivial with his fellow citizens one day and ready to spring a trap on them the next.

ALL THE LEADERS of the Revolution, except Washington, are besmirched in *The Battle of Brooklyn*. There is a subtle change in the playwright's attitude toward the commander-in-chief; the criticism seems muted in comparison with that of Stirling and Putnam. Washington is slandered, but there is an ambiguity about the author's intentions. He sets out to condemn the American leader but he is indirect and vague, and this lack of a direction has confused historians of the nineteenth and twentieth centuries. Paul Leicester Ford comments that Washington "is drawn . . . as the one honest and high-principled man of a band of rogues."[24] Arthur Hobson Quinn notes, "By the introduction of the scene between Lady Gates and Betty, her maid, the author introduces a vileness of slander against Washington that is absent from any of the other dramas upon either side."[25] Moses Coit Tyler is more correct when he observes that in this play "it is perhaps possible to detect some slight forbearance of Washington, to whom is attributed a certain superiority to the men he leads, not extending to such particulars as low lust and political hypocrisy."[26]

One has to take into account that these critics wrote when the idolatry of Washington was still unchallenged. The obvious facts of the attack in *The Battle of Brooklyn* remain: Washington is represented as a pathetic hero caught up in the snares of self-delusion and ambition. He is not made ridiculous nor is he satirized, but he is subtly attacked and indicted for his weakness of character. The reasons underlying such an approach to Washington are difficult to ascertain; one supposition is that he was considered by many to be a Virginia gentleman, sincerely attempting to be a great leader but devoid of the qualities demanded of his position.

Washington first appears in the council scene, which is immediately preceded by a lurid commentary on him by Lady Gates, wife of General Horatio Gates, and her maid Betty. Lady Gates interrogates Betty about the young woman's relations with Benjamin Harrison, member of the Continental Congress from Virginia, and George Washington. It is this particular scene in the play which shocked later adulateurs of Washington, because it explicitly states that Harrison bought Betty for fifty "hard" dollars only to turn her over to Washington. Betty tells Lady Gates that she could not abide Harrison for even half a night and subsequently was transferred to Washington for less money. Betty assures Lady Gates that the exchange was satisfactory to her, because Washington is the "sweetest, meekest, melancholy sighing Gentleman; and . . . such a warrior!" The playwright intended no satire at this point, only calumny.

In the following scene Washington appears before the council as a sycophant to his own generals. He flatters them (one has only to note the elaborate language) and is vacillating and indecisive. Later, when alone with Sullivan, he reveals that he is not in sympathy with the American cause. He feels that the military and the Congress have become tyrants and that the people will eventually know that they have been deceived. "My heart never consented to this ruin of my native country!" he says. After Sullivan leaves he condemns himself for being too ambitious and regrets that he has become a tool of Congress, responsible for a civil war.

In suggesting that Washington bought women from others the playwright had obviously drawn on a published letter that in all probability had been altered from the original, a letter written by Benjamin Harrison to Washington, which had been intercepted by the British and published in the Tory press. (The technique of slander by letter was commonly used by both the Americans and the British. Often letters were seized as they passed from courier to courier across enemy lines, and were then altered and printed as if they had been untouched. The technique was a conventional one in the propaganda war: additions were made in original material to cast aspersions on the writer or recipient.) The Harrison letter, written in July, 1775, was stolen by the British and published in *The Massachusetts Gazette and Boston Weekly Newsletter,* a Tory journal, on August 17, 1775, a year and ten days before the battle of Brooklyn. The content of the letter was well known when the play was written. It contained one scandalous paragraph that may not have been in the original but was used by the playwright as a basis for the scene between Lady Gates and Betty. The damning statement is sprightly and has a jocose air, typical of the sexual hyperbole of the eighteenth century.

"As I was in the pleasing Task of writing to you, a little Noise occasioned me to turn my Head round, and who should appear but pretty little Kate the washer-woman's Daughter over the Way, clean, trim and rosey as the Morning; I snatch'd the golden glorious Opportunity, and but for that cursed Antidote to Love, Sukey, I had fitted her for my General against his Return. We were obliged to part, but not till we have contrived to meet again; if she keeps the Appointment I shall relish a Week's longer stay—I give you now and then some of these Adventures to amuse you, and unbend your Mind from the Cares of War."[27]

The playwright's intention obviously was to embarrass the principals, but there is evidence that Harrison's reputation as a "rough" man was well known. John Adams wrote that he was "another Sir John Falstaff, excepting his Larcenies and Robberies, his Conversation disgusting to every man of Delicacy or decorum, Obscaene, profane, impious, perpetually ridiculing the Bible, calling it the Worst Book in the world."[28]

Adams was not the only person who had a jaundiced opinion of the man who would be the father and great-grandfather of Presidents. In 1774 Silas Deane of Connecticut wrote to his wife that Harrison was "an uncommonly large man, and appears rather rough in his address and speech."[29]

The qualities of vacillation and uncertainty in the portrait of Washington lie closer to the truth than do the other criticisms. In the early days of the Revolution he was unsure of himself, as is apparent in the letter informing his wife of his election as commander-in-chief. The appointment is, he states, "a trust too great for my capacity," but he adds that he could not avoid it without bringing dishonor to himself.[30] What made him resolute, however, was his firm belief in the justice of America's cause.

Washington would make many serious errors in the field as well as many brilliant recoveries. And among the worst of his judgments is the disaster on Long Island. John Adams, writing to General Parsons from Philadelphia in October, 1776, was furious. Although Adams usually sided with Washington, in this instance he castigates the "Marks of Negligence, Indolence, Presumption, and Incapacity on our Side, by which scandalous Attributes We lost that Island wholly, and Manhattan Island nearly." He is appalled that Washington could be surprised by day and "caught in a State of wanton Security, from an overweening presumption in his own Strength."[31] Adams indignantly concludes that such incompetence is a capital crime for which there is no pardon.[32] There were others who deplored the catastrophe on Long Island. Members of Congress were alarmed: Josiah Bartlett of New Hampshire, writing to his colleague William Whipple, also a member of the Continental Congress, remarked that "Our people were ensnared, and, what vexes me, in a very careless manner."[33]

Washington was to make many more mistakes, and the British were to fall into incredible errors as well. If nothing else, the battle of Long Island and Brooklyn Heights pointed a mortal lesson for Americans, overconfident and unprepared. *The Battle of Brooklyn* makes excellent propaganda out of these weaknesses of the colonial command. The constant reiterated theme of provincial military incompetence and personal ineptitude is reinforced by dialogue that gives credibility to character while caricaturing the principal targets of contempt, the American generals, and such lesser men as Lasher, Clark, Snuffle, and Skinner.

The play probably was never produced, but it must have been widely circulated in the colonies and abroad if its three editions may be taken as proof of its popularity. As a literary piece, the work has its obvious limitations, but as theatrical propaganda it has the merit of vitality, a quick pace of action, and direct satire of the American leaders. *The Battle of Brooklyn* crows prematurely about British triumph, but it contains some home truths.

Notes

1. Whittemore, *A General of the Revolution: John Sullivan of New Hampshire* (New York, 1961), p. 42.

2. Dunlap, *History of New Netherlands, Province of New York, and State of New York, to the Adoption of the Federal Constitution* (New York, 1840), II, p. 61.

3. Johnston, *Campaign of 1776 around New York and Brooklyn* (Brooklyn, N.Y., 1878), pp. 124-25.

4. Wertenbaker, *Father Knickerbocker Rebels* (New York, 1948), p. 93.

5. Dunlap, *op. cit.,* p. 66.

6. Sargent, ed., *The Loyalist Poetry of the Revolution* (Philadelphia, 1857), p. 14.

7. Miller, *The Triumph of Freedom* (Boston, 1948), pp. 246-47.

8. Mitchell, ed., "Historical Notes of Dr. Benjamin Rush, 1777," *Pennsylvania Magazine of History and Biography,* XXVII (April, 1903), p. 147.

9. Corner, ed., *Autobiography of Benjamin Rush* (Princeton, 1948), p. 157.

10. Duer, *Life of William Alexander* (New York, 1847), p. 261.

11. *Ibid.,* p. 125.

12. Alden, "Alexander, William," *DAB* (New York, 1957), I, Part 1, p. 175.

13. Syrett and Cooke, eds., *The Papers of Alexander Hamilton* (New York, 1961), I, p. 523.

14. Duer, *op. cit.*, p. 98.

15. Lossing, *The Pictorial Field-Book of the Revolution* (New York, 1890), II, p. 602.

16. Butterfield, ed., *Adams Family Correspondence* (Cambridge, Mass., 1963), I, p. 347.

17. Quoted by Duer, *op. cit.*, p. 260.

18. Burnett, ed., *Letters of Members of the Continental Congress* (Washington, D. C., 1921), I, p. 137.

19. Butterfield, *op. cit.*, II, p. 165.

20. Syrett and Cooke, eds., *op. cit.*, I, p. 358.

21. Cutter, *The Life of Israel Putnam* (New York, 1858), p. 368, quoting Dwight's inscription on Putnam's tomb.

22. Winsor, ed., *Narrative and Critical History of America* (Boston, 1888), VI, p. 314.

23. Whittemore, *op. cit.*, pp. 4-5.

24. Ford, *Washington and the Theatre* (New York, 1889), p. 25.

25. Quinn, *A History of the American Drama from the Beginning to the Civil War* (New York, 1946), p. 58.

26. Tyler, *Literary History of the American Revolution* (New York, 1897), II, p. 209.

27. French, "The First George Washington Scandal," *Proceedings of the Massachusetts Historical Society, 1932-1936,* LXV (November, 1935), pp. 460-74.

28. Butterfield, ed., *Diary and Autobiography of John Adams* (Cambridge, Mass., 1961), III, p. 371. It must be noted that Adams made this statement about Harrison between 1802 and 1805 when he was preparing his *Autobiography*, written with "an unaided memory, never stopping to consult his own Diary or files of correspondence or the contemporaneously published *Journals* of the Continental Congress which he had in multiple copies on his bookshelves." (Observation by L. H. Butterfield, editor of the *Diary and Autobiography,* I, p. xlv.) This method of writing gives an almost extemporaneous quality to his work, but as his editor indicates, he eventually reviewed the *Journals,* his diary, and his letter books, and the results of such reviewing enabled him to be more exact in his recollection of events and persons of the past.

29. Burnett, ed., *Letters of Members of the Continental Congress,* I, p. 28.

30. Flexner, *George Washington; The Forge of Experience* (Boston, 1965), pp. 343-44.

31. Butterfield, ed., *op. cit.*, p. 444.

32. Adams was eager to establish some form of independence, not necessarily a complete rupture but a realignment that would place America on almost equal balance of power with England. Such a status was never openly advocated, even though it was inherent in the Galloway Plan proposed at Philadelphia in 1774, about which Adams had grave doubts. There were many patriots, however, including Adams himself, who realized that the thirteen colonies were potentially a nation, one not necessarily separated from the mother country but held to her by links of fine ore, not chains of iron. There is every reason to believe that the conservative patriots, or moderate men, did not want a complete break. John Adams at first wanted adjustment, but his cousin, Sam Adams, saw that compromise and delicate balance would be honored only in the breach and was determined that there should be complete separation and a new nation. John Adams eventually came to this point of view, expressing it obliquely even in 1775 in letters to his wife, intercepted at the same time as was the Harrison letter. But he needed time to recognize what severance from Britain meant realistically.

33. Burnett, ed., *Letters of Members of the Continental Congress,* II, p. 66.

✯✯✯

THE
BATTLE OF BROOKLYN
A
FARCE
OF
TWO ACTS

As it was Performed on
LONG ISLAND,
ON TUESDAY the 27th Day of August, 1776.
By the Representatives of the Tyrants of
AMERICA,
Assembled at PHILADELPHIA.

✯✯✯

For as a Flea, that goes to bed,
Lies with his tail above his head:
So in this mongrel State of ours,
The rabble are the supreme pow'rs;
Who've hors'd us on their backs, to shew us
A jadish trick, at last, and throw us.

Hudibras.

✯✯✯

NEW YORK:
Printed for J. RIVINGTON, in the Year of the
Rebellion. 1776.

✯✯✯

Dramatis Personae

Men
WASHINGTON
PUTNAM } *Rebel Chiefs*
SULLIVAN
STIRLING

LASHER *A Shoemaker of New-York*
CLARK *A Retailer of Rum in Connecticut* } *Colonels*
REMSEN *A Farmer of Newtown, Long-Island*

EBENEZER SNUFFLE *A New-England Parson, Chaplain to General Putnam*
JOE KING *Servant to Stirling*
NOAH *Servant to Sullivan*
SKINNER *A Thief, employed by Putnam*
OFFICERS and SOLDIERS

Women
LADY GATES
BETTY *Her Servant*

SCENE, partly within the Rebel Lines at Brooklyn;
and partly at Gwanas.

ACT I

Scene 1

An Apartment at Brooklyn.

[Enter Stirling, as from his bed room, rubbing his head.]

Stirling
Joe! honest Joe!—Damn the Fellow, where can this King be; *(looking at his watch)* odso,[a] almost twelve o'clock.

[Enter King.]

King
Why here, my Lord—Devil damme, Sir. pray, who do you damn so?

Stirling
My dear Joe, the cares that distract and split this poor head of mine—

King
Split!—Yes, by heaven! you drank stinkabus[b] enough last night to split the head of an Indian!

Stirling
Insolence!—In future know me for your master—your lord! who has disposal of your life.

King
I must hold a candle to this Devil.[c] *[Aside.]* My Lord, I ask your pardon; I meant no harm, but only as an old acquaintance.—You know, my Lord, I am given to joking, and you formerly encouraged me in it, when we were concerned together in the paper manufactory.

Stirling
Forgive me, honest Joe—the public cares so hang upon me, that they quite destroy my constitutional good humour. The Regulars are near to us, and every moment we expect them over the hills.

King
Your Lordship has so long, and so uniformly wished to meet them, that I thought, the nearer the prospect the

---

[a] *odso* A variant of *Godso*, expressing surprise. The Brooklyn edition reads: odss.

[b] *stinkabus* stinkibus or stinkubus: bad liquor, especially rank, adulterated spirits. The British propagandist begins one of his attacks on an American officer, emphasizing Stirling's drunkenness.

[c] *hold a candle to this Devil* To be actively evil, or to placate with a candle, thus treating the devil as a saint.

better you would have been pleased. You have no doubt, my Lord, of splitting, and roasting, and pickling these red coat fellows.

Stirling
We are to meet at the church this day, to determine in council, what to do with them. I am for surrounding—surround! is the word with me: if they were twenty times the number, I say surround them all!—But these gripes, Joe, and my canteens are empty: you must procure me something for them.

King
O heavens, the gripes!—Zounds![d] a puncheon of Jamaica[e] to have the gripes. *(Aside.)* I have some peach brandy, my Lord.

Stirling
The best of all possible things: it so admirably fits a man for the cabinet and the field. [*A knocking at the door.*] What can that mean; run, Joe, and see who knocks.

King
I go, Sir. *(As he goes, he observes Stirling's countenance.)* Pale and trembling, by that august body the Congress. *(Aside and exit.)*

Stirling
These bloody fellows, I fear, are in motion. I hope to God that damn'd rascal King will be shot; he has been my evil genius, ever since I was concerned with him in counterfeiting paper currency.

[*Enter King.*]

Dear Joe, what is the matter?

King
Nothing, but to desire you to meet the other Generals in council, two hours hence, at the church.

Stirling
O, is that all; I shall attend; in the meantime, go to the Commissary of Rum, and get my canteens filled; and by all means, my good Joe, be at home when I return.

[*Exit Stirling.*]

King
Canteens filled—and then thy whole soul will be in thy canteens. That is, if he has credit enough with the Commissary, to get his canteens filled with rum, he will belch it out of his stomach in the damn'dest lies, that ever disqualified a man for the character of a gentleman: and yet, parson McWorther, bellows from his pulpit, that this most *ignobleman* is a chosen vessel, to execute the Lord's work. —Ill-fated country! when will this delusion end? *(Exit.)*

---

[d] *Zounds!* God's Wounds, a mild oath.

[e] *puncheon of Jamaica* A large cask of varying capacity, in this instance to hold rum, which Stirling hopes will assuage the spasmodic cramps he has; a compound castigation of Stirling as an alcoholic American general, thereby inept because of his generally recognized weakness.

The Scene changes to a small House, in a Field: Cattle and horses grazing.

[*Enter Lasher and Clark*]

Clark
Behold, Colonel, these flocks and herds; with the sword of Gideon[f] have I made them mine; and honestly collected them, in the district allotted to me by our agreement.

Lasher
I rejoice with you in the acquisition. My harvest from the Wallabocht,[g] is like the miraculous draught;[h]—two hundred and seven head of horned beasts, and thirty-seven horses, graze where by guards direct.

Clark
Favor has not been so amply manifested unto me; for, from the farthest verge of Gwanas, even from Caspar's house, till you come to Brewer's mills, one hundred and nine horned, and twenty-eight beasts of burden, were all I could collect: nor was there compassion in my soul, [i-]to spare one of the kine for milk, to the offspring of a people, who believe that men cannot be saved by faith alone, without works.[-i]

Lasher
Impious and blasphemous tenet; destructive of Republicanism and Intoleration.¹ I doubt whether such people should be spared from the sword.—But, brother Clark, to secure what we have thus obtained by a strong hand, and mighty arm, was assigned to your care and prudence.

Clark
That I am not unworthy of the trust, you are to know, that nine of our sloops will, this day, be discharged from the continental service: tomorrow, they will be ready at the ferry to receive the spoil. Every fifth beast, by lot, is to be the wages of their safe delivery, at New Haven, in Connecticut, the residence of the faithful.[j] But we being fellow-laborers, if you approve—Tabitha, the wife of my bosom, shall be charged with the care of your cattle.

Lasher
Be it as thou hast said: at her hands I will require them; and as I had allotted to myself a large brass Kettle, in a former division of the spoil, with the Cattle let it be convey'd, as a testimony of the love I bear unto her.

Clark
Whatever is in thy heart to do, that do and prosper. I hear that twelve thousand are to keep the hills today; spies proclaim some motion in the camp of the Philistians.[k]

Lasher
What the end of these things will be, I know not; but as

BATTLE OF BROOKLYN | 187

---
f
sword of Gideon Gideon, an Israelite with a small band of followers, defeated the Midianites by "the *sword* of the Lord and of Gideon" (Judges 8: 18), and ruled Israel for forty years. The allusion to a small force, the Americans, against a larger force, the British, is clear.

---
g
Wallabocht Dutch for Wallabout; a large proportion of the population on Long Island was Dutch in origin.

---
h
miraculous draught A reference to the "draught" or haul of fishes by Peter, James, and John as commanded by Jesus on the lake of Gennesaret; one of the miracles, a reference that would have been clearly understood by the Scripture-minded colonists.

---
i-i
to spare . . . works Clark and Lasher, American "colonels," both modeled on actual persons, are castigated by the playwright as beneath contempt. They are represented as thieves who have been stealing cattle and horses from the inhabitants of Long Island. To add to the villainy of their characters, these colonial officers compound evil by giving a religious justification for their thefts. The victims of their depredations are Anglicans, who believe in salvation by faith and works. Clark, a Congregationalist, believes that faith alone is sufficient. In his simple way, he is using religious controversy to underline political differences. Such metaphor fits naturally into the pseudo-scriptural style of writing in this scene.

---
j
the residence of the faithful (*Faithful* in the Edinburgh edition.) The irony of this phrase would have been obvious to British readers. The faithful are no more than illegal receivers of stolen goods in the stronghold of strict nonconformists who professed honesty and integrity.

---
k
Philistians (Modern spelling: Philistines. The original peoples

came in the twelfth century B.C. from Crete or Asia Minor, arriving on the coastal regions of southwest Palestine, naming their country Philistia.) The modern Philistians, therefore, are the British who have come from islands to control the peoples of a continent.

1
inspiration Within the Biblical rhetoric of this scene "inspiration" takes on the context of a divine influence or action affecting the lives of certain persons (the Generals), qualifying them to receive and communicate sacred revelation, being inspired by God. For any anti-American reader, the obvious cynicism of this passage is apparent no matter what official lip-service might be paid to Congress, its appointed generals, and divine illumination.

---

m-m
Marylanders . . . Europeans This supposition is false. It is introduced for purposes of propaganda in order to antagonize the Irish and Germans and others of foreign extraction who naturally would resent being sacrificed for the native born or well established. The playwright bases his assumption on the fact that within the ranks of the Marylanders and Pennsylvanians there were many who were descended from European settlers or who were themselves lately arrived in America. Pennsylvania had many Irish as well as German colonists, and Maryland, which was founded by Roman Catholics, received large numbers of Irish before the colony became officially Anglican in 1702. The "alien" issue, althongh a minor one, was pertinent enough so that the use of these foreigners would have been considered an exploitation. The propagandist, therefore, is reversing the coin: the British may have used mercenaries but, the playwright suggests, the Americans were using "native foreigners" to serve their military purposes.

n-n
Heere . . . regiment Remsen, a Long Island resident, is

---

my soul liveth, I mean not to budge a jot beyond the summit of the hill; keeping in full view, and practical acquisition, the fort called GREEN.

Clark
Know you not, the wise determination of the Congress on that head; stimulated thereto, by the prudence of our Generals; who, I do believe, received it by inspiration?[1]

Lasher
Ignorant have I been kept; but unfold the mighty tidings, for I already perceive they are big with joy.

Clark
Have you not observed, with what address the southern militias are drawn hither?

Lasher
That they are here I know, but am yet to learn the secret cause, if any secret cause there be.

Clark
Know, then, that the [m]-Marylanders, Pennsylvanians, and the rifle regiments, are mostly composed of Europeans;-[m] a great majority of which are Irish and Germans.

Lasher
These things I am no stranger to, but still lack information.

Clark
Which way soever the battle tends, the burden and heat of it will be theirs; for thus it is resolved, to spare the natives, and make no account of the expenditure of the Europeans: feel you not the power of inspiration now?

Lasher
Wonderful! truly wonderful workings of wisdom indeed!

Clark
But for some twenty head of cattle, the gleanings of Gwanas, in the orchard of one Bergen, I would not go so far: these once obtained, we will be near each other.

[*Enter Remsen without a hat; his hair on end; his coat torn, and every mark of fear about him.*]

Lasher
Mercy! mercy! O Lord, where are they?

Clark
O heavens! he is wounded, and out of his senses! Dear Colonel, can you speak?

Remsen
Oh! [n]-Heere Godt! what merciful scape I get this time.— Shentlemen, have you seen my regiment?-[n]

Clark
No, where did you leave it?—Lord help us! how near is the enemy?

Remsen
O Godt! O Godt! O Godt!—Comt the bloedt[2] out of me in any place?

Lasher
Blood, no; nor can I see anybody coming after you: your hurt, I fancy, is fear! Colonel; and your wound must be sought for in your breeches; but, compose yourself, and tell us what has happened.

Remsen
Well, I will tell you then. I was, yust now, van the head of my regiment, close up behind Shon van Dinen's field. I keep my eye op Arian Mortes's lane. I see, yust by the groundt, something creep: I say regiment, take care of yoursalf boys. I peep mit both mine eyes, and see nothing: I say, boys, 'tis close up with us now—they begin to run; my horse he see the danger too, and carry me off: Godt knows I get here; I believe the rest is all killed, or taken prisoners.

[*Enter an Officer.*]

Godt bless you ayndant, where is the regment?

Officer
Where! damn them, scattered in every cover between this and the place where you started.

Remsen
Heere Godt! all killed?

Officer
Killed! no, nor any of them hurt, except four or five that you rode over: why, there was not a regular within a mile, when you took fright.

Lasher
O you ungodly coward! out from the presence of the brave!

[*Kicks him off and exits after him.*]

Officer
That fellow kicks as awkward, as if he soon expected the same discipline: but I will go and try, if possible, to collect our heroes.

[*Exit Officer.*]

Clark
What credulous stuff, these New-Yorkers are made of. The bill of lading for the cattle and horses will be in my name only: Poor Lasher! not a hide of them shalt thou have, to

represented as an untutored farmer of Long Island. Many parts of the island had been colonized by the Dutch and the dialogue and accent indicated the origin of the inhabitants. Remsen's language in this scene is written in imitation of the Dutch dialect then prevalent.

put a stitch in:—and then there is the Kettle, too! a! ha! ha! *(Exit laughing.)*

SCENE, a Room at Brooklyn Ferry.

[*Enter Lady Gates and Betty.*]

Betty
After Council, Mem, General Washington will wait of you; till then he begs your patience, as the time is near that he is to meet[3] the rest of the Generals.

Lady Gates
Council! A pretty collection of Councillors, indeed: but since it must be so, you shall comply with your promise to me, girl, by giving me the narrative of Harrison and your General: it will beguile the time.

Betty
La, mem, you so discomfit me, by claiming this promise, that I am a blush all over.

Lady Gates
Why, Betty, you must have assumed the blushing trade lately; it was not always so with you.

Betty
Indeed, your Ladyship does not make proper allowances for necessity and inexperience.—Fifty dollars, and hard ones too, with a promise of fifty times as much, was irresistable: but Oh! the nasty beast! I almost puke at the recollection.

Lady Gates
Oh! that must be affectation, for, bless me, what could raise such ideas?

Betty
Why, he is such a slobbering, odious, unsavory smelling creature, that I wonders any woman in the world could sleep a night by his side.

Lady Gates
And yet, you see, that fifty hard dollars, made you put up, for a night, with all the inconveniency of bad smells.

Betty
A night! your ladyship wrongs me very much; why, he snored within an hour! and the first snore was a signal for my retreat. I am sure, I should have been a corpse, if I had been obliged to stay the night.

Lady Gates
Fifty dollars, is a good deal of money, Betty; but did he make no claim upon you afterwards?

Betty
Indeed, mem, he stay'd from Congress on purpose to tease me: why he cry'd, and said he was in liquor that night, and did everything, I think, that could make me despise him; but all would not do.

Lady Gates
And there your affairs ended with Harrison, did they not, Betty?

Betty
Not quite, my Lady; for when he found I could not abide him, he proposed to introduce General Washington to me. The General was a very pretty gentleman, and I consented to it, on purpose to get rid of Harrison.

Lady Gates
This I should have imagined a favorable change myself, Betty, was it not?

Betty
The General is the sweetest, meekest, melancholy, sighing Gentleman; and then he is such a warrior—O mem, I shall always love the General.

Lady Gates
And among his other qualifications, the most liberal.

Betty
Why, my Lady, I will tell you honestly: his Excellency gave me a thirty dollar bill; he assured me it would have been more, but he was obliged to pay Harrison the fifty hard dollars, that he had given me: now, mem, is not Harrison a dirty fellow, in every shape that you can view him?

Lady Gates
No great things, girl, to be sure, from your account of him; neither is your meek, melancholy hero, from my own observation.

Betty
Lord!—lord!—mem, did he not make codfish of them all at Boston! and has he not seen tory men rid upon rails at New-York, by the tailors and cobblers of the town! And more, my Lady, did he not order the °·King's statue to be pulled down, and the head cut off!·° for God's sake, mem, what would you have of a hero?

Lady Gates
*Codfish at Boston!*ᵖ it is really an odd term, Betty: but he

---

o-o
King's ... off At the repeal of the Stamp Act in 1766, the grateful people of New York erected an equestrian statue of King George III. On July 9, 1776, the Declaration of Independence was read in New York to the troops and the excitement was great. After the reading, the soldiers and the citizens were determined to demonstrate their patriotism. They marched to where the king's statue stood, pulled it down, and proceeded to cut off the head, an act that infuriated the Loyalists. The trunk was carried through the streets to the accompaniment of the "Rogues March." Wertenbaker, in *Father Knickerbocker Rebels* (pp. 84-85) reports the subsequent history of the statue: the head was rescued by the British military engineer Captain John Montressor, buried for a while, and eventually sent to Lord Townshend in London. The body and horse were cut up and sent to Litchfield, Connecticut, where part of the material was cast into bullets. "Four other pieces, among them the tail of the horse, were plowed up on a Connecticut farm in 1871, and later purchased by the New York Historical Society." That Washington ordered the destruction of the statue is in all probability another of the playwright's exaggerations.

---

p
Codfish at Boston! Washington forced the evacuation of the British from Boston, making them "swim" to Halifax and thus turning them into New England's favorite seafood.

O Horatio! Horatio Gates was commissioned major-general of the Continental Army on May 16, 1776. Previously he had been an officer in the British army. He joined the patriot cause partly because he was opposed to the English class system; it was rumored that he was embarrassed by his humble origins. (His father may have been in the army or he may have been in trade as a greengrocer; his mother was housekeeper to the Duke of Leeds.) At the time of the play, however, Gates was at Ticonderoga, where he was jousting for position with General Schuyler. Gates later was to become the hero of Saratoga when he defeated Burgoyne. He was also a rival of Washington, but all these matters are subsequent to the period of the play. Lady Gates was not entirely in sympathy with her husband's association with the rebel cause, and her dialogue in the play may have been in character. Apparently Mrs. Gates was overly ambitious for her husband. According to John C. Miller (*The Triumph of Freedom*, pp. 252 and 521) General Charles Lee, a neighbor of Gates in Berkeley County, pitied the latter because he was honest and had many good qualities but that "Daemoness his wife occasions him to make a very ridiculous figure." Lee also declared, "That Medusa his wife governs with a rod of Scorpions." In the play Mrs. Gates is not shown to be a Lady Macbeth. The laurels to which she refers are those gained in the service of the British; Gates had yet to earn any in the American command, although he had been effective as an administrative officer during the siege of Boston. The playwright's principal observation is that Gates has demeaned himself by supporting a tyrannical revolution, which would be true of any American officer.

---

r

runnagate Renegade.

did not more than that old fool Putnam would have done: his not forbidding that insult to humanity, at New-York, was countenancing an act of barbarism; and none, but a little-minded barbarian, would have suffered the Arts to be trampled under foot, as he did, in the case of the King's statue.

Betty
You know of these things best, mem, to be sure: but I have heard the New-England officers say, that he should be their General no longer than he pleased them, and may be, they would have it so.

Lady Gates
Be you assured, girl, that if he had native dignity of heart, he would have soon convinced the rabble, that they must be governed by him, notwithstanding that he may have obtained his power by an usurpation from themselves— but, hark! what clamorous noise is that in the street? run and learn. (*Exit Betty.*) There appears to be some commotion, and it grows late; I begin to despair of seeing the General.

[*Enter Betty.*]

Betty
O, my Lady, do not let us wait to see the General. The New-England Colonels are in a mutiny; and say they will not fight, if the boats are not all ready to carry their men off to New-York, when they run away: let us go, dear mem, for I do not think we shall be safe, on this side of the Alleghany mountains.

Lady Gates
I will take your advice, girl. O Horatio!q that you should sully your laurels in the abominable cause of republican Tyrants, and Smugglers in power:—to be a runnagater for such miscreants, almost distracts me.

[*Exeunt.*]

The Scene changes to Brooklyn Church.

[*Washington, Putnam, Sullivan and Stirling in Council.*]

Washington
Gentlemen, spies from Flatbush inform, that the regulars are making a disposition to cross the hills, near that place. —General Putnam's wisdom in ordering that road to be flanked with breastworks, is now apparent. Lord Stirling, with his usual intrepidity and precision, has reconnoitered their numbers, which he finds to be about seven thousand.

General Sullivan has appointed the hill with exquisite judgment; where the Brigades under him and Lord Stirling, are to take post, and act as occasion may require: twelve thousand men are allotted for the service of sending them back to their ships. I, with eight thousand, will stay within these lines, to be called out to the slaughter and pursuit; unless our present deliberations, alter this plan of operation. My Lord, the Council expects your opinion.

Stirling
I rise to give it, to the most respectable, and most puissant council of general officers, that this or any other age ever produced. I would not presume, Gentlemen, to speak in this place, without being conscious that I possess the energy and oratory of a ˢ⁻Burke! or even write on the subject, but that I feel the powers, and the pen of a Junius!⁻ˢ That I reconnoitered them is most true; and if my weak opinion has any weight in council, I am for surrounding them, and when we have got them hemmed in, I am for sending to our noble Commander-in-Chief, in these lines,—to know what to do with them.

Sullivan
Pompous, flimsey, drunken fool. *(Aside.)* The noble Lord has said nothing against the disposition that the General had pointed out, and of which I approve.—His Lordship's ideas are exceedingly surrounding; I wish the practice may be as easy as the theory, and that their numbers may not exceed seven thousand:—but if the council holds the opinion of General Washington and myself, our deliberations are at an end; and we cannot be too soon at our different posts.

Putnam
I this morning gave the chaps another pill, and I will tell you how: you know the road to Bedford, a little on this side the house that the bandy-legged Jew lives in; well, d'ye see, there is on each side of the road, a stone wall, near three feet high; beyond that, on each side, are clear fields—what do you think I have done there?

Stirling
Why something like a great officer, nobody doubts.

Putnam
Swamp me,ᵗ if I have not hove up a breast-work, right across the road from wall to wall:—but, before we break up, determine, Gentlemen, what I am to do with my prisoners.

Stirling
Right, General; I should have gone to my post, and been at a loss of this head.

Washington
Send them to me: a great part of Fort Green is allotted for

---

s-s
Burke! ... Junius! Edmund Burke (1729-98) was one of the most important orators of the eighteenth century, if not of all political time. That Stirling should compare himself to Burke is patently ridiculous, which is the obvious intent of the playwright.

Junius, even today, remains a mystery. He was the author of anonymous letters, published between 1769 and 1772 in the London *Public Advertiser,* attacking the political opponents of William Pitt, Earl of Chatham, and John Wilkes, friends of America. The letters are vituperative and loaded with invective. They follow the pattern of personal abuse common to English political propaganda, making use of Latin models in the satires of Juvenal and the elevated sarcasm in the speeches of Cicero. They indicate English satirical influence as well.
J. H. Plumb says of Junius that he was "perhaps the ablest and most devastating political commentator this country has known." (*The First Four Georges,* 1957, p. 113). It is obviously absurd for Stirling to consider himself an equal to Junius.

---

t
Swamp me New England for "swelp" or "s'welp" for "(God) so help" or "so help (me, God)."

their reception; but be sure that they are disarmed, and well guarded.

Stirling
O, to-be-sure; undoubtedly, Sir, we will take care of that. I am for my post: Gentlemen, farewell.

Putnam
A little business dispatched, and I will call upon you there. *(Exit Stirling.)* If your Excellency should have any commands for me an hour hence, I may be found upon the Flatbush road: your servant, Gentlemen. *(Exit Putnam.)*

Washington
Good betide them both.—After this fustian, a little sober reasoning, General Sullivan, may fit the mind for the doubtful events of war. My apprehensions from the King's troops, believe me, are trifling, compared with the risk we run, from the people of America at large. The tyranny, that our accursed usurpation has made necessary, which they now feel, and feeling, I fear, will soon make them see thro' the disguise. Their rage, no doubt, will be heightened, by the slaughter that will probably ensue; and we, as members of the Congress, fall the first victims of it.—O Sullivan! my heart never consented to this ruin of my native country!

Sullivan
My dear General, the moments for reflection are elapsed, and irrecoverable. Our safety is first in conquest; if that is denied to our endeavors, I am sure, we can obtain better terms, from our much injured Sovereign than from our more injured country:—but wear a less rueful countenance; it is a proverb among the troops, that their General is much melted down, since the fleet arrived.

Washington
Our soldiers are a standing miracle to me: they define sensibly upon matters that are unimportant to them, and resign their powers of thinking to us, in a case where their all is at stake; and do not yet discover, that we make them the engines of our power, at the expense of all that is dear and sacred to them as men!—but, avaunt reflection! Our hope, my dear Sullivan, is in you; every command of ground is ours, with a perfect knowledge of all the woods and defiles: these advantages, at the least, double the strength of our men; and if we cannot defend these, I know of no place we can.

Sullivan
All things that depend upon me, will, I hope, meet with your approbation; and I shall aim to infuse such sentiments into the troops, that our next meeting may be ushered in, with greetings of congratulation: till then, my dear General, farewell. *(Exit Sullivan.)*

Washington
Greetings of congratulation!—Oh, could I congratulate myself, on finding my lost peace of mind!—on the restoration of my honor! O! cursed ambition! what have I sacrificed to thee? An ambition, too, of ᵘ·foreign growth; obtruded upon me by the most artful, insinuating villains, that ever enslaved a once, free and happy country. To behold myself, against my principle and better judgment, made the tool of their diabolical determinations, to entail a war upon my fellow-subjects of America.·ᵘ—Heigh ho! *(looking at his watch.)* Bless me, so late, and my engagements to a lady not complied with. *(Exit.)*

SCENE, a Room, in a House at Brooklyn.

[*Enter Putnam and Snuffle.*]

Snuffle
My dear General, the great, the important day advances; big with the fate of empire, in the united States⁴ of America.

Putnam
True, good Sir: and I laugh to think, that when we have established our power, and driven these Red-coats into the sea, what ripping reformation⁵ you Gentlemen will make in church affairs. Down goes Episcopacy and Quakerism,ᵛ at least: I hope you won't leave one broad-brimʷ on the continent.

Snuffle
Why really, General, we shall be very apt to make free with those Gentlemen. We have long beheld, with a jealous eye, the growing power of the Episcopal Clergy; and considered them as the only obstacle to our becoming the heads of the Church, in America; a dignity, that so properly belongs to the Elect, and for which, they have the assurance to contend with the Lord's own people. As for the Quakers, who in general have joined the tories against us, we shall not fail to produce "an ancient testimony"ˣ in their behalf: I mean the testimony of our forefathers; till with fines, whipping, imprisonment, and the gallows, we have extirpated them from the face of the earth.

Putnam
In the meantime, we shall not be behind-hand with the Tories: for, as the best estates in America belong to them, it is but cooking up some new-fangled oath, which their

u-u
foreign . . . America Washington is depicted as a good Loyalist or Englishman would prefer to see him, driven to a foolish act by ambition and abetted by men of ill will.

---

v
Episcopacy and Quakerism To cry havoc against two such disparate points of view as Episcopacy and Quakerism would seem to be an anomaly. Yet those who professed belief in either were recognized as foes to the American cause.

Putnam and Snuffle, therefore, would eradicate Episcopacy and Quakerism, raising still another element of propaganda in the play, the suggestion that the Revolution is a religious war against an established and sanctified king. The Anglican clergy in America were ordained in the British Isles, they were bound by oaths of allegiance to the king, and treason against an earthly sovereign meant rebellion against God. To the clergy, submission to Great Britain was a religious duty. As for the Quakers, the indictment against them was that they declined to respect the right of man to destroy kings, for this prerogative belonged to God. "Vengeance is mine, saith the Lord." (For further elaboration of these concepts *see* Larabee, "The Nature of American Loyalism.")

---

w
broad-brim The reference is to the broad-brimmed beaver hats worn by the Quakers on almost every occasion; a contemporary print of George Fox, their founder, shows him wearing such a hat. It became a symbol of the sect. William Penn, because of his close relations to the royal family, was permitted to wear his hat in the presence of royalty, an almost unheard of distinction.

---

x
"an ancient testimony" A play on the Quaker words "to give

testimony"—as the spirit moves one to make revelation concerning God-inspired conviction—transposed here to mean the Congregational testimony against Quakers in early New England.

y-y
whip . . . ninepence The estates will disappear as quickly as the juggler makes the ninepence vanish; the ninepence was the old Spanish *real,* worth in New England about twelve and a half cents.

z
upon the lay A criminal occupation or, in modern parlance, an illegal venture, "a racket."

aa
Governor of Rhode-Island Identification of the governor depends on which reading one accepts. In the following speech by Putnam, the word *filch* was changed to *Fitch* in the Brooklyn edition (*see* note 6 to *The Battle of Brooklyn*). The editor apparently assumed that the reference was to Fitch, the governor of Rhode Island ten years before the play was written, and did not realize that *filch* was a colloquialism for *thief.* In all probability, the governor referred to was Nicholas Cooke, governor from 1775 until 1778. His "infamy," as it concerned the playwright, was that he was a stanch patriot *after* he had supported the Loyalists, so that he was considered a turncoat, arousing the enmity of the British and making him a fit subject for attack.

bb
Congress notes In order to give financial support to the War for Independence, the Congress resorted to authorizing paper money—nothing more than bills of credit—even though it lacked the power to tax. These Continental notes could not be redeemed or considered legal tender; the states declared them to be so but were reluctant to redeem them. The result was an

squeamish consciences won't let them swallow; then, y-whip go their estates, like a juggler's ninepence,-y and themselves to prison, to be hanged as traitors to the common-wealth.

[*Enter Skinner.*]

Snuffle
Very true, my dear General: but here comes one of your officers. I will retire, to offer up my prayers for the success of our arms; while you pursue, the more important business of your department. (*Exit.*)

Putnam
Adieu, Sir. Well, Skinner, what news with you?

Skinner
The horses are delivered, as your Excellency directed. They are, by this time, well on their way to Connecticut; and so elegant a string of nine horses, are not to be pick'd up again, on all Long-Island.

Putnam
My letter tells me they are clever horses:—but that horse of Polhemus—O, my heart was set upon that horse: you let him slip through your fingers carelessly, Skinner; or did the owner of him, tempt you with a bribe, to leave him—I wish to know where he is?

Skinner
I know where he is, to the length of my whip.—I careless! I take a bribe!—Why the General should know me better; the horse is at Haerlem.

Putnam
At Haerlem!—why what notion of deviltry could send him there! Is there anybody but us upon the lay,z on this island?

Skinner
What's his name brought him there—damn his name, I can't remember it: he is son, however, to the Governor of Rhode-Island.aa

Putnam
O ho! then I quite excuse you; you are too young in the business, to be a match for young filch:[6] he inherits his father's talents. I had expectation, though, that we should have done better, with your knowledge of the country, and other advantages.—I had reckoned upon twenty horses.

Skinner
I myself, Sir, thought that number sure, but he lay in my rear, and brought off six that I had reconnoitered.

Putnam
Well, Skinner, as the business is over for the present, and we expect bloody noses in a few hours, there is a hundred dollars for your encouragement. (*Gives him a handful of Congress notes.*bb) Go over, now, and join your regiment.

Skinner
I hope your Excellency will reconsider the matter, and make it more: there is not one of the horses, but what is worth more than a hundred and fifty *soft* dollars;[cc]—consider, Sir!

Putnam
Consider!—why you are an unreasonable whelp! do you consider, that I took you from serving drams to Negroes, for your mother Foster at Rockaway, and robbing the neighboring henroosts for a livlihood! From petty larceny, you cur, I put you at the head of the profession;[dd] procured you a lieutenant's commission, and a separate command to hunt tories on this island, in order to push you forward,—and dare you grumble?

Skinner
I do not grumble, Sir;[7] but fifty dollars more, would enable [me][8] to take the field with credit: it would [ee]make my regimentals my own.[ee]

Putnam
I seldom mistake my men: I knew that you had talents, Skinner, or I should not have employed you: I will therefore point out a fund for you, to raise the fifty dollars more. Remember, Sir, the fuzee[ff] you filched at Merrick; item, the two watches, rings, etc., etc. at several other places; you gave me no account of these, though I had an equitable demand upon you for half. There is a fifty dollar fund for you,—don't you think, youhg man, to [gg]catch old birds with chaff.[gg] It is near night: I must to my post, and get you over the ferry to your duty.

   [*Exit Putnam.*]

Skinner
What a damn'd old scoundrel he is: how the devil did he know of the gun, and the other things?—In future, I will do business for myself. (*Exit.*)

---

increasing depreciation. "Not worth a Continental" meant anything worthless, and it is little wonder that Skinner is dubious of "Congress notes."

cc

soft dollars The minted coins of gold or silver were rare, and paper was the common currency, but as indicated in the preceding note, paper money was difficult to redeem. To purchase any item one would have to pay more in "soft dollars," the Continental currency, than in the hard dollars of silver or gold. Readers, therefore, were reminded of spreading inflation and the growing financial crisis in the colonies.

dd

profession (The Brooklyn edition reads: head of the procession.) To make him a professional thief.

ee-ee

make . . . own The money would enable him to make the final payment on his uniform, and thus he would owe no man for it.

ff

fuzee Flintlock gun.

gg-gg

catch old birds with chaff To "trip up" knowing persons with banter or humbug; or, employing another kind of metaphor, to capture old birds (experienced people) with worthless bait (the husks rather than the grain).

ACT II

SCENE, a Hill at Gwanas about two miles from the Brooklyn lines, with an encampment on it. Time, about three o'clock in the morning.

[*Enter a Soldier.*]

Soldier
Where's General Stirling? — hollo, General Stirling! — Zounds! how dark it is.

[*Enter Stirling, half dressed.*]

Stirling
For God's sake! what is the matter, sentry?

Soldier
Here, Sir! it is I that call, to inform your Lordship, there has been a great deal of shooting towards the Red Lyon,[a] within this little while.

Stirling
Dear sentry, which way did it come from?

Soldier
I can hardly tell, Sir; but it seemed tight work for a little while:⁹—there! there it begins again.

Stirling
It does indeed: do you think it comes anything nearer, sentry?

Soldier
Rather nearer, if anything; though much in the same place.

Stirling
Run, sentry, to the rear; make my respects to General Sullivan, and beg him to come hither.

Soldier
I will, my Lord. There it goes again: ripping work,[b] my Lord!

[*Exit Soldier.*]

Stirling
Now I will endeavor to get button'd up, and my garters tied.

[*Enter Clark.*]

O Colonel Clark! from whence—from whence are you come?

---

[a] *Red Lyon* The Red Lion tavern near the Narrows Road.

[b] *ripping work* Excellent; very fast.

Clark
From where our out-sentries are attacked.—I see you are getting ready, my Lord.

Stirling
But where are they attacked? Where is the enemy? Are there many of them—are they coming forward—is anybody killed—say dear Will?

Clark
I cannot tell you half of what you have already asked me; but I will tell you all I know. They sent a Captain to relieve me; I would not be relieved by a Captain, so I went to sleep at one Bergen's, from whence the out-sentries were relieved. This Bergen awaked me awhile ago, and said there was shooting in his field.

Stirling
God bless me! shooting in his field! was it near the house?

Clark
Very near—so I stole out, for I knew the road, dark as it was. Everything was as still, as if nothing had happened; except some groans of dying men, that appeared to be at a little distance. But I have seen nothing, nor heard anything by the way.

Stirling
Then their numbers are still a secret?

Clark
I will be bound there are not fifty of them, or there would have been some noise.

Stirling
O damn it! 'tis nothing but a scouting party.—Come, Colonel, we will take a whistle from my canteens.[c]

Clark
With all my heart, my Lord.—Poison, take the canteens; I have lost the cattle, that were in Bergen's orchard. *(Aside.)*

[*Enter five soldiers.*]

What are these! Who are you?

First Soldier
We are the remains of the out-post guard, your honours.

Stirling
And where are the rest of the guard, my good lads?

First Soldier
In Sarah's bosom,[d] I hope.

Second Soldier
In Abraham's bosom, he means, noble General.

[c]
whistle from my canteens Variation of "to wet one's whistle" or, to take a drink.

[d]
Sarah's bosom A biblical reference in Luke 16:22-25, where it is stated that a beggar died and was carried by the angels into Abraham's bosom, for it is a precept of Jewish faith that Abraham welcomes his righteous descendants to the bliss of Paradise; hence the God-fearing rest in "Abraham's bosom." The joke here is a slight one, reminiscent of the description of Falstaff's death in Henry V, when the Hostess says that the fat knight is in "Arthur's bosom."

First Soldier
Blood-an-oons,[e] is not she his wife? which makes it all one.

Stirling
Leave off this trifling, and tell me what you know.

First Soldier
Your honor must know, that we *was* standing by the end of a side of an Indian corn-field, up yonder a-piece. We heard something rustle among the water-mellon leaves, and saw something move; we bid them stand, and blazed away like brave boys.

Stirling
Well, my lad, and what followed?

First Soldier
Followed! by my soul, a sharp iron thing, that they call a bayonet.

Stirling
And what then?

First Soldier
What then! your honor! why to be sure, the few that could run, run away; and then all was peace and quietness.

Stirling
Do you not know, how many there were?

First Soldier
How many! your honor must know, that they were speechless: they carried their tongues in *them* damn'd bayonets, and most of our guard, I believe, are eating breakfast with their great-grandfathers!

Stirling
What corps do you belong to?

First Soldier
Pennsylvanians, an please your honour.

Stirling
Go, and join your regiment.

[*Exit soldiers.*]

Colonel Clark, as it begins to be light, go and get intelligence. I, every moment, expect General Sullivan: one or other of us, you will find here, to make a report to.

Clark
I shall not stay long, my Lord.

[*Exit Clark.*]

Stirling
I begin to feel easy: it has been but a scouting party; and

---

[e] *Blood-an-oons* God's blood and wounds, an ancient oath.

they have gone back again. It is a devilish raw morning, and I must have something to keep the cold out.

[*Exit.*]

SCENE, a Hill, with troops drawn up under arms. Time, broad day-light.

[*Enter Sullivan and Stirling.*]

Stirling
Well, do you not think, from the examination of these fellows, that it was a mere scouting party, that surprised the guard?

Sullivan
Their silence, my Lord, with me, marks order and good conduct: besides, they do not make war by scouting parties—but here comes Colonel Clark.

[*Enter Clark.*]

Clark
Gentlemen, the regulars are in motion: they are numerous, and will be here within an hour. From yonder hill, I looked down upon them.

Stirling
Good Colonel, have they any artillery with them?

Clark
I know not, my Lord; but I must away and join my men O, what a scrape, those cattle have brought me into. I am afraid, I shall be obliged to fight at last.

[*Aside and Exit.*]

Sullivan
Well, my Lord, will you make a disposition for your favourite scheme of surrounding?

Stirling
For God's sake, dear General, don't mention it. I did not expect them this way: our whole dependence is upon you, my dear General; but do not let them cut off our retreat.

Sullivan
Let four[10] brigades immediately take post in the bottom, and extend from the small house below, as far as the stone house upon the left; and farther, if the hill gives them cover: let them approach as near the road as possible, without being discovered. The Pennsylvanians are to draw up, at the foot of this hill, in full view of the enemy. From their uniform, they may be taken for Hessians; and the fire from the brigades, be more completely surprising and effectual.

Stirling
It shall be done—Oh! it shall be done. [*Exit Stirling.*]

Sullivan
If they should force these brigades to the hill, we can easily maintain this post, against the united force of Britain, without loss: and make the retreat to our lines, when we please, unmolested.

[*Re-enter Stirling.*]

Stirling
The brigades are disposed, as your Excellency directed, and the regulars are nearly up to them: you will see their advanced guard pass the stone house, directly.

Sullivan
There they are, and have discovered the Pennsylvanians; for they have quitted the road, and push towards them.

Stirling
I hope to God, they will push back again, as soon as our fire begins. O! There they go—well fir'd my boys! They cannot stand this! You'll see, they will push directly, General.

Sullivan
I see they do push, but it is with their bayonets; and our men are scampering toward us.

[*Enter a Pennsylvanian, hastily.*]

Stop soldier, you are far enough.

Pennsylvanian
I will be judged of that, ᶠmy dear; for, by my soul, honey, you have brought old Irelandᶠ about your ears, at last; and we can find the way to eat now,¹¹ without asking such vermin as you for victuals. (*Exit.*)

Stirling
Dear General, what shall we do now?

Sullivan
Ply the artillery, as fast¹² as possible.

[*Enter an Officer.*]

Officer
Towards the south, an incessant firing has prevailed for half an hour, nor has it ought approached: my post is that way advanced, but I thought my duty bid me quit it, to give you this information.

Sullivan
You have my thanks. To your post again, and let me be speedily informed, if the firing approaches. (*Exit Officer.*) While they are kept at bay, my Lord, we are safe upon this hill.

ᶠ-ᶠ *my dear ... Ireland* Terms of endearment among men, even though used sarcastically in the context of the play, were not uncommon in speech or written word. They were usually used by the upper classes, the officers and gentlemen; the playwright may have used such terms in the speech of a common soldier to emphasize the contempt the ordinary American was supposed to feel toward those of higher class. "Old Ireland" could be a reference to General William Howe, whose father was second Viscount Howe of the Irish peerage, or to the number of Irish troops involved in the Battle of Long Island.

Stirling
But yet we should prepare for a retreat.—For see, where they fearless climb up yonder hill.

Sullivan
There is nothing to obstruct us in our rear, my Lord: we will retreat in good time.

[*Enter Clark.*]

Clark
Lost! O Lord, undone! ruined! destroyed!

Sullivan
Amazement! what ails the man?

Clark
In the rear—there, in our rear—no retreat! no retreat!

Sullivan
Too true—there is part of the royal army, indeed, between us and our lines.

Stirling
O General Sullivan! General Sullivan!—what do you think of it now?

Sullivan
This I now know, my Lord, that we heaven-born Generals, are exceedingly apt to lead our troops to the devil.

Stirling
But my dear General Sullivan, what shall we do?

Sullivan
Just what you please: every man is now his own general, so, Gentlemen, farewell. (*Exit.*)

Stirling
Do not leave me also, Colonel Clark. O Lord, incline their hearts to mercy.

Clark
Amen, and amen. I hope, however, that we are not of consequence enough to be hanged. This way, my Lord, this way. (*Exeunt.*)

SCENE, Fort Green, in Brooklyn Lines:

A Centinel on one of the Merlins,[g] looking out.

[*Enter Washington.*]

Washington
What do you look so earnestly at, Sentry?

[g] *Merlins* Correct spelling is Merlons and means battlements, one of the solid supports between embrasures of a parapet at Fort Green.

Centinel
At our people, Sir, that are setting fire to the houses and barns, in their retreat.

Washington
What, are they retreating then?

Centinel
Look this way, Sir; there they run, like so many deer, and will get in: but the poor souls yonder, that come across the meadow, and attempt to cross the mill creek; O! what a number of them stick in the mud, and the stronger ones make a bridge of them.

Washington
All other retreat must be cut off: but I shall soon know the event, for here comes Putnam galloping.

[*Enter Putnam.*]

What is the disaster? What news do you bring me General Putnam?

Putnam
This is no Boston work,[h] Sir; they are in earnest! Orders must be immediately issued for the Boats to be in readiness, to carry our people over to New-York.

Washington
There is time enough for that General Putnam, after we have defended these works: the account of the Battle is what I wish to hear.

Putnam
Defend Sir! we cannot defend these works; our people won't defend them: if they do not see the boats; they will swim over, they won't be hemm'd in to be made minc'd of. If you don't give your orders I will give the orders myself.

Washington
If it must be so, the orders shall originate with me; and as soon as you have satisfied me on the fate of the day, proper measures shall be taken.

Putnam
Accursed fate, indeed, and most impious, for they took us fasting[i]; and then they deceived us—a devilish deception, too; for they did not come any one way, that we had marked out for them.

Washington
Well, but you had the woods, and the hills, and every other advantage. The rifle-men did great execution from behind the trees, surely!

Putnam
Zounds! Sir, the regulars did all the execution! They know

---

[h]
Boston work Putnam's reference is to the Battle of Bunker Hill where the British attacked in regular lines from below Breed's Hill. Howe had been in command in that battle, and it was anticipated that he would repeat the same tactics on Long Island, but he did not do so. (*See* the introduction to *The Battle of Brooklyn.*)

[i]
they took us fasting Fast days were often proclaimed in the Congregational settlements as days for reflection and prayer and sermons. They were part of the religious calendar, and from Putnam's point of view it was unpardonable for the British to attack on such a day.

that rifle-men are deer killers!—Rifle guns and rifle flocks, will be as cheap in their camp to-morrow, as cods-heads in Newfoundland.—But the orders, Sir; no time is to be lost: they are at our heels.

Washington
Have patience, General. What is our loss? Where are the other Generals?

Putnam
How can I tell, where they are, or what our loss really is; but I am sure it is thousands. Good! God, Sir, let us make haste, to save what is not lost.

Washington
This, General Putnam, is against my will; but I wait on you, to execute yours.

[*Exeunt.*]

SCENE, a Room, at Brooklyn Ferry.

[*Enter Noah, solus; his clothes covered with creek mud.*]

Noah
Notwithstanding your dirty condition, Mr. Noah, I congratulate you, on your safe arrival into your old quarters; neither hol'd by musket balls, nor swelled up with salt water and creek mud. Thanks to my activity, that I am not crab's meat with the rest.

[*Enter King.*]

Welcome, Joe: dripping from the creek, I see: but I am glad to see you alive!

King
Confirm it, that I really am alive, for I feel some doubts about it.

Noah
Don't you know me then?

King
As well as I know myself, Noah: but are we not both in the other world!

Noah
Why, man, look about you; and you will find this to be the very room, that we have inhabited, for some time past.

King
My senses, good Noah, claim conviction: something, first, to cherish me, and then I may be convinced, that I can, with propriety, talk upon sublunary subjects.

Noah
Behold, Joe, this pocket bottle; one half of it's contents, I prescribe to your conviction and restoration.

King
(*Drinks.*) Now I return your congratulations, and am heartily glad to find you on this side of the grave—but, Noah, what has become of our Generals?

Noah
Killed or taken prisoners; but I suppose the latter.—My poor General, I quite lament him.

King
Mine is under the same predicament, but I have not a pity for him:—nor should I love you very much, if I thought you serious in your lamentation.

Noah
Consider; he and I were brought up together: we went together to sea, before the mast; and since he commenced lawyer, he maintained a suit for me against my mother, and got the cause.

King
Confound the dog! But was he really a lawyer, and did he influence you, to commence an action against your mother?

Noah
He!—why, that fellow, drank flip[j] every night with the common people of our town of Berwick, and had art enough, to influence them to all his ends.

King
And some hundreds of the common people, has he influenced to their end, this day.—But for God's sake, Noah, how came a man of your standing,[13] in the capacity of this fellow's servant?

Noah
Without doubt, I might have started with a regiment, and probably, have been, myself, a general by this time. But I saw through their topsy turvy schemes;—though I was obliged to float with the tide, I knew, the post of honor, would be the most private station. But Sullivan will be a loss to his family.

King
So will not Stirling. He will be a loss to no body, but those that find him. Had Sullivan any property?

Noah
Most excellent property, for he made a property of weakness and ignorance, and consequently had an extensive fund.—But your's was a titled general, and I suppose

---

[j] *flip* A hot small beer and brandy, occasionally sweetened and spiced.

very full of property; as he has often declared, he was of principle.

King
His principle, Noah, has for years past, been to withhold other people's property from them; and when all the resources of art failed, his estate was exposed to sale by virtue of an execution: But he resisted the Sheriff and declared himself a partisan of confusion, because law and order, would compel him to acts of justice.—But, do you recollect that this is the fast day?

Noah
Is it, really! then it is one of the baits, which the Continental Congress threw out, for the people of America to bite at; and the event gives the lie to the inflaming and prophetic oratory, this day resounded from the pulpits of New-England. A day, on which, heaven has discarded them, and disavowed their cause, in a remarkable manner. O King, our preachers prevented this unhappy dispute, from coming to a bloodless issue.

King
It is a maxim with the Congress at Philadelphia, that by the marvelous, the vulgar are to be robb'd of their reason; but heaven has rejected the sacrifice, that the people may open their eyes, and be no longer the dupes of their tyranny, deception and bloodshed.

Noah
From the first meeting of that Hydra at Philadelphia, its sixty-four mouths, have been open to devour two strangers!

King
Devouring mouths I know they are; but what strangers do you point at?

Noah
Power! and Riches!

King
True, very true — strangers, indeed, to most of them: the first they have amply usurped from the people, and have had art enough, to make use of them as instruments, to confirm the usurpation.

Noah
They are, indeed, such monopolizers of liberty, that they do not suffer other people to follow their inclinations: but as we know, and consequently detest, their machinations; let us avail ourselves of the character of servants, and the confusion of retreat, to lie concealed, until they are clear of the island.

King
Agreed; and in order that we may claim the mercy, that

our good old master has extended to his erring servants, and return to that authority which never oppressed a subject; let us renew our allegiance to the most amiable and virtuous Prince, that ever sway'd a sceptre; and join our weak endeavors, in supporting a constitution, that has been, at once, the envy and admiration of the whole world.

Noah
I honor your sentiments, because I, experimentally, know them to be just. And O! almighty disposer[14] of human events, open the eyes of my deluded fellow-subjects, in this, once, happy country: encourage them to a free exercise of that reason, which is the portion of every individual, that each may judge for himself: then peace and order, will smile triumphant, over the rugged face of war and horror: the same hand that sows, shall reap the field; and our vines and vinyards be our own.

[*Exeunt omnes.*]

Notes

The copy text is that published in New York in 1776; subsequent editions were printed in Edinburgh, 1777; Cork, 1777; Brooklyn, 1873. In the notes recording substantive changes from the copy text, the abbreviation *E* is used for the Edinburgh edition; *C,* for the Cork edition, and *B,* for the Brooklyn edition.

1. The interpretation of the sentence in terms of propaganda is difficult because "faith with works" in its religious sense would hardly seem to be destructive of republicanism and intoleration. In order to clarify the remark, a response to Clark's preceding statement, Republicanism and Intoleration should be treated separately. Faith without works, the Congregationalists believed, ensures salvation. It is heresy to think otherwise, for man's inspired belief comes directly to him from God alone. Faith is God's action in his soul. It involves personal assent and trust in atonement. Therefore, faith alone to justify man in the eyes of God is imperative for the believer. The concept is widely individualistic, and it moves directly into the area of politics, for it must be remembered that early New England Congregationalism upheld the principle of democracy in the government of the church—self-government by covenant—and that the founders of New England bound church and government inextricably together.

There is, however, a subtle difference from the situation that obtained in England where church and state were one, at least in the symbolic headship of the king as protector of the faith after the pope had been denied authority. The difference is that the New England protestants believed in Christ as sole head of his church with no intermediaries—popes, kings, or priests—and that all members of the church were priests in their own right, consecrated by their faith, and elected to the congregation after they had been sufficiently tested by examination. They may not have been able to speak with the tongues of angels, but they could communicate as individuals with a common trust. This condition was a heritage of "natural rights," of "life, liberty, and property," as Locke had stated it, and consequently, "faith alone, without works" was a religious as well as a political tenet. "Faith with works" is inimical to Republicanism because such a concept was one part of the motivation of *The Thirty-Nine Articles,* becoming jurisdictional under Elizabeth I, Head of Church and State. The coalescence of religious and political matters in this respect, as well as in others, was anathema to the theocrats of New England and bore a connotative stigma that offended the intense individualism of eighteenth century American patriots.

The explanation as to why "faith with works" is destructive of intoleration is another problem. I can discover three possible answers. The first and the most superficial interpretation is that the playwright simply wishes to make a point for the purposes of propaganda. He links republicanism and intoleration, but they need not be equated. They might, however, well go together from the tory or the English point of view. In the English system with its obvious constitutional advantages, monarchy and toleration were synonymous. The Glorious Revolution of 1688 had ensured that condition. The rebels were fools to have forgotten it.

A second interpretation is that "faith alone, without works" is the belief of the patriots, making a common cause, closely allied to a political credo. Those who adhere to "faith with works" are opponents of the crusade for liberty—one that is both religious and political.

A third interpretation, probably closer to the intention of the playwright than are the other two, is that the "Impious and blasphemous tenet"—faith with works—is Anglican and thus destroys intoleration upon which the Americans, particularly those in New England, pride themselves. Thus the sentence is a satirical riposte against the well-known intoleration of other sects by the New England "meeting-house" communities.

2. *E* and *C:* Comt the Bloedt; *B:* Count the bloodt.

3. *E* and *C:* near that he is to meet; *B:* near when he is to meet.

4. *C* and *B:* united States; *E:* United States.

5. *E* and *C:* reformation; *B:* information.

6. *C:* filch; *E:* Filch; *B:* Fitch.

7. *Sir* is omitted in the Brooklyn edition.

8. The word *me* appears in the Edinburgh and Brooklyn editions but is omitted in the New York and Cork editions.

9. In the Brooklyn edition three lines are missing, beginning with Stirling's statement "Dear sentry . . ." and ending with the soldier's first sentence, "I can hardly . . ."

10. *E* and *C*: four; *B*: your.

11. *E* and *C*: eat now; *B*: eat iron.

12. *E* and *C*: as fast as possible; *B*: as far as possible.

13. *E*, *C*, and *B*: man of your understanding.

14. *E*: Almighty Disposer; *C* and *B*: almighty disposer.

****
THE DEATH OF
GENERAL MONTGOMERY,
IN STORMING THE
CITY OF QUEBEC
****

Introduction to
The Death of General Montgomery

OF THE seven plays in this anthology, *The Death of General Montgomery*, published in 1777, is the only one that is nonsatirical. It is a eulogy to the glory of those who died for a cause, essentially a tribute to the fallen and heroic, a moving, dramatic poem of persuasion to arouse the colonists against the British.

Hugh Henry Brackenridge, the author of the piece, was in some ways quixotic and equivocal, and yet he had a sturdy independence of spirit. While still studying to become a Presbyterian minister, he served as a chaplain in Washington's army (from 1776 to 1778). During this period he questioned the creed and the articles of his faith, and after much self-evaluation, decided to turn to another career. In his biography of the playwright, Brackenridge's son offers the following explanation:

He could not think of publicly maintaining doctrines, in which he did not privately believe—he resolved to turn his attention to the study of law—a circumstance, to which may be ascribed the unfriendly feeling manifested toward him afterwards by some of the clergy, who looked upon him as an apostate; denounced him as one of the wicked; and which led him on more than one occasion, to retaliate.[1]

One of the principal fascinations the ministry held for Brackenridge was the opportunity it gave him to deliver orations. He was particularly effective in the pulpit in spite of the inflamed invective and resounding periods that are characteristic of his political sermons when he served as chaplain. He sought to arouse patriotic emotions in order that the soldiers would identify themselves more closely with the cause and remain with the army. One of the major problems Washington had to face almost to the end of the conflict involved voluntary separations and desertions.

Brackenridge had a fiery sense of mission and he knew that his oratorical skills made him an effective agent in the war:

There are two ways in which a man may contribute to the defence of his country, by the tongue to speak, or by the hand to act. To rouse with words and animate with the voice is the province of the orator. To execute with promptitude, and resolution is that of the soldier. These mutually subserve and assist each other. . . . Let it not therefore be thought useless that I address military men. The talent of speech is mine, and that alone is my province.[2]

Fidelity to a cause was inbred in Brackenridge; of strongly independent

Scottish stock, he had from boyhood to make his own way; eager to attain the best education possible, he often exchanged manual labor for tutoring. At fifteen he took charge of a school in Maryland to earn money to attend college, and in 1768 he entered the College of New Jersey (later called Princeton), receiving his bachelor of arts degree in 1771 and a master of arts in 1774. It was at Princeton that he was nurtured on liberal ideas under the guidance of Dr. John Witherspoon, the president of the college.

The College of New Jersey was unique in a number of respects. Witherspoon, a common-sensical kind of person, established a curriculum that—

> differed from those which had led to the founding of the older colonial institutions: education was conceived primarily as training for civic responsibilities, and the English language was given a place beside Greek and Latin as a proper subject of college study. . . . Regular opportunities for practice in English rhetoric and oratory were provided in disputations and literary exercises held in college halls. The ideal college graduate in the middle colonies was thus not primarily the polished country gentleman or the learned minister but the useful and responsible citizen, skilled in the elegant and persuasive use of his mother tongue.[3]

The atmosphere of the College of New Jersey was cosmopolitan; the students came from all the provinces, from the West Indies, and in a few instances, from Europe. In addition, everyone was encouraged to inquire, to question, and within limits, to rebel. Two rival fraternal literary clubs that later became famous were established during Brackenridge's undergraduate term: The American Whig Society, which included Brackenridge, Philip Freneau, and James Madison; and the Cliosophic Society, a Tory rival, which included Samuel Spring, who is the chaplain in *The Death of General Montgomery*. The satires, written by Brackenridge, Freneau, and others in the "paper wars" against the Cliosophic fraternity were of minor importance in the literature of the Revolution to come, but they demonstrated Brackenridge's talent for ridicule, which eventually gained him popularity in his celebrated novel *Modern Chivalry*.[4]

Satire was Brackenridge's forte, although when he was a student and young teacher, emotional and patriotic effusions also came from his pen. His belief in the future importance of America as a nation is evident in the Commencement Ode he delivered at Princeton on September 25, 1771. The poem, by Philip Freneau, bore the hyperbolic title *The Rising Glory of America*. (Another title, *The Rising Glory of the Western World*, was reported in *The New York Gazette and Weekly Mercury* for October 7, 1771.) Such lines as the following give evidence of the youthful extravagance that was "received with great applause by the Audience."[5]

> —By persecution wrong'd
> And popish cruelty, our fathers came
> From Europe's shores to find this blest abode,
> And plough'd th' Atlantic wave in quest of peace;
> And found new shores and sylvan settlements
> Form'd by the care of each advent'rous chief,
> Who, warm in liberty and freedom's cause,
> Sought out uncultivated tracts and wilds,
> And fram'd new plans of cities, governments
> And spacious provinces;[6]

Because of the Whig Society's paper war against the Tories, Brackenridge grew more and more aware of the realities of the political situation. By 1776, two years after the playwright received his master of arts degree, he had written *The Battle of Bunker's-Hill* "for his pupils to act."⁷ Although a dramatic poem about defeat, it made apparent the fact that even though momentarily repulsed, the Americans were determined to win the war, that they had been capable of inflicting a near-disaster on the British, and that they would continue to be dogged and relentless.

The Death of General Montgomery is concerned with another defeat, but once again Brackenridge raised the hope that "out of this nettle danger, we pluck the flower, safety." Both *The Death of General Montgomery* and *The Battle of Bunker's-Hill* were written as exercises for students while Brackenridge was master of an academy in Somerset County, Maryland. Both were published—*The Battle of Bunker's-Hill* in 1776 and *The Death of General Montgomery* in 1777. Their call to arms, their insistence on patriotism, their fierce declamation against the British, ensured them a place in the protest literature of the day. The enemy was clearly identified; he wore a red coat and his master was George III, the once and sometime king of America.

THE ACTION of the play takes place on the night of December 31, 1775, and the early morning of January 1, 1776, on the Plains of Abraham before the citadel of Quebec. In blank verse it relates the salient facts of the attempt by the Americans under General Montgomery and Benedict Arnold to attack the city and capture it, ending in defeat for the Americans, the death of Montgomery, the wounding of Arnold, the capture of 426 prisoners, and the final triumph of the British commander, Sir Guy Carleton.

In order to understand the relationship between the actual event and the action of the play, the following newspaper account from *The New York Packet* of February 1, 1776, is useful. It was Montgomery's plan to—

have attacked the upper and lower town at the same time, depending principally for success upon the upper town. But discovering, from the motions of the enemy, that they were apprised of his design, he altered his plan, and, having divided his small army into four detachments, ordered two feints to be made against the upper town, one by Colonel Livingston at the head of the Canadians, against St. John's gate, the other by Captain Brown, at the head of a small detachment, against Cape Diamond, reserving to himself and Colonel Arnold, the two principal attacks against the lower town.

At five o'clock this morning, the hour appointed for the attack, the general, at the head of the New York troops, advanced against the lower town. Being obliged to take a circuit, the signal for the attack was given and the garrison alarmed before he reached the place. However, pressing on, he passed the first barrier, and was just opening the attempt on the second, when, by the first fire from the enemy, he was unfortunately killed, together with his aide-de-camp, Captain J. McPherson, Captain Cheesman, and two or three more. This so dispirited the men, that Colonel Campbell, on whom the Command devolved, found himself under the disagreeable necessity of drawing them off.

In the meantime, Colonel Arnold, at the head of about three hundred and fifty of those brave troops (who with unparallelled fatigue had penetrated Canada under his command,) and Captain Lamb's company of artillery, had passed through St. Roque's gate and approached near a two-gun battery, picketed in, without being discovered. This he attacked, and though it was well defended for about an hour, carried it with a loss of a number of men. In this attack, Colonel Arnold had the misfortune to have his leg splintered by a shot, and was obliged to be carried to the hospital. After gaining the battery, his detachment passed on to a second barrier, which they took possession of. By this time, the enemy, relieved from the other attack, by our troops being drawn off, directed their whole force against this detachment, and a party sallying out from Palace gate, attacked them in the rear. These brave men sustained the whole force of the garrison for three hours, but finding themselves hemmed in, and no hopes of relief, they were obliged to yield to numbers, and the advantageous situation the garrison had over them.[8]

In Act I, Scene 1, the wild blizzard, wind, and cold are effectively described, and the contrast between the well-equipped, well-rested British soldiers and the ragged, exhausted patriots is strongly emphasized. The final plans are swiftly made: the feint against the Upper Town, the two attacks against the Lower. In the remainder of the act and in Act II, Scene 1, three important characters who are to fall—Montgomery, Macpherson, and Cheesman (Cheeseman)—express thoughts on imminent death. The language here is not, however, sentimentally melancholic; there shines through the poetic dialogue of these three a nobility and heroism and a determination to fight for justice without compromise. Macpherson knows that death is terrible, Montgomery grieves that he will not see his wife and friends again, and Cheesman declares that his fatalism is not cowardice. They are bold, defiant heroes whom Brackenridge wished to provoke his readers to emulate.[9]

In Act II, Scene 2, the emphasis is on the patriot's youthful eagerness to begin the attack on the city and to succeed or die. A secondary theme is the hatred of the British and the call for vengeance against the enemy, emotions that increase as the play progresses. Philosophical and religious considerations inform Act III, Scene 1. The chaplain speaks of God's control over every enterprise of man, guiding his every action toward prosperity or defeat. He iterates the concept of poetic justice and concludes that the American cause shall inevitably triumph, an encouragement much needed in early 1777.

A slight hiatus in the action of the play before the battle begins enables Montgomery to recall the achievements of Wolfe, a hero to both the English and the Americans because of his capture of Canada from the French in September, 1759. Brackenridge extols Wolf's patriotism and insists that he would not have aided Britain had she been as corrupt then as she is now: Wolfe's personal integrity was too great for him to have obeyed a tyrant king. These passages serve to reinforce the contrast between the freedom and justice of England in the past and its corruption in the present, and are reminiscent of John of Gaunt's speech in *Richard II* in which he sees England, "now bowed down in shame."

Until the middle of Act IV, Arnold and Montgomery recall the long and hazardous trek Arnold made with his ill-equipped soldiers to the Heights of Abraham to storm the citadel of Quebec. Montgomery reminds his soldiers of their duty to the cause of liberty and freedom and calls on the chaplain to bless the enterprise. At this point Brackenridge, himself a chaplain, anticipates the *Six Political Discourses* of 1778. God is asked to soften the heart of George III so that he will not wish to reduce the Americans to slavery, for they are justly fighting against oppression.

As the chaplain completes his prayer, a messenger arrives to announce that Carleton has been alerted and lies in wait for the Americans. Montgomery in desperation harangues the troops, who are reluctant to move forward, a reflection of the actual circumstances when Montgomery was harassed by desertions and illness among the troops. He upbraids them in a kind of frenetic desperation because he realizes that to fail at this juncture is to jeopardize the whole campaign. Unfortunately for the success of the assault on Quebec, Carleton was almost unassailable in Quebec. His knowledge that the attack was imminent made him as determined as his foes to compel decisive action. The fierce snowy blizzard militated against the attackers; within a short space of time the intrepid Montgomery fell, and the force now under the command of Campbell retreated, demoralized.

If Brackenridge had not written in such haste, or if he had considered the work for the stage, he would probably have made the death of Montgomery a high point of the action. As it is, we hardly realize that Montgomery has been slain. His last speech anticipates his death, and immediately thereafter Burr announces that he is dead. There is no action indicated, and the remainder of Act IV is a eulogy by Burr over the bodies of Montgomery, Macpherson, and Cheesman. The scene culminates with the appearance of the ghost of General Wolfe, which castigates Britain, bemoaning the fact that Wolfe sacrificed his life for a Medea-like monster. America, the ghost says, shall be inspired by the death of these heroes and will separate from the "step-dame" rule and create a new empire, a United States. Thus Wolfe bids adieu to these noble warriors and comforts Burr with the hope that from their devotion to a sacred cause a new nation will emerge.

The first four scenes of Act V are full of the action of Arnold and his officers. Arnold, wounded, is withdrawn to the hospital, and the English are triumphant, repulsing the enemy and capturing many prisoners. Carleton then appears upon the walls of the Upper-Town with the body of Montgomery displayed on a bier, a scene reminiscent of classic tragedy when the bodies of the fallen are exposed to the populace. Carleton offers the rebel prisoners peace with honor or death without burial. They take him at his word and lay down their arms, upon which Carleton attacks them for their "moon-mad liberty." He intends to give to his Indian allies three Bostonians who will be tortured to death; when they plead with him to be merciful he decides that he will spare the victims because the rebels are still at the gates. But he warns them that if the Americans persist in defying the British, there will be no quarter given and hideous death shall await those who oppose the majesty of Britain.

The play ends as Morgan compares the British with the savage Saracens and Turks, and the vilest of human creatures. Worse than all of these will be that creature at whom the human race will point and declare: "That was an Englishman," a vicious condemnation that would have been applauded by the patriots.

IN HIS prefatory note, "The Author to the Public," Brackenridge makes it clear that his work was not intended for the theatre. Brackenridge's apologia is apt, although there are scenes in the play that have inherent theatrical quality, such as the speeches of Arnold and Montgomery in Act IV, the reported action of the battle and its consequences, the appearance of the ghost of General Wolfe, and the threat of Carleton to punish the rebels even though they have surrendered in good faith. All these scenes have a muted effect, undynamic for the stage and more suited for the closet or for a small group of auditors.

Brackenridge's close adherence to the conventions of heroic tragedy lessen the effectiveness of *The Death of General Montgomery;* yet in spite of weaknesses in the writing and obvious sentimentality, there are scenes that are moving, even though Brackenridge sometimes writes as if he were carving epitaphs. The characters, however, are little more than marionettes, dangling from the strings of propaganda, shown against a panorama of war in the cold and desolate region of New Canada.

The nobility of sacrifice is the theme that is constantly reiterated, and the simplistic nature of the play takes its genesis from the encounter between good and evil forces. Montgomery is the gentle perfect knight, an enlarged heroic model for young men to emulate. Montgomery's counterforce, Sir Guy Carleton, is a heartless, bloody villain, contemptuous of prisoners of war. Although contemporary letters and accounts would indicate that Carleton treated his prisoners with humanity, *The Death of General Montgomery* gives a different impression. There are, however, conflicting statements. In the *Pennsylvania Gazette* for January 24, 1776, the following report is given:

New York, January 18
Copy of a letter from General Montgomery to General Carleton, dated Holland House (near Quebec) Dec. 16, 1775.
Sir,
Notwithstanding the personal ill treatment I have received at your hands, notwithstanding the cruelty you have shown to the unhappy prisoners you have taken, the feelings of humanity induce me to have recourse to this expedient, to save you from destruction which hangs over your wretched garrison. Give me leave to inform you that I am well acquainted with your situation; a great extent of works, in their nature incapable of defense, manned with a motley crew of sailors, most of them our friends; of citizens, who wish to see us within the walls; a few of the worst troops that call themselves soldiers; the improbability of relief, and the certain prospect of wanting every necessity of life, should your opponents confine themselves to a simple blockade, point out the absurdity of resistance—such is your situation. I am at the head of troops accustomed to success, confident of their righteousness of the cause they have engaged in, inured to danger and fatigue, and so highly incensed at your inhumanity, illiberal abuse, and the ungenerous means employed to prejudice them in the minds of the Canadians, that it is with difficulty I restrain them till my batteries are ready—from assaulting your works, which afford them a fair opportunity of ample vengeance and just retaliation.[10]

On the other side of the ledger, Benjamin Trumbull, chaplain with the First Connecticut Regiment, wrote: "General Carleton is said to have some humanity, disavows his having ever set the savages on the Americans. The harsh and inhumane things which have been done this way are rather ascribed to General Prescot, St. Luke La-Corn, Captain Frazier and others of their character and the nobles."[11] It was Prescot who claimed later that all violent acts against prisoners, particularly the treatment of Ethan Allen, were ordered by Carleton. It would seem that the black portrait painted by Brackenridge needs some revision in the light of historical fact.

Brackenridge wrote the play for his students to act, and it was probably performed by them at the academy in Maryland. The author hoped that other schools might give readings of his two dramatic pieces, and they may very well have been acted at Harvard, if one is to believe the report of Abbé Robin (see the introduction to this anthology). *The Death of General Montgomery* is a bravura piece of propaganda, intended to teach that even in disaster heroism would prevail.

Notes

1. Quoted by Newlin in *The Life and Writings of Hugh Henry Brackenridge* (Princeton, 1932), pp. 42-43; from H. M. Brackenridge, *Biographical Notice of H. H. Brackenridge,* in *Modern Chivalry* (edition of 1856), pp. 155-56. This biographical notice first appeared in the *Southern Literary Messenger,* VIII (January, 1842), pp. 1-19.

2. Newlin, *op. cit.,* p. 37, quoting from H. H. Brackenridge, *Gazette Publications* (Carlisle, Pennsylvania, 1806), p. 265.

3. Spiller *et al,* eds., *Literary History of the United States* (New York, 1949), I, p. 93. One might ask if the pretheological student in New England at Harvard and Yale or the William and Mary student were not also useful and responsible. The editors of the *Literary History* appear to consider that the effects of a training in ancient language as well as in the tradition of English from Chaucer through Milton to Pope, not excluding neoclassical dramatists, both French and English, was more limiting than the curriculum at the College of New Jersey. Witherspoon himself taught French and upheld Addison and Swift as models.

4. Newlin, *op. cit.,* pp. 10-11; Moses, ed., *Representative Plays by American Dramatists* (New York, 1918), I, p. 237. (There is an obvious error in Moses; he refers to a manuscript book in possession of the Historical Society of Pennsylvania, giving as its title "Satires against the Whigs," when he means "Satires against the Tories.")

5. Nelson, ed., *Documents Relating to the Colonial History of the State of New Jersey* (Paterson, N. J., 1905), XXVII, p. 584.

6. Pattee, ed., *The Poems of Philip Freneau* (Princeton, 1902), I, p. 61.

7. Newlin, ed., *Modern Chivalry* (New York, 1937), p. xii.

8. Quoted by Moore, ed., *Diary of the American Revolution* (New York, 1860), I, pp. 185-187.

9. Cheesman tells of carrying with him a purse of gold so that he would have a decent burial if killed in action. The story is retold by Lossing, *The Pictorial Field-Book of the Revolution* (New York, 1850), I, p. 201n. Lossing, whose source may have been Brackenridge, finishes the anecdote by reporting that "A sergeant and eleven men fell with him. Cheesman was not instantly killed, but arose to press forward to charge the battery. It was a feeble effort, and he fell back a corpse, in a winding-sheet of snow."

10. *Pennsylvania Gazette,* January 24, 1776.

11. "Journal," *Connecticut Historical Society Collections,* VII (1899), pp. 162-66, quoted by Commager and Morris, eds., in *The Spirit of 'Seventy-Six* (Indianapolis, 1958), I, p. 192.

✦✦

THE DEATH OF GENERAL MONTGOMERY, IN STORMING THE CITY OF QUEBEC

✦✦

A Tragedy.

With an ODE, in honour of the Pennsylvania Militia, and the small band of regular Continental Troops, who sustained the campaign, in the depth of winter, January, 1777, and repulsed the British Forces from the Banks of the Delaware.

✦✦

By the AUTHOR of a DRAMATIC PIECE, ON THE BATTLE OF BUNKER'S HILL. TO WHICH ARE ADDED ELEGIAC PIECES Commemorative of Distinguished Characters. By different Gentlemen.

Hic, manus, ob patriam pugnando, vulnera passi. Patriots who perish'd in their Country's Right.

Pitt's Virgil.

✦✦

NORWICH: Printed by J. Trumbull, for and sold by J. Douglass McDougall, on the West Side of the Great-Bridge, Providence, 1777.

To His Excellency
THOMAS MIFFLIN, Esquire:
of the
STATE of PENNSYLVANIA:
MAJOR GENERAL
in the
CONTINENTAL ARMY:

May it please your Excellency.[1]

I EMBRACE the opportunity of this publication, to express my veneration of your character; not from any of those smaller motives which are attributed to Authors in their dedications; but simply, because it is my "delight to do you honour."

Indeed every friend of virtue and of mankind, must esteem a Gentleman, who, from the beginning, has so warmly asserted the cause of liberty, and hence may be reckoned in the number of those pure patriots, who with underived heat and lustre, first shone out in opposition to the British counsels. For I count them but a second class of men who have slowly taken fire at the patriotism of their neighbors. They may deserve true praise, yet they have not attained to the honour of the "first worthies."

Every officer and soldier who has fought under your command, since the commencement of the war, speaks of your nobleness of spirit, your frank demeanor, humane and generous deportment, with a warmth of approbation which only true love and real admiration could inspire. The inhabitants of Philadelphia attribute to you, under God, and the good conduct of General Washington, the salvation of their city. For perhaps no other person could so effectually have roused the Militia of the Pennsylvania[2] State to encounter the hardships of a campaign, in the depth of winter, even though the object of their enterprize was noble, the repelling[3] the British forces from the banks of the Delaware.

I shall not detain you longer from more important services, but take my leave by wishing you a continuance of life beyond the AEra of the war, that you may behold the matured Blessings of that Liberty and Glory, which you have so gallantly assisted to establish.

Sir, I am, with the greatest respect,
Your very humble Servant, The AUTHOR.

The AUTHOR
to the PUBLIC

It is my request that the following Dramatic Composition may be considered only as a school piece. For though it is written according to the prescribed rules of the Drama, with the strictest attention to the unities of time, place, and action, yet it differs materially from the greater part of those modern performances which have obtained the name of Tragedy. It is intended for the private entertainment of Gentlemen of taste, and martial enterprize but by no means for the exhibition of the stage. The subject is not love but valour. I meddle not with any of the effeminating passions, but consecrate my muse to the great themes of patriotic virtue, bravery and heroism.

With respect to the particular merit of the piece, I have only to say, that I flatter myself it would have been more deserving of attention, had it been drawn up in less haste.[4] It is found by all who have attempted it, that at least one year is necessary to the composition of a good Tragedy. The following was made out at different intervals in the space of a few weeks, and therefore, according to the rule before mentioned, it must be supposed to come far short of perfection. Writing in this way is my amusement not my business. But here it may be observed, that no man pays attention to the time spent in composing, but to the merit of the performance when it makes its appearance. Could not I have kept this small affair to myself some time longer, if after that period, it would have been in my power to have produced it more elegant and pleasing? I answer, that one great foundation of the merit of any performance is its being seasonable. An oration, eulogium, or production of any kind, in honour of our brave countrymen who have fallen, or of those who do not yet contend in the glorious cause of freedom, is likely to do greater good and will be more acceptable at present, than hereafter, when the foe is entirely repulsed and the danger over.

For this reason I submit it in its present state to the candid and generous, with my promise, that when it shall be in my power to afford time to revise and amend it, I will endeavor to give it to the world in a Second Edition, more correct and finished.

PROLOGUE to the DEATH of GENERAL MONTGOMERY
By Colonel J. P.

Once more the advent'rous band, my lays explore,
From Charlestown heights, manur'd with British gore;
From Cambridge barriers, frowning on the foe,
Who harmless bluster on the depths below;
Through howling desarts, many a weary'd mile,
The dreary forest and the dark defile.
The dashing torrent, and the deep morass,
Braving, like Hannibal, the tow'ring pass;
But Fancy quits those realms where horror reigns,
And welcomes Arnold to Canadia's plains.
Those plains where mighty Wolfe in triumph bled;
Britain subdu'd and vanquish'd Bourbon fled:
Thy sons, America, with chearful heart,
In all her conflicts took a willing part,
With steps resolv'd ye trod the hostile wood,
Where famine threatens and where murders brood.
For Britain's glory, flow'd the purple vein,
Warm from the heart to prop a Brunswick's reign.
How chang'd the scene! no more with friendly hand
To aid thy pow'r, we leave our native land.
Burst are those ties, alas! and scatter'd wild,
That join'd the Parent to the faithful child:
Fatal ambition, to each vice ally'd,
Dire mischief's progeny, the child of pride;
These wars malign, from thy curst genius flow
Those fields of slaughter, and those scenes of woe;
Death marks thy steps, while o'er our land high waves
Destruction dire;—deep yawns the op'ning graves,
Portentous ill! see hecatombs expire,[a]
And cities falling! 'midst th' unhallowed fire.
'Midst thundering Culverins,[b] and dread alarms,
Crush'd to their base, by tyranny in arms.
Thro' the bleak arctic clime thy spirit glows,
While blaz'ing ramparts banish soft repose.[5]
Montgomery, glorious from his conquest won,
To Abra'ms plains now leads his cohorts on.
Where hostile batt'ries stern resistance shew,
And dare the fury of th' advent'rous foe.
While Britain's union streams upon the walls,
Our hardy troops to fierce encounter calls.
Now round each heart, fair freedom spreads her flame,
That glows and kindles at the voice of fame.
E'en Carleton trembles from his bastion'd height,
Nor dares, 'gainst freemen, risk the dubious fight.
   Tho' Autumn black'ning on the mountain lowrs,
And o'er the dreary heath the tempest roars,
Tho' o'er his head the sweeping whirlwind flies,
And blazing mortars rend sea, earth, and skies—
Fearless of danger, for he smiles at pain,
Spreads his wide flag and opes the bold campaign.

---

[a]
hecatombs expire Hecatombs were the ancient Greek or Roman sacrifices consisting of 100 oxen or cattle; in this instance the sacrificial slaughter of many victims: the British sacrificing the Americans.

---

[b]
thundering Culverins The long cannon, often an eighteen pounder, with serpent-shaped handles.

Dramatis Personae

MONTGOMERY   *General and Commander in Chief of the Expedition to Canada*
ARNOLD   *Commander in Chief of the Division which effected a March to Canada by way of the river Kennebec*
CAMPBELL   *Colonel in the Division under General Montgomery, and Deputy Quarter Master General*
MEGGS   *Major in the Division under General Arnold*
MACPHERSON   *Aid-de-Camp to General Montgomery, and from the Delaware State*
BURR   *Aid-de-Camp to General Montgomery*
HENDRICKS   *Captain in the Pennsylvania Forces*
CHEESMAN   *Captain in the New-York Forces*
OSWALD   *A gallant Volunteer from the State of Connecticut*
MORGAN   *Captain in the Virginia Troops*
CHAPLAIN   *The Reverend Samuel Spring*
SURGEON, GUIDE, SOLDIERY, ETC.
GHOST OF GENERAL WOLFE
CARLETON   *Commander in Chief in Quebec, and Governor of Canada*
MACLEAN   *Colonel in the British Forces in Quebec*

ACT I

Scene 1

Camp Before Quebec

[*Enter Montgomery and Arnold*]

Montgomery
The third-hour turning from the midnight watch,
By no ray visited of moon or star,
Marks to our enterprize, its proper date.
Now from above, on every hill and copse,
The airy element, descends in snow,
And with the dark winds, from the howling north,
Commix'd and driven on the bounded sight,
Gives tumult privacy, and shrouds the march;
So that our troops, in reg'ment or brigade,
May undistinguish'd, to the very walls,
Move up secure, and scale the battlements:
May force the barr'd gates, of this lofty town,
On all sides, bound, with artificial rock,
Of cloud-cap'd eminence, impregnable.
Impregnable, so long, and fully proof,
To all our batt'ry, and sharp cannonade;
But yet assail'd with vigour, and full force.
This morn, I trust, we enter it, in storm,
And, from its bosom long defiled, pluck,
This scorpion progeny, this mixed brood,
Of wild-wood Savages, and Englishmen,
Who 'gainst their brethren, in unrighteous cause,
With cruel perfidy, have waged war.
Against their brethren, did I say? O God!
Are we the offspring of that cruel foe,
Who late, at Montreal, with symbol dire,
Did call, the Savages, to taste of blood,
Life-warm, and streaming, from the bullock slain,
And with fell language, told it was the blood,
Of a Bostonian, made the sacrament?
At this, the Hell-hounds with infernal gust,
To the snuff'd wind, held up, their blood-stained mouths,
And fill'd[7] with howlings, the adjacent hills.

Arnold
Yes, brave Montgomery, I have heard the tale;
When from the brow, of many a desart wood,
And wolf-resounding mountain top, came down
The yelling Savage, [a]-Onondago wild,
Fierce Outawae, and half extinguish'd brood,
Of aged Huron, native habitat,
Of those high plains, where long their wigwams stood,
And margined the banks of Quebec's streams.
With these the Mohawk, from the nether lakes,
Oneida, Shawnese,[a] and an hundred names

a-a
Onondago . . . Shawnese The fury of the Americans against the British use of the Indians for inhumane slaughter knew no bounds. Horrible massacres occurred, especially in the frontier communities.

Of uncouth accent; Savages inspir'd,
With horrid passion, of inhuman war,
By these our butchers—butchers of the ox
First slain, symbolical, in place of us.
For, while the blood, ran streaming from the wound,
The Indian warrior, tasted it, and sware,
By that fell Demon, whom he hates and prays,
That thus the blood of each Bostonian shed,
Should slake his appetite; which God avert,
And on their heads, the imprecation turn,
Who, with dire artifice, of story feign'd,
Wrought up the Savage, to such pitch of rage.
But, as for us, let indignation fire
Each patriot bosom, to resent the thought,
And turn to them, the meaning and the curse,
Of this dire cantico,[b] at Montreal.
All things, are favouring to our enterprize;
The scaling-ladders, for the assault, prepar'd.
And Heaven, the signal, which we waited for,
In this snow-driven storm, presents to us:
Nor is there one man, in that well tryed band,
Which many a region, hath travers'd with me,
But will exult, to hear the orders given.

Montgomery
I know it Arnold, and revere their worth,
Who swiftly roused, at their country's call,
And nobly resolute, have brav'd all pain,
In such long march, of fifteen hundred miles.
Far from the south-west of Virginia's bounds,
To Massachusetts-Bay. Thence, after toil,
Sustain'd, in combat, with tyrannic foes,
O'er many a region, dolorous and drear,
Have pierc'd the wilds, to Canada's cold clime.
O gallant souls! A sacrifice more rich,
If such should fall, was never offer'd up,
On hill or mountain, to the sacred cause
Of Liberty; not even when Cato died
At Utica, or many a Roman brave,
With noble Brutus, on Pharsalia's plain.

Arnold
Nor less eulogium, have those merited,
Who, from New-England's happy streams, more north,
With me experienced, and saw the fate
Of war's sore tragedy, on Bunker's-Hill.
And since, in common, with the embodyed force,
Have borne sharp famine, and severest toil.
While up the rapid Kennebec, they stem'd,
The impetuous torrent, or at carrying place,
O'er broad morass, deep swamp, and craggy wild,
Urg'd their rough way. Thence over hill,
And dreary mountain top, to where Chaudiere

---

[b] *cantico* A lively ceremonial dance of the Algonquin tribes.

Doth mix his wave, with the St. Lawrence tide.
And now encamp'd on the Abraham heights,
Await your orders to attack the town;
This proud-wall'd town, whose haughtiness hath mock'd,
The incessant batt'ry, and sharp cannonade,
T'effect a breach; but soon possess'd by us,
Shall amply recompense the watching, cold,
Famine, and labour, which we have sustain'd;
And yet sustain, while with the wintry year,
We now contend, digging the ice-bound soil,
In deep entrenchment, and laboriously
Erecting batt'ries of hard frost congeal'd,
'Midst arrowy sleet, and face-corroding storm.

Montgomery
Then gallant officer, be this our plan.
First Livingston, with the Canadian troops,
March to the Palace gate, and with a feint,
Of swift annoyance, to the Upper town,
Keep them attentive, and their guns aloof;
While with the main force, by the river bank,
We storm the Lower town. I on this side,
Along the precipice, and that sad stream,
Which washes their redoubts, with equal force.
You, at the conflux, of the kindred tides,
St. Charles and St. Lawrence, force your way.
Thus, under God, we haply may succeed,
And see, with joy of victory, today,
Our standards planted, on Quebec's high walls.

Arnold
The disposition, for the bold attack,
With all alacrity, shall be obeyed,
No shape of danger, shall deter my steps,
Swift moving, in this gallant enterprize.
I shun no combat, and I know no fear,
But count the honour a full recompense,
For ev'ry peril in this furious war,
If men in after times, shall say of me,
"Here Arnold lies, who with Montgomery fought,
"Stemming the torrent of tyrannic sway."

Scene 2

[*Montgomery and Macpherson.*]

Montgomery
It seems to me, Macpherson, that we tread,
The ground of some romantic fairy land,
Where Knights in armour, and high combatants,
Have met in war. This is the plain where Wolfe,
Victorious Wolfe, fought with the brave Montcalm;

And even yet, the dreary snow-clad tomb,
Of many a hero, slaughter'd on that day,
Recalls the memory, of the bloody strife.
I believe not superstition, or the dreams,
Of high wrought fantasy, that fill the brain,
But yet methinks, Macpherson, that I feel,
Within this hour, some knowledge of my end;
Some sure presentiment, that you and I,
This day, shall be with them, shall leave,
Our breathless bodies on this mortal soil.
But this allotment, should it be our case,
Fear not young soldier, for our cause is just,
And all those failings we are conscious of,
Shall in the bosom, of our God repose,
Who looks with mercy, on the sons of men,
And hides, their imperfections, with his love.
Say not young soldier, that thy life was short,
In the first bloom, of manhood, swift cut off.
All things are mortal, but the warriors fame;
This lives eternal, in the mouths of men.

Macpherson
The light is sweet, and death is terrible;
But when I left my father, and my friends,
I thought of this, and counted it but gain,
If fighting bravely, in my country's cause,
I tasted death, and met an equal fame.
With those at Lexington, and Bunker's-hill.

Montgomery
Sweet fame, young hero, shall attend thy years;
And link'd, in friendship, as we are link'd in death,
Our souls, shall mount, and visit those fair hills,
Where never-dying bards, and heroes stray.
There, Wolfe, shall hail us, and the great Montcalm,
Shall bind the amaranth[c] around our brows.
For mighty warriors, though opposed here,
There live serene, in heavenly amity,
And walk, and taste, of conference sublime.
Go then, young soldier, and these orders bear,
To Colonel Campbell, and to Livingston.
The disposition, for the attack, is here.
Bid them be ready, when the morning breaks,
To try this city, by an escalade.

Scene 3

[*Montgomery, Solus.*]

I fear not death, but yet it gives me pain.
When the soft passion, of my soul, flows out,
In sweet remembrance of Amanda's love,[d]

---

[c] *amarinth* (amaranth) A legendary flower supposed never to fade, used often in poetical connotation.

[d] *Amanda's love* Montgomery married Janet Livingston, daughter of the prominent and wealthy Robert R. Livingston of New York. They were married in July 1773 and two years later Montgomery was on his way with the American forces to invade Canada. Mrs. Montgomery outlived her husband by many years, and there were no children.

Whom I have left, where the swift Hudson's stream,
Circles the shady hills; left to the chance,
Of various war, and the rude Savage foe,
Who yet may penetrate, that happy clime,
And mix the mother's with the infant's blood.
Yes, sweet Amanda, soon disjoin'd in life,
And the connubial-cord, loos'd and cut off,
I must resign thee, to the will of Heaven.
The child unborn, that in thy womb thou bear'st,
Its father may not know, may never climb
The knee paternal, or call forth a smile,
From his fond countenance. To thee O God,
I leave my spouse, sweet children, and each friend,
That mourns behind. Shew them thy grace,
And tender mercy in the walks of life,
And from its changes, rescue them at last,
To the fruition of thyself, in joy.

ACT II

Scene 1

[Macpherson and Cheesman.]

Cheesman
The hour is dreary, and all Nature dark;
But yet, Macpherson, there is something more,
In melancholy, and a mind o'ercast:
In this presentiment of some sad chance,
This throb of heart, that bodes fatality,
And is not cowardice,* but God himself,
That in the knowledge, of the future ill,
Doth touch the mind, with apprehension strange,
And feeling sensible of its approach.
You see, Macpherson, I am gayly dress'd.
Say, is it pride of the departing soul,
That one should chuse, to have the body fair,
And vestured in comely, decent garb,
E'en, when it lies, yet tombless, on the field?
Or is it hope, that thus the victor foe,
May feel a kinder fault, and shed one tear,
While it surveys the body trim and neat,
By their own hand, of the sweet life bereft?
Here is a purse, my brother, some small gold,
Which found upon me, by the ruthless search,
Of plundering soldiery, in quest of spoil,
May pay for burial, should I fall this day,
In this attempt, upon Quebec's high walls.
Haply, for sake of this, they may forbear,
To treat my pale corpse with indignant rage,
To dogs, and fowls of Heaven, casting it,
Or to the beasts, and mountain wolves, a prey.

Macpherson
O gentle Cheesman, such prophetic touch,
On the warm casement of the busy mind,
Doth oft forewarn with certainty, and oft,
Is but illusion, and the fancy's dream:
But be it so, that death should be our lot.
On this sad day, it is the price we give.
For that rich ever-green, of peerless praise,
Which they receive, who for their country die.
The ev'ning past, when first the twilight grey,
With sober step, came o'er the western hills,
In meditation, to that spot I came,
Where, the victorious Wolfe, in battle fell.

---

*It is remarked by critics on the poet Homer, that the courage of his favourite Achilles appears in the highest point of view, from this circumstance, that though it was foretold by the oracle, that he was to fall at the siege of Troy, yet he had the bravery to engage in that expedition, and in every attack, led the van of his countrymen.

There as I stood, profound in mighty thought,
It seem'd to me, a consecrated ground,
Not to be trod on with unholy feet.
I lov'd the laurel bush that grew just by,
And, could have kiss'd the stones, that round about,
Lay scatter'd on the soil; so much the worth,
And praise of this great man, intranced me,
In pleasing reverie. O, thought I then,
One day, it may be mine, in the green earth.
To lie, while the young warrior, visiting,
The solitary spot, shall bless my fame,
And say, Macpherson, I could die with you.
For my ambition, is to die like Wolfe,
Wept by his country, and by many a bard,
Of silver-tongue, high storied in his urn.

Cheesman
Come then my brother, let one soft embrace,
Seal up our souls, in expectation firm,
To the fair bliss above. One soft embrace,
And bid farewell—with this sweet chearing hope,
That if we fail, and leave the earth today,
Our names shall live, and with immortal Wolfe,
And the ennobled of the future world,
Be ever mentioned, and prais'd in song.

Scene 2

[*Burr and Macpherson.*]

Macpherson
What says my friend, to the heroic thought,
Of storming the fair capital today?

Burr
'Tis full of peril, but it gives me joy,
And, wakes the bosom, with ideas warm'd,
Of high invention, and bold thought in war.
First in the van, let me bespeak a place,
Close by the General, for he loves to lead,
His gallant troops, and not to send them on,
With, go my lads, and scale that lofty wall.
But come, brave soldiers, of fair worth approv'd,
And follow me, this bright illustrious day,
Through yielding foes, to triumph and to fame.
You say, this day, we shall attack Quebec?
O, I have long impatient, waited it;
And indignation, brac'd up every nerve,
When I have thought, of this fell British foe,
Who still insatiate, with full revenue,
Drawn from our commerce to their shores confin'd,
Must needs enslave us, and mark all their own.
Whether we land possess, or property,

Of freer nature; still at their command,
We must resign it, and content ourselves,
With some ᵃ˙peculium, slave-like article,
Which these our masters, may vouchsafe to give.⁻ᵃ
Yes, as the culprit Gibeonite, the Jew,
Did serve ingloriously, so we
Must draw them water, and hew for them wood,
That these our task-masters, may then forbear,
To cut our throats. O wond'rous lenity!
'Tis passing gracious of these generous men;
And better far than the Egyptian King,
Who sentenced the Israelites to toil,
And slew the children, on the mother's breast.
Not yet the Englishmen, have come to this.
Perhaps, let me indulge the thought, perhaps,
Not, till increasing numbers, give alarm,
Will they denounce, in proclamation dire,
Unpitying slaughter to the softest age.

Macpherson
With equal hate, I scorn their purposes;
And on my mind, my father's parting words,
Make deep impression, for he knew them well.
My son, said he, take this, your father's sword,
For I have grasp'd, and often wielded it.
Yes, I have fought, in the severest war;
And in Britannia's very cause I fought,
Who now would stab me, and drink from my veins,
The poor remainder of the blood I spilt.
Come here my son, look on this wounded joint—
This injured joint—remainder of that arm,
Which I have lost for baneful Englishmen.
O Britain, Britain, I will hold this up,
To the wide world, as witness of the love,
Which once, I bore you, and did testify.
I say, my son, look on this injured joint—
And let the idea, to revenge, wake up,
The hottest passion of a warrior's soul.
Where you shall meet an Englishman, tell this,
And in his ear, exclaim—ingratitude.
Exclaim—and with a filial piety,
Give, for your father, one life-severing blow,
Making his head start from his shoulders. God!
Will they devour me, who have fought for them?
Let not soft mercy, turn your weapon's edge.
Fight valiantly—in every charge be first:
Nor with the name of cowardice, disgrace
Your father's reputation. Go my son,
And Heav'n protect you in its cause and mine.
These words, sweet Burr, yet harrow up my soul;
And urge me forth, impetuous, to the field.
Come on, and with our General place ourselves,
We must attend him, where he leads to war.

---

a-a
peculium . . . give Brackenridge is referring to the laws of Trade and Navigation, requiring the colonists to send raw materials to Britain and purchase their manufactured goods in England. They could not trade with other countries, and thus American commerce was isolated and free enterprise strangled. The peculium, a gift given to Roman slaves by their masters for obedience and servility is like the ironic gift from England—"permission" to the colonists to buy products made from their own materials.

ACT III

Scene 1

[Hendricks, Oswald, and Chaplain.]

Oswald
Hail! noble Hendricks, this auspicious morn.

Hendricks
To our fair arms, auspicious, let it be.
But to the foe indignant, and severe,
Like that sad day, when in ᵃ·Beth-horon's vale,
The Jewish Captain, smote the Canaanite,
By Heaven's assistance, which, upon them rain'd,
Her rocky hail·ᵃ - - - -

Oswald
—Look not for miracles,
Or hand of Heaven, heroic youth, to day,
For the late world enjoying what is past,
Of supernatural display to man,
Is left to general laws; no more vouchsaf'd,
Uncommon aid, of the dividing sea,
So swift o'erwhelming the Egyptian King,
Or of that ᵇ·Angel, who in one night slew
So many squadrons of the Assyrian host.·ᵇ

Chaplain
I grant, sweet youth, we may not hope from Heav'n,
The sudden vengeance of red fiery wrath,
To blast the foe; but yet the Almighty reigns,
O'er every act, and enterprize of man,
To frown upon, or bless it with his smile.
He unperceiv'd, can from the unchanged course,
Of Nature's settled laws, with ease bring forth,
Events particular; with equal ease,
As when its mound, the mighty ocean pass'd,
In Noah's day, and deluged the world.
Or when an earthquake, rending the deep earth,
Took in its bosom, those that mutined,
Against their Captain, in the wilderness.
Rest then assur'd, that heavenly Providence,
In this late age, accompanies our steps,
And guides our every action, prospering them,
Or laying the expectation, and high hope, in dust.
He can give courage to the warrior's breast,
Or, if it please him, can deject the soul,
With power invisible. He has his cloud,
To wrap the starry firmament of night,
When the skill'd General steals upon the foe,
Or when he prudently, in some retreat,

---

a-a
Beth-horon's . . . hail Upon the appeal of the Gibeonites, under attack by five nations or tribes, Joshua and the Children of Israel under the direction of God, responded to the plea and the combined forces put to flight their enemies, assisted by a deluge of hailstones. Joshua 10:11.

b-b
Angel . . . host The angel of the Lord slaughtered more than five thousand Assyrians encamped before Jerusalem, and the enemy departed in fear and haste after this miracle. II Kings 19:35; Isaiah 37:36.

Draws off the wearied troops. He has his fog,
Which providentially may form a veil,
In the sun's face, and the deep council hide.
The Almighty reigns, distributing to each,
That which we call our lot. Not one hair falls,
Of our head, to the ground, but it is numbered.
He reigns, and gives to innocence, its due reward.
But to the guilty, punishment and death.

Oswald
Then if the guilty shall have punishment,
May we not hope, that this proud cruel foe,
Shall meet an ample share, and yield this day,
In battle vanquished. If Heaven protect,
Distressed innocence, and injured right,
We sure may hope, that this our patriot cause,
Shall triumph finally, and scorn the rage,
Of Britain's parliament and bloody King.

Chaplain
A firm persuasion hath possess'd my mind.
That this fair cause, shall triumph finally.
But the complexion, of the ensuing hour,
We cannot tell. It may be fortunate,
And yet as partial, to the whole event,
It may be clouded, and deep wrought with woe.
Just so the morning of an April day,
When spring repulses the rude wintry year,
Is buried oft, in the descending rain;
But soon, the warm sun bursts the watery cloud,
Gives chearful noon, and bids the evening mild.
On herbs and flowers, shed only her soft dews.

Hendricks
I am resign'd to the dispose of Heav'n,
Let whatsoever be our fate today,
Or my particular lot. Yet I could wish,
Once more to see the Susquehanna banks,
My native rocks, and sweet resounding hills,
Where I have fondly stray'd, delightful stream,
Where I have sported, in the summer's day,
And bath'd my limbs, and angling from a rock,
Caught with my father, the too credulous fish,
That silvered the tide. My father lives
With aged hoary locks, the frost of years.
'Tis mine to aid his swift-declining strength,
And hold his trembling steps—

Oswald
Come Gentlemen,
The troops, have early snatch'd a short repast,
And now to arms, brave Arnold, leads them forth;
In his division rang'd, we scale the wall.

Scene 2

[*Hendricks and Arnold.*]

Arnold
'Tis yours, brave Hendricks, to command the guard,
Of this encampment, while we storm the town.

Hendricks
Since you vouchsafe the epithet of brave,
Let me deserve it, and go forth with you.
Some may be found, who would prefer this post,
Which, I shall hold, reluctantly. No Sir;
If I have merited one thought from you,
Of praise, or confidence, in this long march,
And perseverance, thro' the wilderness,
Have me excus'd, from such inglorious task.
I would go forth, and mingle in the attack,
That when old age comes on me, and slow years,
I may have things to tell, achiev'd in war,
Of which, I bore a part. Then shall the youth,
Encircling me, request the hoary head,[8]
Of this fam'd siege; who first assail'd the wall—
What warriors fell—who wounded in the attack—
How long 'twas fought—and how we gain'd the town.

Arnold
I honour, Sir, the high heroic worth,
Of this fair choice; and shall immediately,
Supply that station, with some other troops.
I count it happy that I go with men,
Who thirst for danger, and renown in arms.
Your station shall be chang'd, and in the van,
You shall have scope to shew your fortitude,
And purchase glory, that shall never die.

Scene 3

[*Montgomery and Campbell.*]

Campbell
We hold ourselves, in readiness, what time,
We have your orders to parade in arms.

Montgomery
In some few moments, when the early day,
Shall mix its breaking with departing shades,
And give a dubious light. This interval,
In conversation, we may here, exhaust.
Far other thought, O Campbell, fill'd my mind,
When first, a soldier, on the Abraham's heights,
I stood in arms. Then, in Britannia's cause,

I drew my sword, and charg'd the rival Gaul.
I felt for her a patriot's generous heat;
And step'd, exultingly, when fair Quebec,
Saw British standards on her rocky walls.
Full, in my memory, I retain the view;
Each circumstance, as if but yesterday.
Here Monckton stood; there Townshend rang'd himself;
And here, great Wolfe, in noble strength of soul,
Array'd the battle, and the men in arms.
O mighty Wolfe, if yet, thy warlike shade,
Revisitest these heights, and rocky streams,
Be witness here, in this unnatural strife,
Where a mad mother doth her children stab.
You, when you fought, did not unsheath the sword
Against your countrymen, and younger sons;
Did not excite, with cruel artifice,
The wild-wood Savage of the gloomy hill,
To drink Bostonian blood. No mighty shade;
Britannia then was free herself; her King,
Call'd not for butchers, to secure his sway
Tyrannical, and to be held with blood.
Unhappy reign of an inhuman George!
I saw it early, and withdrew myself,
To sweet retirement, on the Hudson's banks,
And am persuaded, that had mighty Wolfe,
Surviv'd his victory, his native isle,
O'er-run with parasites, that drink the looks
Of flatter'd Majesty, and base-born Lords,
Would have disgusted him. This western land,
With shades, and solitudes, and wood crown'd hills
Had better pleas'd. He could have lov'd her glades,
O'er-hung with poplars, and the bending beech,
Fan'd by the Zephyr's gale. He could have lov'd,
The budding orchard, and the oak tree grove,
And thought, no more, of luxuries enjoy'd
With prostitution of the free-born mind.
If Wolfe had liv'd, would he have drawn his sword,
In Britain's cause—in her unrighteous cause,
To chain the American, and bind him down?
O no, his soul, by Nature elegant,
With liberal sentiment and knowledge, stor'd,
Would not have suffered it; I rather think,
Nay, I well know it, that himself had led,
Perhaps, once more, an army to Quebec,
To drive the tyrants out. He had obey'd,
Rather, the dictates of an upright soul,
Than the commandment of a tyrant King.
But now the time, that we draw forth in arms,
Resolves to us. Then, through the standing tents,
Let us return, and with high thought of war,
Fire every bosom, with a martial glow.

ACT IV

Scene 1

[Arnold, to his Division.]

Heroes and patriots, who with me have borne,
Cold, watching, famine, and a thousand toils,
O'er dreary mountain, river, bog, and lake,
To these fam'd heights, and that besieged town,
Where your oppressors, and fierce foes are lodg'd.
Fierce foes, in hate, but not in battle fierce,
Since we have waited, and long challeng'd them,
To equal combat, and fair chance in war;
But yet they come not forth, on this wide plain,
To meet our arms, as when the warlike Gaul,
Led by Montcalm, did face the British foe;
And tho' their fortune, gave them not the day,
Contended long, and bravely fought for it.
Yes, we have waited, but they come not forth.
On equal ground, to mix in gallant play,
Of fair hostility. 'Tis then resolv'd,
In storm, brave souls, to storm the city gates.
And, with firm valour, from their dens drive out,
These cut-throat homicides. Shall we brave souls,
Lie on the cold ground, thus unsheltered
From rain, deep snow, and binding ice, and storm,
With but Heaven's canopy, while they possess
Yon noble buildings; chearful residence?
On then my countrymen, and drive them out,
To us, surrendering up the ample halls,
Aspiring domes, and structures of Quebec.

Scene 2

[General Montgomery to his Army.]

My friends, and countrymen, of worth approv'd,
And nobly resolute, in this campaign,
From that first day we gain'd Ticonderogue,
To Crown Point taken, and the fort Chamblee,
St. John's strong garrison, and Montreal.
The hour is come, when one important stroke,
Against this capital, this proud Quebec,
May wrest from Britain, her possessions claim'd,
And to the Thirteen States, add Canada.
The Frenchmen wish it, for they hate the rule,
Of sway monarchial, experienced,
And left unwillingly, when mighty Wolfe,
Subdu'd them into happiness, of which,

They since are sensible, and scorning laws,
By Britain 'stablished, now risk themselves,
On our fair patronage. Let then, my friends,
Our swords protect them, in each privilege,
And sacred right, which we claim birthright to.
Peers of the vicinage, shall try their suits.
No hand shall drag their free-born yeomanry
To death, and punishment, in climes remote.
No standing army shall remain, to spoil
The daughter's virgin innocence, or bathe
Their hands, in the sons blood, relentlessly.
Yes, fellow soldiers, if you exercise,
That noble spirit, which our cause inspires,
This day shall terminate, the bold career,
Of early tyranny in this north clime,
And drive far hence, the hell-born progeny,
With speed precipitate and fear compell'd
To leave the dry land and embark the wave—
To leave the dry land, which beneath them groans,
And feels the pressure of malignant sin.
Yes, these sad plains, beneath their pressure, groan;
St. Lawrence stream, weeps as it passes by;
Quebec's high buildings, echo in complaint,
And Nature sickens with the infernal crew.
Nor strange is it, for sure the miracle,
Would rather be, if earth, and conscious Heaven,
Could bear their rank impiety, their deeds
Of damned horror, shocking mortal ears.
As late, when offering up a roasted ox,
They called the Savages to taste the blood,
Till a Bostonian roasted in like sort,
Should give sweet relish and appease their rage.
Come on brave souls, and spoil their appetite.
But halt my troops—let first with upright thought,
Our prayer ascend to that Almighty Power,
Who guides the wheels of Providence, and rules
In empire over man, to bless our arms
With unstain'd victory. The Chaplain this,
As it is usual, in our names require.

Chaplain
O thou, the God, and framer of the world,
High thron'd in light, and glory excellent!
The tempest and the wind obey thy word;
At thy command, the ebbing tide steals off,
With humble waters, from the assaulted shores;
And, as the wild waves, so the heart of man,
Is turn'd, at thy rebuke, Turn then, O God,
The imagination of Britannia's King,
From this fell purpose of reducing us
To slavery dire. Or, if his heart more obdurate
Than rock of adamant, resist thy grace;

Let not the hostile, and oppressive acts,
Meet triumph, and o'erwhelm us in the effect.
Our cause is just, we dare to call it so,
Even in thy presence, whom bright truth surrounds,
And sun-beam judgment gilds thy radiant throne.
O then, let uprightness, and truth prevail,
And these rude Britons, like Leviathan,
In the rough sea, be hook'd and turned back;
Or with the dragon of the infernal pit,
Chain'd down from hurting us. Soon may those years,
Those thousand years, in smooth-stream flow, succeed,
When the Arch-tyrant, Belzebub, confin'd
With perjured Kings, and Ministers, below,
Shall leave the world, to harmony and peace.
Wash clean, O God, our sin-affected souls,
In the Redeemer's blood; that, no soul slain,
Of taint original, or act of ours,
Yet unrepented of, may form a shade,
Between thy smiles, and our fair hopes to day.
Inspire each bosom, with celestial heat
Of sacred fortitude, steel up the soul,
To resolution, and heroic might,
Of extreme hardiness, and o'er our heads,
Raise thy broad shield, to turn aside the aim
Of swift-wing'd death, and anguish-giving wounds.
But, if in Sovereignty, it is thy will,
To cloud the scene, and rather bear from us,
Some spirit doom'd to meet the approach of death,
O let it flourish in thy immortal love,
And take sweet floods of elemental joy,
With kindred spirits, and seraphic just,
Made pure, and perfect, and resembling thee.

Montgomery
God's will be done, and let us humbly trust,
Not in ourselves, but in his grace divine.
Come, march the van—March yet more speedily.
But stop, dear Sir, your place is not the field;
I would not have a gowns-man take the sword.

Chaplain
The cause is sacred, and doth sanctify,
An action singular; I would go on,
If you forbid it not; it is my choice,
Full in the center of the war, to mix
In the hot combat, and the battle's rage.

Montgomery
It is permitted, Sir, I see you have
A warrior's spirit, in a gowns-man's breast.
I love a clergy-man, the aid-de-camp,
As I may say, of the great God, to man;
Or rather him that holds the flag of truce,

And tells of mercy to the sin-stain'd soul.
But I have thought too little, of these things.
O, had I time, I could talk much with you,
Of man's prime happiness, and Heaven's grace.
Come on brave soldiery, and linger not—
I could talk much with you, of penitence,
High faith, and love—Move on brave countrymen—
A swift approach, may save us much hard toil—
Yet unalarm'd the town lies fast in sleep—
But here a messenger—see what he brings.

Messenger
Alas! the intention of our arms is known.
I saw a scout just turning from the walls,
And have out ran him, who inform'd me thus,
That a deserter, from our camp, this night,
Gave swift intelligence, and now the foe,
Lie on their arms, and wait our first attack:
Each barrier full; the engineers prepar'd,
With matches lighted, and directed guns.

Montgomery
Unhappy circumstance! but God our aid;
We may achieve, and carry the assault,
E'en in the face of their collected force.
Come, give the wide-stream'd standard to the gale,
And march, brave souls. Say guide is this the way?
Say, must we march along this precipice?

Guide
Along the precipice, by these redoubts.

Montgomery
My God! the task is amply perilous;
But why, alas, why halts my infantry?
Come then, brave officers, march on with me;
They sure, will follow, where their General leads—
March on with me, and storm this first redoubt.
One fire, brave souls, and push with bayonet.
The battery's ours. These slave-born renegades.
Dare not confront us. Slavery, slavery dire,
Cowards the spirit, and unmans the soul.
Now to the next, my gallant officers;
Mean time, young Burr, wait and conduct the troops.

Burr [**Aid-de-Camp**]
Why, Gentlemen, with such slow tardy steps,
Moves up the van? See where your General leads,
With few attendants; yet the first redoubt,
So well defended and secur'd is ours.
Move up brave soldiers, and preserve your fame.

Montgomery
The post is ours; the second barrier storm'd;
But in our troops, why such a tardiness?

I must fall back, and with deep-piercing words,
Prevent their ignominy. Gentlemen,
What means this phlegm, this cold and mildew damp,
Which turns the current of the life-warm blood
To winter's ice, and freezes up the tide,
Of noble, bold, and manly resolution?
Why, Gentlemen, so slow and heavily
Moves up the van-guard, to attack that foe
Which oft we vanquished? Ticonderogue
Could not defend them, nor strong-barred Crown-point.
Driven o'er the lakes, we beat them, at St. John's;
At Montreal; and now it were a stain,
Of ignominy, not to be retriev'd,
If sickly cowardice, phrenetic power
Of some sad circumstance, prevent, this day,
To storm this capital, this last retreat,
Where they have shut themselves. O this,
This is juncture critical, the point
Of time elapsing, which may not return,
Which makes it ours to crush the tyranny,
By vengeful Britain, here established.
The poor Canadians, whose effects and lives,
Hang on the fortune of our enterprize,
Shall imprecate dire curses on our steps,
If falling back, from such fair promises,
We now desert them, senseless and unarm'd,
A certain prey, because they gave us aid,
To savages, and haughty Englishmen.
Come on my soldiers, let me pray your haste,
By all that lives in man, of noble fortitude.
By this your country, and those natal ties,
Which binds the memory to the place of birth;
By your spoil'd liberty, and injur'd rights;
By the religion, which you owe to God;
By your own safety, and the love of life.
Come on my gallant countrymen, come on;
Or if you come not on, at least do this;
Advance to me, and in this deep-pained breast,
Pour one sure shot, and ease my amazed soul,
My bleeding soul, of what I feel for you.
Move on, my countrymen, move on;
I first, myself, will in the charge advance.

Cheesman
Nay, rather, Sir, do not expose yourself;
For much artillery, that strong pass defends,
Which soon must rake us; and should you the head,
And source of action, be cut off from us,
The trembling limbs must loose their energy,
And the fair enterprize abortive prove:
Let me advance, with this small chosen band,
And bear the first fire of the cannonade.

Montgomery
Your warm benevolence, heroic youth,
Demands my gratitude; I honour you.
And this small band, that bears me company;
But such, the backwardness, of these my troops,
That of necessity, I risk myself.
Can I survive their infamy, their shame?
Nay death, swift death, is rather my sad choice;
And God hath sent it—But alas, for you,
My sons, my brothers, who are join'd with me,
In equal fate, on this unhappy day.

Burr [Aid-de-Camp]
Let Heav'n be clouded, and her face wrapt up,
In equal gloom with this deep tragedy.
Montgomery slain, and all my fairest hopes,
In this sad hour, cropt off and withered!
O father, father, groaning, fainting, dead!
Let me embrace thee to my grief-sick heart,
And pour my warm soul in thy bleeding vein,*
Wet with the crimson of thy noble blood,
Unchang'd, I'll wear these sprinkled garments home,
And shew my countrymen each ruddy drop,
Each ruddy drop, and with my words wake up,
In every breast, susceptible of rage,
The fallen anger of an injured soul.
O, I could follow from the impoverish'd world,
With thy great spirit mingle mighty man,
And visit scenes invisible, and new
To the released soul. O bleeding corpse,
Let me not leave you to the insulting foe,
Who will exult and trample on thy tomb,
Or tear thy body uninhum'd, expos'd
To the wild Savages, or birds of Heav'n.
O, no, the vultures shall not have thy corpse.
If I can bear it from the blood-stain'd field,
On these poor shoulders. Sight deplorable!
What youth is this pierc'd thro' with streaming wounds?
It is Macpherson, who is likewise fall'n:
Fall'n alas, and with him every charm
Of conversation, and behaviours grace,
With comely beauty, ravishing the heart.
Sweet youth, most lovely in thy shape and mein,
Gay, pleasant, chearful, courteous and soft
To thy companion, as the summers gale
Loose scattering roses. See, alas! the change,
The mournful ruins, which grim death has made.

---

*Sir Charles Lisle beholding the sad spectacle, the dead body of his dearest friend, fell upon it and kissed it, as if he meant to breathe into it another soul—Observations on the Life of Sir Charles Lucas, in Lloyd's State Worthies.

Eclips'd and dim the Heav'n-sparkling eye;
The fair skin pallid, and the lithsome joints
Cold, stiff, and motionless. But who is this?
Ah! hapless Cheesman, art thou likewise slain?
Belov'd companion, of my jocund years;
Tall, graceful, manly in thy stately step;
The bloom of nineteen, withers on thy cheek—
The red lip quivers, and is red no more—
Deep sleep sits heavy on thy midnight brow—
O shades illustrious, join'd in equal fate,
Here will I stay and wake your funeral,
Covering your bodies from the snow-cold wind,
And bidding stars, in the nocturnal sky,
Come down and weep with me—

Chaplain
Not so, fond stripling, but retire with me.
The dead themselves, insensible of pain,
Or ignominy to their bodies shewn,
Fear not the tyrant. Haste and save thyself;
For in swift sally from the western gates,
The crafty foe aims to encompass us.
Away, sweet youth, accelerate thy speed,
And save thy valour for a better hour.

Burr [Aid-de-Camp]
Nay, see that form, in obscure march this way.
With shadowy sword, stuck in the incircling zone:
His wrist bound up, and bleeding wound before,
Just where the jasper saint emboss'd in gold,
Sits on his warrior breast. My heart is sad.
O awful, sober shade, if thou art come
From ghostly kingdoms dreary and unknown,
To walk the earth and choose a solemn scene
Congenial with thyself, detain with me.
There lies our General, brave Montgomery slain;
And here sweet Cheesman, gentle, placid youth.
This was Macpherson, whom in life I knew;
And O pale form if you can weep one tear,
Be it for him in soft compassion shed.
He was the flower and hyacinth of youth,
So fair, so lovely, that he ravished
Each heart that knew him—ravished the love,
The heart-warm love of every soul that gaz'd
On his soft beauty, and first rising years.

The Ghost of General Wolfe
From realms celestial and sweet fields of light,
I come once more to visit this sad spot.
New-ting'd and red'ning with a hero's blood;
With thy rich blood, Montgomery, and these youths,
Of this same ground, so immaturely doom'd

Norman Philbrick
Trumpets Sounding

To taste mortality, in their first years,
Amidst the hopes and bright ey'd promises,
Of early life, relentlessly cut off;
Not in contention with the rival Gaul,
But Britain's self, Medea-like, dispos'd
To tear her children, merciless of heart.
False council'd King and venal Parliament!
Have I then fought, and was my life blood shed,
To raise your power to this ambitious height,
Disdainful height, of framing laws to bind,
In cases whatsoever, free-born men,
Of the same lineage, name, and quality?
Have I then fought, and was my life-blood shed,
To lay foundation for such dire event,
That you, my friends, should bleed, alas! to day,
In opposition to the unrighteous aim
Of British power, by my achievements, rais'd?
Yet must it be, for such the will of God,
Who wraps the dark night in a sable shade,
That thence clear light may spring, and a new morn,
Rise with fresh lustre on the hill and dale.
For from your death, shall spring the mighty thought
O separation, from the step-dame rule
Of moon-struck Britain. Rage shall fire the breast
Of each American, and fathers hence,
Shall like Hamilcar at the altar, swear
Their sons and Hannibals of future days,
To hold no more, conjunction, with the name
Of hard and cruel-hearted Englishmen.
But hence remain, as nations of the world,
In war their enemies, in peace their friends.
Yes, from your death shall amply vegetate,
The grand idea of an empire new,
Clear independence and self-ballanc'd power,
In these fair provinces, United States,
Each independent, yet rein'd in and brac'd,
By one great council, buckling them to strength,
And lasting firmness of immortal date.
O happy empire, 'stablished in truth,
Of high wrought structure, from first principles;
In golden commerce, and in literature,
Of many a bard, and wisdom writing sage,
High flourishing, and filling length of time,
With peerless glory and immortal acts.
In this sweet hope, soft-mourning, gentle youth,
That look'st so sadly on this scene of woe,
Be amply chear'd. Full recompence
In retribution, of dire loss in war,
Awaits these murderers, yet hence compel'd
To reimbark, ingloriously struck down
From every hope to win the Continent.

ACT V

Scene 1

[Arnold, with his Division.]

Arnold
Hard by the conflux of these sister tides,
It is determin'd, that we storm the wall.
This is the place, as fame reports to us,
By Montmorenci, where the Frenchmen lay,
T'oppose the British arms, what time great Wolfe
Rode on the bosom of that winding stream,
And meditated a debarkment here.
A shot—come on my veteran soldiery—
The salutation of their cannonade
Return with equal compliment. Wheel round
And circle this redoubt. Some rifle-men
Advance before, in silent ambuscade,
And pick them from that eminence. Long us'd
To strew the swift deer on the mountain top,
You need no council to direct your fire,
Save this, brave souls, take down their officers.
O, if this day, we stumble not, Quebec,
With all her stores and magazines is ours
And thro' America the sound shall ring,
Of unstain'd victory; thro' all her groves,
The bold achievement shall be mentioned,
And every hill shall echo with our fame.
A shot—A full platoon—Sad accident.
My ankle splintered with a musket ball.
I'm like Achilles, wounded in the heel,
And lose much blood. Be not discouraged.
My brave companions, but advance to fame.
I lose much blood, but yet will stay with you,
While one drop circles in the life-warm vein.

Oswald
Nay Sir not so, the wound is dangerous.
Let the men bear you from the ensanguin'd field.
He faints with loss of blood. Support him hence
My gallant soldiers—let the wound be drest.

Morgan
Come gallant souls, and patriots eminent,
Next in command on me devolves the task
Of Generalship; then may I pray from you
Obedience prompt, in this fair enterprize?
Say, shall I draw you off ingloriously,
With speediest step? or shall we yet advance,
And pour revenge on the indignant foe?

Think, Gentlemen, it will be base to leave
The brave Montgomery, who the other wall
By this time storming, will expect our aid,
And rendezvous in the besieged town.

Soldiery
Lead on—lead on—we follow your command.

Morgan
Come then brave Hendricks, in the charge advance,
With these sure rifle-men, and from the mound
Of the first barrier pick the officers.

Oswald
The barrier's ours, and the rude enemy
Lie in vast numbers wounded and cut off.

Captain Lamb
Let some skill'd surgeon dress the wounded men;
For even an enemy, soft pity and love
Should have from us, if low and vanquished
They ask for mercy, and implore our aid.

Surgeon
I dress them, Sir, with my best skill and speed,
For many lie deep wounded on the plain.
Some with their legs shot off, and some their arms
With grape-shot shatter'd. Some a musket-ball
Hath deeply pierc'd—

Captain Hendricks
Bring up the ladders, plant them speedily,
One hundred Dollars Continental Bills,
Or gold of equal value to the man,
Distinguished with honour and fair fame,
Who first ascends the thirty-feet high wall,
Nor needs he doubt of firm and full support,
With the full corps of infantry, sustain'd.
Ye Pennsylvanian's, make the honour yours,
And shew the world, that Sasquehanna's banks
Bred one adorn'd with this bright heraldry,
This standing monument of peerless praise,
That of this army, he the first assail'd
The ramparts of Quebec, swift-planting there,
The wide-stream'd standard, representative
With Thirteen streaks of ivory and blue,
The extended provinces. A fatal shot—

Oswald
Fell tyranny, these are thy vestiges
In crimson battle and vindictive war,
Unpitying wag'd. The hero immature
Full in the vigour and fresh bloom of life,
With eye star-beaming, and high beating heart,
By thee cut down. The roseate glow of health

Fades on his cheek, and the sweet breath no more
Heaves in his bosom, yet soul cheering thought!
Not unlamented, nor unwept he lies,
For many a tear, O Hendricks, shall bedew,
By Sasquehanna's flood, the annual flowers.
When the sad story of thy mournful fate,
Is hence resounded to her rocky stream.

Scene 2

[Col. Maclean returning from his success against the division under General Montgomery.]

Thus far, success, and noble victory
Breathes on our fortitude. The great arch-chief
Of this rebellion, that so rudely pierc'd
Redoubts and barriers hedging in his way,
Is now cut off. The great arch-chief and head
Of this their daring enterprize, struck down
From his rebellious hope of victory,
Lies haply prostrate on the snow-clad earth,
Discolouring with his blood its virgin tint.
Nought then remains, but that we swiftly charge
This other band, which tho fam'd Arnold leads.
This still holds out, and would bespeak sore toil,
In opposition to our arms this day.

Scene 3

[Major Meggs]

We are surrounded by the enemy.
See where Maclean collecting their whole force,
Hems in our regiment, and cuts off retreat.
I did not dream of numbers in Quebec
To face at once our thus divided troops
With such superior force. Sure they have not
Repell'd Montgomery, from the assaulted wall,
And brought their whole force, to resist our arms?

Lamb
Come, engineers, bring that field piece to bear.
Ye gallant veterans, from the mountain stream,
Of Hudson's river visiting New-York,
Shrink not from danger; 'tis the hero's joy
To live in thunder and the noise of war.
Light up with flame, the air's wide element,
And rock the deep ground with your cannonade.

Scene 4

[*Carleton, from the wall of the Upper-Town, exposing the body of Montgomery.*]

Say rebel brood, why stubbornly maintain
That ground, encircled by superior force?
Why so reluctantly give up the field,
When now my squadrons from each fort and gate,
All opposition broke, collect themselves,
Pouring their whole fire on your shatter'd ranks?
Front, flank, and rear, nay, overhead the storm
Of battle rages; but if so much trust,
And hope of conquest plays upon your minds,
Behold the body of your General slain
The great Mongomery bleeds upon the wall.

Lamb
[*To his Countrymen*]
The hapless fortune of the day is sunk!
Montgomery slain, and wither'd every hope!
Mysterious Providence, thy ways are just,
And we submit in deep humility.
But O let fire or pestilence from Heaven,
Avenge the butchery; let Englishmen,
The cause and agents in this horrid war,
In tenfold amplitude, meet gloomy death.
What do I say? can hecatombs of slaves
And villains sacrific'd, repay one drop
Of this pure vital scarlet-streaming blood?
No, not ten thousand of life-gushing veins,
From perjur'd Kings and venal parasites,
Can rise in value, to one heart-warm drop,
Of that pure patriot; yet this alone we can,
That in revenge, the battle be renew'd,
And indignation be the word to day.

Carleton
Once more I offer you the terms of peace,
Ye stubborn combatants. If I'm oblig'd
To hold the battle up, and lose more men
Slain by your obstinacy; rest assur'd,
The gate of mercy shall be shut. No hope
Of quarter shall remain, but the red flag
Of blood hung out, shall amply testify
The irreversible consign of death.
Nor in sepulture of grassy grave,
Shall you meet burial; but your carcases
Shall feed the fowls and vultures of the Heaven,
Left long expos'd, and rotting on the earth;
But on submission you shall be receiv'd,
With arms of love and pity honouring
Your noble valour eminent and great,
Who these three hours such odds have combated,
And struggled hard with us for victory.

Oswald
Methinks no man, my hapless countrymen,
Can throw suspicion of base cowardice,
On my behaviour, or my words this day;
For I have fought and ventured with you,
Where the hot battle did most fiercely rage.
But in my judgment, we contend in vain,
And risk our persons, without equal chance,
Against this enemy. Fair terms and words,
By them are offer'd, better then submit
And take their mercy, than see butchered,
So many brave men, in such circumstance,
That nought avails their courage and bright flame
Of true heroic excellence approv'd.

Morgan
True, gallant Oswald, we attempt in vain,
To urge the war with such unequal strength,
And disadvantage of encompass'd ground,
On our side, visible. Lay down your arms,
Then hapless countrymen, and put yourselves
On that fair law and custom 'stablished
'Mong christian nations, that the life be spar'd,
And with humanity and gentleness,
The victor foe shall treat his prisoners.

Scene 5

[*Carleton to the Prisoners.*]

Now in my power disarmed and reduc'd,
I will give scope, and scorn you with my tongue,
You vile rebellious progeny of wrath,
Fierce and malignant in Don Quixotism
Of moon-mad liberty. You Bedlam-brood,
You viper-lip'd, and serpent-hearted race,
Bred on the poison of foul fraud and hate,
Scum and off-scouring of humanity,
Whom laws of government to the sure cord
Have ever destined; and were it not,
That the black vengeance of your countrymen
Might dare retaliate, and gibbet up
Some British prisoner, each soul should hang,
And die, this day, in execrable form,
The death of traitors. Yet, whatever shape
Of suffering horrible, can be devis'd,
In dreary dungeon, and in obscure jail,
Cold, dark, and comfortless, and lacking bread,
Shall be your lot, snake venom'd parricides.
And first, three victims from your shattered band,
Must, to the Savages be given up.
Some three Bostonians, sacrific'd and slain,

To glut the appetite of Indian chiefs,
Who at our cantico, at Montreal,
Drank of the ox-blood, roasting his large limbs,
Symbolical of rebels burnt with fire.
Take these three men, ye Indian warriors,
And use them wantonly, with every pain,
Which flame's fierce element can exercise.
And with the sound of each loud instrument,
The drum, the horn, in wildest symphony
With our own howlings, shall the scene be grac'd;
Save, that in terror, oftentimes, a while
The noise shall cease, and their own cries be heard.[9]

The Captives
O gentle Sir, where are the promises
Of life untouched and fair acts of love?
Where is the memory of that faith and word,
That sacred honour, which a soldier wears?
Is there no mercy in the soul of man?
But O whatever we are doom'd to feel,
Of death, or torment, let it not be fire.
The flame is terrible, and none can bear,
On the soft eye, the scorching element;
The sinewy nerve bent up and withered;
The body rolling, crisping in the flames.
Let us be sentenced to some dark pit,
Or subterranean cavity, where light
Of sun, or star shall never cast a ray.
In some lone island destitute of food,
Let us be bound, and slowly waste ourselves,
With painful hunger, and life-pinching want.
O could we but obtain immediate death,
By some sharp bayonet, or musket-ball,
Even should our bodies, afterwards be burnt,
And bones reduc'd to ashes in the flame.

Carleton
Hah, I could laugh, to see your skeletons,
Unflesh'd, and whit'nin in the light-wood blaze.

[Aside to Maclean]
But yet, Maclean, we dare not execute,
Stern justice due; for still the rebel foe,
That part of them which with Montgomery fought,
Recruit their forces and block up the gates;
And should we urge extremity of wrath,
It may be ours to taste an equal fate.
The chance of war is various and unfix'd.
Go then Maclean, and countermand the word
Of pain and burning to the Savages.
Restrain their wild rage with the certain hope
Of mirth, and cantico, and the war song,
To be indulg'd, with many a captive burnt,
If we prevail, and drive them from the walls.

[*To the Captives.*]

Yes, I could laugh, to see the flames involve,
With spiral wavings, your black carcases.
For so enhanc'd and aggravate your guilt,
That well it merits every horrid woe
Denounc'd to murder, sacrilege, and sin
Through all its shapes; but yet the gentleness,
And meek-ey'd majesty of Britain's King,
Will not admit all stretch of punishment.
For Heaven's long suffering imitating, still
He waits your penitence, and better mind.
But this receive, in certainty of faith,
That if your countrymen persist t'oppose,
The peace and order of our government,
Our long endurance shall turn into rage
Of tenfold enmity; yet, perjured brood,
If soon they crush not each rebellious thought,
Keen torture shall excruciate their joints;
And if I conquer, Hell lend every plague,
To give them torment, in all shapes of death.
How then, vile scorpions, will you bear your fate;
The deep-struck tomahawk, in the trembling heart;
The curv'd knife, ready to unroof the scull;
And body roasted in slow-scorching fires.

Morgan
Sad thought of cruelty, and outrage dire!
Not to be parallel'd, 'mongst human kind,
Save in the tales of flesh-devouring men,
The one ey'd Cyclops, and fierce Cannibal.
For what we hear of Saracen or Turk,
Mogul, or Tartar of Siberia,
Is far behind the deed of infamy,
And horror mixt, which Britons meditate.
Nature, herself, degenerate from the fall,
In the curs'd earth, can scarcely furnish out,
So much black poison, from the beasts and herbs,
As swells the dark hearts of the Royalists.
The toads foul mouth, the snake's invenom'd bite,
Black spider, asp, or froth of rabid dog,
Is not so deadly as these murderers.
When men far off, in civilized states,
Shall know the perfidy and breach of faith,
The thought remorseless, and dire act of these,
In every language, they shall execrate,
The earth-disgracing name of Englishmen.
And at the Last Day, when the pit receives
Her gloomy brood, and seen among the rest,
Some spirit distinguished by ampler swell
Of malice, envy, and soul-griping hate,
Pointing to him, the foul and ugly Ghosts
Of Hell, shall say, "That was an Englishman."

Notes

The copy text is that published at Norwich in 1777; the play was also printed in Philadelphia in 1777 by Robert Bell. The abbreviation *Ph* is used for the Philadelphia edition in notes recording substantive changes from the copy text.

Following the end of the play, an Ode in honor of the Pennsylvania Militia who were involved in the campaign on the Delaware in January, 1777, and several "Elegiac Pieces" in commemoration of various "Distinguished Characters" who fell in the cause of freedom appear in the Norwich edition. They are irrelevant to the play and therefore are not reprinted.

1. It is not surprising that Brackenridge should dedicate his tragedy to Thomas Mifflin in 1777, for the latter had reached the height of his popularity as a brilliant revolutionary leader and a military man. He had been enormously successful in recruiting men for the Pennsylvania militia for the winter campaign of 1776-77. For these efforts and for his participation in the battles of Princeton and Trenton, he was appointed major-general on February 19, 1777. Having won the admiration of Washington as well as of the common soldiers made him a heroic figure in the eyes of many.

2. *Ph:* Pennsylvaniay.

3. *Ph:* the repulsing.

4. *Ph:* the sentence "I flatter . . . haste" is replaced with: "I know myself to be capable of producing something much better, had I leisure for that purpose, but writing in this way is my amusement not my business." (The latter part of this sentence—"writing in this way"—occurs later in the Norwich edition, giving credence to the strong possibility that Brackenridge superficially revised the Philadelphia printing.)

6. *Ph:* "not repose" substitutes for "soft repose."

7. At this point in the printed edition of the play, Brackenridge includes a long footnote in italics in which he gives his authority for the drinking of the blood—a letter from General Schuyler in Albany to the Congress, concerning Carleton and the Indians. The letter was written December 22, 1775. (See Force, ed., *American Archives*, Washington, D. C., 1843, IV, p. 260.) Schuyler's letter gives a somewhat different interpretation of the affair, although the facts of the business are grisly enough, as reported by Schuyler. Carleton had ordered a special ceremony and the Indians "were invited to feast on a *Bostonian,* and drink his blood—an ox being roasted for the purpose, and a pipe of wine given to drink. The war-song was also sung." Brackenridge, indulging in poetic license, gives the impression that the Indians thought they were eating a human being and drinking his blood. The playwright then draws a parallel between Carleton's action and that described by Aeschylus in *The Seven Against Thebes* where the chiefs slew a bull and plunged their hands into its blood, uttering wild war cries. "This would seem to be," says Brackenridge, "the very original whence General Carleton had copied the idea for his cantico."

8. *Ph:* request the hoary tale.

9. To this speech of Carleton's and to his next speech, Brackenridge has appended long, italicized footnotes defending his character portrayal of Carleton as a vengeful madman. Brackenridge explains that his picture of Carleton is not far from the truth, if one considers the British commander's treatment of American prisoners, particularly the outrage committed in May, 1776, when the Americans surrendered their post, The Cedars, on the St. Lawrence. Under a threat of Carleton, at least five prisoners of war were turned over to the savages for monstrous and prolonged torture to the death.

★★★★★★★★★★★★★★★★★★★★★★★★★★★★★★

THE PATRIOTS

★★★★★★★★★★★★★★★★★★★★★★★★★★★★★★

6

Introduction to
The Patriots

WHEN eighteenth century farce and sentimental comedy are combined, as in *The Patriots,* lively theatre is the result. The play stands comparison with such English counterparts as *The Beaux Stratagem* and *The Recruiting Officer* of Farquhar, Garrick's *Miss in Her Teens,* and the sentimental comedy of Steele, particularly *The Conscious Lovers.* Clichés of plotting and characterization, the comic canon of the century, abound in *The Patriots.* Use is made in the plot of mistaken identity, an almost successful false wedding, recruiting among rustics, reformation of the rake and, finally, discovery of a long-lost heiress.

The work is of particular significance because it is concerned with parochial strife—opposed forces within the colony of Virginia—rather than the struggle between colonists and British. The threefold conflict, involving the American Whig, the Tory, and the neutralist, differentiates *The Patriots* from other plays in the anthology; it recognizes an ideological triangle rather than simply a dualistic conflict. *The Patriots* does not encourage the Tory cause, but it does recognize that Tory had become a word of opprobrium easy to apply to any one guilty of the slightest deviation from "true" patriotism. Robert Munford, the playwright, attacks emotional and loud-mouthed Whigs who enjoy playing "hounds and hare," pursuing any man whose opinion is not blatantly jingoistic. He condemns those who will not tolerate a moderate political attitude as well as those who refuse others the right of dissent. One must grant that it was a difficult problem to follow a middle course when Britain's soldiers were at the gates of the new-found "haven of liberty" (as the political and religious orators characterized America), but in Virginia, as well as in some of the other colonies, it was still possible, even as late as 1777, to see the value of remaining gray instead of black or white.

Munford was conditioned to this point of view, having suffered outrageous attack as a neutralist, if not a Tory, even though he had publicly declared his belief in the patriot cause when he voted for the Virginia Resolutions under the leadership of Patrick Henry. Munford possessed a peculiar combination of resolute determination to support the attack on Britain and an inbred hesitancy to betray his birthright as an English subject. He realized clearly that events were moving toward independence from the mother country, but his connection with the conservative gentry made him uncertain as to whether revolution rather than gradual separation was the answer to the "colonial question."

On his mother's side the playwright came from impeccable lineage, that of the Blands. His uncle, Richard Bland, whose influence on the playwright may be reflected in *The Patriots,* was a delegate to the First Continental Congress and was admired by Thomas Jefferson for his knowledge of constitutional law. His collection of "many valuable public papers" was included in the official documents used by Jefferson to refute attacks by Britain against the colonists.[1]

MUNFORD probably wrote *The Patriots* sometime between 1777 and 1779. Internal evidence suggests 1777 as the earliest date because the battle of Trenton (December 26, 1776) and the battle of Princeton (January 3, 1777), both triumphs for Washington, are reported in the course of the play. Professor Rodney M. Baine observes:

The good humor, serenity, and optimism may suggest that he completed it in 1779, after he was re-elected to the House of Delegates which would have given him confidence because he could assume from public support that he was no longer under suspicion as an uncommitted Whig.

The play was probably written before 1780. Our hero Meanwell suggests to Mr. Summons, "Be a colonel of Militia then, 'tis a fine post for cripples, for they never march." The laugh would not have been in good taste after the rout of the Virginia militia at Camden on 14 August 1780.[2]

Munford did not consider himself a playwright. During his career he was an extensive landholder, a politician, and a soldier. Writing interested him, however, and he produced a "readable translation of the first book of Ovid's *Metamorphoses,* and . . . a mildly humorous narrative entitled 'The Ram,' in the manner and metrical form of Hudibras."[3] He also wrote a farce on the incredible circumstances attending a rural election in Virginia, *The Candidates,* in which he attacked the unethical absurdities of political campaigning in a country community. The play so cleverly pricked the pomposity and chicanery of public officials that it still may be read as a caricature of America of the nineteenth century and even of the present.

The Patriots, however, is of more importance than *The Candidates* because it has an underlying serious theme, a plea for balance in the heated controversy embroiling all citizens. The author urges a reduction of the fever of political passion by bleeding the choleric advocates for both sides, especially the violent Whigs.

The intention of the play is expressed in the opening scene by Meanwell and Trueman, who stress the need for political moderation and describe the true nature of loyalty to the patriot cause. The two are genuine patriots, but because they have not been openly assertive in their patriotism they are suspect. Furthermore, Trueman is in love with Mira, whose father, Brazen, is, as Trueman says, "a violent patriot without knowing the meaning of the word. . . . His political notions are a system of perfect anarchy, but he reigns in his own family with perfect despotism." Meanwell and Trueman share like opinions about the meaning of liberty and abhor the persecution of innocent men simply because they may differ from the majority. The essence of the philosophy of both moderates is summed up by Meanwell when he says that truth shall prevail and that "Men who aim at power without merit must conceal the meanness of their souls by noisy and passionate speeches in favour of every thing which is the current opinion of the day; but real patriots are mild, and secretly anxious for their country, but modest in expressions of zeal. They are industrious in the public service, but claim no glory to themselves."

Essentially a conservative, Munford was, however, keenly concerned with the rights of the colonists and guarded those rights with passion against the infringement of the British Parliament. In this respect he was sympathetic to the political ideas of his uncle, Richard Bland, whose *An Inquiry into the Rights of the British Colonies* was one of the most influential pamphlets written during the Revolution. Published in 1766, this defense of the American cause was an important justification for later events, as it emphasized that those who by their own consent become members of a society must submit to laws made by a legislative body whose members have been chosen by their fellow citizens. If that society does not, however, "conduce to their Happiness," they have the right to remove themselves from it and join a different community, even if they have to settle in another country.[4] This point of view was one of the pillars of Whig belief. Munford was emphatically, if quietly, an advocate of natural independence and was repelled by the users of patriotic hyperbole to prove their unassailable loyalty.

He would also have agreed with his uncle's allegiance to the king:

The existence of a monarch—pledged to protect the people under the terms of the compact, yet wielding a prerogative of whose limits he was the only short-range judge—was a basic assumption of the Whig constitutionists. Again and again Bland acknowledged the necessity of a king, not because he was anxious to appear as a dutiful subject, but because he believed sincerely that a visible sovereign, governing by the consent of the governed, brought stability, dignity, effectiveness, and legitimacy to the best of all possible constitutions.[5]

Although a member of the Virginia aristocracy, Munford was no Loyalist Whig nor was he a neutralist, as were many of his friends and relatives, who adopted a "wait and see" attitude rather than declare themselves. It was this posture of noncommitment that infuriated violent "patriots," such as those represented by Brazen and other members of the Committee of Observation in the play. As public bigotry became more open, unfounded accusations of Toryism became current and popular.

Everywhere apparent in the play is Munford's hatred of excess and his strong belief that men must be respected for their honest views and must have a right to utter them. Meanwell and Trueman speak for Munford and in so speaking are opposed by the prominent "patriots" of the community.

Still another social evil satirized by Munford is persecution of a minority, represented in the play by the Scots. There was an economic bias against the Scots in Virginia because of their position as factors and middlemen in the tobacco trade. The Scotsman had already become a recognizable character type in broadsides and literary essays—dour, miserly, and obsessively proud of his origins. In the rural South he was violently hated. As Courtlandt Canby indicates, anti-Scots sentiment in Virginia in the 1760s and 1770s grew into actual persecution during the Revolution. The general hostility was "the product of a carefully organized and deliberate propaganda emanating from the opposition journals in London, for in such periodicals as Wilkes' *North Britain* anti-Scotch feeling could be—and was—exploited for a political purpose in the same way Hitler and the Nazis exploited anti-Semitism."[6]

Attacks on a minority group are ridiculed by Munford, and he issues a warning to those who condemn without a fair investigation and those who try a man on superficial evidence. He makes a strong case for freedom of belief by condemning the Committee of Observation, of which Brazen is a member. That body had been established to guard against any breakdown of patriotic discipline and eventually became part of the Committee of Safety, a watchdog organization that ferreted out Tories and others suspected of disloyalty. Munford detected in the committee a desire, based on ignorance, to condemn others in order to establish without question the patriotic allegiance of its members. He saw them as gerrymanders who manipulated everything to their own advantage, and they are portrayed as stupid, ruthless men, self-consciously protecting their own rights.

Thus the committee in the play moves against the Scots, and anyone who is a Scotsman is immediately suspect. Act II, Scene 1, opens with Meanwell and Trueman deploring the persecution about to take place. Trueman says that such treatment will alienate persons who might be attached to the country and who would serve it well and points out that there are Scotsmen who have adhered to the common cause.

The members of the committee appear and a "trial" for nonconformist opinions take place. The whole scene has some of the illogical wildness of Alice before the Queen of Hearts. For example, when the Scots demand proof of the accusation that they are traitors, Brazen, the leader of the committee, says, "Proof, sir! we have proof enough. We suspect any Scotchman: suspicion is proof, sir." There is no defense against being born a Scot, and the accused are punished by being disarmed and proscribed as disloyal citizens.

One other point made by Munford in this scene of condemnation involves the Virginia loyalty oath of 1777. "When the responsibility of administering the oath to all males over sixteen became in May of 1777 fixed upon the county courts, Munford found himself, on July 14, 1777, saddled with the disagreeable personal responsibility of administering the oath within his own district."[7] The Scotsmen in the trial scene refuse to take the oath; they will swear allegiance only to the king, and this intransigence on their part adds to their guilt. Although Munford, as a state official, must have taken the oath, he indirectly condemns it in the play as discriminatory. Those who are not loyal to the patriot cause might hypocritically take the oath; those who are loyal did not need to do so.

The middle course of neutralism is constantly emphasized in *The Patriots*. Trueman expresses the point of view when he states:

If suspicion makes a tory, I may be one; if a disapprobation of men and measures constitutes a tory, I am one; but if a real attachment to the true interests of my country stamps me her friend, then I detest the opprobrious epithet of tory, as much as I do the inflammatory distinction of whig.

Munford had had personal experience with the witch hunters of "disloyalty" and with the obligatory oath of allegiance, both of which he disliked as infringements on the natural rights of man in society.

COMPARABLE TO if not better than the general run of comedies of the period, *The Patriots* would have no doubt succeeded on the stage. Whether it was ever acted cannot be proved, for what slight evidence there is rests on circumstantial grounds. Professor Baine flatly states that "No record of any performance has been noted; the play was probably never produced."[8] He adds, however, that Munford may have arranged for a private performance. In his discussion of *The Candidates,* Professor Baine suggests that Munford may have written that play to be presented by the Douglass Company, which performed in Virginia towns in 1770-71. Both *The Candidates* and *The Patriots* were published in 1798 by Munford's son William. The former play was published with a prologue "By a Friend," which gives the impression of having been spoken before an audience, beginning with:

> Ladies and gentlemen, to-night you'll see
> A bard delighting in satiric glee:

The Prologue might not have been written by Munford himself but by his son when the latter published the play, a suggestion made by Professor Baine, although it is possible that the playwright wrote it for a production.

Courtlandt Canby is not so certain that the plays were not produced. He observes that "Munford's two comedies, in fact, may have been written for a group of his friends and neighbors in Mecklenburg County; for we know that sometime before 1798 Robert's son William had composed the prologue for a local Mecklenburg production of Farquhar's *The Beaux Stratagem* in which he also acted a part. And in 1792 we find William attempting to persuade 'the players' in Richmond to put on a farce of his father's writing."[9]

The only conclusion that can be safely drawn is that the Virginia gentlemen liked to read and see plays and, as audience or participants, were often delighted by amateur theatricals. With the enthusiasm for Farquhar's plays in Virginia, especially *The Beaux Stratagem* and *The Recruiting Officer* of which there are many echoes in both Munford comedies, it seems highly possible that his works would have had a strong appeal and might well have been performed.

The Patriots reveals a familiarity with English drama of the period, not surprising because Munford had had a respectable education. He had gone to England with his uncle William Beverley and his cousins in 1750, remaining there for about six years, during which time he was enrolled at Wakefield School in Yorkshire. It was there that he studied Terence and Aristophanes. He would have also had the opportunity to see plays, because the Yorkshire theatrical circuit was becoming a thriving one, and more and more leading players from London appeared in successes from the capital.

In *The Patriots* Munford has cleverly arranged the different plots into a dramatic unity, and the various characters, scenes, and types of dialogue are similar and, at times, superior to English comedies colonial audiences would have seen in Williamsburg (and in the lesser towns of Norfolk, Petersburg, Hobb's-Hole, and Fredericksburg) produced by the Murray-Kean company of 1751 and the Hallam Company of 1752-54.[10] Munford returned to America from England in 1756; by 1758 a new company of actors under the directorship of David Douglass had arrived in the colonies and continued to play in most of them for the next sixteen years until the resolution against theatre performance by the First Continental Congress was heeded by most of the state assemblies. The Douglass Company appeared often in Virginia, and the colonial admirers of the theatre would have been well acquainted with eighteenth century farce, sentimental comedy, romantic tragedy, "improved" adaptations of Shakespeare, and occasional political pieces such as the popular *Cato* of Addison.

Although *The Patriots* has an obvious imitative quality, it has a theatrical vigor and a caustic wit that raises it above a simple pastiche of sentimental comedy or a routine farce. As Professor Baine indicates, there are three romances embodied in the plot: the farcical, the comic, and the serious.[11] It is the first, however, which contains the greatest originality; Isabella, described as a "female politician," has an obsession with arms and the man, the former preferably. She will marry only one who has been in battle and who knows of "war and Washington." She is passionately fond of smart-looking officers even though they may have lost a limb or an eye. "It appears so martial—so—so quite the thing." Isabella in her madness for patriotism is in love with one of the hypocritical members of the committee, Colonel Strut, and she upbraids Mira, who is allied to Trueman, because he is in her eyes a shocking Tory. Isabella proceeds to inform Strut that she will never marry him until he goes into battle and becomes a general.

"Suppose I should be killed?" he asks.

"I should cry a little, I suppose," she answers.

Strut says that there are soldiers enough without him, but Isabella is adamant: he must be a general so that she can be a general's lady, or quit his wooing of her. The farcical romance culminates in a highly comic mock duel in which Strut and Flash, both cowards, are encouraged by Isabella to fight. The men compromise, shilly-shally to such an extent that Isabella seizes Strut's sword and runs at Flash, who flees, whereupon Isabella in disgust quits her "general-to-be" forever.

The comic romance between Pickle and Melinda is simple and direct, involving all the usual clichés and traditional pattern of innocent maid almost seduced by rake. The plot is obvious, yet well contrived, and there are several well-conceived *contretemps,* among them the scene in which Meanwell's butler, dressed as a clergyman, delays the wedding ceremony by pretending he cannot read the service, thereby giving Meanwell time to arrive and prevent the marriage.

The serious romance between Mira and Trueman is in the sententious and labored style often employed by moralistic stage lovers of the period. The two lovers become unbearably sentimental when speaking of their affection. Mira, determined to marry Trueman without her father's consent, remarks, "I wish love and duty could always go hand in hand, but the little tyrant will be obey'd, even when all the virtues oppose him. What can poor Duty do when sole competitor against so formidable a rival. She must submit, I suppose." Trueman, facing Mira's father, Brazen, proudly states, "You see before you, two persons, long united by the ties of love, now waiting only for the solemn, sacred service the rites of honour call for." Whereupon Brazen, gruff squire that he is, punctures the rhetorical balloon with, "I hate your high flown speeches, Mr. Trueman."

Any perusal of the comedy of the eighteenth century will reveal numerous parallels between *The Patriots* and other standard drama. *The Patriots* has an acceptable, conventional, and respectable comic patina, but it rises above the ordinary dramatic fare because of the rigor given it through its re-creation of the environment of Revolutionary Virginia. The play is obviously imitative, but it transcends mere copy work because Munford introduced a particular native quality in the characters of Brazen, Strut, Summons, Thunderbolt, and others. These militant patriots are caricatures of the planter squirearchy among whom Munford moved; the narrowness of their outlook is obvious in their treatment of the Scots and Meanwell and Trueman. All members of the committee are scrubby little men who will do their duty, although they are not certain what that duty is except to be superpatriotic. As smug, self-satisfied men of substance they will persecute all who seem to oppose the majority point of view and all who appear to be guilty by association. They are well-drawn caricatures, although beyond that there is little depth in characterization. Tackabout, the pretended Whig, is also interestingly portrayed. At heart a Tory, on the surface he must appear devoted to the American cause, even if an informer, and his equivocation is presented with comic insight.

The Patriots is valuable as propaganda, despite its muted point of view. After all, if one wishes to stress the importance of tolerance, screaming negates the appeal of the middle course. Thus among the plays in the anthology, *The Patriots* is by its very nature less abrasive than the others. When Meanwell and Trueman and Mira express their opinions about absurdly extremist points of view, the violence of anger is replaced by cold indignation, which in the long run can be more effective than passionate rage.

Notes

1. Boyd, ed., *The Papers of Thomas Jefferson* (Princeton, 1950), I, p. 164.
2. Baine, *Robert Munford* (Athens, Georgia, 1967), pp. 73-81.
3. Hubbell, *The South in American Literature* (Durham, North Carolina, 1954), p. 144.
4. Bland, *An Inquiry into the Rights of the British Colonies*, Williamsburg, 1766.
5. Rossiter, "Richard Bland: the Whig in America," *William and Mary Quarterly*, X, 3rd Series (January, 1953), p. 67.
6. Canby, "Robert Munford's 'The Patriots,'" *William and Mary Quarterly*, VI, No. 3 (July 1949), p. 439n.
7. Baine, *op. cit.*, p. 85.
8. *Ibid.*, p. 73.
9. Canby, *op. cit.*, p. 445.
10. "The Theatre in Eighteenth Century Virginia Outside of Williamsburg," *Virginia Magazine*, XXXV (July, 1927), p. 295.
11. Baine, *op. cit.*, pp. 74-80.

****

THE PATRIOTS

****

A Comedy in Five Acts

****

The Characters Are,

MEANWELL, TRUEMAN } *Two gentlemen of fortune accused of toryism*

COL. SIMPLE
1. THUNDERBOLT
2. SQUIB
3. COL. STRUT } *Members of the committee*
4. MR. SUMMONS
5. BRAZEN
6. SKIP

STITCH   *door-keeper to the committee*
McFLINT, McSQUEEZE and McGRIPE   *three Scotchmen*
MR. TACKABOUT   *a pretended whig, and real tory*
JOHN HEARTFREE   *a farmer*
CAPT. FLASH   *a recruiting officer*
PICKLE   *servant to Meanwell*
TRIM   *a recruiting serjeant*
MIRA   *daughter to Brazen, in love with Trueman*
ISABELLA   *a female politician*
MELINDA   *a country girl*
MARGARET HEARTFREE   *wife to John*
Butler, Cook, Scullion and a Servant to Meanwell
Groom to Trueman

ACT I

Scene 1

[*Meanwell and Trueman, meeting.*]

Meanwell
Mr. Trueman, I am happy to see you. In times like these, of war and danger, almost every man is suspicious even of his friend; but with you I may converse with the utmost confidence.

Trueman
My dear Meanwell, I know your heart, and am sorry that any man can suspect its purity; but our case is much the same.

Meanwell
What? are you too accused of toryism?

Trueman
I am indeed. Unfortunately, I have some enemies who have raised the cry against me. And what is worse, I fear the consequences will be serious, and a little uncommon.

Meanwell
How?

Trueman
They will be bad indeed if they cause the loss of the girl I love. To your friendly bosom I may trust the secrets of my heart. The lovely Mira, daughter of our old neighbour Brazen has won my affections. You know her beauteous form; but that is but an image of her soul, its more charming inhabitant. I had seen and loved her: her father declared his approbation of my passion, and encouraged me to proceed. Heaven seemed to promise me success, and the idol of my soul had with blushing tenderness consented to be my bride. But all our hopes may probably be blasted by this unfortunate circumstance.

Meanwell
Indeed!

Trueman
It cannot be doubted. Her father is a violent patriot without knowing the meaning of the word. He understands little or nothing beyond a dice-box and race-field, but thinks he knows every thing; and woe be to him that contradicts him! His political notions are a system of perfect anarchy, but he reigns in his own family with perfect despotism. He is fully resolved that nobody shall tyrannize over him, but very content to tyrannize over others. I hap-

pened in conversation to oppose some of his doctrines of a state of nature and liberty without restraint, and he blazed out immediately like a flash of gunpowder. I endeavored to moderate his anger; but as reason and he can never be reconciled, I am afraid my sins will never be forgiven; besides, I have a bitter enemy and rival in Captain Flash.

Meanwell
Ay, that is the drawcansir[a] of modern times; a fellow who pretends to eat the smoke of a cannon fresh from the mouth, and to kill all the enemies of his country, as Caligula would the Roman people, at one blow. But I believe he's a coward at bottom.

Trueman
So do I. But Old Brazen is persuaded that not even Washington is his parallel. As I pretend not to extravagant valour, the captain thinks me a puny milksop, and judges it very great presumption in me to pretend to the lady he adores. I expect he has assisted the old man's prepossession against me, and, by his assertions, convinced him I am a tory:—But this is certain, the old gentleman declared that I should never enter his doors with his consent again, and moreover has commanded his daughter to think no more of having me for her husband.

Meanwell
What a pity it is that all heads are not capable of receiving the benign influence of the principles of liberty—some are too weak to bear it, and become thoroughly intoxicated. The cause of my country appears as dear to me as to those who most passionately declaim on the subject. The rays of the sun of freedom, which is now rising, have warmed my heart; but I hope my zeal against tyranny will not be shewn by bawling against it, but by serving my country against her enemies; and never may I signalize my attachment to liberty by persecuting innocent men, only because they differ in opinion with me.

Trueman
It seems for this very reason you are not accounted a patriot; but truth will at last prevail, the faithful heart be applauded, and the noisy hypocrite stripped of the mask of patriotism.

Meanwell
I hope so; and therefore truth, plain truth, shall be the only shield I will use against my foes. Men who aim at power without merit, must conceal the meanness of their souls by noisy and passionate speeches in favour of every thing which is the current opinion of the day; but real patriots are mild, and secretly anxious for their country, but modest in expressions of zeal. They are industrious in the public service, but claim no glory to themselves.

---

[a] *drawcansir* The bully and braggart in Buckingham's *Rehearsal* who kills everyone on both sides.

Trueman
May the armies of America be always led by such as these! Thus will the power of Britain be overthrown, and peace with liberty return—May men like these conduct our government, and happiness, in the train of independence, will bless the smiling land! But before this can be accomplished many temporary evils must be supported with patience.

Meanwell
Yes, and this under which we now labour among the rest. But what do you propose to do in the case of your lovely Mira? you won't give up the pursuit?

Trueman
Give up the pursuit? When I do, may I be hanged as a traitor to love! But it seems a little difficult at present. I have taken the liberty to use your servant already in the business. As he very lately came into this part of the country, and possesses a very genteel air, I thought he might easily pass for a gentleman with old Brazen. I equip'd him therefore as an officer, and sent him to the house of the old gentleman; and ordered him to pass himself for a travelling captain, and to wait for an opportunity of delivering a letter to Mira. He executed the commission with fidelity, and brought me an answer from her, in which she communicates to me all that I have told you.

Meanwell
And what do you intend to do?

Trueman
With your permission I'll make use of your servant upon a second embassy.

Meanwell
By all means; but what do you propose?

Trueman
In the pursuit of honorable love few things are reprehensible. I shall intreat her to elope with me into a neighbouring government, where Hymen shall make us one.

Meanwell
All fair, in my opinion; as you had her father's licence to win her affections, you have an undoubted right to her person.

Trueman
I am happy you do not condemn my plan.

Meanwell
I will be of your party, your aid-de-camp in this affair. Your ambassador shall wait on you immediately. In love and war no time should be lost.

[*Exeunt.*]

Scene 2

A drawing-room.

[*Mira, alone, sings.*]

Mira
The constant dove on yonder spray,
Cooing, tunes a moving lay;
She warbles out a tender note,
And fills with love her little throat,
No anxious doubts annoy her breast;
Her mate, the guardian of her nest,
Her pretty young attends with care,
And frees her mind from ev'ry fear.
So the maid, that's join'd to thee
My lovely Trueman, blest would be,
Thy virtues would attune her breast.
To constant ease, to perfect rest.
Oh, Trueman! nothing but the fear of losing you, gives me pain. Possessed of thee, I could join the lark to welcome in the rosy morn, and sing with Philomel[b] the moon to rest.

Scene 3

[*Enter Isabella.*]

Isabella
How d'ye do Mira? Mercy child, how grave you look? Come, I'll sing you a catch of the new song, that will inspire you, I'm sure.
As Colinet and Phoebe sat,
Beneath a poplar grove;
With fondest truth the gentle youth,
Was telling tales of love.
There's a song for you.—
But ah! is this a time for bliss,
Or themes so soft as these?
While all around, we hear no sound
But war's terrific strain,
The drum commands our arming bands,
And chides each tardy swain.
My love shall crown the youth alone,
Who saves himself and me—
What a noble thought is this, my dear Mira! I am determined never to marry any man that has not fought a battle.

Mira
Your swain then must have a hard courtship. But suppose he should happen to be killed?

---

[b] *Philomel* The mythological Greek princess who was changed into a nightingale.

Isabella
Why then, I should never marry him, you know. But I am resolved not to love a man who knows nothing of war and Washington. War and Washington! don't you think those words have a noble sound?

Mira
They have indeed; and I acknowledge the smiles of beauty should reward the man who bravely asserts his country's rights, and meets her enemies in the bloody field; but do you love war for its own sake?

Isabella
Lord, no, but then there's something so clever in fighting and dying for one's country; and the officers look so clever and smart; I declare I never saw an ugly officer in my life.

Mira
Your fancy must be a great beautifier, as many of them are not much indebted to nature for personal charms.

Isabella
Ay, that's because you are not in love with an officer. When you are, you'll think as I do.

Mira
Are you in love with one?

Isabella
Ah! now that's an ill-natured question, I tell you, child, I am in love with nothing but my country. If, indeed, a man should approach me, who would lay his laurels at my feet, who could count his glorious scars gained in the front of victory, I might look upon him.

Mira
I suppose, then, if he wanted an arm, a leg or an eye, it would be all the better; or a great cut over his eye-brow, would be a beauty spot.

Isabella
Certainly. Nothing can be more elegant. It appears so martial—so—so—quite the thing.

Mira
Well! I'm afraid my taste will never be quite so grand as your's, tho' I hope I love my country as well as you.

Isabella
You love your country! your sentiments are not refined enough: they are not exalted to the level of patriotism; for my part, I scorn to think of any thing else.

Mira
Well, but my dear, don't you think the politicians are capable of settling these matters better than you or me?

Isabella
The politicians! and who are such politicians as the women? We fairly beat the men, it is universally acknowledged. And why may not I have talents that way? who knows but I may be a general's lady, or wife to a member of Congress, some of these days?

Mira
I heartily wish you may; but would it not be better not to lose time in thinking about things so remote, and attend more to those of the present moment?

Isabella
Remote, indeed! not so very remote, I hope! The times are very busy, and great men very plentiful, and no body can tell what will happen. But, my dear, I can't stay any longer. I sent my servant for the news-papers, and expect he is come by this time. So, child, I wish you a good day, and a good husband soon, tho' you don't aspire to marry a general! *(Exit.)*

Scene 4

Mira
That poor girl's head is turned topsy turvy by the little insignificant animal that dangles about her: she has conversed with him, till she has not only adopted his opinions, but caught his ideas. Oh! Trueman, what a difference!

Scene 5

[*Mira and Brazen.*]

Brazen
What damn'd business employs your thoughts, Mira? you are always in a study.

Mira
My principal study, sir, is to please my father.

Brazen
That's clever, my girl. I'll tell you, Mira, I intend to marry you to my friend the captain.

Mira
What captain, sir? There are so many captains now-a-days, that I might guess a fortnight before I hit upon the man, perhaps.

Brazen
Captain Flash, is the man. He's the man, Mira, a fellow

of mettle, spirited to the back-bone. He'll fight for his country: those are the men, girl.

Mira
Has he ever been in a battle, sir?

Brazen
He's in the army, child, that's enough.

Mira
Shou'd I not see him, sir, before I promise to accept him?

Brazen
See him! yes, and feel him too, for what I care; he's a damn'd fine fellow, a fellow of spirit. If you like him, take him; if not, let him alone. I don't care who you take, so he's no tory, d--m all tory's, say I. *(Exit.)*

Scene 6

[*Mira alone.*]

Mira
That was aim'd at Trueman; who will ever be suspected, as long as false patriots and pretenders to heroism have my father's ear. Well, as an obedient daughter, I will endure one tete-a-tete with this fine fellow he recommends. Mercy on me, here he comes!

Scene 7

[*To her, Flash singing.*]

Flash
Lift up your heads, ye heroes,
And swear with proud disdain
The wretch that wou'd enslave us,
Shall spread his snares in vain.

We'll blast the venal sycophants,
Who dare our rights betray.
Huzza! Huzza! Huzza! Huzza!
My brave America.

Noble, by God! d--m me! here's the stuff, *(drawing his sword)* shall make the cowardly dogs skip, we'll let the scoundrels see what Americans can do; ha! Miss, your most humble—do you know that I have a vast propensity to quit the army for your sake?

Mira
For shame, sir, what! desert the service of your country, when she most stands in need of your assistance?

Flash

Why really, madam, I should be damnably miss'd. Upon my soul I don't know what they wou'd do without me.

Mira

Then by no means quit the service, captain.

Flash

By God I think I have served long enough. Others should try their luck as well as I: for a whole year have I been fighting, thro' heat and cold, wet and dry, hunger and thirst; poor Flash! were you not a heart of oak, a compound of steel and gun-flints, you cou'd not stand it, by heavens! here's he that fears nothing. *(Sings.)*
Shou'd Europe empty all her force,
We'll meet her in array,
And shout and fight, and shout and fight,
My brave America.

Mira

Bravo, captain!

Flash

Mars, I adore thee; Mars, was a fellow of spirit, I'm told, the Flash of his day, I warrant it. By God, I wish the lad was here now, that he and I might have a game at tilts together: *(draws his sword and pushes at the wall.)* Ha, ha; there I had him! I'god, now I cou'd gizzard these English dogs, if I had 'em here.

Mira

Pray, captain, put up your sword, I declare you frighten me.

Flash

Frighten you! 'Sblood, madam, the ladies now-a-days should be all amazons, nothing shou'd please them more than a naked sword: however, to please you, up love *(puts up his sword.)* entre nous, d'ye see, Miss, I do think you are a devilish fine girl. Your father, ma'am, has given me leave.—

Mira

Fie, captain.

Flash

By my soul, he has.

Mira

For shame, sir, a soldier talk at this rate! fighting shou'd be your theme, captain.

Flash

Fighting! 'tis victuals and drink to me. I could breakfast upon fighting, dine and sup upon fighting; but after supper, a fine girl, you know—

Mira

War and love can never go hand in hand. Love enervates the soul, and wou'd make the bravest man upon earth a coward.

Flash

Coward. *(Draws his sword.)* Coward! damn the word, how it makes my blood boil.

[*Mira shrieks, and runs out.*]

Scene 8

[*Flash, alone.*]

Flash

Coward! ha! If you had not been a woman, well, *(puts up his sword.)* 'Tis no matter, but I'll be damn'd, if ever I speak to you again. *(Exit.)*

Scene 9

[*Melinda and Pickle, dressed like an officer, crossing the stage, meeting each other.*]

Melinda

Here am I forced to walk three miles to warp a piece of cloth. Mammy says I was born for a fine lady, but I am sure this does not look like it.

Pickle

(Seeing her.) Ha, a beautiful creature, by my soul! artless and innocent no doubt. (I'll try my luck with her by God) let me see *(musing)* I'll take her in the old way, I believe; address her in heroics, talk of my honourable intentions, and promise marriage. Come to my assistance, dear cunning, and sweet dissimulation; ye true harbingers of lust and love.—Sweet Miss, your most humble.

Melinda

Miss! Lord, how charming that is.

Pickle

Charming girl! By God, I'm at a loss how to begin *(aside)*.

Melinda

(Looking at his hat.) What a pretty feather! are you in the wars, sir?

Pickle

I have served several campaigns, Miss, (under the banners of Venus) *(aside)* I have been in many engagements.

Melinda
I hope you never got hurt, sir.

Pickle
A trifling scratch or two is all the injury I ever received.

Melinda
Do you intend to continue a soldier?

Pickle
Nothing but a wife shall ever induce me to quit the service.

Melinda
Do you intend to marry, sir?

Pickle
As soon as I can get any one in the humour to have me.

Melinda
Any one would not do, I guess: you'll choose some rich lady, no doubt.

Pickle
No, Miss, riches are not my object; I have a sufficient fortune of my own, thank God; I would marry a woman without a shilling, if she hit my taste, such a sweet angel as yourself.

Melinda
Thank you, sir, for your fleers.[c]

Pickle
As I hope for salvation, I would rather have you (for a time, *aside*) than any woman I ever saw.

Melinda
'Tis not worth your while to make your fun of a poor girl.

Pickle
Fun! upon my soul I'm in earnest.

Melinda
A gentleman like you wou'd never marry a poor girl, I'm sure.

Pickle
There, Miss, you are mistaken: I had rather marry a poor girl than a rich one. My reasons are the best in the world: a poor girl wou'd think herself obliged to me, wou'd love me from gratitude, and make me an industrious, frugal, good wife; a rich one would think she obliged me, and would want a thousand things, a fine house, fine servants, fine clothes, a fine equipage, all her requests to be granted, and never to be contradicted in any thing: If I marry a poor girl, I get a wife; if a rich one, I get a mistress.

Melinda
You don't mean what you say.

---

[c] *fleers* Usually a smile of scorn or contempt, but also defined as a false grin, simulating civility; a hypocritical approach that Melinda mistakes for sincerity.

Pickle

I do upon my soul, my intentions are honourable; your name, my dear.

Melinda

Melinda Heartfree, sir.

Pickle

Well, my dear, it shall be Mrs. Meanwell, if you please.

Melinda

Is your name Meanwell, sir?

Pickle

It is, madam. No doubt you have often heard of me, perhaps seen me before: my name and character will remove any suspicion you may entertain of my integrity and honour, I hope.

Melinda

I have often heard daddy talk of you, sir.

Pickle

What is your father's opinion of me, Miss?

Melinda

He likes you mightily, and so does mammy too; you stood for sister Bibby, when you set up for burgess.

Pickle

True, my dear, I well remember it: and are you the daughter of my old friend Heartfree? Come to my arms, *(embraces her)* my dear girl, I shall be proud to be son-in-law to a man of his worth and goodness.

Melinda

You surely are not in earnest, sir!

Pickle

I am, and to convince you of my sincerity, I would immediately wait upon you home, and communicate my intentions to your friends; but I have some business to-day that prevents me: however, I shall be this way to-morrow; will my dear girl be so kind as to meet me?

Melinda

There is no harm in coming here, sir: I can do it to oblige you; but you will forget me, and every thing you have said to me, before to-morrow.

Pickle

Impossible that I can ever forget that sweet face! *(He kisses her, she seems coy.)* will you meet me here about twelve o'clock, to-morrow? Don't be cruel, my sweet girl; you know I love you: my words, my looks, my actions must discover it.

Melinda
Well, sir, I'll be a fool for once, I'll come.

Pickle
Charming creature, one kiss my love *(kisses her)* 'tis ecstacy by heavens! *(Exit Melinda.)* Well! these ignorant girls are the finest game in the world: heave a sigh, look languishingly, and swear a little, the poor things drop their heads into your bosom, and die away as quick as a sensitive plant. Well, Trueman, having plann'd a scheme of amusement for myself, I'll now proceed to the execution of your commands. *(Exit.)*

ACT II

Scene 1

A court-house.

[*Trueman and Meanwell.*]

Trueman
What, is the committee to meet to-day, Meanwell? I hate these little democracies.

Meanwell
Take care, sir, both property and characters lie at the mercy of those tribunals.

Trueman
What weighty business calls their high mightinesses together?

Meanwell
Most of the Caledonians are suspected of disaffection to the American cause, and either from friendship or attachment to their own country, disapprove the public measures: from this cause, our holy inquisition are for the very moderate correction the Jews received in Spain.

Trueman
Banishment, or a renunciation of their error, I suppose.

Meanwell
This may be the cause; at present an oath is to be applied as a mirror to their breasts, which reflecting their private opinions and sentiments, must lay them open to the public eye. This is to be offered as a touch-stone of public virtue, as a trial of faith; and woe be unto those who are found faithless.

Trueman
The ungracious treatment that some Scotchmen have met with, the illiberal reflections cast out against them all, give little hope of their attachment to a country, or to a people, where and with whom they have already tasted the bitter herb of persecution: some there are, who have behaved well, conform'd to the public will, nor given any cause of offence; yet even those have not met with the common offices of civility among us.

Meanwell
Of this character are those who are cited before the committee to-day.

Trueman
Hush, sir, here come two of the guardians of our state.

[*Enter Col. Strut and Mr. Summons.*]

Strut
We delegates, Mr. Summons, have a very hard time of it.

Summons
Men of abilities must give themselves up to the service of their country.

Strut
True, sir, the people will exact the services of those they can depend upon.

Summons
Your wise men, as they call them, cut but a poor figure in these times.

Strut
They are dangerous men: they are always starting doubts and creating divisions; divisions are dangerous. United we stand, divided we fall, is the American motto, you know.

Summons
Very true Colonel, very true. When I became a delegate, I was told it was the ready way to some profitable post. I long to serve my country.

Trueman
Enter into the army, sir; that is the way to preferment.

Summons
I am a cripple, and can't be a soldier.

Meanwell
Be a colonel of militia then, 'tis a fine post for cripples, for they never march, but they have no pay, Mr. Summons: you want a post that will bring you something.

Summons
I love my country and wish to serve her, and I wish some folks were as true to their country as they ought to be.

Meanwell
And as disinterested too, and then men of real merit, would be in her service, in lieu of them who get into office, to catch a few sixpences from her treasury.

[*Enter Brazen, Thunderbolt, Squib and Skip.*]

Brazen
How goes it? How goes it? Well, what business do we meet upon today?

Strut
The Scabbies[a] are to be tried according to the ordinance.

Brazen
Let's duck the scoundrels.

Thunderbolt
Duck 'em! let's burn the scoundrels.

---

[a] *The Scabbies* Obviously a term of contempt, meaning scurvy rascal or scoundrel, used by Munford to indicate the biased attitude toward the Scots held by those who were to judge them; another example of the playwright's condemnation of the superpatriot and self-righteous Whig.

Skip
Let's hang them.

Squib
Ay, ay, hang them, that is the best way.

[*Enter Colonel Simple.*]

Simple
Gentlemen, your servant.

Brazen
How goes it, old cock?

Simple
Why, praise be to God, thro' mercy, I'm reasonably well, I thank you.

Brazen
I understand those gentlemen take part with the Scotch (*pointing to Trueman and Meanwell*).

Thunderbolt
It is a common talk.

Squib
The people don't like it.

Skip
Some talk very hard of it, I assure you.

Trueman
If to treat the unhappy with kindness be an offence, I shall always be an offending sinner; meanness dwells with oppression, and cowardice with insult.

Meanwell
Justice is the birthright of all, and public virtue is displayed by an impartial distribution of it.

Strut
Wou'd you protect our enemies, gentlemen? would you ruin your country for the sake of Scotchmen?

Meanwell
Prove them to be enemies, shew that they plot the downfall of my country, and courtesy itself shall revolt against them.

Brazen
There is sufficient proof that nine hundred and ninety-nine out of a thousand of them are our enemies.

Trueman
Some may be enemies, others guiltless. 'Tis ungenerous to arraign this man for the offence of his neighbour; illiberal to traduce all for the transgressions of a few.

Meanwell
Justice would blush at such proceedings: Pity, drop a tear at the outrage.

Brazen
Here comes the Scotchmen.

[*Enter McFlint, McSqueeze, and McGripe.*]

Simple
Gentlemen of the committee, pray take your seats. *(they sit round a table.)* I was requested by colonel Strut, to summon these men here *(coughs)* I have a bad cold, tell me, if you please colonel, what it is about.

Strut
(Rising.) These men, gentlemen, are cited before this committee, agreeable to an ordinance of convention.

McFlint
What is our offence, pray?

Strut
The nature of their offence, gentlemen, is, that they are Scotchmen; every Scotchman being an enemy, and these men being Scotchmen, they come under the ordinance which directs an oath to be tendered to all those against whom there is just cause to suspect they are enemies.

Brazen
(Rising.) As these men are Scotchmen, I think there is just cause to suspect that they are our enemies. Let it be put to the committee, Mr. President, whether all Scotchmen are not enemies.

Strut
A good notion, Mr. Brazen, I second it with all my heart.

Thunderbolt
We have some Scotchmen in our army; they are our friends, I hope.

Squib
To be sartin they must be our friends.

Skip
Yes, yes, they are our friends, no doubt.

Brazen
They are excepted of course.

McSqueeze
I wish the country very well, I never did it harm, gentlemen.

McGripe
I've gi'en nae cause to suspect that I am an enemy. The

ordinance says, ye must hae just cause. Bring your proof, gentlemen.

Brazen
Proof, sir! we have proof enough. We suspect any Scotchman: suspicion is proof, sir. I move for the question, Mr. President.

Trueman
In the catalogue of sins, I never found it one before to be born on the north of the Tweed *(aside to Meanwell)*.

Meanwell
In nature's lowest works, I never saw before such base stupidity *(aside to Trueman)*.

Strut
The question, Mr. President.

All
The question, the question.

Simple
Is all Scotchmen enemies, gentlemen?

All
Ay, ay.

McFlint
Before you determine so precipitately, gentlemen, I should have been glad to say somewhat in my own defence.

Simple
What is it, my dear sir?

McFlint
I was bred in Scotland, but not born there.

McSqueeze
What, Sandy, do you deny your country mon, tak shame to yoursel, Sandy.

McFlint
It is time to deny man, when they make it a crime to be born there.

McGripe
I'll lose my life for dear old Scotland, before ever I'll blush for it.

Thunderbolt
As Mr. McFlint says he's no Scotchman, we have no right to suspect him more than any other man.

Brazen
As he's no Scotchman, he may be a very good man; I move that he be discharged.

All
Agreed, agreed.

Strut
I rise to move, sir, *(coughs)* I say, sir, I move that the oath be tender'd to these men, according to the ordinance.

McSqueeze
What oath?

Strut
The test oath, sir; you must swear to be true and faithful to this country.

McSqueeze
I'll take nae oath, the like o' that.

McGripe
I'll no swear allegiance to any man but my king.

Strut
There, gentlemen, you see what they are, they are all so to a man.

Brazen
I move that they be disarmed, as the ordinance directs.

All
Agreed, agreed.

Simple
Well, gentlemen, the business is done; I suppose we may rise.

All
Ay, ay. *(They rise.)*

[Enter Mr. Tackabout.]

Tackabout
Is the committee up? I'm sorry I was not here a little sooner. I had an information or two to lay before the committee.

Brazen
We can sit again, sir; order the committee to sit again, Mr. President.

Tackabout
Upon second thoughts, we'll decline it for the present: I have not all the proofs about me; besides a witness I expected, is not here, I find.

Squib
I'll lay he has found out some tory.

Skip
He has got some tory in the wind, depend upon it.

Squib
I declare he is the prettiest spokenest man I ever saw.

Skip
Yes, between you and me, he ought to have been our delegate.

Tackabout
Well, gentlemen, you have trounced those Scotch gentlemen, I hope.

Brazen
We have.

Tackabout
So, colonel, you have resigned your commission, I'm told *(to col. Simple)*.

Simple
Yes, my friend; I grow old and infirm: I thought it best to decline in time.

Tackabout
There's some prudence in retreating from danger: the times are perilous, colonel.

Simple
Young men, like you, Mr. Tackabout, are the properest persons for commissions: such old folks as I, are better out of the way.

Tackabout
Out of harm's way, you mean, colonel.

Simple
I think such men as you ought to step forth: I have often heard you boast of your courage, Mr. Tackabout; now's the time, sir—now or never.

Tackabout
Why sir, I have some expectations in England: the reversion of a considerable estate, or—

Brazen
Poh! damn the estate; let it go.

Tackabout
My ancestors lost an estate by their loyalty; I should not choose to lose mine by my disloyalty.

Simple
'Tis a sin to lose an estate any how; that's certain.

Tackabout
A man's patrimony, in my opinion, is a sacred depositum, especially when an expected title gives lustre to the possession.

Brazen
Damn the title—take a commission: that's better than all the titles in the world.

Simple

Take my commission, Mr. Tackabout: it is expected you should do something, indeed it is.

Tackabout

I have done enough already, sir.

Simple

But I observe, you keep out of harm's way, Mr. Tackabout.

Tackabout

Where is the man that has done more than I have? I have damn'd the ministry, abus'd the king, vilified the parliament, and curs'd the Scotch. I have raised the people's suspicions against all moderate men; advised them to spurn at all government: I have cried down tories, cried up whigs, extolled Washington as a god, and call'd Howe a very devil. I have exclaimed against all taxes, advised the people to pay no debts; I have promised them success in war, a free trade, and independent dominion. In short, I have inspired them with the true patriotic fire, the spirit of opposition; and yet you say it is expected I should do something.

Simple

There are many to be found, who do all this.

Trueman

And few who do any thing else. *(Aside.)*

Meanwell

Can this be the person we were in company with the other day, Trueman? *(Aside.)*

Trueman

The very same, only ᵇ⁻Proteus like, he can change from a man to a brute, from a brute to a serpent, or to any thing he pleases.⁻ᵇ *(To Meanwell.)*

Tackabout

Trueman, your servant; Meanwell, your's. I beg pardon, I really did not observe you were present.

Trueman

We should not have been offended if you had overlooked us altogether, sir.

Tackabout

Poh. Never mind what I say to these fellows, you know my private sentiments.

Trueman

As well as they do, I suppose, Mr. Tackabout; but, sir, the man who privately condemns, and publicly approves either men or measures, shews himself a knave, and proves himself a coward. *(Aside to Tackabout.)*

---

b-b

Proteus like ... pleases Among his other powers, Proteus, the sea god, could assume various shapes and was a master of disguise; thus it is with Tackabout who can be Whig or Tory, according to the company he keeps.

Tackabout
Come, sir, no more, sir, I beg of you; I talk to these fellows always in their own style, to avoid suspicion; nothing else, upon honour, sir, *(aside to Trueman)*.

Trueman
So, sir, you inculcate principles subversive of every public and private virtue, you encourage oppression and spread sedition, merely for your own security.

Tackabout
Prudence requires something of this kind.

Trueman
What you call prudence, I call baseness, Mr. Tackabout: however, I leave you to the pleasures of your prudent duplicity—Meanwell, I wait upon you.

Meanwell
I'll attend you, sir.

[*Exit Meanwell and Trueman.*]

Brazen
You and the tories were at cross-questions, I believe, Mr. Tackabout.

Tackabout
It is always the case, sir: I wish to reclaim the fellows, and cannot but repeat a little of my political catechism to them whenever we meet.

Simple
'Tis a pity such clever men should be enemies to their country.

Strut
They are dangerous men; shew me a clever man, and I'll shew you an enemy; let me advise you to keep a strict eye upon those men. Mr. President.

Brazen
D-mn all tories, say I. Come, let us go into the muster-ground.

[*Exit omnes.*]

SCENE, a muster-field (in the court-yard).

[*Flash, Thunderbolt, Soldiers, Mob, &c.*]

Flash
(*Holding a news-paper in his hand.*) Ha, damn me, I thought so; yes, yes, honies, you have got it, nine hundred

at a clip. Well done, Washington, by God! We'll trim the rascals, d----me.

Thunderbolt
What's that, captain?

Flash
Great, very great; we have done it at last.

Squib
What have we done, captain?

Flash
Every thing, by God; a noble stroke, old fellow; we have killed and taken nine hundred of the damned infidels.

Thunderbolt
Read it, captain, read it.

Flash
Poh! damn it, you know I hate reading; can't you believe me? there it is, in black and white.

Thunderbolt
(Reads.) "A copy of his excellency general Washington's letter to congress, dated, Trenton."

Flash
That's it; d--n my buttons, if I would not give a million that I had been there.

Thunderbolt
This is great news, really, captain.

Flash
It will do; but it might have been better, and more complete. Some got off, you see; if I had been there, I'll be damn'd if a single scoundrel should have escaped; and here am I doing nothing, but encouraging a set of poltroons to enter into the service; ever perplexed, vexed, and disappointed—not a breath of applause; not a sprig of laurel for poor Flash, while others are reaping it by handfuls.

Thunderbolt
Never mind, captain, it will be your time, soon.

Flash
Soon! The enemy will be driven to the devil, before I shall arrive at the scene of action.

[*Enter Trim.*]

Trim
Noble captain, your servant—we shall soon get our complement of men; there are several fine fellows that intend to list.

Flash
Noble fellows: have you any thing for them to drink.

Trim
I have the recruiting jugs full to the brim.

Flash
Of what?

Trim
Peach brandy, the best liquor in the world.

Flash
Produce it, d----me, and give the lads a drink.

Trim
Never mind me; never mind me, captain, I'll do it. *(Sings.)*
Come on my brave fellows, a fig for our lives,
We'll fight for our country, our children and wives;
Determin'd we are to live happy and free,
Then join honest fellows, in chorus with me.
We'll drink our own liquor—our brandy from peaches;
A fig for the English—they may buss all our breeches.
Those bloodsucking, beer-drinking puppies retreat,
But our peach-brandy fellows can never be beat.
Where's the spring?

Mob
We'll shew it you.

Trim
Come on, my brave fellows.

Mob
Huzza! for the noble serjeant.

[*Exit shouting.*]

Flash
My serjeant has enlisted several fine fellows for me; but persecuted with the wheedling of wives, or the entreaties of parents, I am obliged to discharge the cowards as fast as I get them.

Thunderbolt
You should not let your good-nature prejudice the service, captain.

Flash
Prejudice the service! D----me, sir, I don't know what you mean.

Thunderbolt
I beg pardon—I only meant to say, you ought not to be too good-natured.

Flash
D--n good nature, sir, I scorn it. If I let a man off, 'tis for his money; he pays for his peeping,[c] honey.

Thunderbolt
That's right; it makes the more bounty-money[d] for others.

---

[c]
peeping Sleeping: 17th-18th century meaning of the word; i.e., if the recruit prefers sleeping to fighting, he pays for the former.

[d]
bounty-money Munford is attacking the growing evil of the scandalous bounty system. At the beginning of the war recruits were given a bounty to enlist in the Continental Army. Soon after, the various "states" offered bounties to recruits in the separate militia, such as Connecticut, Pennsylvania, etc. The competition between the Continental Congress and the colonies grew out of all proportion. Many of the so-called patriotic soldiers enlisted, deserted, reenlisted in states where bounty was higher. The recruiting officers were also often venal. As Flash indicates, when a man paid him to be released from the obligation to fight, the recruiting officer would keep the money, not adding it to the general fund for bounty. Such practices would have been bitterly deplored by Munford who was a recruiting officer of great integrity.

Flash
No, no, thank you, none of that, my dear; where are my expences to come from, do you think?

Thunderbolt
I thought the public allowed for these.

Flash
The public allowance is nothing, if it was not for a little smart-money, and now and then a run of luck, I should absolutely perish.

Thunderbolt
Do you ever play at cards?

Flash
A pretty question, d----me! Why gaming and whoring are the two first qualifications of a soldier.

Thunderbolt
What say you to a crack at all-fours,[e] now?

Flash
Agreed.

Thunderbolt
Let us go into yonder house, and set to it like brave fellows: my lieutenant shall play with you for what you please.

Flash
Here's he that never flinches.
    [*Enter Trim.*]
Well, Trim, what luck?

Trim
Why, sir, I got ten clever fellows to promise me to enlist *(hickups)* do you see me, just as the brandy gave out, they kept punctually calling for more grog, I told them, says I, *(hickups)* I am very sorry, says I, the brandy is out. e'god, sir, the words were no sooner out of my mouth, *(hickups)* than away they went, every soul of them.

Flash
I am glad of it, for I may perhaps find another use for the bounty-money. Trim meet me at old Brazen's tonight. Come, gentlemen.

    [*Exeunt.*]

SCENE, Brazen's house.

    [*Isabella and Mira.*]

Isabella
Prithee, Mira, lay aside those demure looks; when every

---

[e] *all-fours* An old card game, dating as early as 1674; it was popular with the lower classes and would have appealed to a common soldier such as Flash.

creature is running mad for joy at the glorious news from the northward, here are you like an Egyptian mummy—without sense or motion.

Mira
I have a fit of the horrors, Miss, whenever I hear of a battle.

Isabella
So have I, if it goes against us.

Mira
Victory is attended with the widow's lamentations, and the orphan's tears; I cannot rejoice at any thing, that sounds with funeral dirges, or makes joy smile in the face of affliction.

Isabella
Were I a lump of clay, or an image of wax, the word victory would make me spring into life, and sing *Te deum*.

Mira
The untimely death of a parent, husband, or child, might prevent your vivacity, Miss.

Isabella
Was I to be made a widow by every victory, I verily think I should rejoice.

Mira
Parental and filial tenderness are too nearly allied to our natures, connubial bliss too valuable, the sweet affections of sympathy and compassion, are too much the ornaments of the human heart, to be cast away for the foolish exultations that flow from the vain triumphs of ambition.

Isabella
Ha, ha, ha! Do you imagine that I am such a blockhead as to believe the widow's lamentations, the orphan's tears have any effect upon your spirits, Mira? No, no, I know better.

Mira
What do you know, madam?

Isabella
I know that a poor creature of the masculine gender, has high notions of connubial bliss as your ladyship; that he thinks of the great duties of parental and filial tenderness as you do, and that he esteems all victories horrid, unless they are graced with hymenial triumphs.

Mira
You are extremely pleasant, madam.

Isabella
Positively, Mira, I am surprised at you.

Mira
Surprised at me! for what, pray?

Isabella
Why, child, that you should ever think of being in love with one of those horrid creatures, called tories; Trueman is a shocking fellow.

Mira
Really, Miss, I am as much surprised at you.

Isabella
Why, child?

Mira
That you should ever be simple enough to esteem a filly coxcomb in politics, who puts on the name of patriot, as all coxcombs do their clothes, to be distinguished, and to be laughed at.

Isabella
What do you mean, madam?

Mira
My meaning requires no interpretation, ma'am.

Isabella
If you imagine your satyrical scoffs have any effect upon me, madam, you are much mistaken. The shafts of envy fall short of their mark, when aimed at the well guarded, public protected principles of an honest whig.

Mira
Irony, is a harmless weapon, when pointed either at folly or meanness.

Isabella
You are in your own house, madam.

Mira
Where I shall always be glad to entertain you, when you are disposed to treat me with decency.

Isabella
How have I transgressed?

Mira
Trueman's merits are above the scandal of the times; yet, Miss, it gives me pain to hear his name mentioned in terms of reproach.

Isabella
I hate tories so abominably, that I cannot, for my soul, think of them with patience: As long, madam, as you persist in your fondness for such animals, I shall refrain my visits, I assure you.

Mira
Do as you please, Miss.

Isabella
Madam, your servant; mercy, that any creature can love a tory!

[*Exit Isabella.*]

Mira
So, I have lost one patriotic acquaintance—here comes a male bird of the same species, to torment me; but I'll avoid it. *(Exit.)*

[*Enter Flash.*]

Flash
D—mn me, if I am not the most unlucky dog that ever cut the cards. *(Seeing Mira.)* so, honey, are you there? Push off, for I'll be damn'd if I'll have any thing to say to you.

[*Enter Brazen.*]

Brazen
How goes it, captain?

Flash
It goes damn'd hard with me, old fellow; I'm sick.

Brazen
Sick!

Flash
Beat to death, trimmed most damnably; a round hundred —nothing less.

Brazen
What! Lashes?

Flash
Lashes! d----me, what a thought! no, no, here's the stuff, *(laying his hand upon his sword)* here's the stuff.

Brazen
How beat then?

Flash
A round hundred, good continental, lost with a militia fellow, a d-mn'd milksop lieutenant.

Brazen
I'll give you satisfaction.

Flash
Satisfaction, sir!

Brazen
Yes, sir; the satisfaction that all gamesters require, a chance to win your money back.

Flash
You meant to use me ill, sir.

Brazen
No, upon my honour, nothing but a joke.

Flash
If that's all, here's my hand, I'm at you, for twenty dollars a game, if you dare?

Brazen
A match, come on.

   [*Exeunt.*]

ACT III

Scene 1

A dressing-room.

[*Enter Isabella, and sings.*]

Isabella
No sounds but drums shall please my ear,
Farewel, soft folly; love, adieu:
No grief's but heroe's griefs I'll share
Nor sigh, but Washington, for you

Well, what would I give to hear of another victory! I had a horrid dream last night: I dream't that I saw the congress running out of Philadelphia, frighted to death; some barefooted, others bareheaded, that they run into a great croud, where I soon saw, as I thought, my dear little colonel, bold as a lion, calling out, to arms, arms! but I was surprised to see the men have clubs and sticks, instead of guns; and my dear little colonel with a corn stalk to his side, instead of a sword. It was a horrid dream.

[*Enter Strut.*]

Strut
Your servant, madam.

Isabella
Colonel, I am glad to see you.—Do you ever mind dreams, colonel?

Strut
Pleasant dreams are not amiss, madam.

Isabella
Well, but bad dreams, I meant. I dreamt of you last night.

Strut
Was that a bad dream, madam?

Isabella
Very bad, I thought the congress were running away, and that you, without a sword, was at the head of a number of men without arms.

Strut
Dreams are illusions; but we have had another battle with the enemy, madam.

Isabella
When, where! how, tell me, dear colonel?

Strut
We attacked them at Prince-Town, and have killed, and taken prisoners, a prodigious number.

Isabella
Thank God: but is it true?

Strut
As true as the gospel ma'am: 'tis in the papers.

Isabella
At Prince-town, did you say? where's that?

Strut
Prince-Town, is a town, somewhere about . . . where general Howe is encamped.

Isabella
Don't you long to be there, colonel? Lord! If I was a man, how fond I should be of it!

Strut
If my affairs . . .

Isabella
Affairs: prithee no more of that: when do you think you will set off?

Strut
It is impossible for me, madam—I have some affairs . . .

Isabella
Affairs, again! every thing should give way to the service of your country.

Strut
If I had the constitution of some men . . .

Isabella
Constitution! why are you sick? positively, colonel, if you persist in making such foolish excuses, I shall hate you.

Strut
Upon my honour, madam.

Isabella
That's in my custody, sir: you pawned it to me long ago, as a pledge for the patriotism and courage I have given you credit for.

Strut
I hope you don't suspect me of wanting either.

Isabella
Why really, I never did, but I most certainly shall, unless you go into the army.

Strut
'Tis not necessary that all patriots should be soldiers.

Isabella

'Tis necessary that you should be a soldier, tho': for, to be plain with you, colonel, I am determined to be a general's lady, or never to marry.

Strut

Positively, madam, the service will kill me.

Isabella

You'll be killed in the service, you mean: That's what you apprehend.

Strut

I could die on the field of battle with pleasure, madam, but,—

Isabella

No but's, colonel, you must be a soldier, indeed you must.

Strut

Well, madam, if it is your desire—but I've one favour to request of you, first.

Isabella

Any thing: what is it?

Strut

Will you condescend to marry me, before I go?

Isabella

No faith, won't I: the conditions upon which I engaged myself to you were as follows: First, you were to be a delegate, next a colonel, then a general. The material condition remains yet to be complied with, on your part; that performed, perhaps I may have no objection to give you my hand.

Strut

Suppose I should be killed?

Isabella

I should cry a little, I suppose.

Strut

My dear madam, there are soldiers enough without me.

Isabella

You must be a general, or quit your pretensions to me.

Strut

I can apply in a neighbouring state, and be made a brigadier-general, without being a soldier.

Isabella

No, no, you shall fight for your commission: I'll have none of your chimney-corner generals, I assure you.

Strut

Will no excuse do?

Isabella

None, sir. I bid you adieu for the present; unless you set off for the army immediately, it shall be for ever. *(Exit.)*

Strut

The devil take this: I have vapour'd away to a pretty purpose, faith! By pretensions to patriotism, I became a delegate; and putting on the appearance of a man of courage, I became a colonel; all to tickle the vanity of this girl—and now, truly, I must expose my life that she may be a general's lady! I can't do it: I never thought of fighting in my life. What! stand and be shot at! Indeed, Miss, if these are the terms you are to surrender upon, you may keep your citadel forever, for me: I'm for a whole skin, if I do pennance in it, as an old bachelor, all my days. *(Exit.)*

SCENE, a field.

[Enter Pickle.]

Pickle

Simple creature! how soon she blushed her consent to every thing I proposed? here she comes, fair as Venus, and as Dian chaste.

[Enter Melinda.]

My dearest girl. *(Kisses her.)*

Melinda

I have turned fool, you see, sir, and done as you desired. If you were in earnest in what you said yesterday, I shall always be ready to oblige you in any thing.

Pickle

A pretty forward hint, by God. *(Aside.)* Why, do you see, *(scratching his head)* as to that, my dear, we'll talk it over another time. I have a few preliminary articles to propose to you, which if you agree to, you may name the happy day.

Melinda

I don't understand you, sir.

Pickle

Why, my dear, I have some preparatory measures to take, respecting my friends, and a previous agreement to make with you and them.

Melinda

Speak plain, if you please. I don't understand these fine words.

Pickle
I should be much to blame, you know, to marry any woman without knowing whether she would suit my purpose.

Melinda
As to that matter, you can best judge: you cannot look for much breeding from a poor girl like me, without any bringing up.

Pickle
My dear, that is not my objection. I only wish to examine my commodity before I purchase. *(Taking her hand.)* I wish to know more of you, my dear.

Melinda
(Pushing him off.) You know as much as you shall know, 'till you have a better right than you have at present.

Pickle
My dearest girl, as we are man and wife in the face of heaven, do you see, you should not be so vere scrupulous with me.

Melinda
It will be time enough to take such freedoms, sir, when I am your wife.

Pickle
Wife! mercy on us! *(Aside.)* The liberties I wish to take, my dear, are licensed freedoms. Love requires something of this kind to keep itself alive. 'Tis as necessary to love as fuel is to fire. If you don't let me toy and play with you a little, by my soul, my love will go out.

Melinda
I can't help it; but you shall take no immodest freedoms with me.

Pickle
Poh! a little harmless play, my dear, is mere pastime, don't be afraid. *(Attempts to be rude.)*

Melinda
You don't behave like a gentleman, sir. I assure, you, tho' I might, perhaps, consent to be your wife, I never will agree to be any thing else.

Pickle
Who the devil would have thought it? *(Aside.)* My dear, I humbly beg your pardon. The violence of my passion is the cause of these transports. Alas! with what delight would I take you for my bride—but the objections of my friends ...

Melinda
What friends?

Pickle
I have some particular friends from whom I have great expectations; and your fortune and family would be with them insuperable objections.

Melinda
As to my fortune, and family, it is out of my power to make either of them better than they are: you had better then give over all thoughts of the match.

Pickle
No: it is impossible. My friends shall not controul me. I am resolved upon it, and you shall be mine.

Melinda
But your great expectations, sir.

Pickle
Oh! as to that: I hope, in time they may be reconciled, when they find the marriage is over, and cannot be prevented. For this reason, I think it would be best not to have a public marriage. I will beg you therefore, to keep the marriage a secret for some time, 'till I can reconcile them to it.

Melinda
When I am your wife, you shall direct me in all things.

Pickle
Well, my dear, my servant will wait upon you at this place, about six in the evening, and will conduct you to a friend's house. I'll be there with a clergyman, and proper witnesses.

Melinda
Well, sir, if you do marry me, I will study night and day to please you, and to make you happy. In the evening, you say?

Pickle
Yes, my love.

Melinda
'Till then, I wish you well.

Pickle
Adieu.

[*Exit Melinda.*]

Little did I expect this resistance in so artless a creature. I made as sure of my game, as if I had caught it. However, I'll entangle my pretty linnet yet, in a net often set by us true sportsmen, for these shy birds. Our butler shall be the parson, the cook and scullion the witnesses. The butler has a most demure sanctified face, and will make a tolerable good priest. E'gad, the idea of what is to follow, gives me a palpitation at the heart already. Well, Trueman, your business: then my own. *(Exit.)*

SCENE, Brazen's house.

[*Flash and Brazen at a gaming table.*]

Flash
(*Rising in a passion.*) Damnation seize me, if you did not pack the cards.

Brazen
It is a damn'd lie, sir.

Flash
Dare you give a soldier the lie, sir?

Brazen
Yes, I dare, when he tells one.

Flash
Come, old fellow, I don't mean to quarrel with you. (*Offers his hand.*)

Brazen
Pay the money you have lost.

Flash
Don't be hard, old fellow; I've no money but the public's, not a *shilling* . . .

Brazen
Public or private, pay, I say.

Flash
Consider, sir, the service must be injured, if I apply the public money to any purposes, but those for which I receive it.

Brazen
Damn the service: what's the service to me? pay sir.

Flash
I'll give you my note on demand.

Brazen
Your note! damn your note, I'll have the money.

Flash
Lord! how I tremble with rage, (*sees Pickle coming*). A brother officer, by God! a reinforcement (*aside*) my note, sir, is as good as any man's note. Damn you, sir, you have raised my blood. I demand satisfaction. (*Draws his sword.*)

Brazen
Lay down your stickfrog, and I'll give you satisfaction. (*Puts himself in the attitude of boxing.*)

Flash
What! you are for fifty cuffs? Oh! no, no, honey, I am no black-guard. Come on, my dear. Here's the stuff, honey.

[*Enter Pickle.*]

Pickle
Gentlemen, your servant.

Flash
Your servant, my dear, *(stands in the attitude of fencing)*.

Pickle
What! at points, gentlemen!

Flash
Draw, my dear, for the honour of the profession, draw—Sir, 'tis a disgrace upon a soldier to have a fist cock'd in his company.

Pickle
Your antagonist has no other weapon. Here's my sword, sir, *(offering his sword to Brazen)*.

Brazen
Sir, I thank you. Now, come on, you scoundrel.

Flash
What! Aid the enemy! Hark'ye, my dear, your name! *(to Pickle)*.

Brazen
That's captain Feather, of the flying camp. Come on, sir, I say *(to Flash)*.

Flash
I have nothing to say to you, sir, *(to Brazen)*. Captain, I should be glad to speak with you. Walk out, if you please, sir *(to Pickle)*.

Pickle
The sword, if you please, *(Brazen gives the sword)*. Come, sir, I'll attend you.

Flash
But upon second thoughts, my dear, I can say, what I have to say, here. You seem from the northward, from your uniform.

Pickle
Perhaps not, sir.

Brazen
You are a scoundrel, sir, *(to Flash)*.

Pickle
Do you hear that, captain?

Flash
Washington has done wonders to the northward, sir, *(to Pickle)*.

Brazen
You are a damn'd coward, I say *(to Flash)*.

Flash
Are you from the northward, captain? *(to Pickle).*

Pickle
I am, sir.

Flash
In what corps? in the service of what state, sir?

Brazen
Damn your impertinence; what right have you to catechise any gentleman in my house? *(Kicks Flash out.)*

Flash
I'll be reveng'd, damn'me, I'll make you pay for this, honey. *(Exit.)*

Pickle
Can that fellow be an officer?

Brazen
Yes; and, I once thought, a fellow of spirit. But he is too mean to talk about. I thought captain, you had taken your departure for the southward, yesterday.

Pickle
It was my intention when I left this place, Sir. But hearing of Washington's fresh success, I am now hastening to the scene of action, hoping that I may partake of the glory acquired by our noble commander in the frequent rencountres with the enemy.

Brazen
Noble, captain! give me your hand. You are for the place of danger, I find.

Pickle
Danger and honour are two associates that go hand in hand. We must encounter the one to obtain the other. Honour is the idol I worship; to that I would sacrifice my life and limbs.

Brazen
What can British mongrels do with such men as these. Thirty thousand of them will be but a breakfast for us.

Pickle
Rather hard of digestion *(aside)*. I should be glad to pay my respects to the ladies, sir, if you please.

Brazen
By all means. They are all from home except Mira. I'll send her to you. She'll be glad to see you, I'm sure. *(Exit.)*

Pickle
I make no doubt of it. Now, hat under arm, a low bow, and a most obsequious face.

[*Enter Mira.*]

Mira
So, Mr. Slyboots, are you here again?

Pickle
At your service, madam, and upon an errand of a similar nature to the last.

Mira
You have a letter for me, then.

Pickle
Yes, madam, upon my knees I present it; and in token of the great respect I have for the writer, I must kiss the hand that receives it.

Mira
(Reads.) "On Edgehill—at six in the evening—Meanwell and his trusty squire—your affectionate Trueman." You are the trusty squire, I suppose, and can inform me more fully, perhaps, of Mr. Trueman's intentions, than he has ventured to communicate in his letter.

Pickle
Yes, madam, I can tell you Mr. Trueman's intentions, I believe.

Mira
Do, sir.

Pickle
His intentions are to run away.

Mira
Run away!

Pickle
Yes, madam, with a beautiful angel like your ladyship, and to marry her as soon as he can get a person legally authorised to perform the ceremony.

Mira
So the plot is out. Well, Trueman, love sweetly supplicates for worth like thine; I surrender.

Pickle
What a charming creature! (Aside.)

Mira
Here, sir, deliver this ring to Mr. Trueman; tell him what he gave me as a token of his love, I now send as a token of my fidelity to him.

Pickle
What a pretty way these fine women have of winding themselves round a man's heart! (Aside.)

Mira
Inform him, I will play the obedient mistress that I may sooner learn to act the dutiful wife.

Pickle
Upon my soul, you say so many fine things I shall forget: Do write.

Mira
Time will not permit, adieu. *(Exit.)*

[*Enter Brazen.*]

Brazen
Well, captain, did Mira know you again?

Pickle
Perfectly, sir. Miss and I had some conversation yesterday; she recognized me at once.

Brazen
I did not observe you had a word to say to any body but my old woman.

Pickle
A little acquaintance gives the tongue a privilege with people of my profession.

Brazen
Soldiers are seldom at a loss for talk, they say.

Pickle
Very seldom. I'm at a damnable loss tho' to contrive an excuse for getting away decently. *(Aside.)*

Brazen
Come, captain, lay by your sword. You'll stay with me to-night.

Pickle
Excuse me, good sir, when duty commands, the inclination must obey. I should be happy to stay with you many days, but the honour of a soldier compels me to repair to the scene of action.

Brazen
The honour of a soldier! That's true: Well, noble captain, success attend you.

Pickle
I thank you, sir, for your civilities, and am your most obedient servant. *(Exit.)*

Brazen
A decent, well-bred lad, and a fellow of spirit, I warrant. Well, I'll go in pursuit of that cowardly scoundrel, and cudgel the rascal, or make him pay me my money. *(Exit.)*

ACT IV

SCENE, a Court-house.

[*Enter Col. Simple and Mr. Tackabout*]

Simple
(*With a newspaper in his hand.*) This is great news, glory to the Lord for it. The Lord is on our side, I am taught to believe, for we have great success, Mr. Tackabout.

Tackabout
Nothing but the tories can hurt us; nothing else, sir.

Simple
Praise be to God they are vastly scattered.

Tackabout
There are many in this country. I am surprized the committee don't handle the fellows. I am determined, unless something is done with them, to head a mob myself, and burn down their houses.

Simple
With the Lord's will, something ought to be done. Indeed, there should.

Tackabout
You, as president of the committee, should cite the scoundrels. Let them be stigmatized; mark them out, and it's an easy matter to set a mob upon their backs that shall drive them to the devil.

Simple
Why, sir, we have had several before the committee, already, but it has pleased goodness that nothing could be made appear against them.

Tackabout
You have tories in the committee, sir.

Simple
God forbid.

Tackabout
Two of the members dined with a Scotchman the other day.

Simple
Dine with a Scotchman? that was dreadful.

Tackabout
Dreadful, sir, why, they deserve to be hang'd. I was told they were in a private room, shut up. The person who told me, says he, peeped thro' the key-hole, and saw them wink

to each other, and then drink; that they would every now and then, break out into a horse laugh. He heard them drink damnation to all scoundrels—very plain.

Simple
That was meant for somebody, I reckon.

Tackabout
It was intended for the committee, sir.

Simple
Well, sir, the committee is to meet to-day, you know, at your request. You'll inform them of all such things, I hope.

Tackabout
I'll do my duty, depend upon it.

[*Enter Brazen, Strut, Thunderbolt, Squib and Skip.*]

Thunderbolt
Not pay! I thought the captain was flush of money.

Brazen
He's a damn'd scoundrel.

[*Enter Flash*]

Flash
Mighty well! very fine! excellent terms, indeed, if the guardians of their country are to be abused by every fellow!

Simple
What is the matter, my dear, sir?

Flash
You know I dare not accept or give a challenge: It's contrary to ordinance. My hands are tied up you see; yet truly, I am to be kicked, cuffed, and trod upon. I'll be damn'd if I would not give a million that I durst cut that fellows head off *(pointing to Brazen)*.

Simple
Surely, my friends, you have not used the captain ill?

Tackabout
Use a soldier ill! They are our dependence—our support—our every thing.

Squib
Yes, yes, and we should keep them from all harm.

Skip
No soldier ought to be hurt.

Flash
Gentlemen, I lodge my complaint with you. If soldiers are to be abused, d'ye see me, because they dare not give a challenge, and by a man too, d--n my soul if ever I pull trigger again. *(Cries.)*

Simple
Gentlemen, we really ought to sit upon this matter. *(They all huddle round a table.)*

Brazen
That is not a business that comes before the committee, sir.

Tackabout
The committee; sir, begging your pardon, have a right to take up what business they please; and to give any opinion.

Simple
So I always thought.

Thunderbolt
Except against one of their own body. They have no right to try one another. A lawyer told me it would be *imperium sub imperio*.

Simple
Why, as you say, my friend, I don't think that would be right, nor safe neither, indeed.

Thunderbolt
As Mr. Brazen is a member, we have no business with any matter that touches him.

All
No, no, by no means.

Simple
Well, gentlemen, as that is your opinion, Mr. Brazen, do take a seat; I say, gentlemen, as that is your opinion, captain, we can't do any thing in it, you see!

Flash
Mighty well! very fine! So I am to be abused, and to have no satisfaction. D--nation seize me if I don't.

Brazen
(Rising.) What will you do?

Flash
'Tis no matter, sit still, if you please, I'm done with you, sir. But I'll be d--m'd if I don't—*(Brazen goes towards him.)* I swear the peace, gentlemen, I swear the peace.

Brazen
You are an infamous coward, sir.

Flash
Very pretty! noble doings! If I fight, I am to be broke; if not, to be abused; eh!

Brazen
Walk out, if you please. *(Turns him out.)*

Flash
Yes, yes, I'll go, sir, but D----me if I don't . . . . *(Exit.)*

Tackabout
Upon my soul, Mr. Brazen, I am surprised at you.

Brazen
For what, sir?

Tackabout
That gentleman is an officer in the service of the country.

Brazen
Suppose he is.

Tackabout
Our leading men treat our officers and soldiers with the greatest respect, sir. Whatever they do or say, is overlooked for the good of the service.—They would not have one of them offended for the world, sir: they would not, you may depend upon it.

Brazen
He is a scoundrel; as such I have treated him: if you have a mind—take up the quarrel.

Tackabout
I take up the quarrel! D--n the fellow, I don't care a farthing about him. No, no, old friend, here's my hand; I would not quarrel with you for a dozen such fellows. Well, Mr. President, are the culprits cited, agreeable to the list I gave you?

Brazen
This fellow has more smoke than fire in him, I find. *(Aside.)*

Simple
I told the doorkeeper to summon them.

[*Enter Stitch.*]

Mr. Stitch, have you summoned them men as I told you of?

Stitch
I have summoned four; Mr. Trueman, Mr. Meanwell, the reverent Mr. Preachwell, and a Scotch pedlar, an't please your honour.

Brazen
What are they charg'd with?

Simple
Why, Mr. Tackabout there, gave me a paper, with all their crimes set down in it, but *(searching his pockets)* I've lost it, I believe, some how or other. Howsomever, I can remember as how that Mr. Meanwell and Mr. Trueman are to be tried for dining with a Scotchman, Mr. Preachwell for eating upon a fast day, and the Scotch pedlar for drinking the king's health.

Brazen
Well, where are they?

Stitch
Mr. Meanwell, and Mr. Trueman, promised to come. The parson snuff'd up his nose as bad as if he smell'd a stink. I'm sartin, says I, it's not me that has let a———, mentioning the thing itself, an't like your honour. The words were hardly out of my mouth, before spang he took me with his foot.

Simple
The parson strike!

Stitch
Yes; look, your honour, just here an't please your honour. *(Shewing his b--k si-e.)*

Simple
Praise be to God, our holy teachers detest fighting.

Stitch
I said so, an't please your honour. You a parson, says I! By jing, he ran at me as vigue-rous as a lion, with a monstratious stick; but durn the heels, thinks I, that lets the body suffer; so off I ran.

Simple
Did he say nothing?

Stitch
He call'd me a dirty fellow, an't like your honour.

Brazen
Where is the pedlar?

Stitch
He got the wind of me, and has made his escape out of the precincts, I believe.

Brazen
You say, Trueman and Meanwell promised to attend?

Stitch
Yes, an't please your honour.

Brazen
Suppose we adjourn, Mr. President, for half an hour, 'till the tories come?

Simple
Agreed. *(The committee rises.)*

[*Exeunt.*]

SCENE, the Court-house yard.

[*Enter Trueman and Meanwell, meeting Tackabout.*]

Trueman
Let us secure our pockets Meanwell.

Tackabout
Fie! my dear Sir, that is too severe.

Trueman
The viper that gives a wound, then licks it with an envenomed tongue, is not more noxious, more offensive, than the base reptile thou art.

Tackabout
'Pon honour, gentlemen, I have the greatest veneration for you both.

Meanwell
So talk'd the artful serpent, when with shew of zeal, and love, he seduced our first parents.

Trueman
It is at your instance, Mr. Tackabout, we are called here: What is our offence?

Tackabout
At my instance! you astonish me: at my instance! I scorn it.

Trueman
If your baseness was not perfectly plebeian, Mr. Tackabout, the exteriors of the gentleman might perhaps keep you concealed, but—

Meanwell
Nature is too true to her bias not to make Mr. Tackabout always appear the complete villain she intended him for.

[*Brazen, Thunderbolt and Simple crossing the stage.*]

Brazen
Mr. Tackabout is giving the tories a little more of his political catechism, I expect.

Thunderbolt
Come, Mr. Tackabout, no favour to tories: let's have no pleading off; bring them before the committee.

Simple
Yes, yes, let's have them before us.

Tackabout
I have nothing to say against the gentlemen. I have no charge against them.

Simple
Why, dear me! did not you have them cited. Did not you give me a paper?

Tackabout
That's lost, thank heaven. *(Aside.)*

Simple
Did not you give me a paper with their names?

Tackabout
I give you a paper! I might give you a paper and their names might be wrote upon it, but not by me, I assure you. You should never betray your informers, sir. It will stop all your proceedings. It's a breach of faith and confidence that I little expected, sir, *(aside to Simple).*

Simple
Oh, dear me! Mr. Stitch, Mr. Stitch.

[*Enter Stitch.*]

Where's the paper I gave you with the names of the men you were to summon.

Stitch
An't please your honour, happening to meet with Mr. Pettifogger, the attorney, I shewed it to him. He told me it was a precept, and that I must leave a copy of it at every place I went to, but being a poor hand at writing, tho I have pretty good larning too, I bethought me as how it would do as well to leave the thing itself, so I gave the paper to that gentleman *(pointing to Trueman).*

Tackabout
Blown, by heavens! *(Aside.)*

Stitch
The paper Mr. Tackabout gave me, I lost.

Trueman
Here is the paper he gave me, and in my house this was found. *(Aside to Tackabout.)* Do you know this handwriting?

Tackabout
Hide it, for God's sake, my dear sir. *(Aside.)* Come this way, and let me talk with you: Gentlemen, I wish to have a little conversation with Mr. Trueman. Will you give me leave?

Thunderbolt
Ay, ay, try what you can do with him.

[*The committee retire.*]

Tackabout
Do, my dear sir, be advised. You know I'm a tory; if these fellows find me out, I shall be tore to pieces.

Trueman
To this gentleman *(pointing to Meanwell)* and myself, you profess yourself a tory; with these people you have the

merit of being a whig. It's high time, Mr. Tackabout, for you to be shewn in your proper colours; for, under your present disguise, you are a nuisance to all parties.

[*Enter Thunderbolt, Squib, and Skip, listening.*]

Tackabout
I am a tory, sir, 'pon honour, sir, I am.

Trueman
Then you are the base villain I always found you to be.

[*Enter Simple, Brazen, Strut, and Summons.*]

Simple
Come, Mr. Tackabout, these gentlemen were cited at your request. Let's have 'em before us.

Tackabout
I have no charge against them, gentlemen. I have talked the matter over with them, and am proud to find they are innocent.

Simple
Well, well, what a pity! is there nobody here that can make any thing appear against them? We shall be laugh'd at if they get off so; indeed we shall, my friends.

Trueman
You appear anxious, sir, to have us arraign'd: By interrogating us, you may be furnished with answers respecting any thing you wish to be inform'd of.

Simple
As that is the case, I shall come to the point at once. Are you tories, gentlemen?

Trueman
Explain what you mean by the word tory, gentlemen.

Simple
Tory! why surely every body knows what a tory is—a tory is—pray, gentlemen, explain to him what a tory is.

Strut
A tory, sir, is any one who disapproves of men and measures.

Brazen
All suspected persons are call'd tories.

Trueman
If suspicion makes a tory, I may be one; if a disapprobation of men and measures constitutes a tory, I am one; but if a real attachment to the true interests of my country stamps me her friend, then I detest the opprobrious epithet of tory, as much as I do the inflammatory distinction of whig.

Simple
How is that? this gentleman is neither whig nor tory.

Trueman
Neither, sir!—Yes, neither. Whenever the conduct and principles of neither are justifiable, I am neither; as far as the conduct and principles of either correspond with the duties of a good citizen, I am both.

Simple
Well, really, I don't understand him. Do any of you, gentlemen?

Skip
I understand as how he says he is a tory, or no tory, a whig or no whig, just as the maggot bites.

Simple
How is that?

Skip
Why, mayhap, at this present time of asking, he may be a whig, as we pretend to be. By and by he may be a tory, as occasion offers.

Trueman
I detest the mean subterfuge: this low cunning I leave to your sycophant, Mr. Tackabout.

Simple
Mr. Tackabout is no tory, I'm sure.

Trueman
Ask him, sir.

Simple
Well, for the joke's sake. Mr. Tackabout, the tories have a mind to turn the tables upon you. They seem to signify as how you are a tory.

Tackabout
You are better acquainted with me, sir, than to suspect any thing of that, I hope.

Simple
Why, to be sure I am.

Thunderbolt
Mr. Tackabout and the tories seemed very thick, a little while ago, while he was talking.

Skip
Let me tell, Mr. Thunderbolt.—While he was talking with the tories just now, Mr. Squib, and I bethought us of listening a bit.

Squib
Yes, and he purtested it was not owing to him these gen-

tlemen were summoned. He signified he was a tory himself.

Skip
So he did.

Squib
Fair play, is fair play, that gentleman call'd him a villain for it. *(Pointing to Trueman.)*

Skip
The truth is the truth. That gentleman is lesser a tory than Mr. Tackabout.

Squib
So he is.

Brazen
(To Trueman.) Give me your hand, you are an honest fellow: every tory is a villain. Henceforth, all malice apart.

Thunderbolt
It seems as how the gentlemen are whigs and Mr. Tackabout the tory.

Brazen
They are honest fellows, I find. There's my hand *(to Meanwell)* gentlemen, I move that they be discharged.

All
Agreed, agreed.

Simple
What must be done to Mr. Tackabout?

Brazen
Duck him.

Skip
Tar and feather him.

Thunderbolt
Advertise him.

Meanwell
He should be duck'd, as an incendiary, tarr'd as a nuisance, feather'd as a foul traitor, hang'd—

Trueman
And advertis'd as a coward. *(Kicks him.)* I beg pardon, gentlemen, but Mr. Tackabout's errors are so fundamental, that I can't help applying a certain specific. *(Kicks him out.)*

Simple
Well, really, he is rightly serv'd.

All
Very right.

Brazen
Let us adjourn, and drive the fellow out of the yard.

All
Agreed.

[*Exeunt all but Trueman and Brazen.*]

Brazen
(*Taking Trueman by the hand.*) You are an honest fellow, a fellow of spirit.

Trueman
I once esteemed you as a friend, respected you as a father, Mr. Brazen.

Brazen
Well, well, all malice apart, it shall be so.

Trueman
What, good sir?

Brazen
You shall have her to-night, if you please.

Trueman
I am at a loss for words.

Brazen
Poh! poh! keep your words to yourself; you are welcome to her, that's enough; as I find you are no tory, that's enough; I say. Come, let's mob that rascal of a fellow. (*Exit.*)

Trueman
So in spite of all the malice and censure of the times, I am at last dubb'd a whig. I am not wiser or better than before. My political opinions are still the same, my patriotic principles unaltered: but I have kick'd a tory, it seems: there is a merit in this, which, like charity, hides a multitude of sins. Well, Mira, I have once more obtained your father's consent to our union, and lest some suspicion or other should again tickle his brain with the patriotic itch, I am determin'd to be thine this night.

[*Enter Pickle, not observing Trueman; sings.*]

Pickle
The flocks, the herds, the pretty birds
Nature alone, obey;
Like them I'll range, like them I'll change,
As free, as blest as they.
What he gave as a token of love, I now send as a token of my fidelity to him. So much for my lesson. (*looking at the ring*). Alack! alack! how many poor creatures do these little magic circles make miserable!

Trueman
What fine soliloquy are you meditating, most noble captain?

Pickle
Taken up with your business altogether, I assure you.

Trueman
It becomes intricate, I fear, if it puzzles a man of your adroitness.

Pickle
I was studying how to convey to you, in the best manner, the sweetest message that ever came from a fond mistress.

Trueman
A lady's message can lose nothing of it's merit, when conveyed by so great an adept as you, sir, but I expected a letter—

Pickle
A letter! Lord, sir, never ask a letter from your mistress. 'Tis the worst way of procuring a tender of the affections in the world. A woman, when she commits her sentiments to paper, is so very cautious, so nicely circumspect, lest the warmth that animates the expressions of love, should carry her beyond the usual prudence of her sex, that the glowing ardor of the passions, gives way to a cold prudish reserve, which I call the grave of love; tho' some are pleased to call it the nursery of virtue. However, sir, your mistress assents to all your proposals, and here are my credentials. *(Presents the ring.)*

Trueman
I know the token too well, to doubt the faith of my dear girl, or the fidelity with which you have transacted the business entrusted to you. Take this as a small acknowledgment. *(Offers a purse.)*

Pickle
I never receive wages for conducting a love-intrigue. These little offices of friendship circulate the affections so sweetly, that I always find a reward in my own feelings without any adventitious one.

Trueman
The youngster's expressions and sentiments favour little of the footman, methinks. *(Aside.)*

Pickle
Have you any farther commands, sir.

   [*Enter Meanwell.*]

Meanwell
Well, Trueman, you have got your pleni-potentiary with you, I find. The preliminaries are all settled, I suppose; and you have nothing to do but enter the fortress.

Trueman
I have always had a friend in the citadel, the little traitor, love: but I have obtained by treaty, what I lately thought was only to be atchieved by stratagem.

Meanwell
What? is the old governor in your interest again?

Trueman
Yes, he assents to the surrender, and the terms of capitulation are all my own.

Meanwell
I congratulate you with all my soul: when is to be the happy day?

Trueman
This. I am determined to take the old fellow while he's in the humour. At six in the evening, I expect our plighted troth will be mutually exchanged. Even that happy hour will have a shade upon it unless dispelled by your presence: the old gentleman has been rude to you; can you forgive it?

Meanwell
The interest you have in his affection leaves no room for my resentment. You may expect me: 'till then, adieu.

[*Exeunt Meanwell and Trueman severally.*]

Pickle
Well, since this affair of Mr. Trueman's is to be settled in the old hum drum style; I have nothing to do but to bring my amour to as speedy a conclusion as possible. You to your Mira, Trueman, and I to my dear Melinda. *(Exit.)*

SCENE, a field.

[*Enter Flash.*]

Flash
Poor Flash! to be broke if you fight, to be kick'd if you don't! *(Pulls off his coat.)* Lie there, commission and cowardice, together. *(Draws his sword.)* Now, d----me, come on, ha, hah! *(pushing at the ground)* how I could fight, if I durst.

[*Enter Strut, escorting Isabella.*]

Strut
Well, ma'am, I have taken a commission, purely to oblige you.

Isabella
Your courage must be tried, indeed it must, colonel, before I can consent. Stop, *(seeing Flash.)* A man fighting his own shadow. See, my dear colonel; now is the time to attack him: do fight him colonel; I long of all things in the world, to see a duel.

Flash
Hah! there I had him. Hah! again, by God! through and through d----me! *(Isabella pushes Strut up to him.)* Mercy on me! *(starts back and drops his sword.)*

Isabella
Speak to him, colonel.

Strut
(Putting his foot on the sword.) Who are you, sir?

Isabella
But stay, colonel, let the man have his sword. *(Takes up the sword and gives it to Flash.)*

Strut
May I take the liberty to enquire your name, sir?

Flash
My name! d----me, sir, what right have you to my name?

Isabella
He curses you, colonel; pick a quarrel with him; do, dear colonel.

Strut
What! quarrel with a madman? The man is deranged in his mind. Are you not frantic, sir?

Flash
Frantic, my name Frantic! D-mn you, sir, I'll not be nick-named by any scoundrel living.

Isabella
Scoundrel! now we shall have it, draw, colonel. *(She takes Strut's hand, and puts it upon the hilt of his sword.)*

Strut
He did not call me scoundrel, madam. He only said he would not be nick-named by any scoundrel living. I have not nick-named him, madam.

Flash
It is a lie, sir.

Isabella
What say you to that, colonel?

Strut
The man is mad, absolutely mad, madam.

Flash
Blood and fire.

Isabella
(Draws Struts sword and puts it in his hand.) Now, colonel.

Flash
A pretty blade, let's see it my dear.

Isabella
Let him feel it, colonel. Up to him. *(Pushes up Strut.)*

Flash
(Puts up his own sword, and advances to look at that of Strut.) With your leave, my dear, from France, no doubt. I have heard they are all the best polishers in the world.

Strut
Stand off, sir; what did you mean by calling me a scoundrel?

Flash
I call you a scoundrel! Upon my soul, my dear, you are disordered in your mind.

Strut
This lady says you did, sir.

Flash
D-mn all ladies, say I; they are always making mischief, by setting honest fellows by the ears.

Strut
I told you, madam, he did not call me a scoundrel.

Isabella
I heard him give you the lie in plain terms.

Flash
Don't believe her, my dear. You and I won't quarrel about what a woman says: they will tell fibbs, d--n'd fibbs, sometimes.

Strut
You hear, madam; he did not give me the lie.

Isabella
Was there ever such a paltry coward! to put up with such an affront, and then stand parleying with a fellow who only apologizes for it, by abusing his mistress? give me the sword. *(Takes the sword and runs at Flash.)*

Flash
A man in petticoats, by God! oh, ho! my dear, I smell a rat. Yes, yes, honey, catch Flash if you can. Two to one! Oh! no, no, my dear; I'll not be assassinated by God. *(Runs off.)*

Strut
That last reproach of yours, my dear madam, raised my blood to such a pitch—if he had not gone off—D--n the fellow, I must have kill'd him.

Isabella
Colonel Strut, your most obedient. Henceforth, I disclaim all connexions with you. Never dare to speak to me, nor

hope ever hereafter, to see my face again. This I will take as the trophy of my victory.

[*Exit with Flash's coat.*]

Strut
Well, I don't know whether I am not better without her. She has such a cursed stomach for fighting, she would certainly have brought me into some scrape or other, in spite of my teeth.

Honour's a bubble, fame a sound
Not worth a man's pursuing;
Women at best, are evil's sound,
And oft bring men to ruin.

ACT V

SCENE, Maxwell's house.

[*Enter Pickle.*]

Pickle

My master's servants are a set of honest fellows. The butler made a few scruples at first, but upon his trying on the canonical habit, and my telling him he would make a charming methodist preacher, by God, the old fellow kick'd conscience out of doors, and immediately became a new creature—

[*Enter the butler, in a clergyman's gown.*]

Sage father, your most humble. A little more gravity, and you'll top the hypocrite so perfectly, that tho' true sanctity may blush at thee, yet iniquity will own thee her's for ever.

Butler

I don't much like the business you have set me upon, Mr. Pickle.

Pickle

Poh! you shall have a buss of the bride, a reward that would make lechery kick up the beam, tho' weigh'd against the charity of a bishop. Besides, as my tenure will be of short duration, I expect you may like her in reversion; a gratuity that a lecher of the Romish church would lick his chops at, with avidity.

Butler

It goes against my conscience, Mr. Pickle.

Pickle

Conscience! ha, ha, ha, as long as you are in that habit, you may defy the devil, and all his imps. Conscience only serves as a bugbear to the laity, the clergy are above it's trifling fears. For shame, don't disgrace the cloth, old fellow.—Go take the cook and scullion with you. You know our master is to be at Mr. Trueman's wedding tonight, we shall not be miss'd.

Butler

It is a sin to deceive a poor innocent girl, Mr. Pickle.

Pickle

Poh! poh! curse your canting, come along.

Butler

All the sin must lie upon your head.

Pickle
Well, I don't care, so I have the pleasure somewhere else.

Butler
You must bear me harmless.

Pickle
Yes, yes.

Butler
Well, I must go then, I suppose.

Pickle
Come on. *(Exit with the butler.)*

[*Enter Meanwell, with a letter in his hand.*]

Meanwell
My old friend, Mr. Worthy, writes me that his nephew, George, had arrived from England, about the beginning of our public disturbances; that being too free in discovering his political opinions, he was cited before one of their courts. To avoid the treatment he expected to receive from these guardians of the rights and liberties of their fellow-citizens, he absconded without informing his friends of his route or designs. I am requested to make enquiry after him. We have no asylum with us to which persecuted integrity would fly for shelter. No, no, he is not with us.

[*Enter Groom.*]

Groom
Mr. Trueman presents his compliments to your honour: says he is gone off to Mr. Brazen's, and desires you will follow him as soon as possible.

Meanwell
(looking at his watch.) Six is the hour. Tell your master, I'll be with him at the time appointed.

[*Exit Groom.*]

My butler just informed me that an old tenant of mine, formerly one of my best and most faithful domestics, has sent to me very pressingly to call on him in my way to the wedding. He has urgent business with me. I must comply with his request, and not to be too late, I'll prepare immediately for my journey. Who's there?

[*Enter a servant.*]

Where's Pickle?

Servant
An't please your honour, I don't know. But since he turned captain, I suppose as how he's after some of his wild vagaries. I saw him go out not long ago, with somebody wrap'd up in a gown.

Meanwell
You did! Farther enquiry should be made into this. Do you think any of the servants can tell whither he is gone?

Servant
They say it is a profound secret, but I thinks your honour, it can't be after any good.

Meanwell
Don't be too suspicious of a fellow-servant, but which of them told you it was a secret?

Servant
The cook, your honour: says he to me, Mr. Pickle is a sly cock, says he, and knows what to do, says he, but I hope your honour won't tell as how I told you.

Meanwell
Get ye gone, and tell the cook to come hither. *(Exit servant.)* That young man is out of the way at a very improper time, and may probably have some trick in view. He appears to be a faithful and honest, and at the same time the most ingenious and genteel servant, I ever saw; but nevertheless, it is not impossible but he may have a mixture of the rake in his disposition. Let me see, what girl is there hereabouts whom he can have in view? It is not my wish to pry into all the actions of my servants, but no improper conduct must be permitted.

[*Enter the cook.*]

Meanwell
Well, sir, can you give me any account of Mr. Pickle?

Cook
Your honour won't be offended, I hope. I don't wish to raise mischief against a brother servant.

Meanwell
You know my authority when I choose to exert it on a proper occasion, must not be disputed. I understand that Pickle has gone out with some person muffled up in a cloke, and as secrecy is generally the veil of iniquity, I am confident he has some evil design. If you know any thing of his schemes, I insist upon your faithfully disclosing them to me.

Cook
Why, indeed, your honour, he never told me any thing about it; but I have good reason to believe, and I'll tell your honour all I know about it; for tho' I am a poor sarvant, I hope I may be an honest man. Don't your honour think a sarvant has a soul to be sav'd as well as great folks?

Meanwell
They have indeed, and for that reason should be attentive to their duty. But my time is short, be quick in giving your information.

Cook
Well, your honour must know the butler is gone with Mr. Pickle, and he wants me and John the scullion, to go too. The butler told me Mr. Pickle was going to be married, and we were to be the witnesses.

Meanwell
But if that was all, where was the necessity of secrecy.

Cook
Ah! your honour ha'n't heard all yet! This marriage, the butler said, is to be all a trick. He is to marry her with your name, and the butler is to be the parson, so that Mr. Pickle will gain his ends without any wedding in reality; the butler said as how he did not approve such doings, and he would endeavour to let you know in time to prevent it.—Howsomdever, as he is gone too, without telling your honour any thing about it, I suppose Mr. Pickle may have overpersuaded him.

Meanwell
Bless me! what a scheme of iniquity! But what girl is this he intends to deceive?

Cook
Melinda Heartfree, sir, the daughter of your honour's old servant John. Ah! he is a good old soul, and dame Heartfree too: they are so kind and good, every body loves them; and the young girl, too, is as good a creature, and as pretty as ever a man might wish to see. Indeed, your honour, I think it would be a pity to do her any harm.

Meanwell
I applaud your sentiments, and wish that many in higher stations, who delight in betraying innocence and beauty, could think as justly. To prevent the intended villany no time must be lost. Pickle and the butler may expect you now. You shall go with me. I'll not stay to dress for the wedding; when suffering virtue is to be relieved, or innocence protected, the moments are too precious to be dedicated to ceremony.

[*Exeunt*]

SCENE, John Heartfree's house.

[*Enter John and Margaret Heartfree.*]

John
Well, my dear, are you ready to take a walk over to neighbour Homespun's?

Margaret
Yes: I believe there's nothing more to be done about the

house, and I'll go as I am, plain and simple. You know neighbour Homespun don't stand upon finery.

John
No, and God forbid he should; for neither he nor I have much of that to brag of. But where's Milly?

Margaret
Milly had rather stay at home, she says.

John
Well, let her stay; we can go without her. Come, child.

[*Exeunt. Enter Pickle and Butler.*]

Pickle
Come, I have enquired, and find the old folks are from home. Melinda is within, and will make her appearance immediately.

Butler
What am I to do?

Pickle
Be all gravity, sir, and with a demure face and most audible voice, read the ceremony.

Butler
The ceremony! where must I find it?

Pickle
Here, sir, *(opens the book)* you are to begin here.

Butler
Yes, yes, how much is there of it?

Pickle
All this. *(Shews him.)*

Butler
Why it would take me a month to read all that—

Pickle
Zounds! man, can't you read?

Butler
Great D-e-a-r, dear, l-y-ly, darly, b-e, be, l-o, lo, belo, v-e-d, ved, beloved, darly beloved.

Pickle
Pish! try here.

Butler
Great Wi-l-t, wilt, t-h-o-u, tho', h-a—

Pickle
Hush you clodheaded fool; here comes Melinda.

[*Enter Melinda.*]

Pickle
My dearest girl. *(Kisses her.)*

Melinda
Lord bless me, how my heart aches!

Pickle
What's the matter, my love?

Melinda
I'm so scar'd; you'll pardon my folly, I hope, sir.

Pickle
Yes, my dear, and reward your love; this worthy clergyman—

Melinda
Is that the parson? how my heart aches!

Pickle
He is a learned and sage divine, a true Orthodox minister of the church, a man of letters, and hard reading (literally true! *aside*). He has an impediment in his speech.

[*Enter Meanwell, Cook and Scullion, on one side a little behind.*]

Cook
There is the poor girl, as I was telling your honour he intends to trick.

Meanwell
Is that the butler in the parson's gown?

Scullion
Yes, sir, but he said he would keep them apart 'til your honour came.

Meanwell
(*Clapping Pickle on the shoulder.*) So, sir, you have dar'd to make use of my name, in order to deceive an innocent girl.

Pickle
Blown, by heavens. (*Aside.*)

Meanwell
When virtue stands upon her guard against the protestations of lust and treachery, the professed libertine flies to a new object. 'Tis only the sly hypocrite and accomplish'd villain, who under the mask of honour, makes war upon simplicity and innocence, by prostituting the sanctity of marriage, to the base purposes of seduction.

Pickle
I am asham'd to look him in the face. (*Aside.*)

Meanwell
Young man—I could have pawn'd my life upon your principles: I have found in your fidelity, sincerity, and truth, an understanding and disposition far above your rank in life. In your breast I once thought virtue might have liv'd in concord with the graces. Sorry I am to see a

mind such as yours polluted and abased by the low cunning, of intrigue, and the base arts of sensuality.

Pickle
How much like a scoundrel must I appear!

Meanwell
(*To Melinda.*) It is happy for you, miss, that my other servants are men of better principles than your fond lover, here.

Melinda
Bless me! what do I hear? pray, sir, what is the matter?

Meanwell
My name is Meanwell, child.

Melinda
What is yours, then? (*To Pickle.*)

Pickle
Pickle.

Melinda
Pickle!

Pickle
Yes, and a most woeful pickle I am in. (*Aside.*)

Melinda
What a fool have I been?

Pickle
Pardon me, good sir; and you, my dear girl, forgive me. Tho' your virtue deserves a greater reward, yet, if you will condescend to marry me, it shall be the future study of my life, to atone for my base designs upon your unsuspecting love, by making you a kind and most affectionate husband.

Melinda
Your friends will object to your marriage, unless you get a woman of family and fortune, perhaps.

Pickle
My principal friend is here present: If he consents, and you are willing, there can be no other objection to our union.

Meanwell
The generous tender you make of your hand and affections, to this poor injur'd innocent, gives me hopes that you have not travelled far in the road of vice. Her example will, I hope, recal you to the paths of virtue. If she is willing, I not only consent to your union, but will present you with a sufficient sum to begin the world with.

Pickle
Noble fellow. (*Aside.*) Well, my dear Melinda, you hear this, can you forgive me?

Melinda
It was your person I lov'd, not your fortune: Your person is still the same, I must still love.

Butler
Here's my hand.

Melinda
With mine take my heart.

Butler
Well, as all matters are settled, I may read the ceremony, I suppose. I can read much better now, Mr. Pickle.

Meanwell
Come sir, be merciful, when virtue rides triumphant on the smooth surface of our affections, you should never ruffle the fair prospect by stirring the passions.

Melinda
Instead of a fine lady, I must be poor Melinda, still, and instead of the master I've got the man. *(Taking Pickle by the hand, sings:)*
But come, my Pickle, to my arms,
With all thy love attracting charms,
And free my mind from all alarms.
No sordid views, in thirst of gain,
No hopes of riches giving pain,
Shall e'er disturb my simple brain.
My loom shall tell, my wheel declare
That no domestic feuds, or war,
Shall drive my Pickle from my care.
I'll spin his coat, I'll knit his hose,
With white the legs, with blue the toes,
And keep him neat where'er he goes.

Pickle
My dear Melinda, it is with pleasure I shall now discover to you my real name and character.—After the proofs I've had of your virtue and disinterested love, I can no longer hesitate in making you mistress of a fortune equal to that I falsely pretended to be master of.

Meanwell
What is this I hear?

Melinda
More wonders still!

Pickle
That gentleman *(pointing to Meanwell)* will be able to inform you that there are few families in this western hemisphere superior to mine, either in estate or other circumstances. By the death of a tender and careful father, I am possessed of an ample fortune.

Meanwell
(Aside.) My suspicions increase every moment.

Pickle
The phrenzy of the times, and an unhappy attachment to sentiments and opinions inculcated into me from my early youth, reduced me to the necessity of abandoning both friends and fortune for a time, and to seek an asylum under the roof of a man held high in the esteem of my poor deceased father, and revered by all his dependents.

Meanwell
(Shewing a letter.) Do you know this hand writing?

Pickle
It is my good uncle's, or I'm much deceiv'd.

Meanwell
Come to my arms, my dear George; son to the companion of my youth, the fond associate of my riper years. He will always live in my remembrance, and to thee I will pay the debt of love I owed him.

Pickle
Add no more to what I have received, lest you oppress me with accumulated kindness.

Meanwell
My dear George why did you come to me in the character of a footman? you know the interest you had in my affections which entitled you to a station far above the lowly homage paid to a master, or that pliant duty service too often requires.

Pickle
Hearing that you were a suspected person as well as myself, and apprehending I might be held out to public odium, as the phrase is, I fear'd if I announc'd myself to you, you might be induced to do something in my behalf, which would render you still more obnoxious than you are at present.

Meanwell
Is it not sufficient that public virtue sometimes yields to the torrent of political enthusiasm, but are the social virtues to be confined within the narrow circle of self-preservation, or hid under the disguise of time-serving civility?

[*Enter John and Margaret Heartfree.*]

My old friend, I am glad to see you *(shaking John by the hand)*. Madam, your servant *(to Margaret)*.

John
I am proud to see your honour. Heaven's bounty be prais'd, your honour bears a good face yet.

Margaret
And a good heart too, I hope *(curtseying)*.

Meanwell
Thank you, my good old lady; you wish me a boon far above the treasures of the world.

John
Well, but, Milly, how comes it that the gentlemen are all standing, child? Come, sir, take a seat; nobody welcomer, your honour knows.

Meanwell
I thank you John, I had rather stand. (*Pulling out his watch*) I have no time upon my hands, I find. Well, what business have you with me, John?

John
Business! bless your honour, I am proud to see you: it always does me good, whenever your honour comes a near me.

Butler
(*To Meanwell.*) It was a feign'd story of mine to bring you here, sir.

Meanwell
Is that it? I'll say no more about it, then. So, John, you were near having a wedding in your house to-day.

John
I don't know how that could be, unless Milly would have wedded one of the bed-posts. There has not been a soul here, that I remember, off and on these two months and better.

Margaret
Except the mad captain; he was here anon.

Meanwell
What do you think of this gentleman?

John
I don't recollect that ever I saw him before.

Meanwell
This is a young gentleman of fortune, the son of an old friend of mine. His name is Worthy, and would be happy to marry your daughter, if you will grant your consent.

John
Your honour must be joking now.

Meanwell
Indeed I am not; certain circumstances compelled him, for a while, to pass himself on the world for my servant, by the name of Pickle; but his passion for Melinda has induced him to discover his real name and family.

John
I cannot doubt your honour's word: But how come he acquainted with Milly?

Pickle
Love, tho' blind, by instinct finds his way. I confess, with shame, that when I first saw this beauteous maid, I was tempted to entertain dishonourable designs upon her, but

I found her pure as spotless snows, and firm as adamant against all improper proposals, tho' soft as wax to the impressions of tenderness. I have always wished to find a maiden who could love me for myself alone; in this artless fair I have found one, who when my base attempt to impose upon her by a pretended marriage, was discover'd, mov'd by affection, forgave it all, and deign'd to receive the repentant sinner, tho' seemingly poor and humble. To her then, I bow, and she, if you object not, shall be the partner of my future life.

John
All this is new to me; but the gentleman is welcome to Milly, with all my heart. However, as it is come to this, another secret must be explained, for that girl is no more my daughter than I am a governor.

All
How?

John
No, your honour, she is of a much better family than I shall ever boast: she is nearly related to your honour.

Meanwell
To me!

John
Yes, your honour; but a short story will make all clear. You remember you had a sister once who is now dead?

Meanwell
Yes, one whom I have always remembered with lively regret. She marri'd unhappily.

John
There, your honour, was the beginning of all the mischief. You know Mr. Spendall, her husband was a very extravagant man. He liv'd at a great rate, and gam'd and horse-raced it very much, so that he soon brought himself to ruin. But that was not all, for, besides all this, he treated the lady, his wife, very ill, indeed. She had brought him a fine fortune, and he had spent it: so he thought her heart always upbraided him for it, and that made him worse, but Lord help the poor lady, she was so sweet and kind hearted, she bore no malice to any body.

Meanwell
(*Weeping.*) Your tale touches me too tenderly.

John
No wonder it should, your honour, but as I was about to say, the poor lady you know had a child, which was generally supposed to have died when it was two months old. Her husband was at that time gone upon a long journey which he took indeed to keep out of the way of his creditors, and the report was spread to deceive him, and a pretended funeral was had.

Meanwell
I remember it, and I attended on the occasion, but I did not examine the coffin.

John
Neither did any body else: but the poor lady had brought the child to me. I shall never forget her looks. It was not long before she died. John, says she, I know I shall shortly die, my heart is broken, and I am going to a better world than this. My only tie to earth is this tender infant: may she never feel her mother's sorrow! This infant I cannot leave in the house of a man who has forgotten all the feelings of a husband, who would educate her in vice, and perhaps leave her to beggary. I can preserve her from the pollution of bad example only by removing her from him. With you she will be plain and virtuous. When I am dead, and my husband is no more, who I know when alive, will never permit her to reside with him, convey her to my brother if he shall then be living. I know his generous soul: he will be indeed a father to her: as a proof of her birth, present him with this picture of his wretched sister, which he gave her himself. Here it is, an't please your honour. *(Shews a miniature picture.)*

Meanwell
It is indeed, the same.

John
Tell him, she said, that is the picture of his once dear Caroline, tell him it is the only valuable pledge of affection I had to leave him. She went away weeping so bitterly, that every time I think on't—*(wiping his eyes)*.

Meanwell
(Taking Melinda in his arms.) My dearest girl—say, John, is this my poor sister's child?

John
I'll be sworn.

Meanwell
How can I doubt it? These eyes tempered with sweetness, these looks of mildness declare the fountain from whence they take their origin *(embracing her)*.

Margaret
Blessings upon her, she is as good a child, tho I say it, and had the bringing of her up, as ever suck'd its mother's milk.

Meanwell
(To Pickle.) Come hither, George; the generous tender you have made of your person and fortune to this girl, shall be amply rewarded. Take her, not as poor Melinda, but as my niece, and with her a fortune equal to your wishes.

Pickle
Her merit is a sufficient dowry; her beauty would tempt the miser to forget his gold, and even think of happiness.

Melinda
(*Runs to John and Margaret embracing them alternately.*)
My dear father, my dear mother, how comes it that I am not your daughter? I am, I must be, indeed I must.

Meanwell
Their kindness, my dear, well deserves a filial attachment. It shall be my part to acquit you, in some measure, of the obligations you are under to them, by something more substantial than words.

John
Come, Milly, place your mind upon your uncle; he is worth a dozen such fathers as I am, child.

Melinda
My uncle, I shall respect, no doubt, shall love; but must I forget my poor good old father and mother, who have fed me, rais'd me, cherish'd and loved me so long? I could as soon forget my victuals, and drink, as forget those to whose kindness I have so long been indebted for both.

Meanwell
When gratitude displays itself, it is with a meridian brightness, that almost casts a shade over the sister virtues.— But, John, why did you keep this matter a secret from me?

John
Your honour married, you know, soon after my young mistress went away. Ever since your poor lady died childless, I have been thinking of telling your honour, but some how or other, my heart has always misgiven me 'till now.

Meanwell
Well, my dear niece, I must redeem the time you have been lost to my affections, by redoubled tenderness for the time to come. Your old friend, Mr. Trueman, is to be married this evening, John; will you and the old lady go with us to the wedding?

John
I am always ready to obey your honour's commands. Milly, you must go behind your spouse, I suppose. The old woman and I can walk.

Meanwell
By no means, take my servant's horses. They can wait here 'till our return.

John
Well, well, your honour's will is my pleasure.

Meanwell
Come, let's away.

   [*Exeunt.*]

SCENE, Brazen's house.

   [*Enter Mira.*]

Mira
I wish love and duty could always go hand in hand, but the little tyrant will be obey'd, even when all the virtues oppose him. What can poor Duty do when sole competitor against so formidable a rival. She must submit, I suppose.

(Sings.)
Hail, Cupid, god of love, to thee
Henceforth I'll bend the suppliant knee;
Hymen, to thee my bliss I'll owe,
And fearless to thine altar go.
I have long given up to filial piety, all the little gratifications and amusements so ardently pursued by the gay and giddy of my years, but I can never resign to an arbitrary injunction, proceeding from mere caprice, the fair prospect I have of a happy establishment thro' life.

   [*Enter Trueman.*]

My dear Trueman, how came you here? surely, my eyes deceive me; it can't be you.

Trueman
My love, my life, my every hope! *(Embracing her.)*

Mira
For God's sake, my dear sir—I expect my father, every moment.

Trueman
Let him come. *(Kissing her.)* This prattling talk of love, would make the angry tenants of the forest club their songs, and all the winged race chirp to the melody.— *(Kissing again.)*

Mira
If he should come, and find you here!

Trueman
Lay aside your fears; your father has again consented to our union. What his inducements are, 'tis needless to relate at present. Let it suffice, that here I am by his permission.

Mira
Is it possible?

Trueman
True as my love, doubtless as your fidelity.

[*Enter Brazen.*]

Brazen
So, so, give these young dogs a scent of the scut, and away they fly, regardless of whip or horn. Well, I am glad to see you, sir; Mira, how goes it, child?

Trueman
(*Taking Mira by the hand.*) You see before you, two persons, long united by the ties of love, now waiting only for the solemn, sacred service the rites of honour call for.

Brazen
I hate your high flown speeches, Mr. Trueman.

Mira
My dear father, at your request, I was induced to accept a tender of this gentleman's affections.

Brazen
You begin upon your high ropes. Hush, take him, that's enough, (*joining their hands*) here, now, you are both satisfied, I hope.

Mira
(*Kneeling.*) Accept my thanks.

Brazen
Kneel to your maker, child, not to me, get up. You may have him, I say, that's enough.

[*Enter Meanwell, Pickle, Melinda, John, and Margaret Heartfree.*]

Trueman
My dear Meanwell, (*presenting him to Brazen*). Mr. Meanwell, sir.

Brazen
Poh! I know him well enough. I have eyed him many a time, damn'd sharp, too, you may depend. However, as he is no tory, I have nothing more to say. Here's my hand. I'm glad to see you, sir. Who have you with you?

Meanwell
Mr. Worthy, sir. (*Introducing Pickle.*)

Brazen
Worthy! no tricks upon travellers. I am glad to see you, captain.

Meanwell
Miss Spendall. (*Introducing Melinda.*)

Brazen
Milly Heartfree, as I live! You have a mind to be funny, sir, but you can't cheat me in my neighbour's children,

neither. *(To John and Margaret.)* How goes it, neighbours? I am glad to see you. Come, take seats. I'll go, and have a rouzing fire in the great room. *(Sees Trueman kissing Mira.)* How they bill like two pigeons! The parson will be here presently. He'll set you to kissing, with a vengeance. *(Exit.)*

Trueman
(To Meanwell.) You were quite funny with the old gentleman.

Meanwell
I never was more serious in my life. This, sir, is George Worthy, of Maryland, nephew to our good friend and acquaintance, Charles Worthy, Esq; and this, can you believe it? is my niece, my dear sister's daughter.

Trueman
I am astonished.

Mira
I never was more so in my life.

Meanwell
Let it suffice for the present to inform you they are affianced to each other. The circumstances which have led to a discovery of their rank in life, and the generous proofs each has received from the other, of a disinterested affection, I will give you in full at a more convenient season. Their wedding is to follow yours. Will my Trueman and his lovely bride, favour us with their company?

Trueman
Doubtless.

Mira
With pleasure, sir.

[*Enter Brazen.*]

Brazen
Come, adjourn into the next room, if you please. Old Thump-the-cushion is arrived already.

[*Exeunt omnes.*]

****
THE
MOTLEY
ASSEMBLY
****

7

Introduction to
The Motley Assembly

IN CONTRAST to the other plays in this anthology *The Motley Assembly* is, in the main, a social satire with some political overtones. The play has no real plot; it is the playwright's subtly etched commentary on a small incident of social life, and the attack is consequently more like the thrust of a rapier than the heavy blows of a broad sword.

The revelation of character in *The Motley Assembly* is of greater interest to the reader than is the plot or incident, and the emotions conveyed by the playwright are disgust and impatient anger, rather than the deep hatred of some of the earlier plays. The setting is one in which elegant and "genteel" ladies and gentlemen sit amid tea and coffee cups cutting their friends and acquaintances into little pieces. Such scenes of gossip are reminiscent of Molière's *L'Impromptu de Versailles* and *Le Misanthrope* as well as Sheridan's *The School for Scandal*, which had been produced in London in 1777.

Mercy Otis Warren has been credited with the authorship of *The Motley Assembly*.[1] The acerbic condemnation of society in the play is similar to the social satire of *The Adulateur*, *The Defeat*, and *The Group*—all attributed to Mrs. Warren. *The Motley Assembly* is also like the other plays in that it reveals a keen observer of the foibles of human nature in an affected society, where the elite in this instance are largely influenced by the delights of recollected Tory amenities.

That Mrs. Warren could write such a mockery of the insipid delights of the elite is verified by her approach to the same kind of people in her political satires and particularly in two nondramatic poems published in 1790: "The Squabble of the Sea Nymphs,"[2] and an untitled poem that first appeared in the *Royal American Magazine* of June, 1774. The poems reveal the same social wit and satirical point of view found in *The Motley Assembly*.

"The Squabble of the Sea Nymphs" is a Popian fragment describing the confusion among classic nymphs of the sea when quantities of tea are suddenly dumped on them in Boston Harbor. The second poem is a satire on ladies who must somehow rationalize their love of finery in the face of the interdiction of the Boston Port Bill (which took effect June 1, 1774), a parliamentary act prohibiting all but "necessaries" from being imported or exported. The poem lists what a fine lady considers "necessaries" even though they are designated luxuries under the law:

> Wimples, mantles, curls, and crisping pins
> Need not be ranked among the modern sins.[3]

Hannah Winthrop, writing to Mercy Warren on September 27, 1774, states that she has "Lately receivd great pleasure from an ingenious Satire on that Female Foible Love of dress in the Royal American Magazine" and assumes, rightly, that Mrs. Warren is the poet.[4]

A remarkable letter to Mrs. Warren from her husband on June 6, 1779, may throw some light on the authorship of *The Motley Assembly*. James Warren advises his wife to take up her pen once more, if for no other reason than that such an exercise in satire might be therapeutic. He urges her to overcome her current lethargy and write a "Satyr on Villains—there are enough of them. If not—take in the Fools then I am sure you will have enough. I am sure the remedy will succeed and you will feel a Laudable Pride."[5] This letter might well have inspired *The Motley Assembly*, which was published in 1779.

That Mrs. Warren had a ready wit, that she knew the works of the dramatists of the seventeenth and eighteenth centuries, and that she was clever in the uses of satire is attested to by her writings. She admired Molière, and his views of a deteriorating society could easily be transferred to the American situation in 1779 when changes in the moral climate were obvious to an old-line Republican such as Mrs. Warren.

Writing to Abigail Adams on January 19, 1774, she remarks:

the solemn strains of the tragic Muse have been generally more to my taste than the lighter Representations of the Drama. Yet I think the Follies and Absurdities of Human Nature Exposed to Ridicule in the Masterly Manner it is done by Molière may often have a greater tendency to reform Mankind than some graver lessons of Morality.

The observation that he Ridicules Vice without Engageing us to Virtue discovers the Veneration of my Friend for the latter. But when Vice is held up at once in a detestable and Ridiculous Light, and the Windings of the Human Heart which lead to self deciption unfolded it Certainly points us to the path of Reason and Rectitude.[6]

The Motley Assembly attacks the moral attitudes of the day. It rails against those who shift with the wind and against those who actually preferred Boston under the siege. Mrs. Warren was impatient with social pretense and affectation, and she had a particularly intense disgust for those who still clung to the manners and fashions of the English court. She hated the Loyalists, looking upon them as traitors to their country, and especially deplored the "summer patriot," the man who gave lip service to the patriot cause but longed for the pleasures of the British social round. There was suffering in Boston even after the siege was lifted, but the characters in *The Motley Assembly* knew little of it or at least give no account of it. They resent the loss of gaiety, the rustle of silks in the drawing room, the bidding at whist, the charming suppers served at midnight balls, and the delightful interchange of gossip and social amenities. Under all the false attempt at a mannered society, Mrs. Warren saw that the new nation, still fighting for its life, might lose the battle because of an increasing decadence within society, a decline that would undermine all the patriotic resolves of the early days of the Revolution. *The Motley Assembly* reflects the ideals found in Mrs. Warren's letters and reinforces the possibility that she wrote the play.

By July 29, 1779, the probable time of the writing of *The Motley Assembly*, Mrs. Warren was perturbed by the evidence she saw of rot in the body politic. She wrote to John Adams that prominent members of government—

Deify the phantom Fashion, whether she appears in a French, a British, or American Dress; while others worship only at the shrine of plutus. Yet the old Republicans (a solitary few) with decent solemnity and confidence still persevere, their Hands unstained by Bribes, though poverty stares them in the face, their hearts unshaken by the Levity, the Luxury, the Caprice or Whim, the Folly or ingratitude of the times.

In the same letter she castigates the dishonesty she sees around her and asks:

How much longer shall we be Embarrassed and Distressed by the selfish insidious arts of Gamblers, Courtiers and Stock Jobbers among ourselves, while a Mercyless Foe is laying waste our Borders, Burning our Defenceless Cities, and Murdering the Innocent of all ages and ranks.[7]

Such scorn is also reflected in *The Motley Assembly*. The obsessive and absurd devotion of quasi patriots to the social charms of the Loyalists, and particularly to the trivial amusements afforded by dances, is the theme of the play. (The most brilliant event of the winter season was The Assembly or Patriarch's ball with which the play is concerned.)

Paul Leicester Ford observes that in *The Motley Assembly* "the young Continental officers are held up to scorn and derision because the charming faces of the Misses Hubbard, Sheefe, and Bowdoin [daughters of families sympathetic to the Tory cause], who are as thinly disguised under alias in the cast as they were probably thinly clad at the ball, were attractions strong enough to make them attend a function managed by the 'Tory crew.' "[8]

Throughout 1778 and 1779 the disintegration of moral standards in Boston alarmed the older patriots, as is evident in Charles Warren's account of the correspondence of General Warren, Mercy Warren's husband, and Samuel Adams. General Warren observes:

"All manner of extravagance prevails here in dress, furniture, equipage and living, amidst the distress of the public and multitudes of individuals. How long the manners of this people will be uncorrupted and fit to enjoy that liberty that you have long contended for, I know not." And later, he wrote that "assemblies, gaming and the fashionable amusements engage the genteel people." During the year, 1779, Adams wrote to Warren of that "inundation of levity, vanity, luxury, dissipation, and, indeed, vice of every kind, which I am informed, threatens that country."[9]

The Revolution was not yet won, but because Boston had been secure from enemy depredations since 1776 a sense of security pervaded the colony, and life assumed a more normal pace. In other parts of the country, however, the British appeared to be winning. By the end of 1779 and the beginning of 1780, the rebel cause was in danger. The English had had military success in the South where they invested Georgia and South Carolina. Boston remained calm, primarily because of its distance from the South, and consequently social life became more elaborate and free. It is against this background of British triumph that the characters in *The Motley Assembly* play their several parts.

The characters in the play are all Loyalists with the exception of Captain Aid of the army and Captain Careless of the navy. Mrs. Flourish and her friends, however, are careful not to commit themselves publicly to the Royalist cause, even if Mrs. Flourish is friendly to the British prisoners of war encamped in Cambridge.

The playwright indirectly satirizes the general Loyalist opinion that the French, although coming to the aid of America, will never fight or, if they do, will be destroyed. This idea was generally accepted, but the truth of the matter was very different. As John Miller points out:

> The fact that a large body of French troops could be stationed in the United States and live in amity with the American people confounded Englishmen who had comforted themselves with predictions of the early end of the Franco-American alliance. It was an object lesson in international relations: the more the French and Americans saw of each other, the better they seemed to get on.[10]

Mrs. Flourish and the rest of the ladies might have done well to have shifted their allegiance to the French rather than to remain nostalgically loyal to the departed British. Although they are compelled to disguise their allegiance, they are less than civil to the American officers, and they damn Washington with faint praise, worship the past, deplore the uncomfortable present, and hope for the return of an unreconstructed future.

There is little of the theatrical in *The Motley Assembly;* most of the action is the to and fro rushing of the gossips, and there are no scenes of conflict or confrontations. The atmosphere is quiet and the value of the piece lies in a juxtaposition of wit, having much of the flavor of the "bon ton" comedies of the eighteenth century without the incisive analysis of human behavior found in the comedies of Sheridan, Colman, and Garrick. In all probability the play's audience was limited to readers of pamphlets in Massachusetts and other colonies where distribution was possible. That the play was ever staged is extremely doubtful.

Notes

1. Among the writers who assign *The Motley Assembly* to Mrs. Warren are Montrose J. Moses, who notes, "indeed, so closely identified was she with things satirical, that 'The Motley Assembly' was attributed to her." (*The American Dramatist*, Boston, 1925, p. 48).

Worthington Chauncey Ford also states that the play was "attributed to Mrs. Warren." ("Mrs. Warren's 'The Group'," *Proceedings of the Massachusetts Historical Society*, LXII [October, 1928-June, 1929], p. 21.)

Paul Leicester Ford is more definite: "In the *Motley Assembly*, an anonymous farce published in Boston in 1779, we have a piece so much in the same style as Mrs. Mercy Warren's plays as to suggest the possible author." (*Some Notes towards an Essay on The Beginnings of American Dramatic Literature, 1606-1789*, New York, 1893, p. 24.)

Katharine Anthony states definitely that Mrs. Warren wrote the play. Miss Anthony offers no absolute proof but assumes that the play is so much like earlier efforts that there can be no question as to authorship. (*First Lady of the Revolution*, New York, 1958, p. 112.)

Arthur Hobson Quinn also attributes the play to Mrs. Warren. (*A History of the American Drama from the Beginnings to the Civil War.* New York, 1946, p. 53.)

Moses Coit Tyler devotes two pages to the play and in a footnote remarks, "That this play was by Mercy Warren, is the not improbable suggestion of P. L. Ford." (*The Literary History of the American Revolution,* New York, 1897, II, p. 227n.)

2. The poem first appears as an enclosure in a letter from Mercy Warren to Abigail Adams, written from Plymouth, February 27, 1774. (L. H. Butterfield, ed., *Adams Family Correspondence,* Cambridge, Massachusetts, 1963, I, p. 99.) It was then published as "Squabble among the Celestials of the Sea," *Boston Gazette.* March 21, 1774; the poem finally appears as "The Squabble of the Sea Nymphs" in Mercy Warren's *Poems, Dramatic and Miscellaneous* (Boston, 1790).

3. Warren, *Poems, Dramatic and Miscellaneous* (Boston, 1790).

4. Ford, ed., *Warren-Adams Letters* (Boston, 1917), I, p. 33.

5. Ford, ed., *Warren-Adams Letters* (Boston, 1925), II, p. 103.

6. Butterfield, ed., *Adams Family Correspondence* (Cambridge, Massachusetts, 1963), I, pp. 92-93.

7. Ford, ed., *Warren-Adams Letters* (Boston, 1925), II, p. 114.

8. Ford, *Essay on the Beginnings of American Dramatic Literature.* pp. 24-25.

9. Warren, "Samuel Adams and the Sans Souci Club in 1785," *Proceedings of the Massachusetts Historical Society,* 1926-1927, LX (May, 1927), p. 319.

10. Miller, *The Triumph of Freedom* (Boston, 1948), p. 529.

✳✳✳✳✳✳✳✳✳✳✳✳✳✳✳✳✳✳✳✳✳✳✳✳✳✳✳✳✳✳✳✳✳✳✳✳✳✳
THE
MOTLEY
ASSEMBLY
✳✳✳✳✳✳✳✳✳✳✳✳✳✳✳✳✳✳✳✳✳✳✳✳✳✳✳✳✳✳✳✳✳✳✳✳✳✳
A
FARCE
✳✳✳✳✳✳✳✳✳✳✳✳✳✳✳✳✳✳✳✳✳✳✳✳✳✳✳✳✳✳✳✳✳✳✳✳✳✳
Published
For the
Entertainment
of the
CURIOUS
✳✳✳✳✳✳✳✳✳✳✳✳✳✳✳✳✳✳✳✳✳✳✳✳✳✳✳✳✳✳✳✳✳✳✳✳✳✳
BOSTON:
Printed and Sold by Nathaniel Coverly,
NEWBURY-STREET,
M, DCC, LXXIX

Dramatis Personae

ESQUIRE RUNT *short, fat and old, considers himself a gallant; one of the managers of the Assembly*

MRS. FLOURISH *a leader of society, something of a Bluestocking*

MISS FLOURISH *her daughter, a debutante*

MISS TAXALL *friend of Miss Flourish, also a debutante.*

MISS DOGGRIL *another debutante, perhaps slightly older*

CAPTAIN AID *an American army officer.*

MRS. TAXALL *a member of society, but in a precarious financial situation.*

TAB *probably a servant*

MISS P——— *daughter of Turncoat*

MISS B——— *daughter of Turncoat*

TURNCOAT *another manager of the Assembly*

MRS. BUBBLE *a leader of society*

BETTY *her maid*

BUBBLE *her husband*

CAPTAIN CARELESS *an American naval officer*

Following the title page of the first edition of the play is a one-page Advertisement. In it the author notes that *The Motley Assembly* was written at the request of two or three particular friends and that it is published against the writer's "inclination." The public must determine who the characters supposedly are. They may or may not "suit" anyone, but the writer wishes to make it clear that the characters were copied from life and that some of his friends have been satisfied with the likenesses.

SCENE, at the House of Mrs. Flourish

[*Enter Mrs. Flourish and Esq. Runt.*]

Runt
It is a very great mortification to the gentlemen, Madam,—your not permitting Miss Flourish to go to the Assembly.

Mrs. Flourish
I mean it as such Mr. Runt;—if your sex are so weak and undiscerning, as to prefer the fading, short lived, perishable trifle beauty, to the noble exalted, mental accomplishments, which only are of intrinsic value, Mr. Runt;—it is fit they should be mortified.—O why has Heaven permitted our passive sex to be so long deceived and misled by the idle and groundless opinion of the superior wisdom of the male sex!—in animal strength I grant their superiority;—and I have found some capable of pleasing;—but few—very few indeed capable of informing me.—

Runt
But madam you will be pleased to consider, that few ladies are so accomplished as you are allowed to be.

Mrs. Flourish
Say no more, Mr. Runt;—I am almost sick at the bare mention of the word;—it is so horribly prostituted and misapplied upon almost all occasions.

Runt
I beg your pardon madam.

Mrs. Flourish
I do not mean in this instance Mr. Runt:—but pray Mr. Runt how comes it that you are one of the a-managers of this motley assembly?-a

Runt
I was advis'd madam—both for my interest and safety.

Mrs. Flourish
By one of your own sex,—I dare say—

Runt
It was madam:—Mr. Turncoat advis'd me.

Mrs. Flourish
To keep him in countenance I suppose;—well what appearance do they make, compared to our assemblies in the siege?

Runt
I wish you had been there the last evening madam, only to have seen the contrast.

a-a *managers . . . assembly* Runt and Turncoat are both playing a safe game. They manage the assembly under rebel society, although the occasion is actually under the auspices of the Loyalists, but should the British ever return to Boston, they can claim that they were endeavoring to uphold the social tradition of the Tories and would be received once again as devotees of the English cause. Their obvious hypocrisy is an object of the playwright's scorn.

Mrs. Flourish
Contrast indeed! I dare swear:—O Mr. Runt!—when shall we see such happy times again? Will they ever return Mr. Runt?

Runt
Turncoat says he has long been afraid they never would return;—and wishes all the friends of government would do as he has done;—tack about, and make fair weather with the other side.

Mrs. Flourish
How versatile is man! have you known any one of my sex on the side of government to change their opinion Mr. Runt? nay more—have we not openly, in the face of day, and in defiance of our present mock rulers—frequently visited our dear, distress'd ᵇ⁻friends in Cambridge. While the men!—you dastard men!—meanly stole there under covert of the night; and some of the highest Whigs, who in some companies have exclaimed against us, have been glad to make use of our interest for you know what purposes;—and their wives who have sometimes accompanied us, have returned more than half converted, by the gentility, address, politeness, and generosity of the Convention troops.⁻ᵇ—O my God! my heart bleeds whenever I think of the poor distress'd Convention troops:—What will become of them Mr. Runt? It is impossible they can endure such a horrid march:ᶜ—Enough almost to kill our Yankies.

Runt
It is very cruel treatment; and it is a wonder if we dont suffer for it in the end; I never could learn the cause madam.

Mrs. Flourish
The French! The cursed French! Mr. Runt, are the cause of all our misery:—This Rebellion would have been crush'd long before this, but for them—We could not have held out much longer, when they step'd in; but must have submitted to such terms as our gracious sovereign would have condescended to offer; which all who know his goodness Mr. Runt, are convinced would have been just and merciful.

Runt
Your observations are very just madam, and I am entirely of your opinion:—As to the French—everybody says they are a treacherous crew:—I know when I was in England it was the general opinion there; and that they never would fight: and I don't despair but Old England will give them a drubbing yet.—But as to us, I think we are in a worse box than ever;—out of the frying-pan, into the fire; and all this for a trifling duty on tea.ᵈ

Mrs. Flourish
Well we must wait with patience Mr. Runt; I have still

ᵇ⁻ᵇ *friends in Cambridge . . . Convention troops* After the defeat at Saratoga in 1777, Burgoyne's troops were surrendered under the terms of the Convention of Saratoga. They were sent to Cambridge; when Mrs. Flourish refers to all those dear "friends," the British prisoners of war, any true patriot would have been infuriated. An attack is also made against the Loyalist men who are Whig by day and Tory by night, paying secret visits to the English prisoners in Cambridge.

ᶜ *horrid march* Eventually the Convention troops were sent southward on a long march and were not released until after the war.

ᵈ *duty on tea* Runt's statement obviously simplifies the whole matter of the Revolution to a point of absurdity.

hopes, notwithstanding what Mr. Turncoat says;—I never thought him much of a politician.—It was rather unfortunate for him, that he would not even suffer his daughters to go to a Whig-Assembly[e] as it was called the winter before last; and now so warmly to engage in it; because these people are very apt to remember; and may possibly assign this miraculous change to the true motive.

[Enter Miss Flourish.]

Miss Flourish

O Mr. Runt, I am exceeding glad to see you; I wanted to ask you a thousand questions:—What sort of an assembly had you?—Who was there?—Were the ladies very much dress'd?—How did the He-Bears[f] (As Miss Doggril calls them) behave?—How did they handle their paws?—Could you keep your countenance?

Mrs. Flourish

Stop! stop! stop! Miss Volubility,—not quite so fast; who do you think can answer so many questions at once?—Now Mr. Runt, can you think it possible, after all this seeming contempt for the company, that this girl cried a whole day because I would not let her go to the assembly?—Assembly! Good Heavens! It is a burlesque upon the name of an assembly:—I have no patience when I think of it:—Yet there's my sister is fool enough to go; tho' she told me she would not dance, because she could not bear to give her hand to such cattle.

Runt

I observ'd Mrs. —— refuss'd to dance; but did not know the reason before:—Well I think she is quite right.—But Miss Flourish how comes it that you are so anxious to go?

Miss Flourish

Because there is a sett of us who agreed to go on purpose to make our remarks on the droll figures, for our diversion and entertainment when we got home.—

Runt

Ha! ha! ha!—You are a rogue, Miss Flourish.—

Mrs. Flourish

Did you observe Mrs. Bubble's behaviour Mr. Runt? It seems to me that creature tries how ridiculous she can make herself;—the town rings with her silly speeches;—She has not a single advocate in our little polite circle. And is laugh'd at by the very creatures whom she affects to despise, but has not sense enough even to distinguish the ridiculous part of their character.—Excuse me a moment Mr. Runt.—
(Exit Mrs. Flourish.)

[Enter Miss Taxall and Miss Doggril.]

Runt

How do ye do ladies? Give me leave to take your cloaks:—What do you hear abroad ladies?

---

[e] *Whig-Assembly* During the siege of Boston, the ball was strictly a Tory or Loyalist affair.

[f] *He-Bears* A snide reference to the uncouth manners of the Continental officers who attended the assembly.

Miss Taxall

We hear nothing talk'd of now, but the assembly, and Mrs. Bubble's pretty speeches. O Miss Doggril! I wish you had been in town in the seige;—then you would have seen assemblies!—Don't you remember one evening Miss Flourish?—Well tho' they are so impudent sometimes; yet they are so genteel, so easy, so careless, and so agreeable, that one can hardly be offended at anything they say or do:—if you had been with us then Miss Doggril, you would not wonder at my turning off my Yankie spark.[g]

Miss Doggril

Kind fortune! bring them back—"or let us drink of Lethe's fountain, and forget to think."

[*Re-enter Mrs. Flourish in a Hurry.*]

Mrs. Flourish

Take care girls what you say now:—Capt. Aid is coming in;—remember he is an officer in the *reb*,[h] I had like to have spoke treason—in our army.

[*Enter Aid—a little gay.*]

Aid

Ladies your most obedient;—Mr. Runt, I am yours.

Runt

Your humble servant Sir;—How do you do Mr. Aid? Capt.—I beg your pardon Sir.

Mrs. Flourish

Take a chair Captain Aid; will you drink a glass of wine.

Aid

With all my heart madam.—Ladies your health; Mr. Runt your health:—And long life, health, and prosperity, to His Most Christian Majesty[i]; and Godlike, glorious WASHINGTON.

Mrs. Flourish

Thank'ee Sir. (*Speaking very faintly.*)

Runt

With all my heart Captain:—I really take that WASHINGTON to be a very clever fellow.

Aid

Let us be silent on that subject Mr. Runt:—We have neither time, nor talents, to do it justice.

Mrs. Flourish

Why? He is no more than man; Captain Aid.

Aid

Then all mankind beside are less; madam.

---

[g] *Yankie spark* Another sarcastic comment against the provincial beaux.

[h] *reb* In the rebel army, another example of the derogatory attitude toward the patriot troops.

[i] *His . . . Majesty* Louis XVI.

Mrs. Flourish
You have not seen all mankind Sir.—I believe Mr. WASHINGTON:—or GENERAL WASHINGTON if you please,—is a very honest, good kind of a man; and has taken infinite pains to keep your army together; and I wish he may find his account in it:—But doubtless there are his equals;—to say no more.

Aid
If you meant that as a compliment, madam; it is really so cold a one; it has made me shiver;—I will therefore with your leave, drop the subject; and take another glass of wine.

Runt
Ay, ay, that's right Captain: I think there are more fit subjects for a young gentleman's contemplation in this room.

Aid
Still gallant Mr. Runt; But the ladies must pardon me if I cannot readily assent to the justice of your rebuke; when I assure them, that I think such charms as theirs, would justify my inattention to every other object, but what concerns my General, or my country.

Miss Taxall
I believe we are all very ready to pardon your inattention to us at times.

Aid
Curse your impudence. *(Aside.)* Knowing my inclination, and particular attention to please and oblige the ladies; you say what you please without the hazard of offending:—And as you seem disposed at this time to be merry at my expence; I am extremely sorry to deprive you of the opportunity, by being obliged to leave you. *(Exit Aid.)*

Scene changes to the house of Mrs. Taxall.

[*Enter Mrs. Taxall, Miss Taxall and Tab.*]

Miss Taxall
I am afraid Tab we shall be obliged to do something at last.—The gentlemen will be tired by and by: I have found already that some of them do not come so often as formerly; and when they do come, are not so ready to take a hint, tho' pretty broad; and I am really ashamed to speak plainer than I do.

Tab
Why Ma'am! I am sure you have no reason to complain yet:—You remember the last time the gentlemen drank tea here, how very generous one of them was to Miss—, and another very readily took your hint about the—, by what

he sent the next day: And you cannot but acknowledge that they have been exceeding genteel to Miss Taxall;—If any one has reason to complain; I think it is poor Tab.

Mrs. Taxall
I grant Tab they have done very well, considering who they are; but I begin to fear that it will not last; unless we could depend upon a new set every now and then, which is so precarious that I wish we had some other dependence.

Tab
Why you know Ma'am that I have taken in work for some particular people:—But before I would stoop to work for our modern mushroom gentry; I had rather starve.

Miss Taxall
I think Mamma that Tab is to be commended for her spirit; I'm sure I should rather starve than take in work for any body.

Mrs. Taxall
Why, I can't but say I commend such a spirit; It is very humiliating to people of taste and fashion, who have brought up a family so very genteely as I have, to think that any of them must stoop so low.—I am therefore determined to wait till necessity drives me, before I submit to it.—These times cannot last always. Perhaps we may see such days again, as we saw in the siege.

Miss Taxall
O Mamma! I fear we never shall.

Tab
I don't despair yet.

Miss Taxall
Well Tab if you don't despair, I am sure I have no reason.

[*Enter Miss P——— and Miss B———.*]

Miss P———
Your servant ladies!—Miss Taxall when did you see Captain Aid? He passed us just now as if he did not know us.

Miss B———
We heard he was affronted the winter before last, at our not going to the assembly,—and now I suppose he is offended because we do go.

Mrs. Taxall
I have heard several gentlemen remark upon that affair, Miss B———, and the late extraordinary change in your papa's conduct; not much to his advantage:—But I never open'd my lips, tho' I confess I think it looks odd.

Miss B———
Why Ma'am! When my Papa forbid our going to the Assembly, the winter before last; he thought the British

troops would be here again in the spring following, and retake the town; and was afraid it would hurt his and our characters, if he kept company with the liberty people:— But now he thinks they will not come again.

Mrs. Taxall
That may be a sufficient reason for his allowing you to go now; but his being a Manager looks as if he was really fond of such company.

Miss B———
Why Ma'am! He was urged to it, and as it was not like taking up arms; he thought it best to accept.—

[*Enter Turncoat.*]

Miss Taxall
I have been telling Miss B———, that some gentlemen have expressed great surprize at the apparent alteration in your conduct, Mr. Turncoat.

Turncoat
I don't doubt it Madam; and readily guess on what account; —but if those gentlemen wou'd consider the great change in our affairs; and the critical situation of my family, interest, and connections; they could not justly blame me; as they know my determination still is, never to take an active part on either side.

Miss Taxall
Well Sir I believe you are right all things considered. Pray Sir did you hear of the Fracas at the concert the other evening, between two gentlemen? I wish to hear the particulars.

Miss Taxall
La Mamma! it was nothing at all: They went so far as to draw on each other, to be sure; but no blood Mamma. I wish the ladies would adopt the same method of deciding their quarrels as it neither wounds the skin or reputation.

Scene at the house of Mrs. Bubble.

[*Enter Mrs. Bubble and Betty.*]

Betty
I have brought back the silk Ma'am; the lady says you have not sent all and refuses to take it again.

Mrs. Bubble
Well I'll see about it: You may go. *(Exit Betty.)*
Bubble has refused to buy it for me; and I am determined nobody else shall have it.

[*Enter Bubble.*]

Bubble
Do you go to the Assembly to-morrow evening my dear?

Mrs. Bubble
No! that I shan't,—Yes I will too, and in my worst gown—But I am determined not to dance—Yes I will dance a minuet on purpose to mortify you by my dress; why Mr. Bubble! how can you ask me to go to the assembly when you know I have got nothing fit to wear? And yet you have refused to buy for me the genteelist, prettiest thing I ever saw—and every body says it is exceeding cheap for paper money;—only a thousand dollars[j]—

Bubble
Very cheap indeed! Only a thousand dollars!

Mrs. Bubble
And not much the worse for wear neither—Any body who was to see it on me would suppose it quite new—But I have a great mind never to go among such cattle again; for unless one can eclipse them in dress; there is no mortifying them any other way—and that is all the pleasure one can take in going into such company.

Scene changes to Coffee-house.

[*Enter Aid and Careless.*]

Aid
We shall both be in Coventry[k] soon Careless.—Curse on the girls!—There is no keeping company with them without being a rascal.

Careless
Why? What's the matter Aid? ha! ha! ha!

Aid
Hold! hold! Don't you crow:—There's a Devil of a storm brewing for you my lad—I met Tab just now. She is running about brawling like a bedlamite against you.

Careless
Poor Tab! What does she say Aid?

Aid
D--n me if I can tell, tho' I heard her run on for half an hour; I can only recollect—"that puppy Careless—that young coxcomb! Continental shirts, ha! I'll Continental shirts him—a little saucy impudent puppy"—what the Devil does she mean Careless.

Careless
Ha, ha, ha!—why I'll tell you Aid—I was in company the other evening with that pretty set; tho' by the way some of

---

[j] *only a thousand dollars* Paper was the common currency but it was difficult to redeem. One would have to pay more in "soft" or paper dollars, the Continental currency, than in the hard dollar of silver or gold.

[k] *Coventry* To be socially ignored; variation of "send to Coventry"—to refuse to associate with.

them are really pretty; But Entre nous Aid—They are a damn'd set!—It is unnecessary to repeat the conversation; suffice it to say it was upon the old topic; which they handled with so much rancour, and indecency, sparing none of us; and so very lavish of their encomiums, on the British officers;—that I confess I felt not a little vexed; and in revenge.—as well as to divert the conversation;—proposed, their making each two shirts a week, for the continental soldiers.

Aid
Did you by Heaven? Well how was it received?

Careless
As I intended; faith!—it operated so violently on Tab, that I expected nothing short of an hysteric fit, her efforts to contain her rage must have been excessive, if one may judge by her horribly distorted countenance.

Aid
Why I dare swear Careless, it was her natural look, which you took for such an horrible distortion.

Careless
No, no, Aid,—Though we all agree she is dam'd ugly at best, yet I never saw her look quite so much like the devil before. But at last she was relieved by opening upon me.—Heavens and Earth what a volley!—I stood the shock for some time; at length I pretended to be very sorry, and begged their pardon. Then addressing Tab—I had not thought of giving the least offence, said I, my dear young lady; but was really simple enough to think, that while gentlemen were fighting, bleeding and dying for their country;—that the ladies could do no less than I proposed;—Nevertheless, convinced by the force of your arguments I give up the point.—I had scarce finished before I saw symptoms of another explosion from the same quarter:—and seeing not one advocate in the room; but on the contrary, every countenance deeply tinged with the irascible; I thought it best to decamp; which I did leaving them not a little chagrined.

Aid
I am very glad of it.—for between you and I, Careless, I begin to be sick of such company; though I think what they say is of very little consequence.

Careless
It is of so much consequence in my opinion; that I think it is the duty of every whig to discountenance such indecent raillery and abuse, at all times and upon all occasions.

Aid
If many would join in it—it would do—but should two or three only attempt it—they would appear ridiculous.

Careless
Ridiculous, or not; was I to continue here for anytime I should not hesitate to treat them with the neglect and contempt they deserve. Such a conduct invariably pursued by those whom they affect to despise, would soon effect a great change in their conversation and conduct.

Aid
I believe you are right Careless: I wish to Heaven the experiment was tried—O how I should glory in seeing the poor despised, neglected, solitary devils, looking and longing in vain for a bow or a smile, to cheer their indrooping spirits.

Careless
No man is more happy than I am, in the company of a pretty girl:—But shall selfish considerations weigh so much with a man of honour, as to take a little damn'd paracidical viper to his bosom, because it is pretty: Honour and patriotism forbid it.—O Aid! I am ashamed of the conduct of some in this town, who profess themselves whigs;—They are not barely doubtful, but in my opinion the most dangerous characters among you, but I shall leave you soon; and with less regret on this account:—Sincerely wishing, that on my return, I may find a great reformation, or a thoro' extirpation.

Blush B———! blush!—Thy honest sons bewail,
That dance and song o'er patriot zeal prevail;
That whigs and tories (join'd by wayward chance)
Should hand in hand, lead on the sprightly dance,
Or sword to sword as harmlessly oppose.
As all such heroes would their country's foes.
Here lur'd by fashion, opp'site int'rests join,
And lull their cares and rage,—in cards and wine;
Here friends to freedom, vile apostates meet,
And here unblushing can each other greet;
In mix'd assembly—see they crowd the place;
Stain to their country—To their Sires Disgrace;
Hell in some hearts; but pleasure in each face.
All—all are qualified to join this tribe;
Who have an hundred dollars to subscribe.

Bibliography

Bibliography

PLAYS IN THIS ANTHOLOGY

[Author Unknown] *The Battle of Brooklyn.* New York: Printed for J. Rivington, in the Year of the Rebellion, 1776.

Edinburgh: Printed in the Year, M,DCC,LXXVII

New York: Printed for J. Rivington, 1777.

Cork: Reprinted by J. Sullivan, Cattle-street, 1777.

Brooklyn: Private reprint, "New York: Printed for J. Rivington, in the Year of the Rebellion, 1776," 1873.

Brackenridge, Hugh Henry *The Death of General Montgomery, in Storming the City of Quebec.* Norwich: Printed by J. Trumbull, 1777.

Philadelphia: Robert Bell, 1777.

[Leacock, John] *The Fall of British Tyranny: or, American Liberty Triumphant.* Philadelphia: Styner and Cist, 1776.

New England, Boston: John Gill, and Powars and Willis, in Queen Street, 1776.

Providence: J. Douglass McDougall, 1776.

[Mary V. V.] *A Dialogue, between a Southern Delegate, and His Spouse, on his return from the Grand Continental Congress.* [New York], 1774.

Boston: Printed by Mills and Hicks, 1774.

Munford, Robert *A Collection of Plays and Poems by the late Colonel Robert Munford, of Mecklenberg County in the State of Virginia.* Petersburg [Va.]: Printed by Wm. Prentiss, 1798.

[Warren, Mercy Otis] *The Blockheads; or, The Affrighted Officers.* Boston: Printed in Queen-Street, 1776.

[Warren, Mercy Otis] *The Motley Assembly.* Boston: Printed and Sold by Nathaniel Coverly, in Newbury-Street, 1779.

OTHER PUBLISHED PLAYS OF THE REVOLUTION

[Author Unknown] *The Blockheads; or, Fortunate Contractor.* New York; London: reprinted for G. Kearsley, 1782.

Brackenridge, Hugh Henry *The battle of Bunkers-Hill.* Philadelphia: Printed and sold by Robert Bell, in Third Street, 1776.

[Paine, Thomas] *A Dialogue between the Ghost of General Montgomery Just arrived from the Elysian Fields; and an American Delegate, in a wood, near Philadelphia.* [Philadelphia]: Printed, and Sold by R. Bell, in Third-Street, 1776.

[Sewall, Jonathan] *The Americans Roused in a Cure for the Spleen.* New England, printed; New York, reprinted, by James Rivington. [1775]

[Trumbull, John] *The Double Conspiracy, or Treason Discovered but not Punished.* [Hartford]: Printed in the year 1783.

[Warren, Mercy Otis] *The Adulateur.* Boston: Printed and sold at the New Printing Office, near Concert Hall, 1773.

———*The Group.* Boston: Printed and sold by Edes and Gill, in Queen Street, 1775.

GENERAL SOURCES
Books

Adair, Douglass, and Schutz, John A., eds. *Peter Oliver's Origin and Progress of the American Revolution.* San Marino, California: The Huntington Library, 1963.

Adams, John *The Works of John Adams.* 10 vols. Boston: Little, Brown and Company, 1851-1865.

Alden, Edmund Kimball "Alexander, William." *Dictionary of American Biography.* Vol. I, part 1. Edited by Allen Johnson. New York: Charles Scribner's Sons, 1957.

Anthony, Katharine *First Lady of the Revolution: The Life of Mercy Otis Warren.* New York: Doubleday and Company, Inc., 1958.

Archbold, William A. J. "Jenkinson, Charles." *Dictionary of National Biography.* Vol. X. Edited by Sir Leslie Stephen and Sir Sidney Lee. London: Oxford University Press, 1921-1922.

Bailyn, Bernard, ed. *Pamphlets of the American Revolution.* Vol. I. Cambridge, Massachusetts: Harvard University Press, 1965.

Bargar, B. D. *Lord Dartmouth and the American Revolution.* Columbia: The University of South Carolina Press, 1965.

Barker, George F. R. "Dunning, John." *Dictionary of National Biography.* Vol. VI. Edited by Sir Leslie Stephen and Sir Sidney Lee. London: Oxford University Press, 1921-1922.

———"Legge, William." *Dictionary of National Biography.* Vol. XI. Edited by Sir Leslie Stephen and Sir Sidney Lee. London: Oxford University Press, 1921-1922.

———"North, Frederick." *Dictionary of National Biography.* Vol. XIV. Edited by Sir Leslie Stephen and Sir Sidney Lee. London: Oxford University Press, 1921-1922.

Boatner, Mark Mayo III *Encyclopedia of the American Revolution.* New York: David McKay Company, Inc., 1966.

Bowen, Catherine Drinker *John Adams and the American Revolution.* Boston: Little, Brown and Company, 1949.

Boyd, Julian P., ed. *The Papers of Thomas Jefferson.* Vol. I. Princeton: Princeton University Press, 1950.

Bradley, Phillips, ed. *Democracy in America.* 4th ed. New York: Alfred A. Knopf, 1948.

Burnett, Edmund C., ed. *Letters of Members of the Continental Congress.* Vol. I. Washington, D.C.: Carnegie Institute of Washington, 1921.

———, ed., *Letters of Members of the Continental Congress.* Vol. II. Washington, D.C.: Carnegie Institution of Washington, 1923.

Butterfield, L. H., ed. *Adams Family Correspondence.* 2 vols. Cambridge, Mass.: Harvard University Press, 1963.

———, ed. *Diary and Autobiography of John Adams.* 4 vols. Cambridge, Mass.: Harvard University Press, 1961.

Clark, Dora Mae *British Opinion and the American Revolution.* New Haven: Yale University Press, 1930.

Commager, Henry Steele and Morris, Richard B., eds. *The Spirit of 'Seventy-Six.* 2 vols. Indianapolis: The Bobbs-Merrill Company, 1958.

Corner, George W., ed. *The Autobiography of Benjamin Rush.* Princeton: Princeton University Press, 1948.

Courtney, William P. "Barre, Isaac." *Dictionary of National Biography.* Vol. I. Edited by Sir Leslie Stephen and Sir Sidney Lee. London: Oxford University Press, 1921-1922.

———"Glynn, John." *Dictionary of National Biography.* Vol. VIII. Edited by Sir Leslie Stephen and Sir Sidney Lee.

London: Oxford University Press, 1921-1922.

Cutter, William *The Life of Israel Putnam, Major-General in the Army of the American Revolution.* New York: Derby & Jackson, 1858.

Davidson, Philip *Propaganda and the American Revolution.* Chapel Hill: The University of North Carolina Press, 1941.

Donne, W. Bodham *The Correspondence of King George the Third with Lord North.* From 1768 to 1783. 2 vols. London: John Murray, 1867.

Duer, William Alexander *The Life of William Alexander, Earl of Stirling; Major General in the Army of the United States, during the Revolution: with selections from his correspondence.* New York: Wiley & Putnam, for the New Jersey Historical Society, 1847.

Dunlap, William *History of the New Netherlands, Province of New York, and State of New York, to the Adoption of the Federal Constitution.* 2 vols. New York: Carter & Thorp, 1839-1840.

Dwight, Timothy *Travels in New England and New York.* 4 vols. New Haven: T. Dwight, 1821-1822.

Evans, Charles *American Bibliography* Chicago: Privately Printed for the Author by the Blakely Press, 1903-1905.

Fairman, Charles "Ruggles, Timothy." *Dictionary of American Biography*, Vol. VIII, Part 2. Edited by Dumas Malone, New York: Scribner's Sons, 1935.

Fitzpatrick, John C., ed. *The Writings of George Washington.* Vol. 3. Washington, D.C.: U. S. Government Printing Office, 1931-1934.

Flexner, James Thomas *George Washington: The Forge of Experience.* Boston: Little, Brown and Company, 1965.

Force, Peter, ed. *American Archives.* 4th series. Washington, D.C.: M. St. Clair Clarke and Peter Force, 1837.

Ford, W. C., ed. *Journals of the Continental Congress, 1774-1789.* Washington, D.C.: U. S. Government Printing Office, 1904.

———,ed. *Warren-Adams Letters.* 2 vols. Boston: The Massachusetts Historical Society, 1917.

Freeman, Douglas Southall *George Washington.* 5 vols. New York: Charles Scribner's Sons, 1948-1952.

Frothingham, Richard *The Life and Times of Joseph Warren.* Boston: Little, Brown and Co., 1865.

Gipson, Lawrence Henry *The Triumphant Empire.* Vol. XII. New York: Alfred A. Knopf, 1965.

Goodman, Nathan G. *Benjamin Rush Physician and Citizen.* Philadelphia: University of Pennsylvania Press, 1934.

Hammond, Otis G., ed. *Letters and Papers of Major-General John Sullivan, Continental Army.* Vol. 1, 1771-1777. Concord, New Hampshire: New Hampshire Historical Society, 1930.

Humphreys, David *The Life and Heroic Exploits of Israel Putnam, Major-General in the Revolutionary War.* Hartford: Silas Andrus and Son, 1847.

Hutchinson, William T. and Rachal, William M. E., eds. *The Papers of James Madison.* 3 vols. Chicago: The University of Chicago Press, 1962-1963.

Johnson, Edgar H. "Hopkins, Esek." *Dictionary of American Biography.* Vol. V. Edited by Dumas Malone. New York: Charles Scribner's Sons, 1961.

Johnston, Henry P. *The Campaign of 1776 around New York and Brooklyn.* Brooklyn, N. Y.: The Long Island Historical Society, 1878.

Kelsey, Rayner W. "Penn, William." *Dictionary of American Biography.* Vol. VII. Edited by Dumas Malone. New York: Charles Scribner's Sons, 1934.

Kilroe, Edwin P., Kaplan, Abraham, and Johnson, Joseph, eds. *The Story of Tammany.* New York County: Democratic Organization, 1928.

Lossing, Benson J. *The Pictorial Field-Book of the Revolution.* 2 vols. New York: Harper & Brothers, 1851-52.

Mackesy, Piers *The War for America.* Cambridge, Mass.: Harvard University Press, 1964.

Memoirs of the Long Island Historical Society. The Campaign of 1776, around New York and Brooklyn. Vol. III. Brooklyn, N. Y.: Published by the Society, 1878.

Millar, Alexander Hastie. "Wedderburn, Alexander." *Dictionary of National Biography.* Vol. XX. Edited by Sir Leslie Stephen and Sir Sidney Lee. London: Oxford University Press, 1921-1922.

Miller, John C. *Origins of the American Revolution.* 2nd ed., revised. Stanford: Stanford University Press, 1959.

——— *Sam Adams, Pioneer in Propaganda.* 2nd ed., revised. Stanford: Stanford University Press, 1960.

——— *The Triumph of Freedom.* 3rd printing. Boston: Little, Brown and Company, 1948.

Moore, Frank, ed. *Diary of the American Revolution.* 2 vols. New York: Charles Scribner, 1860.

Nelson, William, H. *The American Tory.* Oxford: At the Clarendon Press, 1961.

Nelson, William, and Honeyman, A. Van Doren, eds. *Documents relating to the Colonial History of the State of New Jersey.* First series, vol. XXVII, 1773-1774. Patterson, N. J.: The Call Printing and Publishing Co., 1917.

Plumb, J. H. *The First Four Georges.* New York: The Macmillan Company, 1957.

Ricord, Frederick, and Nelson, William, eds. *Documents Relating to the Colonial History of the State of New Jersey.* Vol. X. Newark, N. J.: Daily Advertiser Printing House, 1886.

Rigg, James McMullen. "Wilkes, John." *Dictionary of National Biography.* Vol. XXI. Edited by Sir Leslie Stephen and Sir Sidney Lee. London: Oxford University Press, 1921-1922.

Robin, Claude C. *New Travels Through North America: In a Series of Letters.* Boston: E. E. Powers and N. Willis, 1784.

Sabine, Lorenzo. *Biographical Sketches of Loyalists of the American Revolution.* 2 vols. Boston: Little, Brown and Company, 1864.

Schlesinger, Arthur M. *Prelude to Independence.* New York: Alfred A. Knopf, 1958.

Sedgwick, Romney, ed. *Letters from George III to Lord Bute.* London: Macmillan and Co., Ltd., 1939.

Syrett, Harold C., and Cooke, Jacob E., eds. *The Papers of Alexander Hamilton.* Vol. I. New York: Columbia University Press, 1961.

Telford, John, ed. *The Letters of the Rev. John Wesley, A. M.* Vol. VI. London: The Epworth Press, 1931.

Thackeray, Francis *A History of the Right Honorable William Pitt, Earl of Chatham.* Vol. II. London: C. and J. Rivington, 1827.

Trevelyan, George Otto *The American Revolution.* 4 vols. New York: Longmans, Green, and Co., 1905.

Van Doren, Carl *Secret History of the American Revolution.* New York: The Viking Press, 1941.

Watson, John F., ed. *Annals of Philadelphia and Pennsylvania in the Olden Time; being a collection of Memoirs, Anecdotes, and Incidents of the City and its Inhabitants, and of the earliest settlements of the inland part of Pennsylvania, from the Days of the Founders.* Vol. 1. Philadelphia: Parry and M'Millan, 1855.

Wertenbaker, Thomas Jefferson *Father Knickerbocker Rebels.* New York: Charles Scribner's Sons, 1948.

Whittemore, Charles P. *A General of the Revolution, John Sullivan of New Hampshire.* New York: Columbia University Press, 1961.

Winsor, Justin, ed. *The Memorial History of Boston.* Boston: James R. Osgood and Company, 1882.

———,ed. *Narrative and Critical History of America.* Vol. VI. Boston: Houghton, Mifflin and Company, 1888.

Wright, Louis B., ed. *The Prose Works of William Byrd of Westover.* Cambridge, Massachusetts: Harvard University Press, 1966.

Journals

Adams, Thomas R., ed. "American Independence: The Growth of an Idea: A bibliographical study of the American political pamphlets published between 1764 and 1776 dealing with the dispute between Great Britain and her colonies." *Publications of the Colonial Society of Massachusetts.* Vol. XLIII (December, 1956), 4-202.

Amory, Thomas C. "The Memory of General John Sullivan of New Hampshire, vindicated from Historical Misrepresentation." *Proceedings of the Massachusetts Historical Society 1866-1867.* Vol. IX (December, 1866), 380-436.

Calkin, Homer L. "Pamphlets and Public Opinion during the American Revolution." *Pennsylvania Magazine.* Vol. LXIV (January, 1940), 22-42.

French, Allen "The First George Washington Scandal." *Proceedings of the Massachusetts Historical Society 1932-1936.* Vol. LXV (November, 1935), 460-474.

Larabee, Leonard W. "The Nature of American Loyalism." *Proceedings of the American Antiquarian Society.* Vol. LIV, Part 1 (October, 1944), 15-58.

Mitchell, S. Weir, ed., "Historical Notes of Dr. Benjamin Rush, 1777." *The Pennsylvania Magazine of History and Biography.* Vol. XXVII (April, 1903), 129-150.

Rossiter, Clinton "Richard Bland: the Whig in America." *William and Mary Quarterly,* 3rd series, vol. X (January, 1953), 33-79.

"Selections from the Correspondence of William Alexander." *Proceedings of the New Jersey Historical Society 1850-1851.* Vol. V, no. 3 (January, 1851), 179-196.

———*Proceedings of the New Jersey Historical Society 1851-1853.* Vol. VI, no. 1 (September, 1851), 41-48.

———*Proceedings of the New Jersey Historical Society 1851-1853.* Vol. VI, no. 2 (January, 1852), 56-64; 93-96.

———*Proceedings of the New Jersey Historical Society 1853-1855.* Vol. VII, no. 1 (May, 1853), 38-48.

———*Proceedings of the New Jersey Historical Society 1853-1855.* Vol. VII, no. 3 (May, 1854), 111-116.

———*Proceedings of the New Jersey Historical Society 1853-1855.* Vol. VII, no. 4 (January, 1855), 136-148.

Warren, Charles. "Samuel Adams and the Sans Souci Club in 1785." *Proceedings of the Massachusetts Historical Society 1926-1927.* Vol. LX (May, 1927), 318-344.

Whitehead, W. A. "Robbery of the Treasury of East Jersey in 1768." *Proceedings of the New Jersey Historical Society 1850-1851.* Vol. V, no. 2 (September, 1850), 51-65.

Newspapers - Pamphlets

Allen, John *The American Alarm, or the Bostonian Plea, For the Rights, and Liberties, of the People.* Boston: Printed and Sold by D. Kneeland, and N. Davis, 1773.

[Bland, Richard] *An Inquiry into the Rights of the British Colonies, Intended as an Answer to the Regulations lately made concerning The Colonies, and the Taxes imposed upon them considered....* Williamsburg: Alexander Purdie, and Co., 1766.

THEATRE AND LITERATURE
Books

Addison, Joseph *Cato.* London: J. Tonson, 1725.

Baine, Rodney M. *Robert Munford.* Athens, Georgia: University of Georgia Press, 1967.

Brown, T. Allston *History of the American Stage.* New York: Dick & Fitzgerald, 1870.

Coad, Oral Sumner, and Mims, Edwin, Jr. *The American Stage.* New Haven: Yale University Press. Pageant of America series, vol. 14, 1929.

Dunlap, William *History of the American Theatre.* New York: J. & J. Harper, 1832.

Ford, Paul Leicester *Washington and the Theatre.* New York: Publications of the Dunlap Society. New Series, no. 8, 1899.

Hewitt, Barnard *Theatre, U.S.A.* New York: McGraw-Hill Book Company, 1959.

Hodge, Francis *Yankee Theatre.* Austin: University of Texas Press, 1964.

Hornblow, Arthur *A History of the Theatre in America.* 2 vols. Philadelphia: J. B. Lippincott Company, 1919.

Hubbell, Jay B. *The South in American Literature.* Durham, North Carolina: Duke University Press, 1954.

Krutch, Joseph Wood *Comedy and Conscience after the Restoration.* Revised edition. New York: Columbia University Press, 1949.

Loftis, John *Comedy and Society from Congreve to Fielding.* Stanford: Stanford University Press, 1959.

———*The Politics of Drama in Augustan England.* Oxford: The Clarendon Press, 1963.

Moody, Richard *America Takes the Stage.* Bloomington: Indiana University Press, 1955.

———,ed. *Dramas from the American Theatre 1762-1909.* Cleveland: The World Publishing Co., 1966.

Moses, Montrose J. *The American Dramatist.* Boston: Little, Brown and Company, 1925.

———,ed. *Representative Plays by American Dramatists.* Vol. 1. New York: E. P. Dutton & Company, 1918.

Newlin, Claude Milton *The Life and Writings of Hugh Henry Brackenridge.* Princeton: Princeton University Press, 1932.

———,ed. *Modern Chivalry.* New York: American Book Company, 1937.

Nicoll, Allardyce *A History of the Early Eighteenth Century Drama.* 2nd ed. Cambridge: The University Press, 1929.

———*A History of the Restoration Drama.* 3rd ed. Cambridge: The University Press, 1940.

Pattee, Fred Lewis *The Poems of Philip Freneau.* 3 vols. Princeton: The University Library, 1902-1907.

Quinn, Arthur Hobson *A History of the*

American Drama from the Beginning to the Civil War. New York: F. S. Crofts & Co., 1946.

Rankin, Hugh F. *The Theater in Colonial America.* Chapel Hill: The University of North Carolina Press, 1960.

Sargent, Winthrop, ed. *The Loyalist Poetry of the Revolution.* Philadelphia: n.p., 1857.

Seilhamer, George O. *History of the American Theatre.* Vol. 1. Philadelphia: Globe Printing House, 1888.
New York: Benjamin Blom, 1968

———*History of the American Theatre.* Vol. 2. Philadelphia: Globe Printing House, 1889.

Sonneck, O. G. *Early Opera in America.* New York: Benjamin Blom, 1963.

Spiller, Robert E., Thorp, Willard, Johnson, Thomas H., and Canby, Henry Seidel, eds., *Literary History of the United States.* 3 vols. New York: The Macmillan Company, 1949.

Trumbull, John *M'Fingal.* Boston: John G. Scobie, 1826.

Tyler, Moses Coit *The Literary History of the American Revolution, 1776-1783.* Vol. II. New York: Putnam's, 1897.

Warren, Mercy Otis *Poems, Dramatic and Miscellaneous.* Boston: T. Thomas and E. T. Andrews, 1790.

Journals

Canby, Courtlandt "Robert Munford's 'The Patriots'." *William and Mary Quarterly,* Vol. VI, no. 3 (July, 1949), pp. 437-503.

Damon, S. Foster "Varnum's 'Ministerial Oppression,' a Revolutionary Drama." *Proceedings of the American Antiquarian Society.* Vol. LV, pt. 2 (October, 1945), 287-298.

Ford, W. C. "Mrs. Warren's 'The Group'." *Proceedings of the Massachusetts Historical Society 1928-1929.* Vol. LXII (October, 1928), 15-22.

"The Theatre in Eighteenth Century Virginia Outside of Williamsburg." *The Virginia Magazine of History and Biography.* Vol. XXXV (July, 1927), 295-296.

Newspapers - Pamphlets

Boston Evening Post: September 29, 1766.

New England Chronicle: September 26, 1776.

Pennsylvania Gazette: January 24, 1776.

Ford, Paul Leicester *Some Notes towards an Essay on the Beginnings of American Dramatic Literature, 1606-1789.* New York: Privately Printed, 1893.